The Governance Public Debt Nexus (1962 to 21st C)

A Case Study of Jamaica with Barbados and Singapore As Comparators

The Governance Public Debt Nexus (1962 to 21st C)

A Case Study of Jamaica with Barbados and Singapore As Comparators

Collette June-Ann Smith
With Foreword by Professor Anthony Clayton

Copyright © 2021 by Collette June-Ann Smith.
First Edition 2021

All rights reserved. No part of this book may be used, reproduced, scanned, or shared in any form, manner, or by any means whatsoever without prior written permission, except in the case of a brief quotation, or quotations embodied in critical articles, theses, and reviews written for inclusion in a magazine, or periodical including newspaper articles.

Cover Design: Oniel Wright

This book is dedicated to the leaders and people of Jamaica, including first, second, third and fourth generation Jamaicans across the diaspora.

Contents

Contents		i
List of Figures		ii
List of Tables		vi
Abbreviations and Acronyms		vii
Foreword		ix
Acknowledgements		xii
Preface		xiv
Chapter 1	Governance and Public Debt in Jamaica Introduction	1
Chapter 2	Governance, Fiscal Policy and Debt Theoretical Foundations	26
Chapter 3	Jamaica's Political Economy 1930s to Present – with Barbados and Singapore as Comparators	76
Chapter 4	Antecedents and Factors Contributing to Public Debt Accumulation in Jamaica	130
Chapter 5	Findings – Public Debt and Governance in Jamaica	177
Chapter 6	Further Findings – Comparators: Jamaica, Barbados, and Singapore	213
Chapter 7	Conclusion	286
References		290
Appendix I	Photographs of Capital Projects Discussed	321
Appendix II	Supplementary Material on Governance Decisions	326
Index		334

List of Figures

Figure 1.1	Jamaica's Economic Growth Relative to Public Debt (%)	4
Figure 1.2	Channels through which Governance Impacts Public Debt	14
Figure 2.1	Link between Social Services and Public Debt	31
Figure 2.2	Fiscal and Primary Balances 1965 - 2010 (5-year Intervals)	73
Figure 3.1	Public Debt-to-GDP: 1960-2010	93
Figure 3.2	Average GDP Growth	101
Figure 3.3	Comparative Population 65 Years and over	114
Figure 3.4	Comparative Contribution fr. Agriculture & Manufacturing	123
Figure 4.1	Comparative T-bill Rates	132
Figure 4.2	GFCF as % of GDP 1960-2010	137
Figure 4.3	Net International Reserves (Jamaica) 1960-2010	144
Figure 4.4	Fiscal Balances (Jamaica) 1962-2010	145
Figure 4.5	External Debt Service (US$) for Jamaica 1971-2011	146
Figure 4.6	Jamaica's Trade Balance as % of GDP	148
Figure 4.7	Comparative Deposit Rates 1980-2010	151
Figure 5.1	Maturity Profile of Jamaica's Domestic Public Debt	180
Figure 5.2	Post-NDX Maturity Profile	181
Figure 5.3	Maturity Profile of Jamaica's External Public Debt	181
Figure 5.4	Currency Composition of Jamaica's Public Debt	183
Figure 5.5	Changes in Social Service Allocations; with Debt	185
Figure 5.6	Changes in Allocated Recurrent Expenditure to Social Service 1965-2010	186
Figure 5.7	Ratio of Social Service Alloc. 1965-2010	187

Figure 5.8	Changes in Contribution to GDP (Mining …) 1970-2010	204
Figure 5.9	Debt Trajectories 1960-2010	205
Figure 5.10	Comparative Gross Fixed Capital Formation	207
Figure 6.1	Barbados' Total Public Debt-to-GDP 1960-2010	214
Figure 6.2	Jamaica's Total Public Debt-to-GDP 1960-2010	214
Figure 6.3	Singapore's Total Public Debt-to-GDP 1960-2010	215
Figure 6.4	Comparative Total Public Debt-to-GDP (% of GDP)	216
Figure 6.5	Public Debt-to-GDP (%) Components: Jamaica 1960-2010	217
Figure 6.6	Total Public Debt-to-GDP (%): Barbados 1960-2010	218
Figure 6.7	Comparative External Debt-to-GDP (%) 1960-2010	219
Figure 6.8	Total Public Debt-to-GDP (%): Singapore 1960-2010	220
Figure 6.9	Singapore's External Public Debt – Components	220
Figure 6.10	Comparative per Capita GDP 1960-2010	222
Figure 6.11	Comparative Per Capita Expenditure on Health 1997-2010	223
Figure 6.12	Comparative Average Life Expectancy 1960-2010	223
Figure 6.13	Comparative GDP per Person Employed	224
Figure 6.14	Comparative GDP Growth (%)	230
Figure 6.15	Percentage Contribution of Key Sectors to GDP – Jamaica	231
Figure 6.16	Percentage Contribution of Key Sectors to GDP – Barbados	232
Figure 6.17	Percentage Contribution of Key Sectors to GDP – Singapore	232
Figure 6.18	Comparative Inflation Rates	234
Figure 6.19	Comparative WGI Ratings	238

Figure 6.20	Comparative WGI Political Stability Ratings 1996-2010	239
Figure 6.21	World Governance Indicators Ratings – Jamaica	239
Figure 6.22	World Governance Indicators Ratings – Barbados	240
Figure 6.23	World Governance Indicators Ratings – Singapore	241
Figure 6.24	Comparative Ratings on Voice and Accountability	242
Figure 6.25	Females in Parliament 1997-2010	244
Figure 6.26	Age Group of Respondents – General Public	262
Figure 6.27	Public's Rating of PNP on Participation	263
Figure 6.28	Public's Rating of JLP on Participation	263
Figure 6.29	Public's Rating of PNP on Effectiveness and Efficiency	265
Figure 6.30	Public's Rating of JLP on Effectiveness and Efficiency	265
Figure 6.31	Public's Rating of PNP on Following the Rule of Law	266
Figure 6.32	Public's Rating of JLP on Following the Rule the of Law	267
Figure 6.33	Public's Rating of PNP on Transparency	269
Figure 6.34	Public's Rating of JLP on Transparency	269
Figure 6.35	Public's Rating of PNP on Responsiveness	271
Figure 6.36	Public's Rating of JLP on Responsiveness	271
Figure 6.37	Public's Rating of PNP on Consensus Orientation	272
Figure 6.38	Public's Rating of JLP on Consensus Orientation	272
Figure 6.39	Public's Rating of PNP on Equity and Inclusiveness	274
Figure 6.40	Public's Rating of JLP on Equity and Inclusiveness	275
Figure 6.41	Public's Rating of PNP on Accountability	276
Figure 6.42	Public's Rating of JLP on Accountability	276
Figure 6.43	Local Perception of Governance Quality in Jamaica	278

Figure 6.44	Public's Awareness of Level of Public Debt	280
Figure 6.45	Respondents' Opinion on FINSAC	280
Figure 6.46	Respondents' Recommended Alternatives to FINSAC	281
Figure 6.47	Respondents' Opinion on Sale of NCB	282
Figure 6.48	Respondents' Opinion on Highway 2000	282
Figure 6.49	Respondents' Opinion on Why HW2000 May Not Benefit Jamaica	283
Figure 6.50	Respondents' Opinion on the Jamaica Debt Exchange	283

List of Tables

Table 3.1	General Elections in Jamaica: 1962-2020	80
Table 3.2	Avg. GDP Growth by Political Term: 1962 – 2011	99
Table 3.3	Gross Domestic Product Growth/Decline: 2011-2020	100
Table 3.4	Comparative per Capita GDP	108
Table 3.5	World Governance Indicators (2010)	109
Table 3.6	World Governance Indicators (2019)	109
Table 3.7	Comparative Rankings	126
Table 5.1	Changes in Public Debt, by Political Administration (J$B)	178
Table 5.2	Pre- & Post-NDX Maturity Profile of JA's Domestic Debt	180
Table 5.3	Jamaica's External Public Debt-to-GDP: 1962-2011	182
Table 5.4	Currency Composition of Jamaica's External Debt	183
Table 5.5	Debt and Recurrent Social Service Exp. as % of Total Expenditure	184
Table 5.6	Jamaica's Human Development Indicator Results and Targets to 2030	189
Table 5.7	Gross Fixed Capital Formation as % of GDP	207
Table 6.1	Total Public Debt-to-GDP (%) Indicators	214
Table 6.2	Comparative Public Debt-to-GDP	215
Table 6.3	Comparative Indicators Prior to and Post-Independence	222
Table 6.4	Comparative Exchange Rates	226
Table 6.5	Other Comparative Indicators	229
Table 6.6	Comparative Indicators Relating to Governance	243
Table 6.7	Triangulation - Summary of Comparative Ratings	277

Abbreviations and Acronyms

AG	Auditor General
BD	Barbados Dollar
BITU	Bustamante Industrial Trade Union
BLP	Barbados Labour Party
BOJ	Bank of Jamaica
BOP	Balance of Payments
CAP	Clarendon Alumina Production
CARICOM	Caribbean Community
CBB	Central Bank of Barbados
CBI	Caribbean Basin Initiative
CD	Certificate of Deposit
CHEC	China Harbour Engineering Company
CPF	Central Providence Fund (of Singapore)
CPI	Corruption Prevention Index
DG	Director General
DLP	Democratic Labour Party (of Barbados)
DPP	Director of Public Prosecution
ECLAC	Economic Commission for Latin America and the Caribbean
EDB	Export Development Board
EDC	Export Development Canada
ESSJ	Economic and Social Survey of Jamaica
EU	European Union
FDI	Foreign Direct Investment
FID	Financial Investigation Division
FINSAC	Financial Sector Adjustment Company
GCI	Global Competitiveness Index
GFCF	Gross Fixed Capital Formation
GDP	Gross Domestic Product
GNP	Gross National Product
GOJ	Government of Jamaica
GOB	Government of Barbados
GOM	Government of Mexico
GOS	Government of Singapore

IBRD	International Bank for Reconstruction and Development
ILO	International Labour Organization
IMF	International Monetary Fund
JIS	Jamaica Information Service
JLP	Jamaica Labour Party
JP	Jamaica Producers
JWTU	Jamaica Workmen and Tradesmen Union
LRS	Local Registered Stock
MAS	Monetary Authority of Singapore
MP	Member of Parliament (Member)
MOE	Ministry of Education
MOFP	Ministry of Finance and the Public Service
NAFTA	North American Free Trade Agreement
NCB	National Commercial Bank
NDB	National Development Bank
NIS	National Insurance Scheme
OCG	Office of the Contractor General
PAHO	Pan American Health Organization
PDMA	Public Debt Management Act
PIOJ	Planning Institute of Jamaica
PM	Prime Minister
PNP	People's National Party
Repo	Repurchase Agreement
RMF	Road Maintenance Fund
SG	Singapore Dollar
SCJ	Sugar Company of Jamaica
SMP	Staff Monitored Programme
SPSS	Statistical Programme for Social Sciences
T-bill	Treasury bill
TI	Transparency International
UN	United Nations
UNESCAP	United Nations Economic and Social Commission for Asia and the Pacific
UNDP	United Nations Development Programme
US or USA	United States of America
UWI	University of the West Indies
WB	World Bank
WEF	World Economic Forum

Foreword

Collette Smith was one of my most brilliant students. She undertook a detailed study of one of the most important questions in economics; why are some nations rich and others poor, and what can we do about it?

In recent decades, a number of formerly poor nations have become rich. In 1950, the average income in Taiwan was about the same as in Sierra Leone and the Democratic Republic of Congo, but Taiwan is now very wealthy while Sierra Leone and the Democratic Republic of Congo have remained poor. What do poor countries need to do in order to prosper?

Many of the studies in this area have focused on the reasons why countries don't make progress. Most agree that unreliable electricity supplies, bad roads, inadequate ports and poor telecommunications certainly cause problems, but these can be solved with well-managed investment in infrastructure. Violence and corruption, however, can be fatal, and condemn a country to decades of failure, and many of the poorest countries in the world are also among the most oppressive, violent and corrupt.

There are a number of studies of countries that overcame their limitations and went on to prosper. There are relatively few examples, however, of countries that appeared set to prosper, made what appeared to be appropriate investments, and then collapsed into long-running economic underperformance. These examples are particularly important, as they can tell us much about the factors that are essential to national development and prosperity.

Collette looked at one of the most remarkable examples of lost prosperity. Jamaica was one of the most rapidly developing countries in the world at the time of independence in 1962, and its stellar economic growth rate continued for about ten years after independence, when it collapsed into a series of debilitating recessions. Today, Jamaica has had nearly fifty years of anaemic growth, its economy is a small fraction of the size it should have been, and it has become one of the most murderous nations in the world, with a homicide rate higher than in most war zones.

This appears to be a paradox. Most of the countries that have become rich have moved up into high-value exports of goods and services. They have invested in human capital, and raised productivity. In most (but not all) cases, these countries also have strong institutions, efficient government, the rule of law and some measure of political freedom.

Jamaica has achieved many of these things. The country now has some good roads and ports, universal education, excellent telecommunications, a free press, two independent political parties who stand in fair elections, an increasingly effective police service and an active anti-corruption agency. So why has Jamaica failed to escape from its long-running pattern of weak growth, high debt, low productivity and intractable social problems?

Collette collected an extraordinary volume of data, including many first-hand interviews, trawled the archives extensively, created a detailed delineation of key macro-economic and related policy decisions and linked them to subsequent events. This study revealed, in meticulous detail, the role that flaws in Jamaica's politics and governance contributed to its decline, and the extent to which vital macro-economic policy decisions and investment strategies were influenced by short-term politics and corruption. The culture of patronage and corruption that was established in the 1970s and 1980s has become so interwoven in the system of national and local government that it has been almost impossible to eradicate. Even the substantial progress made in other areas has been insufficient to overcome the harm done by this largely invisible distortion of economic decision-making.

This has shown that nations like Jamaica have to overcome their own deep internal problems with governance in order to escape from the destructive cycle of weak growth, high debt and corrosive social consequences.

This is an extraordinarily useful insight. It is highly relevant for a number of other developing countries in similar positions, and it has profound implications for Jamaica's

Professor Anthony Clayton, PhD, OD
Alcan Chair Professor
Institute of Sustainable Development
University of the West Indies, Mona

Acknowledgements

This book is a labour of love for my country and people. It is also a gift to Heads of Government, Leaders of Opposition, Permanent Secretaries, and other political leaders and their teams globally.

It is the culmination of a revised version of my doctoral thesis prepared and defended at the University of the West Indies, Mona Campus in Kingston Jamaica.

My first statement of profound thanks goes to Professor Anthony Clayton, the hardest working, most professional, competent academic I have ever met. Though he has guided government policies in several jurisdictions and consulted on key areas relating to Crime, Governance, and Sustainable Development, he still found time to guide us meticulously throughout the entire research process. For this I am grateful. His regularly scheduled cohort meetings allowed us to widen our knowledge base in several areas of research being conducted by each candidate. This will redound to the benefit of the entire Caribbean region, and other areas globally, where our graduates will no doubt, contribute significantly to development, economic growth, and higher levels of integrity within their respective institutions.

I am also very grateful to my family for their patience, encouragement, and support throughout the process (years) of conducting this research, and the many months spent travelling all over the island to conduct surveys, and interviews.

This book would not be a reality, if, during my years of conducting the research forming the foundation for this publication, I did not also have the support and encouragement of others including:

- Respondents: Former Prime Ministers, Ministers of Finance, Financial Secretaries, Central Bank Governors (JA

& BD), MPs, Heads of Government, elites/executives & technocrats, and Jamaicans surveyed;
- The staff of the Library/Document Centre of Parliament at Gordon House in Kingston, Jamaica;
- Faculty and Staff of the Sir Arthur Lewis Institute of Social and Economic Research – UWI Mona
- Faculty and staff of the Institute of Sustainable Development – UWI Mona
- The staff of the Office of Graduate Studies & Research - UWI Mona
- The staff of the Main Library - UWI Mona
- Members of the 2009 – 2015 Ph.D. Cohort – ISD, UWI Mona

This publication has been made possible because you cared enough to extend your support when it was desperately needed. You are all amazing!

Thank you,

Collette J-A Smith

Preface

Jamaica became one of the most heavily indebted nations in the world at various points in its economic history. Successive administrations have argued that borrowing is necessary to finance development and growth, but Jamaica's growth rate has been anaemic for the last four decades. This publication is an offshoot of a study that examined the causes of Jamaica's debt accumulation from 1962 to 2010, with a particular focus on the role of governance, patronage, and corruption in the accumulation of exceptionally high levels of debt, and the associated social and economic consequences.

Barbados and Singapore were used as comparators, as all three islands gained independence from Britain in the 1960s. Until 1967, Jamaica's GDP per capita of US$636 was actually higher than those of Barbados (US$580) and Singapore (US$626). Unlike the other two countries, Jamaica has not prospered. By 2012, Barbados was about three times richer per capita, and Singapore was about ten times richer. Jamaica's development, by contrast, has been undermined by its problems with profligacy, political patronage, and corruption. These have largely driven the accumulation of debt, while simultaneously undermining development and growth.

Using a convergent Mixed Method Research design, this research shows that a number of specific governance decisions, particularly with regard to unproductive investments in infrastructure projects and social programmes have contributed significantly to increasing Jamaica's public debt since independence.

This study identifies some specific mistakes and long-running patterns of failure that have resulted in the country's indebtedness, and makes a number of recommendations (with policy implications and additional recommendations to follow in Volume II) to correct this problem and put Jamaica back on the path to long-term growth, good governance, and stability.

Chapter 1

GOVERNANCE AND PUBLIC DEBT IN JAMAICA – INTRODUCTION

1.1 Introduction

Up to the late 1980s, discussions about development were centred around a country's performance on specific social and economic indicators, including per capita GDP, economic growth, and literacy rates. Since the 1990s, the quality of national leadership (governance) has gained equal importance, especially with regard to macroeconomic management, and control of public debt. Weak governance, incompetence, and corruption can result in high levels of public debt, without commensurate gains in human capital or economic development. In fact, human capital and economic development have largely stagnated for over four decades.

For many years Jamaica was known as one of the most highly indebted countries globally, with Debt-to-GDP reaching 202.6% in 1985. Jamaica's Debt-to-GDP ratio has since fluctuated and was at 130% in 2010. A debt buyback of US$300 million (US$0.46 per US$1) owed to the Government of Venezuela through the Petro Caribe agreement, which permitted Jamaica and other Caribbean territories to purchase oil under preferential arrangements, contributed to a ten percent reduction in Jamaica's 2015 Debt-to-GDP.

Yet, the 2017 ratio of over 120% was still well above sustainable levels, though a reclassification of government debt and policy actions taken by the Ministry of Finance (MOFP) resulted in a downward trajectory.

By 2019/2020, Debt-to-GDP was reduced to 95%, consistent with fiscal consolidation measures agreed, and implemented across political administrations – first under Dr. Peter Phillips as Finance

Chapter 1: Governance and Public Debt in Jamaica - Introduction

Minister, and followed through by Dr. Nigel Clarke, in the same capacity in the new JLP administration of 2016.

Subsequently, however, the country's Debt-to-GDP ratio has been on an upward (unfavourable) trajectory, partly due to the devastating economic impact of the COVID19 pandemic, and partly due to a lack of buoyancy, and economic diversification to drive GDP growth – the numerator of the ratio.

On March 18, 2021, Fitch Ratings reported that Jamaica's Debt-to-GDP ratio was "projected to reach 110.9% by end-March 2021 from 94.8% a year before, largely reflecting exchange rate depreciation and GDP contraction (61% of total government debt is in foreign currency)." Later that day, the World Bank reported that they would be providing a loan of US$150 Million to Jamaica, for COVID-19 resilience. At this rate, with GDP declining significantly in 2020 as a result of Jamaica's heavy reliance on tourism, and the impact of COVID-19 on the fallout in this main foreign exchange earning sector, Jamaica's Debt-to-GDP appears to be heading back to the highs of 2012-13.

With prudent management and a more strategic approach, however, the GOJ can counteract the negative impacts, even as they explore the many options for greater economic diversification presented in numerous studies since the 1960s. The IMF (2020) reported that as part of their debt management strategy:

> In September 2019, the Government of Jamaica conducted buybacks of outstanding global bonds coming due in 2022, 2025, and 2028, totalling around US$1 billion. These buybacks together with new bond issuance through the reopening of the global bond coming due in 2045 led to a substantial maturity extension. (IMF 2020, 19)

Jamaica, like Barbados and Singapore, received independence from Britain during the 1960s. At that time, Jamaica was the strongest economy of the three, with economic growth averaging 5.7% from 1962 to 1972 (STATIN data).

Jamaica also had a more favourable exchange rate of J $0.71 to US$1 in 1962, compared to BD $1.71 for Barbados and SG $3.06 for Singapore. As of July 23, 2021, Jamaica's exchange rate

Chapter 1: Governance and Public Debt in Jamaica - Introduction

was J$153.74 to US$1 (BOJ 2021). In spite of this early economic advantage, poor governance decisions in Jamaica have resulted in economic stagnation, unsustainably high levels of public debt, pervasive corruption, and one of the highest levels of violent crime in the world (PAHO 2010, 13; BBC 2006).

1.2 Framing the Problem

Some policymakers have blamed external shocks, including increased oil prices, structural adjustment, stabilization policies, and recessions for Jamaica's indebtedness. The findings of this study have revealed that a large portion of Jamaica's accumulated debt has been due to failures of governance more so, than to external shocks or International Financial Institutions' (World Bank, IMF, and others) stipulations.

Reports from the Auditor General, Contractor General, Hansard of Parliament, and other records, showed that politicians and their agents, repeatedly bypassed parliamentary procedures and institutional controls, leading to increased indebtedness, excessive expenditure and significant losses. Some have also argued that funds were dissipated through personal/political legacy projects, and for short-term electoral advantage (Moxam 2004; Golding 2008; Buddan 2009).

This publication makes a significant contribution to the understanding of Jamaica's post-independence fiscal problems and expands the literature on the relationship between governance, fiscal management, and development.

An analysis of data gathered from the Hansard of Parliament, surveys, elite interviews, national archives, global reports, International Monetary Fund (IMF), and the World Bank (WB) databases, revealed that several poor decisions in Jamaica, led to rapid public debt accumulation, without commensurate improvements in infrastructure, human capital development, or economic progress. These decisions included costs of more than J$530 billion just for a small subset of projects and programmes examined for this study, inclusive of high coupon rates (interest)

Chapter 1: Governance and Public Debt in Jamaica - Introduction

paid and payable on global bonds, as well as projects and programmes, some of which were deemed non-viable (due to dilapidated infrastructure, and other factors). These amounted to more than a third of Jamaica's total public debt in 2010.

As the Netherlands (2003) noted, Jamaica's recurrent and high Debt-to-GDP levels are unsustainable, as revealed by a lack of capacity to meet debt obligations and maintain reasonable levels of growth (p. 93). This has been clearly demonstrated by repeated debt restructuring - 2 technical defaults in the form of the Jamaica Debt Exchange in 2010, and the National Debt Exchange in 2012. Concurrently, as Figure 1.1 below shows, Jamaica's GDP growth has averaged less than 1% over the last 40 years.

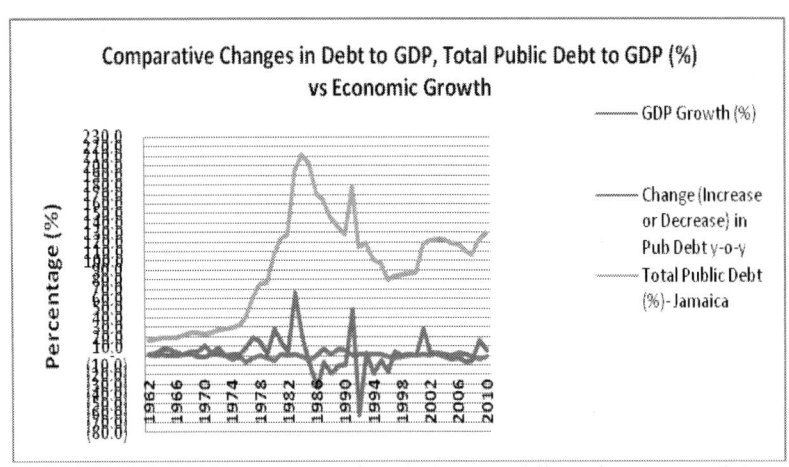

Figure 1.1 Jamaica's Econ Growth Relative to Public Debt-to-GDP (%)

Over the last two decades, governance and public debt levels in Jamaica, as in other developing economies, have come under greater scrutiny by investors and global rating agencies, as high public Debt-to-GDP levels can lead to economic destabilization. Major international financial institutions (IFIs) like the IMF and World Bank have also made improvements in the quality of governance, and structural reforms, prior conditions for providing aid and loans to member countries (UNESCAP 2009, 1).

Chapter 1: Governance and Public Debt in Jamaica - Introduction

1.3 The Conceptual Framework

While this publication has been tailored to meet the needs of a general readership, it is important to provide an overview of the research process that yielded the findings on which it is based. The conceptual framework is an integral component of the research design that introduces the phenomena being studied, and the process involved in answering the research questions posed. Some key terms and concepts used in this study include *Public Debt* which consists of the liabilities created by government borrowing, including the issuance of government securities (GOJ Public Debt Management
Act 2011, 4).

Public Debt Accumulation, which is the build-up of new debt on existing debt, has been a major issue for many developing and emerging market countries. High borrowing costs, as well as heavy dependence on the capital markets, have led to repeated borrowing, and an exponential increase in Jamaica's debt from 1962 to 2010. From 2017 to 2021, the Government of Jamaica continued to borrow heavily for infrastructural and public sector reform projects.

Finance Minister Dr Nigel Clarke announced what he reportedly referred to as "the largest programme allocation to physical infrastructure tabled by any Government of Jamaica in budget history" in his 2021 budget speech. He termed this $60-billion infrastructure programme as the Social Economic Recovery and Vaccine (SERVE) Programme for Jamaica, noting that $33-billion of that would be financed by a one-off Bank of Jamaica dividend (Linton/JIS, 2021), with no clear indication of how the remaining $27-billion would be sourced.

Debt Management involves decisions pertaining to the composition, maturity structure, and cost of debt, as well as the use of the resources acquired through government borrowing (IMF/WB 2002). Public debt accumulation and *Debt Management* are directly related to fiscal management, through the cost and

Chapter 1: Governance and Public Debt in Jamaica - Introduction

impact of the public debt on the government's budgetary decisions.

In fact, *Public Debt Management* (PDM), which the IMF defined as the procedures involved in the establishment and execution of the government's plan to access required financial resources, taking full account of the associated costs, risks, and macroeconomic goals it wishes to pursue (2002, 11), is a crucial area of fiscal responsibility. While public debt accumulation relates to the build-up of debt, *Public Debt Management* relates to strategies employed by the government to manage the components and cost of the debt incurred by the government.

The main variables in this study, *governance* and *public debt* are, therefore, inextricably linked, through government's role in fiscal management, and; the quality of oversight it provides in managing and using borrowed funds.

While *Government* here, refers to the elected officials and their agents, the definition of *Governance* used in this study is "the exercise of economic, political, and administrative authority to manage a country's affairs at all levels, comprising the mechanisms, processes, and institutions through which that authority is directed" (UN 1997, iv).

The term *'character of governance'* then, can be evaluated by examining the distinguishing features and peculiar quality of the institutions, leadership provided, and the consistency or lack thereof, between the stated intent, and consequential outcomes of the decisions that are made.

Institutions in this regard, represent "the humanly devised constraints that structure political, economic and social interactions" (North 1991, 97). This study reiterates that governance is carried out through institutions formed and coordinated by elected officials and their agents.

Since many governance decisions in Jamaica have led to the acquisition, and rapid build-up of public debt, it was important to examine the relationship between the leaders/'governors', the decisions they made in using the country's scarce resources, and the outcomes of those decisions, with particular focus on the public

Chapter 1: Governance and Public Debt in Jamaica - Introduction

debt levels. The quality of governance influenced how borrowed funds were utilized.

Non-developmental public debt accumulation, such as funds borrowed and used for housekeeping expenses, for example, hindered the often stated objectives of achieving economic growth and sustainable development.

Conceptually, and as supported by the theoretical and empirical literature, *public debt* is said to be unsustainable, if the primary balance is insufficient to stabilize the debt at manageable levels (IMF/WB 2002, Kraay and Nehru 2003, Shizume 2007, Tiwari 2013).

The conceptual framework for examining the quality of governance has often been developed by garnering the views of experts, academicians, households, and technocrats enhanced by aggregate data analysis (Kaufmann, Kraay and Mastruzzi 2006, and others). As Saisana et al. noted, trying to simplify governance and its intricate systems may create empirical problems; but metrics derived through rigour, can provide a potent tool for comparison and evaluation of socio-economic circumstances (2009, 12).

Relatively reliable metrics are global indicators of governance. Those of Kaufmann, Kraay, Mastruzzi, and others were examined, to assess Jamaica's position relative to its counterparts (at Independence from Britain) Barbados and Singapore. It was also important to examine the local relevance and validity of these indicators, by comparing them with data gathered through island-wide surveys and interviews, aimed at obtaining the perspectives of locals, elites, academicians, and experts, on the quality of governance in Jamaica, and its impact on debt accumulation. This kind of rigour was highly important, as these respondents had the first-hand experience of the socio-economic consequences of governance decisions in Jamaica, during the period of the study.

As Davis et al (2012) argued "governance can be modelled using a standard triangular schematic which posits relations between the actors (the governors) who allocate resources among or exert influence over the behaviour of other actors, the actors subject to governance (the governed), and other interested constituencies (the public)" (p. 11).

Epistemologically (to understand and appreciate the origin, nature, and foundation), knowledge of *governance* and *public debt levels* were deemed to exist in meaningful forms to the respondents and researcher, with the relationship between both phenomena being elucidated through careful empirical research, involving the experts whose knowledge has been captured through in-depth interviews, published works, archived records, and; surveys.

Lacey (2000) noted that positivist philosopher Auguste Compte adopted this kind of empiricist attitude to observe and verify human affairs (p. 261). The relationship between governance and public debt accumulation was examined from a positivistic perspective, based on the factual realities (empirical truths) of the respondents, and how they interpret their lived experiences. This guided the philosophical stance informing the methodology (strategy/action plan), and choice of methods (Crotty 2006, 3-6).

A convergent mixed methods design was employed to incorporate the qualitative and quantitative aspects of the study, acknowledging the primacy of respondents' practical knowledge, and engaging them through a language that was grounded in their shared experiences and culture. The study neither attempted to reconstruct the tools, nor the process of measuring governance; but as Kaufmann, Kraay, and Mastruzzi (2006) suggested, the author chose to "Exploit the wealth of currently-available indicators, since new ones may be of limited value" (p. 33).

Comparative World Governance Indicators (WGIs) ratings for Jamaica, Barbados, and Singapore were examined to determine trends over time, and evaluate changes as they were observed. These indicators were repeatedly referenced in several empirical studies (see Williams and Siddique 2005; UN 2007; Jalles 2011 and others). They provided a useful framework for comparatively evaluating governance, and; incorporated several features of the United Nation's eight characteristics of good governance, around

Chapter 1: Governance and Public Debt in Jamaica - Introduction

which survey and interview questions for this study were formulated.

Trends in the United Nations Human Development Indicators (HDI) were also analyzed to examine key developmental outcomes related to governance decisions made over the period studied.

1.4 Examining Governance

Governance is an intangible concept that has been examined by researchers and technocrats, using several variables and proxies. Kaufmann, Kraay and Mastruzzi (2006) presented a comprehensive evaluation of more than twenty international governance indicators including their own Worldwide Governance Indicators (WGIs). They differentiated between 'Rules-based' indicators (legislation) and 'Outcome-based' indicators (performance). Some examples of Outcome-based indicators identified were the International Budget Partnership (IBP), Investment Climate, and Global Competitiveness Index. The 'Rules-based' indicators, such as the World Bank's Doing Business, and Global Integrity Indices, are useful for providing clarity about a country's business climate and governance mechanisms.

They noted, however, that 'Rules-based' indicators can be subjective in codifying the features of a country; links from assessment to outcome can be affected by a lapse in time; while constitutional provisions can affect the level, amount, and timing of public expenditure. Yet, most economists assessing governance globally have referenced them, and; many development assistance and investment decisions have been influenced by these indicators over time.

The WGIs are based on a longitudinal study from 1996 to present and enable cross-country comparisons on the quality of governance in more than 200 countries. They are created from data captured in surveys and reports from experts, households, and firms in the private and public sector, the Gallup Poll, Global Competitiveness reports, Global Integrity, Freedom House,

Corruption Prevention Indices, assessments of the World Bank, regional banks, Ministries of Finance, and think tanks. Since the WGIs capture essential elements of many of the global indicators available, they have been selected for this study. The reports are normally presented in ranks, which show the percentage of countries falling below the ranking of the country being evaluated, under the following six dimensions of governance:

- *Voice and Accountability* – perception of the degree to which citizens can freely participate in elections. There is freedom of expression and the media;
- *Political Stability* – perception of the possibility of unconstitutionally destabilizing the government through violence or terror;
- *Governance Effectiveness* – perception of the quality of public service, public policy, and government's credibility;
- *Regulatory Quality* – perception of government's ability to formulate and implement effective policies and regulations, to spur private sector led development;
- *Rule of Law* – perception of the degree of confidence that people have in agents of the State to abide by and respect rules, regulations, contracts, property rights provisions, law enforcement, the judiciary, and; curtailment of crime and violence.
- *Control of Corruption* – perception of the extent to which public power is used for private gain; including through state capture (Hellman and Kaufmann 2001).

Countries receiving better ratings are accorded a higher percentile rank. The researcher aimed for validity evaluating the quality of governance by: (i) utilizing the globally recognized World Governance Indicators as proxies for the quality of governance globally, including Jamaica and the comparator countries, and; (ii) operationalizing 'good governance' in all survey and interview

Chapter 1: Governance and Public Debt in Jamaica - Introduction

instruments, by defining each of the following eight (8) characteristics outlined by UNESCAP (2009), and formulating questions around them:

1. *Participation* ensures that the needs and interests of everyone are factored into the decision-making process.
2. *Effectiveness and Efficiency* are achieved when resources are used in a manner that yields the greatest benefit, at the least cost, to as many as possible; while sustaining natural resources and protecting the environment.
3. *Adherence to the Rule of Law* requires a fair legal framework, impartially enforced by an upright judiciary, and police force, which recognizes and preserves human rights.
4. *Transparency* ensures that decisions taken are guided by rules and regulations, with clear, unambiguous, and precise information that is easily accessible to all.
5. *Responsiveness* requires that people are served in a timely manner.
6. *Consensus Orientation* is achieved when different interest groups are able to find a middle-ground so that the outcome serves everyone's best interest.
7. *Equity and Inclusiveness* suggest that everyone should feel a part of the governance process.
8. *Accountability* is achieved when public and private sector representatives are open and answerable to stakeholders.

This enabled consistency in the interpretation of the questions posed. Classification of the questions under these predefined headings also simplified the process of coding and analysis. Validity was also enhanced by the fact that macroeconomic data provided by the World Bank, and IMF were presented in a common currency – the US dollar, and standardized units such as percentage. This enabled effective cross-country comparison, and analysis of secondary data. Local currency units were used where appropriate.

1.5 Government's Role in Macroeconomic Management

Macroeconomics is concerned with economy-wide aggregates relating to savings, investment, money supply, interest rates, consumption and government expenditure, employment, and inflation (Maunder 1991; Todaro 1997).

The government's key macroeconomic responsibility is to craft, fiscal and monetary policies, and; to determine how, and by whom, these policies are to be implemented and managed.

Monetary policy is geared at regulating money supply, exchange rates, inflation, and interest rates, while *fiscal policy* deals with the management of public finances, through national income and expenditure. Though interest on debt is managed through fiscal policy, public debt is affected by both fiscal and monetary policy, through the impact of inflation and interest rates on the cost and maturity profile of the public debt.

The higher the level of debt accumulated, the greater the pressure on the government to reduce expenditure and/or increase revenues to meet debt service obligations. These reductions have had negative impacts on economic growth and development in Jamaica over the period of the study (from Independence in 1962 to the twenty-first century).

Effective Public Debt Management is, therefore, a central part of the government's broad macroeconomic responsibility. This has gained increasing prominence in the development literature since the 1980s. While the initial global focus at the time was on external debt, not much attention was paid to domestic debt. Consequently, Jamaica's domestic Debt-to-GDP increased from 36% in 1989 to 77% by 2003, without much international attention.

The 1990s financial crises, led to a greater focus on the total debt portfolio, and the governance institutions through which debt management strategies were to be implemented (Kappagoda 2002, 1). Today, the debates about the role of governance institutions in macroeconomic management are as active in developing, as in advanced economies of North America and Europe, particularly

Chapter 1: Governance and Public Debt in Jamaica - Introduction

since the global recession, which started in 2007/08. This has led to intense deliberations in the US Congress, the European Union, the British and other Parliaments, among economists, and in global financial markets, about government's role in managing the economy, and the need to curtail debt accumulation.

Many analysts globally have also questioned whether the government should have been involved in Quantitative Easing (QE), which is the central bank's purchase of longer-term government securities to stimulate economic activity (BIS 2011; Vinals 2012). QE was expected to contribute to a reduction in interest rates, increase in money supply, and expansion in the volume of consumer loans.

While some saw QE as a less than ideal Keynesian approach to drive growth, higher than average levels of growth have been achieved by countries like China and Singapore, with significant government involvement and oversight (Lee 2000, Chang 2002, Kaufmann 2003, and Toye 2006).

1.6 Channels from Governance to Public Debt

The governments of some territories have sought to achieve development and growth by focusing on creating a favourable, enabling environment for the private sector, while others have taken on a more overt role by investing directly in income-generating projects and programmes. The latter strategy depends particularly on there being effective controls, high levels of competence and integrity in government, and robust, well-managed institutions. Otherwise, there is likely to be a temptation to direct public funds towards political allies and supporters, if strong institutional controls are not in place. It was, therefore, important to examine the channels through which governance decisions can and will impact indebtedness, so political leaders, technocrats, and citizens can understand and evaluate the channels that may or may not be functioning effectively, and whether there are features within them that can be altered to curtail indebtedness. These channel are:

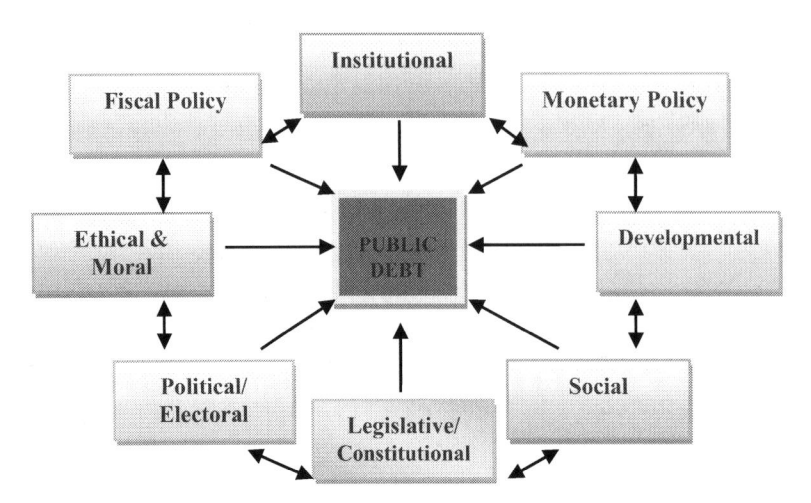

Chapter 1: Governance and Public Debt in Jamaica - Introduction

Figure 1.2 Channels through which Governance Impacts Public Debt © CJASmith

1. **Institutional** – This relates to the capacity and autonomy of agents of the government, as well as the rules and regulations governing acquisition, accumulation, and repayment of public debt.
2. **Fiscal Policy** – The impact of this channel depends on the competence of the team with responsibility for crafting the budget, devising revenue strategies, and meeting fiscal obligations. Accuracy and timeliness are crucial, to ensure that the actions taken are aligned with an effective debt management strategy.
3. **Monetary Policy** – As with fiscal policy, this channel can affect public debt accumulation positively (reduction) or negatively (increase), through the management of interest, exchange and inflation rates. Inefficiency, repeated devaluations, and lack of coordination can, thus, lead to unsustainable levels of debt. Figure 1.2 below outline the manner in which each channel functions to impact public debt.
4. **Ethical and Moral** – This channel can facilitate or curtail corruption, immoral conduct by public officials, and the

Chapter 1: Governance and Public Debt in Jamaica - Introduction

circumvention of institutional controls, which can result in rapid debt accumulation.

5. **Developmental** – If this channel is not managed well, it could lead to a lack of strategic planning, and substandard human, infrastructural and technological development, resulting in wastage, and a resultant exponential increase in the nation's public debt.
6. **Political/Electoral** – This is a very important channel requiring close monitoring, to prevent graft, nepotism, and wanton use of resources. National leaders making governance decisions, including those relating to the acquisition and use of public debt, are chosen by the ballot. Poor candidate selection can result in nepotism, profligacy, corruption, and wastage, and ultimately, further debt accumulation.
7. **Legislative/Constitutional** – The legislative/constitutional channel provides for checks and balances on governance decisions, to ensure that there is probity, accountability, and transparency. Poor management of this channel can have devastating consequences on the economy, and lives of citizens. Legislation must be effective and consistently enforced in tandem with constitutional provisions, to ensure that there are robust constraints to deter profligacy and wanton debt accumulation.
8. **Social** – This is an extremely important channel through which decisions on human capital development, safety, security and health are made. Effective developmental policies and programmes can expand the human resource, and technical capacity, to reduce indebtedness and welfare dependency. This, in turn, working in tandem with the health, and national security programmes, can lessen the likelihood of public debt accumulation for welfare programmes. The government's social service philosophy will influence how these programmes are financed, and the level of debt accumulated.

Chapter 1: Governance and Public Debt in Jamaica - Introduction

1.7 Government's Involvement in the Economy

There are different schools of thought regarding the extent to which the government should be involved in the economy – whether from a capitalist, socialist, or mixed economic system. Yet, there is a consensus amongst leaders and economists of varying ideological persuasions, that there has to be some level of governmental involvement.

Smith ([1776]1981) for example, argued that the government's main role was to provide security, property rights protection, and an enabling environment to drive productivity and growth, with the market determining appropriate levels of supply and demand.

Keynes, on the other hand, presented a more interventionist perspective, focusing on the government's role in the monetary system, to reduce unemployment and increase demand through short-term stimulus spending ([1936]1971).

Though their perspectives differed, both Smith and Keynes were unsupportive of profligate government spending and excessive debt accumulation. In fact, Keynes firmly advocated for the prudent management of national reserves, as he felt that an imprudent government could make unreasonable demands on the Treasury. He also argued that an "Act of Parliament is a very ineffective method of curtailing the powers of a government, and; in almost every known case of stress or strain, in which the note regulations interfere with the wishes of the government of the day it is the former which has given way" (1971, 235).

While Smith ([1776]1981) argued for government to take a laissez-faire approach, Keynes (1971) believed government should play a more activist role. Government activism is more pronounced in economies like China, South Korea, Singapore, and Cuba than in most Western economies. The extent of the government's involvement has often been examined in empirical studies through levels of democracy, frequency of elections, the ratio of trade with other countries, and government expenditure as a percentage of Gross Domestic Product (GDP) (see Williams and Siddique 2005).

Though the literature often highlighted openness and democracy as features that contribute to good governance and development, relatively closed economies like Cuba have still been able to achieve high standards of development, particularly in education and health care. This apparent anomaly has led to empirical works, like that of Sirowy and Inkeles (1990), who evaluated several studies looking at the impact of democracy and development on growth from neutral, pro, and counter positions. After extensive analyses, they concluded that political procedures and institutions were the key factors required to support democracy and spur growth.

Przeworski and Limongi (1993) conducted a similar analysis of twenty-one empirical studies. Eight found in favour of democracy, eight against, and five found no difference. They concluded that "political institutions do matter for growth but thinking in terms of regimes does not seem to capture relevant differences" (p. 51).

It is clear, therefore, that economic performance is affected by the quality of institutions, irrespective of the economic or political system in place. A country like Singapore, for example, with leaders perceived as benevolent dictators, has consistently recorded growth and development comparable to highly democratic ones. Singapore scored between 98 and 100% on the WGI institutional measures of Regulatory Quality every year since the indicators were introduced in 1996.

The works of Coase (1992), North (1990, 1991), Acemoglu et al. (2003) and others, have led to a greater focus on underlying institutional factors, such as rules, regulations, and the quality of decision-making, that influence economic performance. Consequently, the state versus market approach to government involvement has led to new debates within the political, economic, and academic spheres, about how these institutions ought to be structured and managed, to enhance development and growth.

Since the 1990s, many once closed, socialist economies have opened up to market-driven policies, and heavy external borrowing. Some have done so voluntarily, and others, out of an obligation to meet stipulations of multilateral institutions. Particular challenges are presented when highly indebted, low-growth countries aim to achieve sustained growth and development, without effective institutions.

1.8 Governance Institutions – An Empirical Review

There is now an expanding body of literature suggesting that weak institutions result in poor macroeconomic performance, unsustainable debt, and fiscal challenges (Kaufmann, Kraay, and Zoido-Lobathon 2000; Khan 2007; Jalles 2011). Amany and Katsaiti (2010) also noted that a "[w]eak governance and institutional infrastructure could have a direct negative effect on growth by lowering the productivity of the economy" (p. 1), as institutions affect the quality of fiscal management. This view was also shared by Edwards and Tabellini (1991), and North (1991) who argued that political and economic institutions are both essential.

However, Sachs and Warner (1995b) countered these arguments in their study, using data from the 'Bureaucratic Efficiency' index, arguing that an abundance of natural resources could be inimical to economic growth, even if institutions were considered.

Later, Acemoglu et al. (2003) used settler mortality as an instrument of governance institutions for several former British colonies, to examine whether there were correlations between bad macroeconomic policies and economic volatility; or if there were institutional factors at play. They found that weak institutions were characteristic of countries with poor macroeconomic policies, including unrestrained powers given to politicians and elites, lack of respect for property rights, unbridled corruption and political instability (p. 49). They concluded that such countries were more prone to experiencing economic instability. That body of work highlights the nexus between governance institutions and macroeconomic performance. Similar conclusions were drawn from empirical studies conducted by Easterly and Levine (2003), and Rodrik et al. (2004).

Nevertheless, these arguments were refuted by Henry and Miller (2008), who examined the divergence between real per capita incomes for Jamaica and Barbados from 1960 to 2000, and concluded that the macroeconomic policies chosen, and not institutions per se, accounted for differences in economic performance (p. 1). However, when their work was juxtaposed against that of Acemoglu et al., the concluding arguments were found to be related, as the policies highlighted were formulated and implemented within, and through, institutions of governance.

Sachs (2003) also sought to refute Acemoglu et al.'s arguments, using a malaria index, and governance indicators, to argue that when regressed against per capita incomes, the evidence showed that development depended on a confluence of geographical, institutional, and political factors (p. 9).

Notwithstanding these arguments, the works produced by Acemoglu et al. (2001-2003) have been some of the most popularly referenced in the governance and institutions literature (Williams and Siddique 2005, 151).

This focus on governance institutions has continued, as economists, theorists, and academicians have sought to examine the impact of institutions on macroeconomic performance.

An institutional feature that was repeatedly discussed in the literature was the *constitutional protection of property rights*. This was also a key element in the Washington Consensus (IFI economic policy prescriptions) and relates to the important corresponding '*adherence to the rule of law*' characteristic, identified by the United Nations as a central feature of good governance.

There was also a great emphasis in the literature and guidelines published by international financial institutions such as the IMF and World Bank, and bilateral lenders, on the need for institutional reforms in borrowing countries, to improve efficiency, transparency, and accountability in debt management (IMF/WB 2002; WB/IDB 2006; EC 2007). This is consistent with North's

Chapter 1: Governance and Public Debt in Jamaica - Introduction

seminal works (1990, 1991), which highlighted that transaction costs from ineffective institutions can undermine economic performance through weak governance.

1.9 Examining the Quality of Governance

Several metrics have been presented and examined to evaluate the quality of national governance. Among the most frequently cited indicators are the World Governance Indicators (WGIs) presented by researchers from the World Bank. The WGIs present the result of assessments of the quality of governance in more than 200 countries globally.

The IMF, as the world's largest provider of loan funds to governments, has also focused on the quality of governance through its emphasis on the need to reduce corruption and improve resource management. It does this through policy advice and technical assistance aimed at public sector reforms, revenue collection, budgeting, and the encouragement of transparency, efficiency, and effective regulatory controls along with guidelines for public debt management (Camdessus 1997, 3; WB 2002).

1.10 Key Issues Relevant to Public Debt Management

According to the IMF/World Bank (2002), the key goal of public debt management is to guarantee that the government is able to meet its financing needs and pay its bills at "the lowest possible cost over the medium to long run, consistent with a prudent degree of risk" (p. 363). These include market risk and refinancing risk, which take into account exchange rate risk, interest rate risk, liquidity risk, and sovereign debt default, insolvency of businesses and banks, and loss of credibility in domestic and international capital markets. These have also influenced decisions relating to the cost and maturity profile of Jamaica's domestic and external debt.

Effective public debt management (PDM) can be a powerful tool to influence economic development, through tactical maturity

Chapter 1: Governance and Public Debt in Jamaica - Introduction

scheduling, diversified placement, sensitivity analysis, and timely adjustment to changing market conditions (IDB 2007; BIS 2011).

Unfortunately, significant portions of loan funds borrowed by, and granted to Jamaica across successive administrations, have been wasted through poor maturity scheduling and fiscal imprudence. Senior economist Damien King, and financial analyst Dennis Chung agreed that the real problem in managing Jamaica's public debt was the quality of governance (Love 101, 2011).

1.11 The Relevance of Governance to Development and Debt

As societies moved through different stages of development, from bartering to agrarian subsistence, through to industrialization, many found that they had limited resources with which to attain the levels of development required to sustain their rapidly growing populations. Some, like Singapore and China, financed development through savings, and parsimonious (guided by frugality) public expenditure. Others such as Japan opted to borrow externally (Nurkse 1953; Lee 2000).

Jamaica's counterparts, Barbados and Singapore borrowed externally up to the early 1990s, and subsequently focused more on domestic sources of finance (Lee 2000; Moore and Skeete 2010). On the other hand, decision-makers in Jamaica have borrowed heavily from both domestic and external sources and then had to face stringent loan terms and conditions, such as Structural Adjustment and Stabilization policies of the World Bank and IMF.

The problem was then exacerbated, as Jamaica's fiscal and monetary policies for almost sixty (60) years were mainly crafted to reduce budget deficits, control inflation, and manage rapid and unfavourable movements in the exchange rate.

Yet, there are those who continue to blame Jamaica's indebtedness on external market conditions, oil price shocks, natural disasters, global recessions, and the structural and institutional reforms recommended by its creditors, including the World Bank and IMF - effectively presenting the necessary adjustments as though they were the original cause of the problem.

Chapter 1: Governance and Public Debt in Jamaica - Introduction

As then Prime Minister Patterson argued, the oil crisis "triggered the debt crisis, it caused the balance of payment problems, it resulted in the shortage of [foreign] exchange, it led to constant devaluations. That is what drove us into the jaws of the IMF" (2000, 3).

The impact of the oil crisis during the 1970s, financial crises of the 1980s and 1990s, and recent global recessions were not trivial. However, this study found that over the post-independence period, policy failures, profligacy, and weakness in the exercise of political, administrative, and economic authority (governance) have contributed more significantly to Jamaica's public debt than policymakers have admitted, notwithstanding the impact of external shocks. This had not received sufficient analytical attention to date and gave rise to the need for the study resulting in this publication.

1.12 Rationale for Conducting the Study and Key Questions

The main reason for conducting the study was to examine whether the quality of governance in Jamaica since its Independence from Britain in 1962, had played a role in the rapid accumulation of decades of public debt.

It was also important to see how this debt accumulation had affected, and been affected by, development-related governance decisions such as human capital development, education, health, and national security.

The researcher also wanted to examine if there were any correlations between macroeconomic performance, development, and expenditure on social services. The economic and institutional performance of Singapore and Barbados were examined through available publications, global indicators from reputable institutions, interviews (in the case of Jamaica and Barbados), and data made available through their national statistical offices, and archives.

For almost sixty (60) years, Jamaica's public debt has undermined development and economic growth. As Finance

Chapter 1: Governance and Public Debt in Jamaica - Introduction

Minister Phillips noted, "Jamaica has experienced a high-debt low-growth cycle for a number of years, occasioned by persistent fiscal deficits, long-standing structural impediments to competitiveness, and low resilience to macroeconomic shocks and natural hazards" (GOJ 2014, 1). This study seeks to identify how governance has contributed to this problem and to propose possible solutions.

This study is about governance decisions, and the accumulation and management of public debt in Jamaica, with a specific focus on how rapidly this debt has expanded, from 1962 to 2010, and beyond.

Key Questions: The central question asked was:

How has the character of governance in post-independent Jamaica contributed to the country's indebtedness from 1962 to 2010?

When GDP grows faster than public debt, the Debt-to-GDP ratio declines. Conversely, when GDP grows more slowly than the public debt, remains stagnant, or declines the Debt-to-GDP ratio increases, and this is unfavourable.

Some have argued that GDP growth and economic development can be achieved through capital accumulation, foreign direct investments, or borrowing. Jamaica has incurred unsustainably high levels of public debt, arguably, through these channels, to achieve these objectives (GDP growth and economic development). Yet, growth, development, and productivity in Jamaica, have stagnated for more than four decades, relative to Barbados and Singapore.

To examine the underlying factors relating to this, the central question was broken down and answered through four specific questions:

1. What is the extent of Jamaica's indebtedness, and; how has this been influenced by; or influenced, development-related governance decisions?

2. What role has governance played in fostering the build-up of debt in Jamaica from 1962 to 2010?
3. How do Jamaica's public debt and economic performance compare to that of Barbados and Singapore?
4. How does Jamaica rank against Barbados and Singapore in terms of global indicators of governance?

1.13 Growth, Development, Governance and Debt

Growth focuses on movements in a country's real gross domestic product (GDP), while development goes further, to address socio-economic issues related to provisions in health, education, and national security.

Poor governance through weak institutions can seriously undermine long-term economic growth and development (Mauro 1995; Acemoglu et al. 2003).

This creates a conundrum, as a country like Jamaica that experiences negative or anaemic growth, is likely to end up borrowing at premium rates, to meet its expenditure obligations, worsening the problem. This study, therefore, sought to identify some of the governance factors that may have contributed to Jamaica's rapid accumulation of public debt from 1962 to 2010.

1.14 Relevance of the Study

This study is important, timely, and relevant as it presents an objective historical analysis of how governance impacted public debt in Jamaica from 1962 to 2010. It makes an important contribution to the global literature on governance and public debt management in small, open, import-dependent developing countries like Jamaica, and; presents recommendations to assist in correcting the problems identified. While other studies have identified some of the associated problems, none has provided the kind of historical-comparative analysis or the recommendations presented in this study.

Chapter 1: Governance and Public Debt in Jamaica - Introduction

This study also examined public debt challenges in a number of more developed countries (MDCs) in Asia, North America, Europe, and Latin America. And so, given the quality and depth of the analyses and findings of this study, this publication will provide excellent insights for leaders of government globally, as well as their technocrats and advisors, and; contribute to guiding governance decisions, and debt management strategies, in many countries whose authorities are willing to learn from Jamaica's experience.

Chapter 2

GOVERNANCE, FISCAL POLICY AND DEBT
THEORETICAL FOUNDATIONS

2.1 Introduction

As noted in Chapter One, it is important to examine if and how the character of governance in post-independent Jamaica contributed to the country's indebtedness. The character of governance is reflected in the quality of economic, political, and administrative decisions made by national leaders, and the resultant outcomes.

The United Nations (UN) emphasized that good governance is achieved when there is transparency, equity, participation, and accountability in a country's institutions, such as its Parliament and ministries. They further noted that violence, corruption and poverty undermine good governance (2011, 1).

Chapter One provided an introduction to the study, demonstrated the relevance of the publication, and prefaced its content. This segment, Chapter Two, delves further, beginning with an examination of the theoretical and empirical literature on the nexus between governance and macroeconomic performance, with specific reference to growth, development, fiscal management, institutional economics, plantation models of development, deficit financing, and public debt. After all, the main aim of good governance is to ensure prudent management of resources, to achieve equitable and sustainable development.

Some have argued that countries can achieve growth and development objectives by accumulating surpluses, from high levels of productive output, or borrowing. Others have highlighted the negative socio-economic impact of incurring high levels of public debt to stimulate growth and development (Nurkse 1953). However, sustainable growth and development are unlikely, without fiscal discipline.

Chapter 2: Governance, Fiscal Policy and Debt - Theoretical Foundations

2.2 Governance, Sustainable Development, and Debt

The etymology of *'governance'* rests in the Latin word 'gubenare', which means, to steer or captain a ship (Chor Tik Teh 2009). Governance has also been linked to an old French word 'gouvernance', which means control (Cosenza 2007). As Hall and Benn noted, "Our expectations of good governance are not limited to styles of ruling, but also to the provisions which governments make for a civilized life" (2003, 222).

As the United Nations (UN) emphasized, governance is essential for economic prosperity and sustainable human development. In their view, an inefficient government is likely to waste scarce resources, so that even if external help is received it will make no difference (UNDP 1997). This inefficiency in governance can lead to excessive debt accumulation, and curtail sustainable development. According to the Bruntland Commission, sustainable development results in a progressive transformation of societies and economies and can be pursued multi-dimensionally from social, political, and physical paths, recognizing the importance of inter-, and intra-generational equity (1987).

Therefore, the burden of debt incurred by the present generation ought not to be borne by future generations, unless a corresponding accumulation of assets is also transferred. Acknowledging this, the Government of Jamaica (GOJ) under Finance Minister, Dr. Peter Phillips, gave the following undertaking:

> [T]he policy decisions we take now as a Government, will not only be reflective of the immediate impact but will have due regard to the financial implications or burden for future generations. We recognize that the historical pattern whereby both high Central Government fiscal deficits and the recurrent assumption of contingent and direct liabilities of public bodies, financed by public debt and an increasing tax burden is unsustainable. (2014, 3)

Chapter 2: Governance, Fiscal Policy and Debt - Theoretical Foundations

This was a paradigm shift from the past. It provided a useful point from which to pivot the discourse on good governance, indebtedness, and sustainable development. Good governance requires transparency, accountability, and observance of the rule of law in managing fiscal resources, to achieve development goals (IMF/WB 2002). The ultimate objective of good governance is to enhance development (AUSAID 2002; UNESCAP 2009). Development takes into account citizens' access to education, health, security, reasonable incomes, and involvement in the process of decision-making about matters affecting them.

Abdellatif (2003), and Henry and Miller (2008) argued that poor governance, through corruption, mismanagement of public funds, human rights abuses, and misuse of power, impede development. Henry and Miller's research emphasized that countries that had similar resource endowments and circumstances prior to Independence, demonstrated significant differences in performance and social progress, largely as a result of the policies they chose. Transparency International concurred, noting that poor governance and corruption have simultaneously hindered progress, and increased indebtedness in Jamaica (2010, 3).

2.3 The Role of Government

Government has an indispensable role to play in minimizing indebtedness, ensuring security, law and order, property rights, justice, public infrastructure, providing access to education and healthcare (Smith [1776]1981, North 1991; Acemoglu et al 2003; Henry and Miller 2008). While this relates to the government's social responsibility, there are divergent views on whether social services should be provided solely by the government, the private sector, or through public-private partnerships (ECLAC 2001; Nanto 2009).

Some economists have argued that government should concentrate on areas like infrastructural development, and structural transformation to achieve particular social and economic

Chapter 2: Governance, Fiscal Policy and Debt - Theoretical Foundations

outcomes (Keynes 1971; Lewis 1954). Others believe that the government's intervention outside of a few core areas, can do at least as much harm as good (Smith [1776]1981; Ricardo 1955).

One particularly sensitive aspect of this debate is the likelihood of vested interest influencing corrupt practices that may lead to increases in public expenditure, and misallocation of funds. Partly as a result, the general intellectual and policy climate has shifted from majority support for an active role for the state in economic and social matters, towards a generally more sceptical view of the government's involvement in these areas given the proclivity for some politicians to accede to the demands of vested interest groups, and powerful elites (Bucchanan 1984; North 1991).

There is also a challenge to the moral authority of the state to tax and spend, and thereby to reallocate resources from one group to another, and a questioning of the efficiency, competence, and integrity with which this is done. The discussion now is less about whether government is a good or bad thing per se, and more about how much government intervention is required, as well as when, and for what purposes (Karagiannis, Clayton, and Bailey, pending 2014).

2.3.1 Government's Role in the Provision of Social Services

Articles 25 and 26 of the United Nations Declaration of Human Rights states that "Everyone has the right to a standard of living adequate for the health and well-being of himself and his family, including food, clothing, housing, and medical care and necessary social services" (2008, 9). Government has a moral responsibility to ensure that these rights are upheld. However, with these rights come the accompanying moral responsibilities of citizens to contribute productively to society.

Much of the classical works in this area from Smith, Keynes, Ricardo, and Lewis speaks to the role of government in providing

Chapter 2: Governance, Fiscal Policy and Debt - Theoretical Foundations

social services geared at development. Smith, for example, argued that the government's main role was to:

i. Protect its people from violence and attack, through a military force (p. 879);
ii. Protect all members of society from injustices and oppression, through an effective justice system (p. 901), and;
iii. Establish and maintain public institutions for the benefit of all, without any special gain being obtained by a minority of individuals or groups ([1776]1981, 916).

He emphasized that this would enable economic progress, as the government's actions would promote commercial activities, education and training, as it seeks to establish infrastructure and public institutions for development. Smith felt that these were essential for peaceful existence and good order.

Pantin (1989) also highlighted the government's role in the legislative process, and enforcing law and order, noting that irrespective of ideological persuasion, most economists would agree that this role included the provision of security, health, education, and basic social welfare (p. 5).

Those who subscribe to a strictly socialist ideology may advocate for government to exercise direct control over the provision of social services. Capitalists, on the other hand, may expect government to play more of a regulatory role. Notwithstanding these divergent perspectives, much of the debate has surrounded whether this role should be discretionary or developmental (Thomas 2003); or whether the strategies to be employed should be market-led, or state-led (Pantin 1989, 5).

Thomas (2003), for example, noted that there has been a developing trend to integrate governance with social policy, institutional and organizational restructuring, and economic growth (p. 119). This has gained greater attention, as an increasing number

Chapter 2: Governance, Fiscal Policy and Debt - Theoretical Foundations

of international financial institutions (IFI) and donors are now linking their support to the ability of beneficiary countries to meet global governance standards, and benchmarks like the United Nation's Sustainable Development Goals (SDGs). The UN argued that good governance was essential to achieving these targets (UN 2007, 1).

Even in the face of these requirements, aid flows and grant funding for human capital and infrastructural development projects are declining. This poses a challenge for open, import-dependent, highly indebted developing countries like Jamaica, with recurring budget deficits, and a heavy dependence on aid, grants, and concessionary loans to bolster development programmes. Figure 2.1 highlights the inter-relationships between social service expenditure and debt and the national budget.

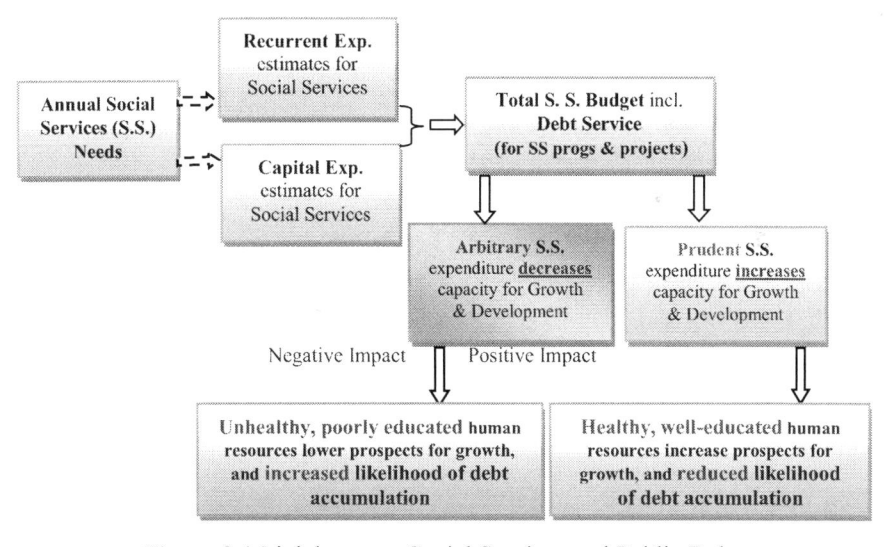

Figure 2.1 Link between Social Services and Public Debt ©CJASmith

There is consensus in the literature that strategic investment in human capital can enhance economic performance and development (Ricardo [1817]2002; Rosenstein-Rodan 1943; Nurkse 1953; Toye 2006). However, the positive impact of this is subject to the constraint that these investments are properly

Chapter 2: Governance, Fiscal Policy and Debt - Theoretical Foundations

evaluated, and directed through effective institutions, with appropriately crafted development plans, aimed at reducing debt dependence, and spurring economic growth. Arbitrary social service expenditure, financed by borrowed funds, can retard GDP growth and increase indebtedness.

2.3.2 Governance Institutions and Macroeconomic Performance

While the early works of economists like Smith, Ricardo, and Keynes have had a significant influence on development policies globally, there was much focus on the responsibilities of government, but not much on the role of governance in macroeconomic performance.

Over the last two decades, some studies have been conducted to examine the relationship between governance, and macroeconomic performance. Buchanan's contribution to *Public Choice,* and the works of *Institutional Economists* like Coase, Williamson, and North have served to emphasize that weak governance, inefficiency, information asymmetry, corruption, and nepotism can result in significant transaction costs, and increased indebtedness. This often occurs through profligacy and state capture, as unscrupulous persons seek to influence the legislative and fiscal processes in their favour (Hellman and Kaufmann 2001).

There is now a popular view amongst many economists that effective institutions are required, to improve governance and macroeconomic performance (North 1990; Acemoglu et al 2003; Rodrik, Subramanian and Trebbi 2004; Amany and Katsaiti 2010). Though the arguments of institutional economists are sound, Henry and Miller (2008) have suggested that macroeconomic policy choices were paramount, in determining economic performance and outcomes.

Sach (2003) also posited that geographical location and natural endowments were more reliable predictors of economic

Chapter 2: Governance, Fiscal Policy and Debt - Theoretical Foundations

performance than institutions. Yet, they have acknowledged the integral link between governance and economic performance.

2.4 Governance at the National Level

Governance is multidimensional and occurs at the global, national, local, and corporate levels. This study focuses on governance at the national level. Still, there are commonalities. In the same way that private companies are expected to adhere to principles of good governance to drive shareholder value, public sector entities are encouraged to institutionalize these principles, to improve economic performance, and create sustainable value for their 'stakeholder citizens' (IFAC 2009, 20).

Understanding the evolution of governance in a particular jurisdiction helps create a better appreciation of how this objective can be achieved, and; provides insights on how power has been devolved to policymakers in Jamaica, to make decisions, many of which have led to rapid debt accumulation.

During medieval times, rulers were thought to have had divine rights. Political philosophy later gained prominence, leading to lively debates among philosophers, statesmen, and economists about the role of government. While Hobbes felt that rulers had divine rights, fifteenth-century philosopher Nicolas de Cusa, who played a significant role in promoting democracy in Medieval Europe, saw human beings as equal and divine (Miller 2013).

On the other hand, Aristotle held the view that political power resulted from natural inequalities in political skill and virtue, arguing that human beings were naturally anti-social, and so the sovereign should be vested with complete control. In the modern era, governments are selected by consent, expressed through voting. Peters (1962) noted that Hobbes' examination of the nation-state involved an exceptional analysis of the interplay of such ideas as rights, law, contract, liberty, sovereignty, and commonwealth, along with an argument that sought to justify government on the basis of an "ethical theory which Hobbes

Chapter 2: Governance, Fiscal Policy and Debt - Theoretical Foundations

deduced from man's desire for peace and self-preservation" (p. 13). Though he embraced autocracy, Hobbes offended Parliament and the royalists, by arguing that government was by consent of the people who had to devolve power to them.

Notwithstanding the objections to Hobbes's views, Members of Parliament in Jamaica, who are the architects of laws and policies governing debt acquisition and use, are chosen by the consent of the people, through democratic elections, within a Westminster system. These Parliamentary procedures are influenced by the customs and practices of the English Common Law, which along with the protection of property rights, have been identified as key institutional characteristics required to achieve long-run economic stability (Smith [1776]1981; Henry and Miller 2008).

In the works of Erskine May which guides Parliamentary practice, "the word 'parliament' was first used in England in the thirteenth century, to describe an enlarged meeting of the King's council, attended by barons, bishops and prominent royal servants" (2004, 12), who were expected to advise him on law-making, administration, and justice.

Throughout the eighteenth and nineteenth centuries, political institutions in British colonies were comprised of governors, council, and assembly (Hall and Benn 2003). Due to the attractiveness and value of the sugar industry in the colonies, the Crown exercised great influence over the institutions formed. This resulted in the Lords of the Privy Council Committee of Trade, taking on the roles of lawmaker and authority over the islands' revenues and expenditures.

Local assemblies later sought to wrest authority from the councils and governors, who represented the Crown. The Westminster-Whitehall system was then introduced to Jamaica in 1953 to protect the Crown's interest. British colonial authorities maintained oversight until the island gained internal autonomy in 1959, and full independence in 1962 (Lal and Myint 1998).

Chapter 2: Governance, Fiscal Policy and Debt - Theoretical Foundations

Westminster deals with Parliamentary operations, while Whitehall refers to the civil service.

> Central to self-government, was the right to order the lives of the enslaved. But to a degree, in practice, legislatures delegated governance of the enslaved to the managers of the estates. It has been asserted that the style of management in public institutions, private corporations and family households today, is the legacy of the style of governance on estates during slavery. (Hall and Benn 2003, 216)

Public sector institutions in Jamaica today, including those vested with debt management responsibility, still reflect this plantation-style of governance, bequeathed by the leaders of the pre-, and post-independence period. The plantation system was an offshoot of the mercantile system. Though steeped in British traditions, and sympathetic to Britain's need for economic dominance, Smith ([1776]1981) argued that, while the stated aim of the mercantile system was to enrich every country and improve their balance of trade, "it seems to follow an opposite plan: to discourage exportation and encourage importation" (p. 815). Ricardo ([1817]2002) concurred, referring to this as the "injustices suffered by the colonies" (p. 228).

Consequently, the governance decisions which supported mercantilism contributed to Jamaica's current account and fiscal deficits, later resulting in the acquisition of debt. Free trade replaced mercantilism in the late 1950s, as a greater sense of nationalism and desire for self-government arose. Members of the council and assembly formed executive committees to exercise authority, prepare estimates of revenue and expenditure (budgets), and enact laws. Subsequently, there were massive capital outflows and rapid debt accumulation in several plantation economies like Jamaica. This historical review is important to provide clarity in the analysis of Jamaica's post-independence budgets and to demonstrate how governance decisions influenced the country's indebtedness and poor economic performance.

Chapter 2: Governance, Fiscal Policy and Debt - Theoretical Foundations

The net budget balance (deficit or surplus) indicates if debt financing is required. Power to borrow is delegated to national leaders through the Constitution, which is the supreme law, containing the fundamental principles and rules to guide the political, legal, and economic activities of the state. Unfortunately, fiscal rules have not always been observed or adhered to in Jamaica, resulting in rapid debt accumulation.

2.5 The Electoral System and Governance

Jamaica, like Barbados, and Singapore, adopted the Westminster Parliamentary model, with a first-past-the-post (FPTP) electoral system, in which the winning candidate is the one who obtains the largest number of votes. While there are arguments in favour of this system, Ryan (2003) argued that small Caribbean states do not provide the best political structures for this 'winner take all' model in which resources are often wasted or inefficiently organized (p. 182).

Mahmood (2001) also noted that the FPTP gives greater significance to the candidate than the political party; candidates win because of personality and are virtually immune from discipline; they depend heavily on localized loyalties, and; many keep enmeshed in parliament through 'pork barrel politics', leading to challenges of vote-buying and campaign financing. He felt that an unethical candidate could, therefore, siphon off resources for personal gain, at the expense of the State.

While Mahmood acknowledged the simplicity of the FPTP system, he argued that it creates problems for good governance and fiscal management. He indicated a preference for a Proportional Representational Party-List system (PRPL), which he argued was fairer, as it secures a close relationship between votes cast and seats won (p. 128-32). He felt that this system gives more power to the party than the candidate, to ensure greater equity in the distribution of state resources.

Chapter 2: Governance, Fiscal Policy and Debt - Theoretical Foundations

While the points raised by Mahmood (2001) and Ryan (2003) highlighted some of the challenges which have contributed to poor governance and indebtedness in Jamaica, the significantly better historical economic performance of former colonies like Barbados and Singapore that have also used the FPTP system, raised further questions. Acemoglu et al (2003) argued that it was the quality of governance institutions created in these former colonies, which accounted for the difference in their performance and economic outcomes.

While in the past, citizens may have been satisfied with having political leaders make decisions on their behalf, there is now a greater focus on the need for good governance, effective institutions, increased participation, and the promotion of ethical behaviour in the crafting of public policy, to achieve sustainable development, through prudent fiscal management.

2.6 The Role of Public Policy in the Governance Process

The key issues surrounding public policy are essentially political, so that "good governance refers to no more and no less than the fundamental character of the relations between citizen and state" (Thomas 1996, 56). An ethical philosopher like Kant, for example, would expect politicians to observe the deontological rule, and act morally, in the citizens' interest. However, one recognizes that while politicians and members of the legislature generally determine the final shape of public policy, the interplay among stakeholders within the policy-making process, influences outcomes (Jones 1974; Stone 1993). Thus, the government's ability to create and implement effective policies may be undermined by the level of influence that interest groups are allowed to wield (state capture).

According to Hellman and Kaufmann (2001) state capture relates to the extent to which firms and powerful individuals seek to influence legislation that is advantageous to their interest, and may provide illicit benefits to those holding public office (p. 1). In

Chapter 2: Governance, Fiscal Policy and Debt - Theoretical Foundations

Jamaica's case, powerful elites have sought and gained generous concessions and waivers, through legislative provisions (Jones 1981; Stone 1985; IMF 2010). As a result, billions of dollars of government revenues in Jamaica have been expended, and tax revenues foregone, without commensurate economic benefit. The IMF (2010) estimated these revenue losses at approximately J$20 billion to $25 billion annually (p. 49).

As Jones (1974) argued, the interactions between administrative and political authority and major economic interests, have defied the assumption that it is purely the executive arm of government, through the state bureaucracy, that determines public policy. In his view, the planter class in the Caribbean exercised dominance over the public policy process. The OCG (2010) highlighted this in a report on the divestment of a valuable property in Jamaica, in which there were questionable private negotiations between public officials and the principals (2010, 34). The challenge worsens when public officials receive private gains from the interactions (Hellman and Kaufmann 2000). Jones (1974) reported that:

> Throughout the "Crown Colony" political phase in Jamaica, through the era of "Representative Government" to "Self-Government", and ultimately to the age of independence, public policy outputs have been largely influenced and dominated by planter interests and at the expense of the lowly social strata." (p. 5)

Jamaica's fiscal challenges and rapid debt accumulation have, therefore, been exacerbated by legislative provisions facilitating concessions, waivers, and subsidies, to powerful elites, (MOFP executive, pers. comm.). Jones further argued that the policies implemented to benefit the lower socio-economic groups were largely formulated in response to mass uprisings and rebellion. Political leaders in Jamaica have capitalized on this since 1938, and gained political control over the distribution of state resources, exacerbating the problem.

Chapter 2: Governance, Fiscal Policy and Debt - Theoretical Foundations

State capture was reported to have occurred even before Independence when the British colonial authorities granted monopoly rights, tariff protection, and significant subsidies, to the Jamaica Match Industry and milk-producing companies in the 1940s and 1950s (Lal and Myint 1998). Other concessions were later granted through the Hotel's Aid Law (1944), Pioneer Industries Law (1949), Export Industries Law (1956), Industrial Incentives Law (1956), Hotels (Incentives) Act, Resort Cottages Acts (1968), the Short Term Incentive Package (2001), and others. The latter allowed for large concessions, duty free importation of raw material, and the writing off of their value, through capital allowances, against profits. The IMF (2010; 2013) stipulated that discretionary waivers must now be reviewed, and significantly curtailed.

Many of the public policy decisions that have contributed to Jamaica's indebtedness, were influenced by the political objectives and ideologies of successive administrations since 1938. Jones argued that in order to correct the historical failures of public policy output, there needed to be a greater level of equitable participation across social classes, better planning, empowerment through capacity building, and the cessation of "crisis-induced public policy outputs" (1974, 16). Poor public policy curtails development, and weakens the economy, leading to a greater need to acquire public debt.

Thomas (1996) noted that many of the governance challenges which have retarded development in the Caribbean region, stem from: confusion about priorities; excessive bureaucracy and centralized power; duplication of functions and authority in public administration; pervasive misuse of resources, and; inequity in representation across socio-cultural lines. This, he said, resulted in low levels of accountability and "a lack of effective governance in the region" (p. 47).

Beckford and Girvan (1989) argued that when local political managers replaced the colonial administration in the Caribbean region, political organizations and state power were based on legal

Chapter 2: Governance, Fiscal Policy and Debt - Theoretical Foundations

authority and control, with power being concentrated in a superordinate (elite) group. The lower class (subordinate group) had to depend on the elites for legislative support (Beckford 1999), so that the ability of the legislators to freely represent the subordinate groups was curtailed. He concluded that "As in all societies, the distribution of real political power is identical to the patterns of distribution of economic and social power" (1999, 78). With such power imbalance, Smith's 'invisible hand' was insufficient to create the enabling conditions for the efficient coordination of resources, to achieve the goal of equity and sustainable development, and reduce the need to borrow extensively.

The Hansard of Parliament (from 1962 to the twenty-first century) showed that after Independence, there were lively Parliamentary deliberations about the need for greater citizens' participation in governance; though the arguments and approaches taken conflicted with this view.

This changed somewhat during the Patterson administration and was succinctly summarized by Member of Parliament Alethia Barker, who reminded her Parliamentary colleagues that transparent and equitable governance required a partnership between the state, private sector, civil society and the legal support systems, as this was paramount to achieving and sustaining human development and growth (2001, 3).

Still, by 2010 the global perception of Jamaica worsened, in these areas of public trust, ethics, fiscal prudence and social service delivery (World Governance Indicators, and the World Economic Forum's Global Competitiveness Index). The World Bank captured this succinctly, stating that Jamaica's "public-private dialogue is predominantly informal, with an alarmingly high amount of ministerial discretion in the provision of exemptions from taxes and customs duties …to the detriment of the wider economy" (2011, 24).

The Jamaican government was subsequently mandated to improve its governance mechanisms, and reform public policy (including tax collection and public sector efficiency), in order to

Chapter 2: Governance, Fiscal Policy and Debt - Theoretical Foundations

reduce public debt levels. Tax compliance requires greater citizen participation, which is an important feature of governance, forcefully demonstrated by the groundswell among civil society groups globally, who are now demanding greater accountability from national leaders.

2.6.1 From Public Policy to Public Choice

The power devolved to national leaders, and the extent to which they are held accountable will influence the quality and outcomes of their decisions. Public Choice or New Political Economy theory was popularised by Buchanan (1984) and others. Its main focus is on the moral aspects of public administration, and the need for self-interested politicians and their agents to be kept in check. It "assumes that politicians, bureaucrats, citizens, and states act solely from self-interested perspectives, using their power and the authority of government for their own selfish ends" (Todaro 1997, 129). According to Buchanan:

> [E]xplosive increase in debt or deficit financing of public consumption outlays can be explained, at least in part, by an erosion of previously existing moral constraints. The political decision-makers did not "discover" a new technology of debt financing midway through this century. Their rational self-interest has always dictated resort to nontax sources of public revenue. (p. 265)

These non-tax sources are often in the form of the rapidly accumulating debt, which has been a less costly political decision, but a very expensive economic one. While Public Choice theory has served to highlight the impact of governance on macroeconomics, a deeper analysis was required to examine how transaction costs from these interactions can influence fiscal outcomes.

Chapter 2: Governance, Fiscal Policy and Debt - Theoretical Foundations

2.6.2 From Public Choice to New Institutional Economics

Veblen, a strong critic of orthodox economics, was considered to be one of the oldest institutional economists (Lawson 1997, 167). Though orthodox economists initially ridiculed institutional economics on the basis that it lacked scientific rigour, Williamson (1986) noted that Matthews contributed to changing that perspective, arguing that "New Institutional Economics (NIE) turned on two propositions.

First "institutions do matter", and; second, "the determinants of institutions are susceptible to analysis by the tools of economic theory (Matthews 1986, p. 903)" (Williamson 2000, 595). Williamson also noted that NIE superseded older forms of institutional economics, by merging economic history and microanalysis to demonstrate why economic institutions emerged the way they did (Arrow 1987, 734, quoted in Williamson 2000).

Ronald Coase has also been credited with the formal introduction of institutional economics, which was later popularized by Williamson, North, and others. New Institutional Economics (NIE) has extended on neo-classical economics to take account of the role of laws, rules, norms, and constraints in economics. It was seen as providing greater objectivity for the analysis of public sector resource allocation and outcomes, than Public Choice Theory.

While North (1991) noted that Coase's popular theorem suggested that there was no need for undue concern about transaction costs in an efficient market, he credited him for demonstrating the essential link "between institutions, transaction costs and neo-classical theory" (p. 2). North saw politics and economics as part of one institutional environment; though a purely orthodox approach in a market that is perceived to be efficient, could lead to a blatant disregard for the very institutional constraints that are put in place to modify behaviour and reduce transaction costs.

Chapter 2: Governance, Fiscal Policy and Debt - Theoretical Foundations

The theoretical principle of 'transaction cost' presupposes a principal-agent relationship, contractually reinforced, with high levels of institutional accountability. North felt that since transaction costs have a major impact on economic performance, attention should be paid to the effectiveness of institutions, and the technology employed within them, to minimize these costs (1991, 98). He also felt that the more sensitive stakeholders are to transaction costs, the greater the likelihood of internal pressure to reduce them. He differentiated between institutions and organizations, noting that organizations are made up of individuals within political, economic, social and educational bodies, bound by a common purpose, while:

> Institutions are the humanly devised constraints that structure political, economic and social interactions. They consist of both informal constraints (sanctions, taboos, customs, traditions, and codes of conduct) and formal rules (constitutions, laws, property rights)... They evolve incrementally, connecting the past with the present and the future; history in consequence is largely a story of institutional evolution in which the historical performance of economies can only be understood as a part of a sequential story. (p. 97)

It is the evolution of this 'sequential story' of Jamaica's weak institutions of governance, and the resultant accumulation of public debt from 1962 to the twenty-first century that this study sought to address. As North emphasized, the "development of an institutional process by which government debt could be circulated, becomes part of a regular capital market and [can] be funded by regular sources of taxation" (1991, 107-8). This is an important point to consider, in addressing deficit financing. He presented five key propositions to effect institutional change:

1. Encourage continuous interactions between institutions and organizations as economic resources are utilized;
2. Compete to survive and attract the best resources;
3. Invest in skills and knowledge to maximize returns;

Chapter 2: Governance, Fiscal Policy and Debt - Theoretical Foundations

4. Change perception and players' mental constructs through 'learning', and;
5. Encourage innovation to drive change (1991, 6).

New Institutional Economics (NIE) has increased in importance, in response to a growing call for improved governance. The popularization of the concept of governance in the development literature has led to greater consensus that the institutions created, and the macroeconomic policies developed within them can have a significant impact on a country's development and fiscal performance (Ali 2001; Acemoglu et al 2003; Grindle 2005; Henry and Miller 2008; UN 2009). North noted that this requires a fundamental policy shift since NIE influences the evolution of different structures from those presented by orthodox economists (1991, 5).

2.7 Heterodox and Orthodox Perspectives

An increasingly referenced body of works by Heterodox economists such as Chang, Onis, and Toye, have contributed to a better understanding of how institutions differ in developed and emerging economies, and; how they impact economic performance. They have often used examples in Asia, and Latin America to argue that developing countries have the capacity to create effective institutions to steer their own growth and development (Onis 1995; Todaro 1997; Chang 2002; Henry 2013).

Chang (2002) criticized the orthodox view that presented politics as interfering with economic rationality. He proposed an alternative theoretical framework which he referred to as the 'Institutional Political Economy' (IPE), which he saw as being better able to evaluate the role of the state in economics. In his view, government in its political role, has a notable impact on markets, as they make decisions about the rights and obligations of market participants. He noted that institutions influence: perception; people's view of what policies are important, and; the

Chapter 2: Governance, Fiscal Policy and Debt - Theoretical Foundations

extent to which people are free to lobby against issues like rent-seeking behaviour (pp. 53-7).

Conversely, most Orthodox economists reviewed tended to focus on the interaction of market forces, with the expectation that improvements in administration, more or less, in line with the Washington Consensus, should drive rapid growth.

Heterodox economists, go beyond this to examine the impact of global and endogenous factors, including the socio-political and cultural interactions within the institutional framework, on the economy. They have reframed the convergence argument to demonstrate that growth in countries such as South Korea, Singapore, and China has been influenced by governance factors beyond those outlined in the Washington Consensus.

In the latter, Williamson (1997) suggested that fiscal discipline, tax reform, protection of property rights, financial and trade liberalization, privatization, and deregulation would drive growth and development. While elements of Williamson's proposal are relevant to improving macroeconomic performance, the one-size-fits-all approach has been questioned, and at times, vehemently criticised. Williamson has subsequently argued that this was not his intention.

Heterodox perspectives also differ from orthodox perspectives, on how governance influences macroeconomic performance. The strongest arguments concern the critical institutional structures and capabilities required; while others relate to the prioritizing of governance and its impact, in conducting economic analysis. Khan argued that while the orthodoxy tended to focus on achieving good governance through market efficiency and reduction of transaction costs, heterodox economists emphasized the importance of building growth-enhancing governance capacities, through productivity-driven technologies, and political stability, to avoid market failure (2007, Abstract).

Stiglitz (2002) argued that the tendency towards financial market failure and weak macroeconomic performance in less developed countries (LDCs) were due to lack of full information,

Chapter 2: Governance, Fiscal Policy and Debt - Theoretical Foundations

high risk, and the contagion effect. Yet, the contagion effect was highlighted as one of the factors resulting in the need for the controversial stimulus packages introduced in the developed markets of the United States and Europe during the most recent global recession prior to the COVID-19 pandemic.

As a result, the focus on institutions and good governance has sharpened, while debates continue to rage among analysts, who link the causes of the recession to weak institutions, poor credit risk analysis, and governments seeking to rescue firms deemed too big to fail.

The governments of many economies globally are now looking for new models to reignite economic growth, some due to the impact of the pandemic, and others due to poor economic performance linked to subpar policy choices, and other governance decisions.

2.8 Development and Growth – A Brief Review

The issue of growth in a country's Gross Domestic Product (GDP) is fundamental to any evaluation of governance and public debt, as GDP is the denominator of the most common measure of indebtedness, the Debt-to-GDP ratio.

Various growth and development models have influenced Jamaica's macroeconomic policies, since independence. This publication will contribute to a better understanding of how governance, through macroeconomic policy choices, institutions, and politics have contributed to Jamaica's indebtedness. The level of development or underdevelopment, facilitated or hindered by the quality of governance decisions, often determines the extent to which a country may have to borrow to meet its fiscal obligations and finance its recurrent and capital expenditure budgets.

Chapter 2: Governance, Fiscal Policy and Debt - Theoretical Foundations

2.8.1 Early Influences on Development and Growth in Jamaica

In the halcyon days of mercantilism, colonies like Jamaica and Barbados served as producers of primary products for Britain. After the Great Depression (the 1930s) Europe's hegemony waned. Still, Adam Smith's views that specialization and trade could provide the required buoyancy to stem economic stagnation remained dominant.

However, Smith's expectation of rational actors interacting in a system of free competition proved to be antithetical to the development of countries like Jamaica. This was not because the market system was faulty per se, but more so, due to the actions which undermined the effectiveness of governance within the institutions created.

As a result, high transaction costs have worsened Jamaica's indebtedness. Smith's focus was on economic growth and wealth creation, propelled through division of labour and specialization, with government playing a limited role (Maunder et al. 1991, 25), as he felt the market would determine levels of supply and demand. This influenced the assembly-line piecework system in Jamaica's Free Zones.

Keynes opposed Smith's theory that the market would self-regulate, arguing that to quickly increase employment and exit the Great Depression, the government needed to stimulate aggregate demand (total expenditure), through investments, capital expansion, deficit spending, regulation of tax rates, and money supply (Maunder et al. 1991, 229). This strategy was initially successful in Britain, though they borrowed heavily to finance public expenditure. In fact, Smith ([1776]1981) argued that England has never had a parsimonious (frugal) government, so that:

> It is the highest impertinence and presumption, therefore, in kings and ministers, to pretend to watch over the economy of private people, and to restrain their expense, either by sumptuary laws, or by prohibiting the importation of foreign luxuries. They are themselves always, and without exception, the greatest spendthrifts in society. (pp. 441-2)

Chapter 2: Governance, Fiscal Policy and Debt - Theoretical Foundations

Hence, while Keynes was in favour of government spending as a stimulus, Smith was not. Interestingly, both of Jamaica's colonizers, Spain and England, borrowed extensively to finance their own development and subsequently experienced fiscal crises, with Spain having three defaults in 1607, 1627, 1647, and; England in 1340, 1472, and 1594 (Reinart and Rogoff 2008, 20). It was shortly after Spain's 1647 default that England took colonial control of Jamaica from them, after the Battle of Rio Nuevo in 1655. At that time, both European countries were in search of land, raw material, labour, and naval bases to drive their industrialization plan and propel their own development and growth.

2.8.2 Harrod-Domar: Growth through Savings and Investments

Whereas Keynes focused on stimulus expenditure to drive growth, Harrod (1939) and Domar (1946; 1957) looked at the mechanistic nature of growth, arguing that in order to drive growth, obsolete or depreciated capital stock should be replaced through savings, since old investments would be insufficient to acquire new inputs and serve new markets.

They highlighted the significance of savings and investment, to increase output per unit of capital, and economic growth (Todaro 1997; Ranis 2004). Their model presented aggregate capital stock (K) as bearing a direct relationship to aggregate national income (Y). This meant that the rate at which income grew ($\Delta Y/Y$) was determined by the level of incremental savings (s), and the ratio of output (k) from additional units of capital introduced. Higher levels of savings could, therefore, finance additional capital to increase labour productivity and economic growth.

Though useful, the model has been criticized for assuming that there is a fixed price for capital and labour. In Jamaica's case, the

Chapter 2: Governance, Fiscal Policy and Debt - Theoretical Foundations

price of capital (borrowing cost) is not fixed and is normally impacted by several exogenous and endogenous factors, including levels of perceived risk, and government's demand for funds to meet debt-service obligations. The worse the economy performs, the higher the risk, and hence, the higher the cost of debt to finance capital expansion.

The Harrod-Domar model was extended upon by Solow (1956) in his highly acclaimed neoclassical growth model. In this, he suggested that changes in the effectiveness of labour augmented by technology could lead to sustained levels of growth (Mankiw, Romer, and Weil 1992; Todaro 1997). Romer (1989) believed, like Solow, that technological improvements would enhance economic growth, as technology and skilled labour could be absorbed in the production process, to enhance industrialization.

2.8.3 Sir W. Arthur Lewis: Growth through Structural Transformation

Jamaica's early focus on industrialization, a part of which has been financed by debt, was influenced by the works of Nobel Laureate Sir W. A. Lewis (1954), though his focus was more on foreign direct investment (FDI) than borrowing. Lewis, who won a Nobel Prize, has been lauded for his contribution to development globally.

A major part of his work focused on how primary subsistence, Third World countries like Jamaica, could be developed through structural transformation. He argued that there were two sectors in the Caribbean, as in Egypt and India - a large traditional agricultural sector, earning subsistent rural wages, and a small urban modern sector, earning a premium above the subsistence wages. He felt that as long as entrepreneurs were willing to provide the capital, labour could be transferred from the traditional sector, up to a point of zero marginal productivity. His stated objectives were: to encourage and increase employment, by redeploying labour from small agricultural land bases; mechanize

Chapter 2: Governance, Fiscal Policy and Debt - Theoretical Foundations

the agricultural sector; increase labour productivity and raise income levels. He believed the answer to persistent poverty rested in achieving higher levels of factor productivity through industrialization. This was his Closed Model (p. 435).

Years later he noted that a finite supply of capital could limit growth; but, economic growth could be spurred if capitalists saved and invested a portion of their surplus. He saw this share of profits in the national income, as a factor required to increase savings, and generate capital to fund the industrialization process. He recognized that profits would decline over time, but believed capitalists could counter this "by encouraging immigration or by exporting their capital to countries where there is still abundant labour at a subsistence wage" (p. 436). In this his Open Economy Model, he changed from a fixed supply of labour, to an unlimited supply, based on greater access to labour and capital globally.

2.8.4 Nurkes: Growth through Human Capital Development

Nurkse (1953), like Lewis, believed that capital formation was central to the development problem faced by LDCs that were "under equipped with capital in relation to their population and natural resources" (1953, 1). While capital formation, through structural change, was a necessary condition, it was not sufficient for development.

As Nurkse noted, "human as well as material capital" (p. 2) could be expanded through investments in skills, education, and health. He believed that foregoing a portion of current consumption, to increase this stock of capital would lead to an expansion in output and future consumption. He noted that "the mere possession of a surplus labour force in the overpopulated countries is no guarantee of progress. It is an advantage only if, and in so far as, the surplus labour force can be effectively used for real capital accumulation" (p. 56). In his view, a curb in consumption was required to generate higher levels of national incomes.

Chapter 2: Governance, Fiscal Policy and Debt - Theoretical Foundations

While neoclassical economists saw capital accumulation and technological advancement as an exogenous process, endogenous strategies were later explored, to spur growth (from within). Critics of endogenous growth theory have argued that some developing countries were limited by lack of skilled labour, high energy cost, and IFI stipulations, which created a dependency relationship. As Girvan et al. argued, "New technologies should be appropriate to local resources and to local needs" (1983, 20). They, like Nurkse, saw this technology as a combination of knowledge, skills, production methods, and procedures. Labour augmentation and technology adaptation continue to be highlighted as key areas to be addressed, to drive Jamaica's development and cauterize the bourgeoning public debt. Plantation economists like Lloyd Best have highlighted some features of Caribbean economies that have slowed this process.

2.8.5 Plantation Economy Perspectives

Smith ([1776]1981) argued that colonies like Jamaica were best suited to agricultural development. These perspectives influenced the colonial institutional arrangements that led to the formation of what is often referred to as plantation economies in the Caribbean.

Renowned Plantation economist Lloyd Best noted that the works of Smith, Keynes, Ricardo, Marx, and Harrod-Domar, provided a framework to better understand the evolution of economic perspectives that have shaped development in the Caribbean. To Best, the structural and institutional assumptions and models explored, evolved through four development stages, being the:

- Garrison– prior to the establishment of the plantations;
- Pure Plantation– sugar and slavery;
- Plantation Modified– sugar, free labour, and domestic agriculture, and;

Chapter 2: Governance, Fiscal Policy and Debt - Theoretical Foundations

- Plantation Further Modified– organized labour with technology for industrialization (2009, 6-7).

He argued that the plantation system was subordinate, lacked community support, from a political perspective, and; had no internal structural dynamic for local wealth creation and technological innovation.

Best and Levitt (2009) also argued that small open economies of the Caribbean are "dominated by total institutions" (p. 2), of self-contained foreign-owned firms, exploiting the raw material sources of the developing countries.

Beckford, in Levitt (2000) also pointed out that the plantation system has "left a legacy of economic, social and political institutions that function in such a way as to perpetuate underdevelopment" (p. 255). In their view, some of the major economic obstacles contributing to this were: differences in ownership of factors of production, making it difficult to regulate supply and demand; inequality in wealth and income distribution; foreign ownership of means of production, limiting finance; export-orientation of low-value primary products and high import demand, leading to unfavourable terms of trade; concentration of linkages for forward and backward integration within foreign-owned enterprises; technological limitations, and; investment flows determined by multi-national firms.

Though these are still relevant today, national leaders have much greater autonomy, to exercise effective economic, political, and administrative authority (governance) in managing the country's affairs, including its public debt. Unfortunately, while the identity and structures of governance have changed in each of the four stages and forms of plantation economy highlighted, the macroeconomic conditions in Jamaica have not changed substantially.

When Best presented this body of work, many developing countries across Asia, Latin America, and the Caribbean were faced with major development constraints. Today, some have

Chapter 2: Governance, Fiscal Policy and Debt - Theoretical Foundations

progressed, while others, like Jamaica, have lagged behind. Thus, we can see some of the governance factors, and challenges that have contributed to Jamaica's indebtedness, though Dependency theorists have sought to place the blame at the feet of international capitalists.

2.8.6 Dependency Theories

International-dependency theorists of the 1970s and 1980s saw Third World economies as being politically, economically, and institutionally dependent, and developed countries as dominant. They classified salaried civil servants in Marxists terms, as proletariat, and the business-class or wealthy, as elites or bourgeois, who enjoyed a high standard of living, while perpetuating the international capitalist system, leading to underdevelopment.

Some also felt that underdevelopment and increased indebtedness resulted from faulty recommendations made by biased, uninformed international advisors, who presented plans that led to inappropriate policies for Less Developed Countries (Todaro 1997). Martinussen (1997) also argued that international lenders were not particularly concerned with the nuances and political institutions through which their recommended policies were to be implemented (p. 6).

Almost a decade later, Stiglitz, a former senior vice president of the World Bank, supported this view, arguing that the IMF often sent its technocrats to countries with which they were unfamiliar, expecting them to quickly analyze numbers and devise programmes to solve economic problems, without fully appreciating the nuances involved (2005, 325). Dijkstra (2008) concurred, noting that the World Bank needed to reform its operations and redistribute decision-making power, as their technocrats have never had to carry out many of their policy prescriptions in their own economies.

Chapter 2: Governance, Fiscal Policy and Debt - Theoretical Foundations

Stiglitz's perspective was similar to that shared by Eberstadt (1989), fifteen (15) years prior, who noted that though multilateral institutions have linked development aid to policy reforms, not much was achieved.

On the other hand, neo-classicists have argued that what was needed was not more foreign aid or reforms of economic systems, but tolerant governments allowing free markets to determine how resources are used. Angresano felt that this neoclassical approach matched the supply-side ideological focus of Thatcher and Reagan at the time (2007, 46). Recall that both leaders – Margaret Thatcher of the United Kingdom, and Ronald Reagan of the United States - significantly influenced the flow of loan funds into Jamaica during the 1980s, when the country's Debt-to-GDP peaked above 200%.

One might then ask, why was it that Jamaica did not achieve significant growth and development from their largesse? Todaro (1997) and other economists have shown that neoclassical prescriptions were not particularly successful in many developing countries, with under-developed capital markets, and an inability to compete equitably with their global trading partners. Todaro argued further, that neoclassical economists "point both to the success of countries like South Korea, Taiwan, Hong Kong, and Singapore as "free market" examples although ... these Asian tigers are far from the laissez-faire prototype ascribed to them" (p. 87). Onis shared similar perspectives (1995, 97).

Even in the most efficient markets, government involvement is required to regulate institutions, communication processes, and standards, as information asymmetries can lead to significant transaction costs, from distortions in the interpretation and application of policy. As Adam Smith noted, "all markets have to work within a certain legal framework and that unless the framework is adequate, the market will cease to be free" ([1776]1981, 112-3).

Successful Asian countries like Singapore have been adept at blending this market-oriented approach with clearly established

Chapter 2: Governance, Fiscal Policy and Debt - Theoretical Foundations

guidelines for the government's involvement, as it seeks to manage the political economy.

2.9 Government's Role in the Political Economy

Political economy combines the analysis of economics and politics, so as to better understand the government's role (Todaro 1997, 711). While Keynesians advocate for an activist government, neoliberals prefer less government involvement, with market forces determining the use of resources.

As developing countries sought to identify the most appropriate models to address their economic challenges, many embraced the Keynesian view, that government should play a leading role in stimulating the economy. Keynes' argument that the economy could be stimulated by increasing real disposable income, and hence consumption, through government expenditure, was premised on the view that humans are naturally disposed to spending more, as their income increased (1936). This argument ran counter to Smith's free markets philosophy discussed earlier.

On the other hand, a monetarist like Friedman believed that an equilibrium level of nominal national income could be achieved by regulating money supply. Friedman's views on the quantity theory of money were, however, ridiculed by Keynesians, but embraced by the liberals (Maunder et al. 1991).

Macroeconomic policies in Jamaica, as in many developing countries, were significantly influenced by Keynesianism and Monetarism at different points in time, with the latter significantly influencing the high interest cost of Jamaica's debt during the 1990s, contributing to lively debates about the extent to which a politically elected government should be involved in these economic decisions.

The literature on the government's role in the economy has largely focused on the ideological and philosophical paradigms (patterns; models) which have informed the relevant structures and arrangements (economic models, systems, and policies). Chen

Chapter 2: Governance, Fiscal Policy and Debt - Theoretical Foundations

(2007) showed, for example, that a change in the ideological paradigm of the Communist Party of China (CPC) in recent times, has led to a "change from a pure socialistic system to a dual capitalistic and socialistic mixed system" (p. 8), with a new culture of growth centred politics based on greater openness. Government is still, however, seen as being integral to the transition from a relatively closed system up to the 1990s, to a gradually, more open economic system in 2021.

Even as China expands its global influence, however, its political system still remains relatively closed and ensconced from global scrutiny or 'intervention'.

From a philosophical perspective, one may take a *Cusan* view, that elected officials are moral agents and should be involved by consent, in deciding what is in the best interest of the people (Miller 2013).

Others may take a *Lockean* view that the sovereign could become an abominable institution, and should focus only on making laws, and the preservation of property rights (Tuckness 2012).

There may also be some, who take the *Hobbesian* view that government should play an authoritarian role. There are yet others who will suggest a balance between the state and the private sector. The latter assumes primacy of the market, seeing it as a natural institution, and; the state as a man-made one (Chang 2002, 50).

Notwithstanding these divergent perspectives, it is generally agreed that government is essential for the effective functioning of the economy. The role government chooses to play will determine how resources are managed, and the outcomes from these processes.

With regards to Jamaica, Stone and Brown (1981) noted that the main policy focus pursued, changed at various stages prior to Independence, even as the State responded to the cries of the people through welfare and social policies to calm them. Stone (1991) outlined three types of political economies and societal

Chapter 2: Governance, Fiscal Policy and Debt - Theoretical Foundations

systems in the Third World through which political and state power is exercised to achieve economic objectives (p. 95):

- Liberal-Capitalism – a liberal democracy with a dominant private sector – found in Jamaica, Argentina, Barbados, Malaysia, India, Venezuela, Brazil, Costa Rica and Sri Lanka;
- Authoritarian-Capitalism – a one-party system, authoritarian and dictatorial leadership, and a dominant private sector in a mixed economy – found in Singapore, Ivory Coast, Taiwan, South Korea, Nigeria and Haiti, and;
- Populist-Statism – a one-party state having economic dominance, with a weak or absent private sector – found in China, Mongolia, Cuba, Vietnam, and North Korea.

China and Vietnam are now more (economically) open, with some amount of governmental control.

Hall and Benn also argued that from as early as the 1930s "there were three competing models of the best way to provide welfare: liberal democracy, communism and fascism" (2003, 223). In a liberal democratic system, there is the protection of individual rights and freedoms, with citizens having the right to choose the leaders who will make macroeconomic decisions on their behalf. As such, political power is conferred on leaders through voting, with conduct being regulated through a Constitution. Property rights are protected by the rule of law.

A communist system is one in which property is publicly owned and controlled by the state (government). Though, in theory, such a system advocates for a classless society in which the means of production (capital, land, labour etcetera) are owned by, and belongs to the community, there is very little autonomy for ordinary citizens to freely determine how these economic goods (resources) are to be used or distributed.

Chapter 2: Governance, Fiscal Policy and Debt - Theoretical Foundations

In a fascist system, a dictator rules by force, sometimes violently, and maintains control by force. Opposition is supressed with the nation-state, and even race being given supremacy over individual rights. These are usually totalitarian regimes. These classifications are relevant, to place governance and debt management in context.

From an Asian perspective, Onis (1995) argued that the state has been more actively involved in development strategies and policies, aimed at supporting specific industries in successful developing economies than neoliberals would wish to admit. He saw government involvement as being important to temporarily shelter key growth sectors until they become globally competitive. Unfortunately, the Jamaican government, which has adopted a democratic model of government since independence, extended support for infeasible sectors, such as sugar and bananas, well beyond their profitable existence.

Though democratic, the two main political parties that have held the reins of government since independence - the Peoples National Party (PNP) and Jamaica Labour Party (JLP) have embraced different ideological paradigms, resulting in vastly different approaches to macroeconomic and social policy, up to the late 1990s. Subsequently, as will be discussed further in this publication, there has been a significant narrowing of the ideological divide, especially with regards to economic development, and growth strategies.

As Stone observed, it is not so much the nature of the political economy that determines economic performance, but the way in which power is managed (1991). He singled out Singapore as having achieved exceptional success in productivity and improvements in the quality of life for its citizens. He believed that the state plays a major role in guaranteeing or preventing progress, by the type of political climate it provides.

Development can be achieved, he argued, through stability, hospitality to investors, empowerment of the people, and effective management of gains from colonial relationships. Countries like

Chapter 2: Governance, Fiscal Policy and Debt - Theoretical Foundations

Barbados have benefited largely from this (Stone 1991; Acemoglu et al. 2003). Stone saw attempts at political control, and obsolete forms of democracy as factors contributing to Jamaica's underdevelopment. During the time of Stone's writing, public finance was bolstered by generous external aid and loans, as with those obtained from Reagan and Thatcher, which masked Jamaica's fiscal problems.

2.10 Public Finance

Government, in its fiscal role, makes decisions regarding sources of revenue, and levels of expenditure. The government's annual Recurrent Expenditure budget outlines allocations for day-to-day operations, while the Capital Expenditure budget involves acquisition and enhancement of physical assets and amortization on debt. When a government earns less revenue than is required to finance its expenditure, this results in a fiscal gap (a budget deficit) for which financing must be found.

Bullock (2010) argued that the debt burden may be eased, if government reduces its constant dependence on debt, to fix the deficit problem since the cost of servicing the debt crowds out "essential social and economic expenditure, and increase the likelihood of expenditure overruns and unprogrammed increases in budget deficits" (p. 1). He noted that increasing taxes and reducing non-debt expenditure reduces nominal GDP growth, making it harder to collect taxes to reduce the fiscal deficit and debt burden. While he felt that there was a place for appropriate Keynesian-type fiscal or monetary stimulus, he argued that problems of major deficiencies in the productive structure posed greater problems than insufficient aggregate demand. These are largely political decisions.

The following observation from Milas and Legrenzi (2002) emphasizes how public expenditures can often be influenced by political objectives:

Chapter 2: Governance, Fiscal Policy and Debt - Theoretical Foundations

> Distinguishing between demand-side and supply-side theories of government growth allows for the distinction between responsive government, whose public expenditure is justified by the electors' preferences, and excessive government, which spends beyond the limits imposed by the demand-side following bureaucrats' or politicians' interests. (p. 58)

They argued that citizens/electors may demand additional goods and services leading to expansion in the public sector, and; increasing inequality, as voting patterns change. On the supply-side, they felt that bureaucracy may lead to big government, as technocrats try to increase their salaries, perquisites, reputation, and status (Niskanen 1971, 38), through political control and selective dissemination of information to citizens/electors (p. 60). These then lead to budget deficits, and the need for further financing. Kimenyi (1990) concluded that expansion in the size of government may, therefore, be achieved at the expense of taking on additional debt.

During the 1980s, under greater scrutiny from the IMF and World Bank, the government was mandated to focus more on the supply-side, by removing distortions deemed to be negatively impacting the market mechanism, to stimulate growth. Still, Levitt (1991) argued that whereas the IMF assumed that the private sector was capable of efficiently using government incentives on the supply-side to stimulate economic activity that did not occur.

During the 1990s and early 2000s, the Jamaican government generally took a demand-side approach, spending generously on social and infrastructure programmes, arguably formulated to stimulate aggregate demand. Still, the budget deficits remained, though reduced since the 2013 IMF agreement.

The crises and challenges of the last three decades have served to counteract the purely orthodox forms of development, as governments in developed and developing countries now grapple with large budget deficits and soaring debts. The deadlock in the US Congress in 2012/13, as well as the verbal sparring in Britain, and other European Union member countries like Greece, has

Chapter 2: Governance, Fiscal Policy and Debt - Theoretical Foundations

highlighted the impact that debt can have on an economy and global financial markets.

Another challenge that arose from government's intervention over this period was to determine how much government is 'too much government'. Whatever the answer, funds must be found to finance the national budgets from one or more of three main sources: seignorage, taxes, or public debt.

2.10.1 Financing through Seignorage

While the use of seignorage - printing money, and the associated costs, was employed even before the 1800s (Smith [1776]1981; Ricardo [1817]2002) it has proven to be deleterious to the economic health of many nations. Consequently, seignorage is generally avoided in modern public finance, though it was actively practised in Jamaica up to the early 1990s.

As Aisen and Veiga (2005) noted, countries wishing to implement policies to strengthen their institutions, and give more autonomy to their Central Banks could "limit the negative effect of political instability on seignorage and thus improve their chances of successfully lowering their dependence on seignorage revenues to finance their governments' deficits" (p. 14).

Kwon et al. (2006) also noted that monetary and fiscal policy could be coordinated, so that heavy demand for government bonds, for example, does not lead to seignorage. According to Moore and Skeete (2010) the relationship between fiscal policy and debt stems from the fact that further borrowing, or seignorage, may be pursued to close the fiscal gap and worsen the problem.

Seignorage employed to meet debt obligations leads to inflation, in countries such as Jamaica with a floating exchange rate regime, and; increased current account deficits in countries such as Barbados, with a fixed exchange rate regime (Downes and Moore 2007; Moore and Skeete 2010). Moore and Skeete also emphasized that monetary authorities should avoid political pressure to use seignorage (2010, 1).

Chapter 2: Governance, Fiscal Policy and Debt - Theoretical Foundations

In fact, during the high inflation period of the 1990s (80.2% for Jamaica in 1991) this exacerbated the debt problem. As Minister Small told parliament, "When the open market operations were conducted by the Bank of Jamaica CDs, the Bank had to pay the interest by literally printing money, because they didn't have an income stream from which to pay the interest" (1993, 1354). Edie (2000) reported that the government of Jamaica started printing money extensively to meet Jamaica's public expenditure obligations, as early as the 1960s and 1970s.

Baran (1957) noted that growth stimulated by "outright budgetary deficits incurred either by printing money or by borrowing from businesses, financial institutions and individuals" would be unsustainable (pp. 123-4). Instead, he recommended, like Harrod-Domar, and Lewis, a greater focus on investment expenditure, and like Smith, equitable taxation.

In 2021, the Government of Jamaica gave greater autonomy to its central bank, the Bank of Jamaica, which is now considering the introduction of a Central Bank Digital Currency (CBDC). While this will negate the need to print money in previous quantities, whether to facilitate transactions, control money supply, or fulfil public sector debt service and other obligations, a deeper analysis is required to see the potential impact of the CBDC on inflation, interest rates, and other monetary policy indicators. The CBDC, no doubt, will further reduce the need for seignorage.

2.10.2 Financing through Taxation

Taxation is the most common strategy employed by a government to finance public expenditure. Maunder et al highlighted three main types of tax systems (1991, 168; 573):

- **Proportional Taxation** – based on a fixed tax rate, that is expected to lead to higher tax revenues as individual incomes increase;

Chapter 2: Governance, Fiscal Policy and Debt - Theoretical Foundations

- **Progressive Taxation** – a higher tax rate is charged for higher levels of income;
- **Regressive Taxation** – as income increases, the tax rate falls.

Jamaica employs a proportional tax system, with low rates of compliance. This has been worsened by predominantly low incomes, inefficiency in collections, and a Keynesian approach to government expenditure, which fails to focus on up-skilling human capital to earn higher wages and salaries from which tax revenues can be earned. Maunder et al pointed out that Keynesian counter-cyclical fiscal policies (raising government expenditure and reducing taxes, during economic downturns), were only effective up to the 1960s. Subsequently, inflation spiralled, and economic performance was worsened by structural problems, which increased unemployment and reduced aggregate demand (p. 492). Smith outlined the following four principles, or canons of taxation (pp. 1043-6) to increase tax compliance:

1. **Equality**: Each citizen should pay taxes according to his/her ability, and the benefits received;
2. **Certainty**: Avoid arbitrary taxation, so that persons may know how much, and when to pay;
3. **Convenience**: Synchronize timing of tax payments to create convenience for the tax-payer, and;
4. **Economy in Collection**: Minimize tax administration costs to avoid over-taxation.

He argued that the latter (over-taxation) could result from excessive staffing, and economic decline if the tax authorities discouraged business operations through forfeitures, penalties, and frequent examination. He believed that in a fair and equitable tax system, the affected entrepreneurs would otherwise provide capital to increase employment.

Chapter 2: Governance, Fiscal Policy and Debt - Theoretical Foundations

Lindahl (1919), like Smith, believed tax levied and paid according to ability, and perceived as just and fair, would yield greater revenues. Jamaica has been faced with a number of related taxation challenges over several years, namely:

- **GCT**: Economists have argued that the GOJ's strategy of exempting Consumption Taxes from certain goods and services benefited the rich, more so, than the poor, and was, therefore regressive.
- **Tax-free Global Bonds:** The GOJ's issuance of high-yielding tax-free global bonds has largely benefited overseas investors and their economies, at Jamaica's expense.
- **Waivers and Incentives**: Arbitrary tax waivers and incentives since Independence (1962) have robbed Jamaica of needed revenues, and contributed to the country's burgeoning public debt, low tax intake, and dismal economic performance (World Bank 2011).

Additionally Pandeiros and Benfield noted that:

> Jamaica currently ranks 170 out of 178 countries in the difficulties associated with paying taxes. This induces extensive informality and contributes to dishonest and illegal dealings in an environment where corrupt practices are a major concern. Powerful established enterprises usually engage in lobbying and rent-seeking behavior in order to maintain their preferences. (2010, 13)

- **Informal Economy**: The informal economy in Jamaica accounts for an estimated 40% to 50% of uncollected tax revenues (IDB 2006, 22; 39).

Some public commentators have also argued that inordinate delays in implementing tax reforms to improve compliance, increase productivity, simplify the tax collection process, and encourage private sector participation, are due in part to the

Chapter 2: Governance, Fiscal Policy and Debt - Theoretical Foundations

potential political cost. Tax policies focused on incentivizing the expansion of key industries and sectors have significantly greater potential for enhancing economic growth and sustainable development, than the current approach, which results in perennial borrowing and rapid debt accumulation, especially public debt due and payable in the rapidly devaluating Jamaican to United States dollar.

2.10.3 Deficit Financing

The third option available to government requiring funds to close the budget deficit is to borrow. While the GOJ was able to access loan funds by issuing Savings bonds and other securities in the 1960s (Hansard 1961-1966), a culture of saving for investment was not fostered. At that time, Jamaica's counterparts Barbados and Singapore focused on increasing savings which helped them to achieve and maintain adequate levels of reserves to finance their physical and human capital development programmes (Lee 2000; Downes 2002).

Jamaica has instead depended heavily on borrowing from International Financial Institutions such as the IMF and World Bank, commercial banks, global capital markets, and domestic investors, to finance its budget deficits and development programmes.

As Smith ([1776]1981) argued, governments tend to focus less on savings when wealthy merchants and manufacturers are willing to advance funds to them (pp. 1157-8). These investors did indeed make use of the Government of Jamaica's high interest/coupon rates securities, especially during the 1990s. Smith concluded that "Bankruptcy is always the end of great accumulation of debt" (1981, 1184).

Domar (1957), like Keynes, took a more liberal view than Smith, arguing that "Whatever effects the existence and growth the debt may have, what matters is its relation to other economic variables" (p. 37). He argued that the effort and time spent

Chapter 2: Governance, Fiscal Policy and Debt - Theoretical Foundations

focusing on debt should instead be channelled into growing the national income (p. 64).

Though Jamaica's political leaders have repeatedly promised that borrowed funds would have been used for projects and programmes to do just that, lack of economic growth and high debt service obligations have led the IMF (2013) to stipulate that the GOJ should significantly reduce public expenditure to create fiscal space. Arbitrary cuts can, however, have serious repercussions, resulting in recurring budget deficits. In Todaro's view:

> Most stabilization attempts have concentrated on cutting government expenditures to achieve budgetary balance. But the burden of resource mobilization to finance essential public development efforts must come from the revenue side. Public domestic and foreign borrowings can fill some savings gaps. In the long run, it is the efficient and equitable collection of taxes on which government must base their development aspirations. (1997, 620)

2.10.4 Ricardo and Barro's Perspective

A deeper examination of the literature on budget deficits showed that there were several proponents, and as many critiques of the works of two of the most popular theorists on deficit financing, David Ricardo, and Robert Barro.

Some economists have argued that David Ricardo saw taxes and debt as interchangeable fiscal policy tools. However, a review of his seminal work ([1817]2002) on the Principles of Political Economy and Taxation, proved otherwise. Ricardo himself did not subscribe to the strict equivalence view. He noted that budget deficits, in fact, led to a diminution of capital; as "taxation under every form presents but a choice of evils; if it do [sic] not act on profits, or other sources of income, it must act on expenditure" (p. 107). In other words, tax policy must provide incentives for growth. He also objected to the collection of transfer taxes on property by an inefficient government, noting that "They are more or less unthrifty taxes that increase the revenue of the sovereign,

Chapter 2: Governance, Fiscal Policy and Debt - Theoretical Foundations

which seldom maintains any but unproductive labourers, at the expense of the capital of the people" (p. 98).

This suggested that unless the government could implement a more efficient tax system, exemption of real property from taxes, could be more economically beneficial. In so doing, the transfer taxes foregone by an inefficient government could result in those funds being used by taxpaying property owners to generate further capital for investment.

Ricardo's work also showed that he, like other neoclassical economists, harboured concerns about government borrowing, and the potential for this to lead to crowding-out of the private sector; producer-driven inflation, resulting from the pass-through effect of taxes into prices, and; the decline of savings, leading to a reduction in the capital required to spur growth.

Rowley, Shughart, and Tollison (2002) noted that while Ricardo's perspectives were largely misunderstood, Barro had in fact modified Ricardo's theorem. This was done, by adding the assumption that intergenerational transfers would cause persons to be indifferent between taxation and the issuance or retirement of public debt, as they could shift consumption across generations, or alter their bequests, to neutralize any differences in the tax burden. This model assumed that the bequest would cause both generations to maximize the utility of this wealth over their infinite lives.

In his 1979 work, Barro placed significant focus on tax-smoothing, by using a budget deficit, or surplus, to reduce distortions in the tax system caused by incentives (Mankiw 2010, 486). He felt that taxation was distortionary by nature so that the optimal debt management policy could be achieved by having a smooth tax rate, to enhance long-term planning. However, it is difficult to be certain about future government expenditure, and so an optimal tax rate may have to be determined using a time value of money approach, considering the present value of government revenue and expenditure. Where there is variance between future expenditure and the estimates, he argued, a new optimal tax rate will be required, with additional funds, to close the budget deficit. The changes in deficits and public sector borrowing requirements (PSBR) will, however, lead to fluctuation in the

Chapter 2: Governance, Fiscal Policy and Debt - Theoretical Foundations

public debt.

Roubini and Sachs (1989) argued that Barro's theory was most appropriate where government borrows during wartime and repays the debt after the war (p. 912). A variant of Barro's theory could be adopted by a government that uses fore-sighting as a planning methodology to craft long-term strategies, making adjustments as required, given changing tax rates. Barro felt that future taxes and tax-financed government expenditures were equivalent (Rowley, Shughart and Tollison 2002, 3).

Afonso (1999) also conducted a comprehensive empirical analysis of the Ricardian Equivalence theorem, using panel data of 176 observations across indebted and highly indebted countries from the Euro area, and highlighted a list of stringent conditions that were required for the assumption to hold. These were:

- Successive generations are altruistic, and have infinite horizons;
- Capital markets are efficient and perfect; with constant interest rates, and no constraints on liquidity;
- Consumers have perfect information;
- Public debt is issued in one period, and reimbursed from taxes in the next;
- Taxes levied are lump-sum, and do not create distortions (p. 6).

Afonso's findings cast doubts on the validity of the equivalence theorem, for the countries examined.

Mankiw (2010) also sought to present the Ricardian Equivalence as a forward-looking theory that did not presuppose that consumers would automatically increase consumption from increased government spending, or tax reduction. Instead, taxpayers were deemed to be futuristic in their analysis of fiscal policy, reasoning that debt-financed tax reductions simply represented a rescheduling of the debt (p. 479).

Chapter 2: Governance, Fiscal Policy and Debt - Theoretical Foundations

Similarly, Barsky, Mankiw and Zeldes (1986) empirically tested the Ricardian Equivalence arguments of Barro relaxing the lump-sum tax assumption, arguing that the marginal propensity to consume from a tax cut, along with an expected increase in taxes, could be substantial. They concluded that "While Ricardian equivalence may be the appropriate benchmark for a world in which taxes are lump-sum, it is probably not the appropriate benchmark for the world in which we live" (p. 688). Tobin (1980) opposed Barro's formulation of this theory, on the basis that it did not hold for childless, uncharitable, or poor households.

2.10.5 Tobin's Portfolio Management Approach

In his 1963 body of work on deficit financing, and debt, Tobin argued that government debt had two types of impacts on aggregate demand, a fiscal impact on private income, through government expenditure and receipts, and; a monetary impact, through the claims on government by lenders. This, in turn, affects their income. He felt that the rate at which the debt increased or decreased (the fiscal effect) was more relevant than the size of the debt. He argued that while government could not easily change the size of the debt without significant budget deficits or surpluses, it could change the composition of the debt, through swaps of securities or other arrangements.

He recommended that the authorities should, therefore, focus on policy measures to reduce the cost of debt. In his view, monetary control and effective debt management could influence economic stability through taxation and fiscal policies targeted at "the composition of output, economic growth, the distribution of wealth and income and economic efficiency" (1963, 211). The cost of debt could then be reduced by, varying the discount rate and reserve ratio; substituting short-term debts with instruments of longer tenures, and; altering the composition of debt to reduce long-term interest costs.

The 2010 Jamaica Debt Exchange (JDX), and 2013 National

Chapter 2: Governance, Fiscal Policy and Debt - Theoretical Foundations

Debt Exchange (NDX) sought to achieve some of these objectives. Still, this study found that there remain major cash flow challenges, due to the current maturity profile, with repayment falling due over the next 2 to 10 years.

2.10.6 Boothe and Reid's Cost Minimization Theory

Boothe and Reid (1992) noted that Tobin's seminal work highlighted the two main objectives of debt management: (1) to function collaboratively with monetary and fiscal policy, and; (2) to minimize interest cost. They argued that these two objectives may, however, work counter to each other, as, while Tobin's Portfolio Management theory may have been constructed for a closed economy, small open economies that use debt as a stabilizing tool, may gain limited benefits. Their study sought to determine if small open economies should base their debt management strategy on minimizing interest costs, using a weighted average cost model, subject to interactions between the prices of short-term and long-term bonds.

They also examined the extent to which authorities could seek to minimize interest cost, with the expectation that bonds of different tenures and T-bills could be refinanced through changes in future interest rates. They argued that cost may be reduced by tactical comparisons of the returns investors expected from holding competing securities (1992, 47).

The holding period returns take into account the coupon rate, plus increases in the value of marketable government securities (capital gains). They believed significant savings could be achieved if the government focuses on a cost minimization strategy. It is important to note that though yields can be evaluated on the basis of trends, it is difficult to accurately predict future returns in volatile underdeveloped capital markets.

2.10.7 Component, Structure and Cost of Public Debt

Ricardo, Barro, Tobin, Booth and Reid have proposed various models of debt financing, with the latter focusing on the cost of debt. Public sector capital projects could be selected more efficiently by evaluating their cost in a portfolio context, with

Chapter 2: Governance, Fiscal Policy and Debt - Theoretical Foundations

specific emphasis on their Internal Rate of Return (IRR), and the cost of each component within the capital structure (debt, equity, etc).

Though Modigliani and Miller (1958) argued that the structure of financing was not very important in an efficient market, the real world is not efficient. So, there will be information asymmetries, where either the lender or borrower has more information. Some may also argue that the Internal Rate of Return would be difficult to quantify since the government's main focus should be to provide public goods. However, this argument does not hold, as notional values can be determined by analyzing the economic value of the services provided.

Government borrowing may also be significantly enhanced by an optimal capital structure approach. As Dooley (2000) argued, developing countries differ from developed ones, so that a simple focus on a risk/return trade-off in a portfolio context may ignore the likelihood of default. He discouraged a strict focus on financial intermediation (where government borrows to lend), as this could mask the potential default triggers and their costs. Instead, he recommended that government should: choose an optimal capital structure with long-term debt over inflation-indexed domestic debt; lengthen maturities if a crisis is expected; live within budget constraints, and; avoid crises and debt structures that are likely to result in a default (p. 46).

While these recommendations are relevant and practical in a stable economy, rapid movements in Jamaica's exchange rate, make it difficult to focus mainly on long-term external debt. As Sir Arthur Lewis noted in Emmanuel (1994) even during times of economic buoyancy "the proceeds must be convertible into foreign exchange" (pp. 2066-8).

Additionally, Jamaica's heavy dependence on external debt, led to principal and interest payments that resulted in very large net outflows from Jamaica during the Seaga administration (Levitt 1991; Panton1993). Some of Jamaica's external debt securities (global bonds) are indexed to inflation.

Chapter 2: Governance, Fiscal Policy and Debt - Theoretical Foundations

2.10.8 Budget Deficits, Inflation and Debt

Proponents of the Fiscal Theory of the Price Level argue that budget deficits are the primary determinants of inflation (Kwon et al 2006; Zoli 2005).

Conversely, a monetary perspective on the cause of inflation holds that increased money supply leads to demand-pull inflation. Consequently, government may employ monetary policy tools (which can increase debt) to control inflation. Another type of inflation is creeping, or cost-push inflation, which Maunder et al (1991) argued occurred in Britain during the 1973 to 1975 recession, on account of:

- Union Power, with wage increases that were not matched by increased productivity – [much like the situation in Jamaica over many years];
- Big Business Power, where corporations raise their prices, increasing the cost of living of workers, who then demand higher wages, and;
- Increasing cost of energy and other raw material inputs.

High inflation and rapid currency devaluations have contributed to persistent fiscal deficits for 34 of the 48 years covered by this study, worsening Jamaica's indebtedness (see figure 2.2).

Chapter 2: Governance, Fiscal Policy and Debt - Theoretical Foundations

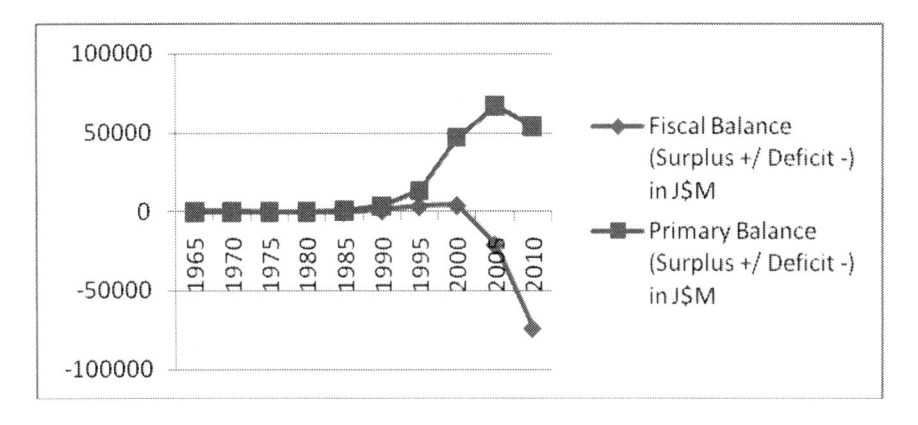

Figure 2.2 Fiscal and Primary Balances 1965- 2010 (at 5-year Intervals)

While the fiscal balance represents the difference between government revenues and expenditure, the primary balance is calculated before accounting for debt service charges. The fiscal balance is also referred to more frequently as the budget deficit/surplus. When reviewed in terms of Solow's growth model, "budget deficit[s] can reduce national savings and crowd out investments" (Mankiw 2010, 201).

During the 1980s, the Seaga administration took a combined fiscal and monetary policy approach, by initiating the restructuring of the revenue areas, cutting the public sector wage bill, and implementing sharp currency devaluations, in an attempt to address the inflation and deficit problem. New fees were introduced; some tax exemptions were removed; while several perquisites were taxed by 1985 (Hansard).

When inflation reached 30% in 1990, the Manley administration employed monetary policy tools such as interest rate adjustments through Open Market Operations (OMO), and changes in reserve ratios, which they said, were intended to stabilize the economy, minimize exchange rate fluctuations, and control inflation and money supply (Hansard 1990-2006).

Blackman (1995) argued that this strategy backfired, as Jamaica's heavy emphasis on the use of OMOs over currency

Chapter 2: Governance, Fiscal Policy and Debt - Theoretical Foundations

management and fiscal restraint in the 1990s, caused interest rates to skyrocket, increasing Jamaica's debt service costs. Jamaica's inflation rate increased exponentially to 80.2% by 1991, masking the challenges that culminated in the FINSAC crisis (former MOFP technocrat pers. comm.).

Conclusion

This chapter has outlined the theoretical foundations supporting this publication on the Governance and Public Debt Nexus, by reviewing the works of some of the most prominent minds that have influenced and shaped the economic development models, and public policy globally. It looked at the role of government in macroeconomic management; the evolution of governance, political systems, and fiscal policy as it relates to taxation, and financing government expenditure. It also discussed how these relate to the growth and development strategies that have influenced, and still do influence macroeconomic performance (including debt to Gross Domestic Product ratios).

Buchanan's seminal work on Public Choice examined the moral dimensions of governance, and how, if not properly monitored, this could lead to an explosion of debt (1984, 265). It was felt that Public Choice theories lacked analytical rigour.

This led to the formulation of the New Institutional Economics theories, in which Williamson, North and others emphasized the need for greater constraints on government, through effective institutions, to reduce transaction costs. These perspectives contributed to a better understanding of how governance decisions, can impact indebtedness.

Factors leading to the need for public finance, and the options generally employed to close the fiscal gap were then reviewed, in relation to their relevance to governance, and deficit financing.

The literature revealed that whether state governance is examined from a philosophical, economic, or political perspective,

Chapter 2: Governance, Fiscal Policy and Debt - Theoretical Foundations

government has a key role to play in steering the economy along a path of development and growth.

It also showed that the structures and institutions formed in the Caribbean to facilitate the governance process have been influenced largely by a plantation history. Over time, these have evolved, though structural, cultural, and ideological retentions have remained. This has largely determined how decisions are made, leading to some unfavourable economic outcomes. Consequently, Jamaica has been plagued by economic stagnation, intractable debt, high levels of inflation, repeated reports of corruption, and relatively poor governance, particularly in relation to lack of accountability, transparency, and lack of full disclosure in transactions financed by taxpayers' funds.

There was, however, minimal emphasis in the literature on how governance contributes to indebtedness and poor macroeconomic performance, in small developing countries like Jamaica. This publication now contributes to closing that gap.

Chapter Three examines Jamaica's political economy from the 1930s to present and juxtaposes this against the comparator countries, Barbados and Singapore.

Chapter 3

JAMAICA'S POLITICAL ECONOMY: 1930's TO PRESENT

With Barbados and Singapore as Comparators

3.1 Introduction

This chapter describes the development of paternalism and patronage in Jamaica, through an examination of economic activity in its political context. The central question asked was:

How has the character of governance in post-independent Jamaica contributed to the country's indebtedness from 1962 to 2010?

Recall that when we speak of the Character of Governance, we are referring to the distinguishing features and peculiar quality of the institutions, leadership provided, and the consistency or lack thereof, between the stated intent, and consequential outcomes of the decisions that are made.

We present this in an outline of Jamaica's political history, cultural and societal nuances, which aids the reader to have a better understanding of how governance has evolved in Jamaica, and its influence on leaders' proclivity to accumulate debt. It also presents the rationale for using Barbados and Singapore as comparators.

3.1.1 General Overview of Jamaica

Jamaica is a part of the Greater Antilles, located to the southeast of Miami, Florida, and the south of Cuba. It is the third largest Caribbean island, with a landmass of 11,420 km^2, and a population

Chapter 3: Jamaica's Political Economy 1930s to Present – with Barbados and Singapore as Comparators

of approximately 2.9 million. Jamaica which was previously inhabited by the Tainos, was settled by the Spanish after the arrival of Christopher Columbus in 1510 (1st visit 1494).

After the Battle of Rio Nuevo in 1655 Jamaica was taken over by the British. Subsequently, significant developments were enabled by slave labour. Slavery ended in 1834, with Emancipation ('full freedom') being granted in 1838. However, mercantilism continued, as Jamaica was a key source of primary products for Britain.

A large sugar estate, Sevilla de la Nueva in St. Ann, was named the first capital of Jamaica. The current capital Kingston is now the hub of government and commerce, hosting the Central Bank, Houses of Parliament, and other key institutions. The seventh largest natural harbour in the world is also found in Kingston; though its advantage has not been fully explored. A logistics hub was proposed for the Goat Island area, to the South of Kingston. Subsequently, the logistics hub has taken on a new dimension, not necessarily having a base on the Goat Islands.

Jamaica gained independence from Britain on August 6, 1962. Since then, the economy has been heavily dependent on bauxite, tourism, agriculture, and services. In 2010, Jamaica's per capita GDP was US$5274 (current); while Debt-to-GDP was at the unsustainable level of 130%. Debt-related decisions are made in Parliament.

3.2 Length of Tenure and Policy Choice

Legislative authority is vested in Jamaica's bicameral Parliament, consisting of the Houses of Representatives, and the Senate. Policy-making authority rests with the Cabinet, made up of the Prime Minister (PM), selected Members of Parliament, and two to four members of the Senate. Each political administration is given a five (5) year term, which can be shortened if the PM chooses to call an election.

Chapter 3: Jamaica's Political Economy 1930s to Present – with Barbados and Singapore as Comparators

According to Gray, Hellman and Ryterman (2004) "the longer the horizon of the executive, the greater its opportunity to implement institutional reforms and the weaker its incentive to strip a country of its resources; however, there are limits to these beneficial aspects of tenure if a government becomes ossified and unresponsive to public demands" (p. 36). It was established earlier in this study that these problems can be curtailed through institutional constraints which guide standards and reduce transaction costs (North 1991).

Length of tenure (term length) of elected officials can also influence the type of institutional constraints embedded within the policies crafted and implemented. Dal Bo and Rossi conducted an empirical study of 'Term Length and Political Performance', and found that while it was difficult to infer causality, "[b]ecause legislators with longer terms have a longer horizon of time during which to reap the benefits of a richer experience, they feel incentivized to exert higher effort" (2008, 17).

Similar arguments were presented by Ozler and Tabellini (1991) who used empirical data to argue that longer tenures can provide leaders with more time and 'degrees of freedom' to conceptualize, formulate and implement policies and strategies that they can see through to completion (p. 1).

Longer tenures and effective institutions may, therefore, lead to better economic outcomes, as highlighted in a study of Taiwan, conducted by Yun-Han Chu (2012). He concluded that "Under the KMT's long political tenure, the state's long-standing policy guideline for macroeconomic management was characterized by its overriding concern over monetary and financial stability as well as fiscal conservatism" (p. 10). The KMT (Kuomintang – the Nationalist Party of China) is Taiwan's ruling political party.

Without focusing purely on the political ideologies of a nation, it has been noted that in a less stable environment, frequent elections can result in a situation where "the policymaker may wish to borrow in excess of the optimum and let his successor 'pay the bills" (Edwards and Tabellini 1991, 19). This brings into sharp

Chapter 3: Jamaica's Political Economy 1930s to Present – with Barbados and Singapore as Comparators

focus, the issue of how political stability and weak institutions can influence debt accumulation and development (recall Chapter 2).

While Prime Ministers in Jamaica, Barbados, and Singapore all have five-year political terms, those in Barbados and Singapore have generally served for relatively longer tenures since each country's independence.

Even during the PNP's three-term period of 1989 to 2007, there were three (3) changes of Prime Ministers. The UNDP (2010) observed that inefficiency in government, and frequent elections in Jamaica have led to resource wastage, lack of support for the government's development plans, and the likelihood of social disintegration (p. 2).

Alesina and Perotti (1995) also noted that frequent elections could lead to policy discontinuities, and decreased investments. Dal Bo and Rossi (2008) shared similar views, arguing that short tenures could lead to failure on the part of legislators to concentrate on their substantive duties, including the development of human capital. In Rodman's view, "Disruption of policy results either because the new Minister must learn from the beginning what is going on or because he insists on starting all over again from scratch (the pseudo-creative response')" (1968, 15).

Jamaica has had ten (10) Prime Ministers (PM Holness twice), through seven (7) changes of administration (JLP and PNP), from fourteen (14) general elections since Independence in 1962. See Table 3.1 below.

Chapter 3: Jamaica's Political Economy 1930s to Present – with Barbados and Singapore as Comparators

Table 3.1 – General Elections in Jamaica from 1962 - 2020

YEAR	DATE	TYPE	PARTY	PRIME MINISTER
2020	Sept. 03	General	JLP	Andrew M. Holness
2016	Feb. 25	General	JLP	Andrew M. Holness
2011	Dec. 29	General	PNP	Portia L. Simpson-Miller
2007	Sept. 03	General	JLP	Bruce O. Golding
2002	Oct. 16	General	PNP	Percival J. Patterson
1997	Dec. 18	General	PNP	Percival J. Patterson
1993	Mar. 30	General	PNP	Percival J. Patterson
1989	Feb. 09	General	PNP	Michael Manley
1983	Dec. 15	General	JLP	Edward P.G. Seaga
1980	Oct. 30	General	JLP	Edward P.G. Seaga
1976	Dec. 15	General	PNP	Michael N. Manley
1972	Feb. 29	General	PNP	Norman W. Manley
1967	Feb. 21	General	JLP	Donald Sangster/Hugh Shearer
1962	April 10	General	JLP	Alexander Bustamante

Source: Electoral Commission of Jamaica (2021)

Frequent changes of administration can undermine policy continuity. Tindigarukayo and Chadwick (2003) conducted a study of local government reform and found that:

> Jamaica represents a classic case of a regular alternation in office of the two major political parties (the PNP and the JLP). However, every change of government implies, in most of the cases, that reforms initiated by the previous regime are either weakly supported, at best, or completely discontinued, at worst. The stiff competition between the two political parties enhances a high level of alienation of each other as they alternate in running the political business of the country. (p. 43)

Two former Prime Ministers interviewed were asked how this has impacted governance and the economy. The first said, "I think perhaps much more attention might be given to a number of social programmes which have received less deserving support than was the case when they were originally conceived" (PM 1). The other emphasized that:

Chapter 3: Jamaica's Political Economy 1930s to Present – with Barbados and Singapore as Comparators

> The political culture is at fault in the abandonment of policies and projects initiated by previous governments. Development plans, Social Wellbeing 1988, Going for Growth 1988, the Solidarity Programme for Youth project was scuttled. I won't talk in terms of projects, there are just too many of them. But if you take the 70s, that was an entirely different type of governance. Socialism was introduced and therefore, everything that was before it was at a standstill or rejected. ... In the 1980s we had to undo that. (PM 2)

In retrospect, this approach has been costly. As Roubini and Sachs (1989) found, "there is a clear tendency for larger deficits in countries characterized by a short average tenure of government" (p. 903). This led, naturally, to an examination of some nuances in political leadership, as each new administration sought to 'place their stamp' on legacy projects, and how these have influenced the quality of governance, anaemic growth, and indebtedness in Jamaica since Independence.

3.3 Jamaica's Political Economy

Political economy combines the analysis of economics and politics, so as to better understand the government's role, which "is increasingly being recognized as necessary for any realistic examination of development problems" (Todaro 1997, 711). Since the 1930s, Jamaica's political leaders have fostered a culture of populism and dependency, by their rhetoric, forms of representation, and the monikers they embraced. Bustamante, for example, was known as 'The Chief'; Manley (Michael) as 'Joshua'; Seaga as 'One Don'; Golding as 'The Driver', and; Simpson-Miller as 'Mama P'. More recently, Jamaica's current Prime Minister Andrew Holness has adopted the moniker of 'Bro. Gad', much to the chagrin of some in the Christian community. Implicit here, as Panton noted with regards to earlier leaders, are connotations of messianic leaders and protectors/providers, within a patron-clientelist system (1993, 26).

This point was also emphasized by Stone and Brown who argued that working-class persons in the Caribbean were

Chapter 3: Jamaica's Political Economy 1930s to Present – with Barbados and Singapore as Comparators

mesmerized by "flamboyant demagogic and charismatic leaders in the square from whom they expect deliverance according to millenarian political expectations" (1981, 25).

Hall and Benn (2003) felt that this was an offshoot from the crown colony period when national leaders were expected to provide welfare for everyone, placing severe pressure on post-independence budgets.

Panton (1993) believed that the objective of those who encouraged this was to gain and maintain state power. Consequently, when austerity measures were to be implemented to instil fiscal discipline, leaders experienced great difficulty trying to change what Williamson (2000) referred to as the 'institutionalized and embedded culture' of dependency and expectation ingrained within the psyche of some segments of society.

Even during periods of crisis, there are still enclaves in Jamaica where 'government' is expected to support entire communities (Virtue 2012). As Abdellatif (2003) argued, deeply embedded social attitudes and culture can have a profound impact on governance (p. 20).

Jamaica's constitutional arrangements make Parliamentarians jointly and severally responsible for governance decisions, many of which have led to increased indebtedness. This being the product of collective policies and decisions made by both major political parties and implemented through their approval in Parliament.

Former Deputy Prime Minister Kenneth Baugh concurred, arguing that both major political parties were responsible for Jamaica's poor economic performance, and dismantled institutions (2010, 4). In his view, this has contributed to Jamaica's poor performance relative to Barbados. Some have linked this to obdurate retentions from the plantation experience, demonstrated through the styles, and decisions of those in leadership.

Chapter 3: Jamaica's Political Economy 1930s to Present – with Barbados and Singapore as Comparators

3.4 Leadership Style and Governance – A Political Overview

It has been argued that Jamaica's plantation history has influenced the electorate's inclination to choose leaders based on personal characteristics, including leadership style. As with tenure, this influences the quality of governance decisions, response of the governed, and economic outcomes (Jones 1981; Panton 1993; Lee 2000; Osei 2002; Milas and Legrenzi 2002). In Jamaica's case, these outcomes include the rapid accumulation of public debt, the antecedent of which can be traced back to weak governance institutions and policies, created and implemented by national leaders.

3.4.1 1930s - 1940s:
Premier Alexander (Clarke) Bustamante, and; Leader of the Opposition Norman Manley

During the Great Depression of the 1930s, there were major upheavals globally. Development strategies were focused on capital formation, territorial expansion, control of money supply, and industrialization. In Jamaica, as in other former British colonies, there was widespread discontent among workers, due to poor working conditions and low wages. Workers expressed their dissatisfaction by challenging the authorities, leading to a massacre among sugar workers in May 1938. These upheavals culminated in the formation of Jamaica's labour unions, and the rise to prominence of union leaders like Norman Manley and his cousin Sir Alexander Bustamante, who later became Premier and Prime Minister (PM), respectively.

Chapter 3: Jamaica's Political Economy 1930s to Present – with Barbados and Singapore as Comparators

The Early Years

Sir Alexander (Clarke) Bustamante, Jamaica's first Prime Minister (pre-Independence national leaders carried the title of Premier), was described as flamboyant, charismatic, and dramatic (Panton 1993; Seaga 2000). His involvement in national affairs started in the 1930s when severe economic hardships led to very high rates of unemployment and cries of injustice. By 1936, the Jamaica Workmen and Tradesmen Union (JWTU) was formed; with Alexander (Clarke) Bustamante becoming the treasurer, and later president. As Seaga (2009) reported, "With no other valve which could be opened for significant employment the pressure increased to a point of eruption in 1938" (p. 36). The ensuing riots reignited the union movement which had started in 1894.

Bustamante left the JWTU in 1938, and formed the Bustamante Industrial Trade Union (BITU), and later (in 1943) the Jamaica Labour Party (JLP). He spoke out vociferously for the people during the 1938 riot and was arrested. His cousin Norman Manley, who was a well-respected barrister, represented him, resulting in his release.

Manley then formed the Jamaica Welfare Limited, to promote rural community development, and; by September 1938 he founded the People's National Party (PNP). Seaga argued that Bustamante was more in touch with the struggles of the working-class than Manley (2009).

Conversely, Panton argued that Bustamante "exercised dictatorial control by declaring himself President-General for Life" (1993, 22). Bustamante has been portrayed as someone who exuded the persona of a strong, fearless leader, who would take on anyone in authority, on behalf of the newly independent citizens of post-colonial Jamaica. In Panton's view:

Chapter 3: Jamaica's Political Economy 1930s to Present – with Barbados and Singapore as Comparators

> Bustamante derived most of his power from his magnetic personality which was able to win over most crowds. Although Manley possessed less personal charisma, his ability to command respect and his personal convictions earned him tremendous admiration from the Jamaican people. (1993, 40)

On 14 December 1944, Jamaica held its first general election after the granting of Universal Adult Suffrage. The Bustamante-led JLP won twenty-two (22) of the thirty-two (32) seats in the Legislative Council. The PNP and Independent candidates won the remaining seats. Premier Bustamante had campaigned on labour legislation and social reform, which the electorate found more alluring than Manley's proposal for self-government. The PNP sought to regain labour support by forming the Trade Union Council, in readiness for the 1949 elections, which it also lost.

3.4.2 1950s - 1960s:
Premier and Prime Ministers Alexander Bustamante, Norman Manley, Donald Sangster, and Hugh Shearer

By 1952 Manley formed the National Worker's Union (NWU). The following year a constitutional amendment made Bustamante Chief Minister. The PNP gained momentum by 1955, as the ideological differences narrowed. The Norman Manley-led PNP won eighteen (18) seats to the JLP's fourteen (14). Panton opined that "[T]he election marked the beginning of the Jamaican clientelist-patronage system" (1993, 26). Clientelism emphasizes the exchange of votes for favour.

Manley introduced full internal self-government, and again won the 1959 election with twenty-nine (29) seats to the JLP's sixteen (16). He then led Jamaica into the 1961/62 Federal elections - a proposed political system that would have had its own Parliamentary structure, federal powers, capital site, and financing, in the West Indies. Bustamante did not support this, but called for a referendum, insisting that Jamaica should pursue independence singularly. Manley delayed the referendum and later conceded that

Chapter 3: Jamaica's Political Economy 1930s to Present – with Barbados and Singapore as Comparators

the people had settled the issue. When Jamaica finally seceded from the Federation, his popularity waned.

Seaga (2009) reported that a group of prominent Jamaicans was then instructed by Cabinet to outline steps to prepare Jamaica for Independence. On 17 October 1961, a Joint Select Committee was formed to draft the Constitution which took effect at Independence. By August 6, 1962 Jamaicans were fully in charge of the governance of their nation state.

Premier Norman Manley (1955-1962)

Mr Manley was soft-spoken, yet firm and decisive. His socialist stance and intellect won the hearts of many; as did Bustamante's charisma and bravado. His governance approach was succinctly captured by Stone and Brown (1981), who noted that in the 1950s and 1960s the State responded to the cries of the people through welfare and social policies to calm them. This showed up in increased expenditure on agriculture, social and public works programmes.

They noted that the socialist goals were promulgated by an elitist middle-class intelligentsia within the PNP; while the JLP opposed them with cries of communist infiltration. The Hansard of Parliament provided ample evidence of this.

"The period between 1953 and independence in 1962 saw an ideological convergence of the two parties, around the common goal of modernizing capitalist development in partnership with North American investment" (Stone and Brown 1981, 18). Agricultural staple exports declined, while economic diversification led to the expansion of the modern sectors, including bauxite and alumina, manufacturing, tourism, food processing, and construction – with economic growth being targeted through foreign direct investment. The service sector was also expanded to include finance, banking, and the provision of utilities. Industrialization had begun in earnest (PIOJ/ESSJ 1959-1962).

Chapter 3: Jamaica's Political Economy 1930s to Present – with Barbados and Singapore as Comparators

Premier/ Prime Minister Bustamante (1962-1967); Prime Minister Sangster (1967)

Premier Manley called and lost the 1962 election taking nineteen (19) seats, to the JLP's twenty-six (26). Bustamante was again in charge of the country, and took it into Independence, with much pomp and pageantry. He became ill and announced his resignation before the scheduled 1967 election. His Finance Minister and deputy, Donald Sangster became Prime Minister in February 1967.

Much of the credit given to Sir Alexander Bustamante for the most consistent period of economic growth in Jamaica from 1962 to 1967 (averaging 5%), ought rightly to be attributed to Sir Donald Sangster who held the reins of leadership, while Prime Minister Bustamante was ill (Bullock 2012, pers. comm.). Prime Minister Sangster died two months after taking office and was succeeded by Prime Minister Hugh Shearer.

Prime Minister Hugh Shearer (1967-1972)

When Prime Minister Shearer took office in 1967 there were great income disparities, high unemployment levels, and a rising black-conscious movement. Black Nationalist groups used various platforms, including the university campus to promulgate their views. In 1968, his administration refused to allow a vocal Black Nationalist lecturer Walter Rodney re-entry into the island. This led to a student riot and mayhem.

Still, the United Nations agreed to declare 1968 as the International Year of Human Rights, after much lobbying by Mr Shearer from 1963. He was lauded by his Parliamentary colleagues as a statesman who avoided political rancour.

Chapter 3: Jamaica's Political Economy 1930s to Present – with Barbados and Singapore as Comparators

3.4.3 1970s – 1980:
Prime Ministers Michael Manley, and Edward Seaga

PM Michael Manley (1972-1980)

PM Michael Manley who took over from his father as party leader in 1969, won the 1972 election against Hugh Shearer, gaining thirty-seven (37) seats to the JLP's sixteen (16). His emphasis on social justice, and the promulgation of an ideology of democratic socialism, made him popular with the masses, but not the private sector.

Worrell and Smith (2000) argued that the elections were won on a populist agenda, based on the redistribution of income. Correspondingly, there were very few backward and forward linkages, to reduce unemployment, and stimulate trade across industries. Panton noted that:

> Although the economy was adversely affected by several external factors, Manley's fiscal expansionism and restrictive controls on private sector production played the crucial role in the severe economic decline which characterized this period. On the positive side, the government managed to contain the trade deficit, improve domestic agricultural production, and provide incentives for informal opportunities, all of which prevented the total collapse of the Jamaican economy. (1993, 32)

Michael Manley went on to win the 1976 election, with forty-seven (47) seats to the JLP's thirteen (13). He was a charismatic leader who used symbols such as a rod, a casual style of dressing, and slogans such as 'I man born ya', to establish a firm identity with the masses. He has (then and even now) been highly regarded for introducing legislation to promote social advancement. Though he openly associated with leaders that many classified as being on the radical left, like Fidel Castro of Cuba and others, he sought to assuage the fears of Jamaicans and foreigners, by denying any widespread communist infiltration of the island's governance structures.

Chapter 3: Jamaica's Political Economy 1930s to Present – with Barbados and Singapore as Comparators

Still, high inflation and economic and social instability led to much unease and disinvestment, resulting in an extended period of negative growth (Stone and Brown 1981). Many continued to look to politicians for sustenance, which the country could not provide. Manley became unpopular, and; Seaga who had been accused of stoking the fear of communism for Manley's entire tenure of leadership, won the 1980 election, taking fifty-one (51) of the sixty (60) seats.

3.4.4 1980s -1990s:
Prime Ministers Edward Seaga, and; Michael Manley

PM Edward Seaga (1980-1989)

Mr Seaga entered representational politics in 1962 and served as Prime Minister and later, Opposition Leader for a total of forty-three (43) years. He was seen as Bustamante's protégé, and; exuded much the same autocratic style, without the charisma. Some even described him as being introspective and aloof. By 1995 he had begun to lose favour with several of his Cabinet Ministers, including his heir apparent Bruce Golding. The infamous move by dissenting Jamaica Labour Party (JLP) members was succinctly captured by Buddan (2009) who reported that:

> The voices for change in the JLP go back to 1995. The strongest of these voices was Bruce Golding's. His was not the first but was the most articulate and the most credible. ... The challenge to the old party order has come in different forms. The first form was to work from within to try and get Mr Seaga to change his style and make the JLP more democratic.

However, Mr Seaga also had a gentler side. During the 2002/2003 budget debate, he concluded a review of his political life, with the following offer to Finance Minister Davies with regards to Jamaica's economic challenges: "I think I have a solution and I am going to sit down with you quietly, you and I,

Chapter 3: Jamaica's Political Economy 1930s to Present – with Barbados and Singapore as Comparators

and I am going to show it to you, spell it out and if you are in agreement I want us to do it together" (p. 415).

Closer to the end of his tenure in 2005, he became more reflective, asking his colleagues to ensure that matters relating to education, human rights, the economy and social services for the haves and the have-nots, be given priority attention. He argued that a system of good governance should focus on, "provision of a secure criminal justice system, there must be operation of an effective education system and there must be the creation of an economy which provides gainful opportunities" (2005, 100).

Even in the face of criticism, he was highly regarded for his attention to detail, ability to expound on social and economic issues, and his work in culture and community development. His tenure as Prime Minister ended in 1989 when he lost to PM Manley.

3.4.5 1990s – 2000s:
Prime Ministers P.J. Patterson; Portia Simpson-Miller, Bruce Golding, and Andrew Holness

Prime Minister Percival J. Patterson (1992-2006)

Mr Patterson QC, was sworn in as Jamaica's sixth Prime Minister in 1992, during Prime Minister Manley's illness. Though some perceived Prime Minister Patterson as a laissez-faire leader, he has been lauded by many for encouraging greater levels of consultation across party lines and focusing on the need for positive 'values and attitudes' in the society.

On the eve of his exit from active politics, he emphasized that "it is time we stopped seeing this thing in terms of oppose, oppose and oppose. Let us instead say, let us create firstly …That is what Independence was intended to mean as we became masters of our own destiny" (Patterson 2005, 281). He served in various ministries throughout his thirty (30) years of Parliamentary service, and; demitted office on March 30, 2006.

Chapter 3: Jamaica's Political Economy 1930s to Present – with Barbados and Singapore as Comparators

Prime Minister Portia Simpson-Miller (2006-2007; 2012-2016)

In 2006 Prime Minister Portia Simpson-Miller succeeded Mr Patterson to become Jamaica's seventh Prime Minister. She has been described as a 'grass roots' politician, mentored by Michael Manley, whom she said saw in her what she never saw in herself. Her style of leadership has been described as democratic, though she was more confrontational than her predecessors.

She has continuously sought to be identified with the poor and dispossessed, even at the expense of being ridiculed. As she said "My lifelong service to politics can only spell one thing, caring and advocacy for the poor, and; this will forever burn in my heart and soul" (2008, 5). She remains one of Jamaica's most popular politicians, though her constituency bears evidence of poverty and degradation, over more than three decades, as she continued to repeatedly win elections in that division.

Prime Minister Bruce Golding (2007-2011)

In 1972 Mr Golding became the youngest Parliamentarian in Jamaica's history, at age 21. He left the JLP and formed the National Democratic Movement (NDM) in October 1995 lobbying for constitutional changes. After unsuccessfully contesting the 2001 North East St. Ann by-election, he returned to the JLP in September 2002, and became Jamaica's eighth Prime Minister, serving from 2007 to 2011. He was highly regarded for his oratory skills, and willingness to question the status quo.

He was, however, perceived as being inconsistent, and admittedly lacked charisma (Buckley 2006). He later noted that though Jamaicans had found themselves in a harsh global environment to which they were very vulnerable, they should not be overwhelmed (Golding 2008, 5). Yet, by October 2011 he tendered his resignation, saying the challenges of the past four years had taken a toll on him.

Chapter 3: Jamaica's Political Economy 1930s to Present – with Barbados and Singapore as Comparators

Prime Minister Andrew Holness (2011; 2016-present)

Mr Andrew Holness was seen as PM Golding's heir apparent, and became Jamaica's ninth Prime Minister in 2011, after Golding's departure. Holness' deportment and role in Parliament as Leader of Government Business, gained him respect and admiration. His style was somewhat autocratic, even as he sought to emphasize the importance of accountability in governance. In 2008 he noted that "Lack of trust increases transaction cost and hinders the formation of political capital" (p. 5).

He called the 2012 election, in a bid to seek his own mandate, and lost to Mrs Portia Simpson-Miller. Political commentators linked his defeat to the Jamaica Labour Party and his predecessor Golding, having lost credibility, after long delays regarding the extradition to the United States of so-called reputed area don Christopher 'Dudus' Coke in 2010. The unrest provoked by this extradition was linked to residents of Mr Golding's constituency (Tivoli Gardens) professing loyalty to Coke, on account of his ability to meet their social needs - a popular role allegedly played by dons, who many have argued, wield significant political authority in Jamaica's so-called garrison constituencies.

This segment provides a perfect segue into the links between governance, social policy, development, and public debt.

3.5   Social Policy and Early Development

The preceding discourse has set the stage and provides the lenses through which we will examine the links between politics, leadership styles, governance, social policy, and how these have influenced the accumulation of public debt in Jamaica, for arbitrary social, infrastructure, and other projects and programmes, during the period 1962 to 2010.

Figure 3.1 below tells a story of the volumes and components of public debt accumulated, across the tenure(s) of each leader. Recall or revisit the leadership time periods provided above.

Chapter 3: Jamaica's Political Economy 1930s to Present – with Barbados and Singapore as Comparators

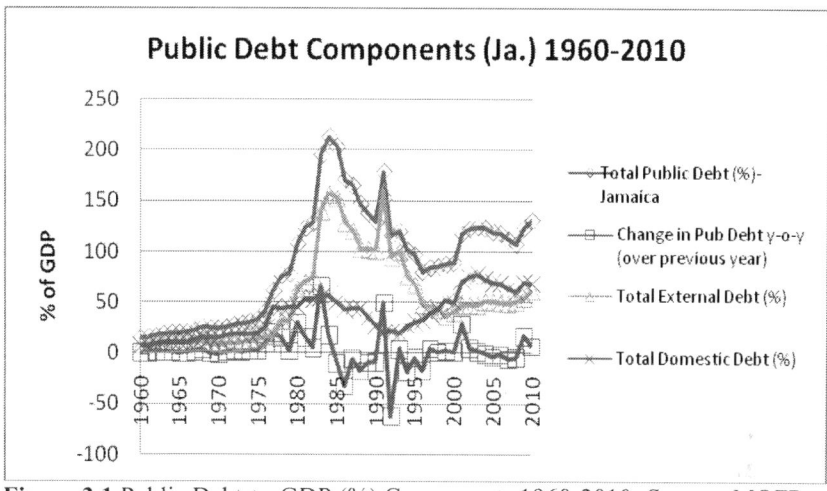

Figure 3.1 Public Debt-to-GDP (%) Components 1960-2010- Source: MOFP

Social Policy – An Overview

Social policy is guided by the needs in society requiring government intervention. It generally seeks to address societal conditions relating to health, education, housing, and social services for the vulnerable (ECLAC 2001). They also emphasized that contemporary social policy is now based on social welfare pluralism in which social services are provided through several channels including the State, Non-Governmental Organizations (NGOs), and private enterprise (2001, 3.1).

From as early as Independence in 1962, concerns have been raised inside and outside Jamaica's Parliament, about the high net cost of social policy decisions, resulting in the expansion of Jamaica's public debt. Despite huge expenditures, "evaluations have shown that the impact could be greater, but for fragmentation, duplication and high administrative costs, resulting in inefficiencies in service delivery" (MP Horace Dalley 2003, 543).

Seaga (2009) also noted that many of the social programmes of the 1970s were not thoroughly thought through, lacked proper planning, and were open to corruption. However, he noted that

Chapter 3: Jamaica's Political Economy 1930s to Present – with Barbados and Singapore as Comparators

"Of all the programmes instituted by Manley in the 1970s, it was the agenda of social legislation that was most successful. This has endured" (2009, 232). These included: The Holiday with Pay Law (1973), Redundancy Act (1974), The Equal Pay for Men and Women (1975), and the Labour Relations and Industrial Disputes Act.

Yet, the Manley administration admitted that "There is a limit on how far the Government can go in the direction of improving welfare and increasing employment through higher Government spending, without dislocating the entire economy" (GOJ 1978, 9). These expenditures contributed to a rapid build-up of debt, culminating in the 1977/78 crisis.

Since Independence, social policy decisions taken by successive political leaders in Jamaica have been influenced by election cycles, a priori assumptions about what was best for the people, and stipulations from International Financial Institutions (IFIs). Still, leaders who focused heavily on social expenditure were often re-elected.

For example, from as early as the 1960's Mr. Seaga, in his role as Minister of Development and Welfare, paid significant attention to social and infrastructural development in the Tivoli (Back o' Wall) constituency he wanted to represent. He described it as a notorious criminal den, in a slum with over 15000 residents, so that:

> In order to both create proper housing and disperse criminal elements, Back o' Wall had to be demolished. In its place I planned a 40 acre community for 4000 residents living in a variety of structures: some high-rise condominiums, other town-house type complexes and some bungalows. (Seaga 2009, 152-153)

In 1986 he presented a Government Guarantee for a United States Agency for International Development (USAID) development loan of US$5 million, to reduce congestion, increase tourism traffic, enhance human development, improve safety and beautify the Parade (in downtown Kingston) area near Tivoli.

Chapter 3: Jamaica's Political Economy 1930s to Present – with Barbados and Singapore as Comparators

Today, not much has changed in terms of the socio-economic conditions Seaga described above. The area is now in a dilapidated condition, surrounded by the hub of commerce and government, with slum dwellings on the periphery. Tivoli has long been perceived as a political garrison. In May 2010 when Jamaica's security forces made an incursion into the community to arrest Coke, an 'impenetrable enclave' existed.

Tivoli's Member of Parliament, PM Golding, former PM Seaga's successor, reported that sections of the community had been barricaded and rigged with explosives; one JDF soldier and seventy-three (73) civilians were reportedly killed; while twenty-eight JDF soldiers and eight police were injured (Golding 2010,1).

Utility companies have also complained that prior to the incursion they could not venture into Tivoli to regularize supplies and collect payment. This was also the case 20 years earlier when Minister Ramtallie informed Parliament of plans to regularize occupancy and utilities in a number of areas where legitimate property owners were being intimidated and their houses vandalized. The response of prominent JLP Parliamentarian Pearnel Charles was, "You go touch Jungle [Tivoli] and see how it go" (Charles 1990, 337). This suggested high-level protection of political turf, leading to the transaction costs of which North (1990) and Williamson (2000) wrote.

3.6 Social Policy Decisions - The NHT and Public Debt

For fifty-one years (1960 to 2011) Tivoli Gardens was represented in Parliament by Jamaican Prime Ministers – first Prime Minister Edward Seaga, followed by Prime Minister Bruce Golding. During Prime Minister Seaga's tenure, more than 700 housing units were built there, by the National Housing Trust (NHT). The cost of these facilities, and utilities allegedly extracted to support them, have been reported as being largely borne by the State, contributing to widening the fiscal deficits and increasing Jamaica's public debt.

Chapter 3: Jamaica's Political Economy 1930s to Present – with Barbados and Singapore as Comparators

Foster (2006) reported that similar NHT funded developments had taken place in Prime Minister Simpson-Miller's South West St. Andrew constituency. They were reportedly slated to receive over 500 apartments valued at more than $8 million each, yet priced at under $1.4 million (Jamaica Observer, September 15, 2006). PM Golding later reported that the related arrears on the project totalled $337 million.

He also argued that whereas PM Simpson-Miller had reported that she left the NHT in a very good financial position, fifteen years of NHT employees' contributions approximating $10 billion ($20 billion with interest) were unpaid; while NHT funds had been reduced from a surplus of $3.5 billion in March 2004, to a projected deficit of $634 million by March 2008. He also pointed out that the Inner City Housing programme (ICHP) in her constituency, had reportedly cost the public purse between "$1½ and $2 million per unit" (2008, 3).

By March 2013, the Simpson-Miller administration took a policy decision to use a further $44 billion of NHT funds, over four years, for fiscal consolidation. Though she declared that this would not affect the Trust's ability to achieve its objectives, there were reportedly cash flow challenges from that action.

These funds held in trust were allegedly used with profligacy, and again later further depleted, to address Jamaica's debt problem. King and Richards (2008) believed Jamaica's fiscal policy went awry because of such poor policy choices. Though promises have been repeatedly made in political manifestos and budget speeches to prudentially manage Jamaica's financial resources, many of the promises were not kept. As the IDB observed:

> The standard economic model of government debt [in Jamaica] posits a benevolent government that uses debt to finance capital accumulation or smooth the impact of natural and financial disasters or economic fluctuations. But in fact, decisions on debt and fiscal policy are made by politicians who may have in mind other issues, such as the result of the next election and the interests of their constituencies. (2007, 171)

Chapter 3: Jamaica's Political Economy 1930s to Present – with Barbados and Singapore as Comparators

Dr Phillips concurred, noting that Jamaica's "politics has become of the short-term calculations of the electoral cycle. And we have abandoned the compromises necessary to be made in the interest of longer term advance of Jamaica, on the road to development" (Phillips 2010, 1).

As Finance Minister, he oversaw significant improvements in fiscal discipline from 2012, due in part to stringent stipulations in the 2013 IMF agreement, and the supervision provided by the private sector led Economic Programme Oversight Committee (EPOC). This was not so in the early years.

3.7 Dominant Ideologies and the Debt/Growth Nexus

The PNP regimes of the 1950s and 1960s led by Prime Minister Norman Manley, emphasized democratic socialism as the dominant ideology, with planned economic progress as the basis for its existence (Levi 1989). Prime Minister Michael Manley reemphasized the democratic socialism rhetoric, defending the right of the state to maintain control over national assets. The promulgation of this socialist ideology invoked fear and paranoia, locally and overseas, resulting in massive capital flight, migration, and brain drain.

Meanwhile, Jamaica's debt obligation to the International Monetary Fund (IMF) and other lenders continued to increase, with limited fiscal resources to meet the public debt obligations. After repeatedly failing the scheduled IMF tests, the Manley administration went to the Soviet Union and other members of the Non-Aligned Movement for assistance. However, as Fine noted:

> From the mid-1980s, the threat of the Soviet Union system as an alternative source of support for development was already on the wane. By the 1990s, it had already collapsed as an alternative model. Also, during the 1980s, the modernization approach to development had given way to the neo-liberal Washington consensus, with its emphasis on market forces and a minimal role for the state. (2006, 213)

Chapter 3: Jamaica's Political Economy 1930s to Present – with Barbados and Singapore as Comparators

The private sector was now expected to be the 'engine of growth'. This was premised on the view that underdevelopment resulted from too much government involvement, corruption, lack of incentives, and inefficiencies in pricing and allocation of resources (Bauer and Yamey 1957; Bhagwati 1978 and Krueger 1978).

While those on the left maintained their socialist stance, the market-oriented approach gained traction, as the way to achieve economic growth. Countries like Singapore and Barbados capitalized on this market-oriented approach, even while retaining some amount of state control. Those economies began to experience growth. Concurrently, Jamaica's exchange rate to the United States dollar devalued from J$1.78/US$1 in 1980 to J$21.57 by 1991. While Singapore's exchange rate revalued from SG$2.14/US$1 to SG$1.73/US$1, and Barbados' held firm (fixed) at BD$2/US1 over the same time period.

An economy that is competitive and experiencing sustained growth has little or no need for external borrowing. Recall that economic growth is essential to reducing the Debt-to-GDP ratio (ceteris paribus). Unfortunately, poor planning and implementation, profligacy, and rapid debt accumulation have been major hindrances to economic growth in Jamaica for decades.

Mr Seaga, who embraced the market-oriented approach to development, argued that over a forty-year period, one party accounted for economic growth in 16 of their 18 years in government, while the other accounted for growth, in only 4 of their 20 years (2001, 826). Prime Minister Patterson countered this, arguing that it was the foundation of industrialization and modernization established by the PNP under Premier Norman Manley in the 1950s, that had "initiated the period of the most rapid growth in Jamaica" (2001, 865).

An empirical review was conducted to examine these arguments. Between 1952 and 1972 the Jamaican economy recorded average annual growth of 6.3%, propelled by the development of the bauxite, alumina and tourism sectors (Lal and

Chapter 3: Jamaica's Political Economy 1930s to Present – with Barbados and Singapore as Comparators

Mynt 1998). Subsequently, growth averaged only 0.6% from 1973 to 2010. Table 3.2 provides a breakdown of average growth, across political administrations.

Table 3.2 - Average GDP Growth by Political Term 962 – 2011

YEARS	PNP	JLP	Election Year
1962-1971	-	5.3	1962
1972-1980	-1.1	-	1972
1981-1988	-	1.6	1980
1989-2006	1.8	-	1989
2007-2011	-	-0.9	2007
Overall Average by Party	0.35	2.0	1962-2011

Source: STATIN; Averages calculated

As Table 3.2 above shows, the average GDP growth for all PNP administrations from 1962 to 2011 was 0.35 percent; while that for the JLP was 2 percent. The average of 2 percent for the JLP was buoyed mainly by the favourable economic outturns of the immediate post-Independence period (1962-1967), and an eight percent (8%) growth rate in 1987 under PM Edward Seaga, mainly from production in the Garment Free Zones.

There were five consecutive years of economic decline after 1975, the worst being -5.7% in 1980. GDP growth then averaged 1.6% from 1981 to 1988; 1.8% from 1989 to 2006, and; -0.9% from 2007 to 2011. GDP growth was 1.5% in 2010/2011.

Subsequently, even with greater fiscal discipline resulting from the combined efforts to meet the IMF targets in the 2013 Extended Fund Facility (EFF) agreement, support from EPOC, and commitment of the GOJ from 2013, economic growth has been relatively stagnant. See Table 3.3 below.

Chapter 3: Jamaica's Political Economy 1930s to Present – with Barbados and Singapore as Comparators

Table 3.3 – Gross Domestic Product Growth/Decline 2011-20

YEAR	GDP Growth/Decline (%)	Administration
2011	1.73	Jamaica Labour Party
2012	-0.614	People's National Party
2013	0.518	People's National Party
2014	0.69	People's National Party
2015	0.921	People's National Party
2016	1.375	Jamaica Labour Party
2017	0.997	Jamaica Labour Party
2018	1.89	Jamaica Labour Party
2019	0.892	Jamaica Labour Party
2020	-10.2 (COVID-19 year)	Jamaica Labour Party
Average	-0.19811 or approx. -0.2	JLP & PNP

Source: Word Bank IBRD - IDA (2021)

When Prime Minister Andrew Holness received his own mandate in 2016, he formed an Economic Growth Council, comprised of prominent businessmen, including Michael Lee-Chin of the National Commercial Bank (Jamaica) and Portland Holdings (Canada), then Ambassador, now Minister of Finance and Planning Dr Nigel Clarke, and other prominent Jamaicans including Adam Stewart of Sandals Resorts International.

PM Holness repeatedly touted that Jamaica would achieve five percent (5%) growth in four years through a number of initiatives including human capital development, and stimulation of greater asset utilization (JIS 2016). As Table 3.3 shows, nothing close to that rate of growth was achieved, even prior to the COVID-19 pandemic.

While one party showed a higher average rate of growth than the other, from 1962 to present, none was particularly impressive, when examined against the exponential growth in national debt (the numerator of the very important Debt-to-GDP ratio). Stone assessed the political antecedents and outcomes of the period of economic performance up to the mid-1980s and concluded that:

Chapter 3: Jamaica's Political Economy 1930s to Present – with Barbados and Singapore as Comparators

> Prior to the October 1980 election in Jamaica, the administration of Michael Manley's People's National Party (PNP) had tried for eight years to turn Jamaica into a show piece of socialist economic management. Shortly after the successes at the polls of the Jamaica Labour Party (JLP) under Edward Seaga, the administration of President Ronald Reagan in the United States promised to turn Jamaica into a show piece of capitalist development in the Caribbean. After eight years of PNP socialism and four years of JLP capitalism, Jamaica's economy has failed to respond to either ideological medicine and continues to drift from crisis to crisis. (1985, 282)

The crises continued. By February 2011, the IMF observed that there had been little or no growth in Jamaica, even as other comparable Caribbean and Central American countries had progressed (p. 32).

Average GDP Growth by Political Party and Term

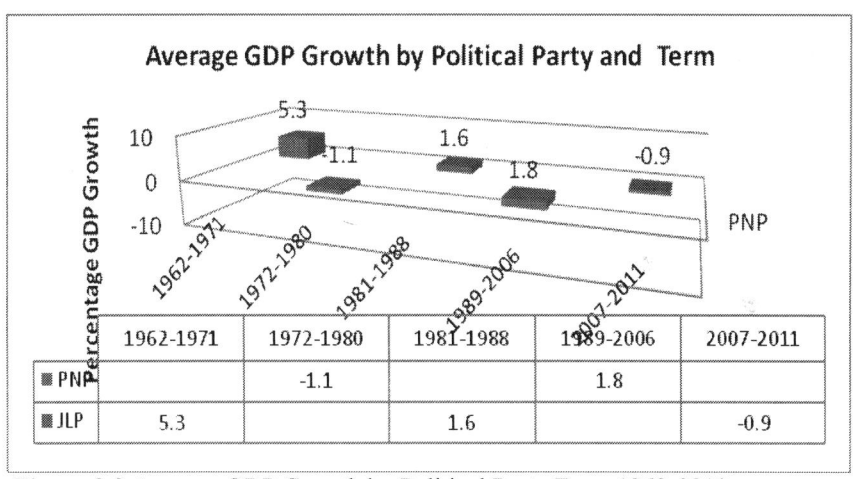

	1962-1971	1972-1980	1981-1988	1989-2006	2007-2011
PNP		-1.1		1.8	
JLP	5.3		1.6		-0.9

Figure 3.2 Average GDP Growth by Political Party Term 1962-2010

Some have argued that leaders' experimentation with various ideologies and development plans, alongside massive ad hoc social and infrastructural expenditure, have served to deplete Jamaica's financial resources, expand its public debt and stymie growth.

Pandeiros and Benfield noted that even after 30 years of macroeconomic and structural reforms and "investment at levels adequate to spur growth of 4 to 6% on average, Jamaica's per capita GDP was almost the same as it was, in real terms, in 1970" (2010, 6).

Concurrently, low productivity, a high crime rate, corruption, and high energy costs have also exacerbated the problem and continued to hamper competiveness, and growth in Jamaica. Comparatively, GDP per capita in Barbados grew three times faster than Jamaica leading to an income gap that was five times wider in 2008 than in 1962 (Henry and Miller 2009, 2). Economic growth is influenced by a country's level of competitiveness.

3.8 Divergent Views on Competitiveness

Jamaica's score on the WEFs Global Competitiveness Index, which ranks more than 130 countries globally on macroeconomic performance and governance, fell from 4.06 out of 10 in 2006, to 3.85 by 2011.

The Hansard of Parliament (1962-2010) was reviewed, to better understand Jamaican Finance Ministers' approach to competitiveness and growth. The two most vociferous Finance Ministers who repeatedly spoke on these matters were Mr Audley Shaw and Dr Omar Davies.

Finance Minister Audley Shaw's Main Focus
- Reduction in Interest Rates -

Mr Shaw's main focus to spur competitiveness and growth was on reducing interest rates, and stabilizing the dollar. In his view:

> [A] high real interest rate regime makes export business activities less competitive, less profitable, creates a huge import subsidy, export jobs, robs the country of potential tax revenues, re-enforces the vicious cycle of fiscal deficit and debt financing and impedes growth. ... [T]o get the economy growing again, as a matter of top priority, interest rates must come down. (2001, 684)

He also emphasized that "sustainable lower interest rates... require synergy in the consistent achievement of critical macroeconomic targets" (2008, 3). By 2010 he presided over Jamaica's first major debt exchange (the Jamaica Debt Exchange or JDX), and a significant reduction in interest rates to single digits. Still, the public Debt-to-GDP ratio continued to increase.

Finance Minister Omar Davies' Main Focus
- Reduction in Inflation Rates -

On the other hand, Finance Minister Davies argued that reduction in inflation rates would be the key to enhancing competitiveness. He repeatedly referred to inflation as the "most cruel form of taxation on the poor and fixed income workers" (2001, 592). He oversaw reductions in inflation rates from 80% in 1991 to 8.8% by 2001.

Yet, the financial sector collapsed during that period, costing the country more than J$140 billion (1/3 of annual GDP in 2001), while growth virtually stagnated. The Financial Sector Adjustment Company Ltd (FINSAC) was established to restore stability to Jamaica's financial institutions. More will be shared on this later in this publication.

Though exogenous factors do impact competitiveness, some basic endogenous factors such as effective institutions, a skilled and competent workforce, technological innovation, consistent savings and investment, and robust development plans, have been identified as key success factors to spur competitiveness and growth (Schumpeter 1939; Solow 1956; Wehmeyer, Clayton and Lum 2002, and; Acemoglu et al 2003).

Dr Davies later acknowledged that while Jamaica lagged behind, its development partners were integrally involved in crafting medium-term social policies aligned to their country's macroeconomic targets (2004).

A key issue that appeared to have alluded these Finance Ministers was the matter of a dwindling pool of resources to meet increasing current and future pension obligations, even as both major political administrations failed to achieve the levels of efficiency and productivity required to justify the size of their public sector wage bills.

3.9 Social Policy: Pension, a Potential Crisis

While the economy continues to underperform, another major fiscal challenge that threatens to worsen Jamaica's indebtedness is inadequate pension and health care provisions for a rapidly ageing population. As PM Patterson lamented:

> What will happen to this country in another 20 to 30 years with an ageing population for which no provisions have been made for their pensions? How will we cope with the enormous pressures and demands that will be placed upon the State to make provision for their security and well-being? (2005, 281)

He emphasized that there would be no sustainable development, justice or guarantee of liberty if the society does not provide appropriate income security and social protection for its people. The situation grew worse when in 2009 PM Golding highlighted the danger of the National Insurance Scheme (NIS) being de-capitalized in 13 to 17 years, as eligible pension contributors were rapidly increasing; while the NIS paid out more than it was collecting.

The Planning Institute of Jamaica (PIOJ 2010) also reported that the dependent elderly over 65 cohort was expected to increase from 7.7% to 11.2% of the population by 2030; with more than one-third of public sector pensioners being over 75 years. The gravity of the problem is clearly demonstrated by an examination of Jamaica's population pyramid.

After more than a decade of deliberation and inaction, the government finally acknowledged in 2011 that the system was administratively inefficient, fiscally unsustainable, and in need of reform (see Green Paper No.2/2011). Though successive administrations had long made commitments in prior IMF loan agreements, to carry out public sector pension, and tax reforms, to

Chapter 3: Jamaica's Political Economy 1930s to Present – with Barbados and Singapore as Comparators

reduce Jamaica's indebtedness, it was not addressed in any significant manner. These decisions remain outstanding, largely due to possible political repercussions (see Hansard), providing evidence that the character of governance, through inaction, and inordinate delays, has further contributed to exacerbating Jamaica's debt problem.

Comprehensive reform is now required, to consolidate more than thirty pieces of legislation governing the public sector pension system. Without these reforms, major challenges will persist. As Kappagoda noted:

> Payments that could arise due to unfunded pension liabilities, health care and other benefits of the public sector, insurance and reinsurance programs of the government, indemnities, comfort letters and other forms of assurances that are not legally binding could be a potential burden in times of crisis. (2002, 1)

While the economy continues to be negatively affected by these delays, worsened by indebtedness, many highly skilled and competent persons have chosen to migrate. A White Paper on Public Sector Pension Reform was tabled in Jamaica's Parliament on April 1, 2016 (MOFP).

3.10 Migration, Brain Drain and the Remittance Cycle

Migration which often results in brain drain, can stymie development and growth. In 2010 the Brain Drain ranks for Jamaica, Barbados, and Singapore were 98, 29, and 4 respectively (WEF). Jamaica was, therefore, most likely to lose its skilled and qualified workforce through migration. As the report stated, "[T]he lack of meritocracy in the labour market limits employment opportunities for young talent and is one of the factors that fuel a brain drain from the country" (p. 39).

While a skilled workforce is essential for sustainable development and growth, migration was seen by Jamaican

Chapter 3: Jamaica's Political Economy 1930s to Present – with Barbados and Singapore as Comparators

policymakers as a "valve to continue to reduce the unemployment pressure" (Seaga 2009, 182).

> Some 175,000 migrated to the United States between 1970 and 1980, about 50,000 of them dependants. ...16,100 professionals, technical, managerial, skilled and semi-skilled members of the labour force migrated between 1977 and 1980. This was an estimated 60 percent of the output of the university and other institutions of higher learning and those trained in various skills in 1979. (Seaga 2009, 182)

In contrast, the World Bank (2011) argued that "the people who migrate [from Jamaica] are more able, more entrepreneurial and less risk averse; the country therefore loses very important assets for productivity, innovation and entrepreneurship" (p. 8).

The impact of this loss may have been overshadowed by the fact that most Jamaicans, who have migrated, regularly remit funds home, making remittances Jamaica's second largest source of foreign exchange.

However, as Chami et al. (2008) noted, while worldwide remittances totalled US$114 billion in 2003, the relationship between remittances and governance cannot be ignored, as in countries where remittance recipient households are able to maintain an acceptable standard of living, poor governance results in substandard infrastructure and limited economic growth. Consequently, profligate government expenditure, high Debt-to-GDP ratios, and continued heavy external borrowing create economic pressures, resulting in greater levels of unemployment, and more persons choosing to migrate.

Chami et al. felt that those receiving remittances do not exert pressure for governance to be improved, as the remittances moderate the impact of poor government policies (p. 82). The effect of remittances on the work ethic and productivity of the recipients also arose in an interview for this study. A Central Bank executive interviewed noted that:

Chapter 3: Jamaica's Political Economy 1930s to Present – with Barbados and Singapore as Comparators

> Because we have not been growing on our own steam and have been depending so much on either remittances or official aid, we have been able to survive without the effort that other people would have required to maintain that kind of international commerce. Part of the reason for our reliance has been insufficient attention paid to developing our skill sets. We see it in every family. Every day you run into hundreds of people who are unemployable. They have been to school but they didn't learn anything. Yet they survive just by going to 'Western Union', or through some programme where they get handouts. So we have sort of adapted to an environment where so many people are dependent on the few who work, that it even dissuades those who work from working harder. (pers. comm.)

Jamaica's dependence on remittances may, therefore, be deemed unsustainable, inimical to good governance, and counterproductive to growth and development. Like migration, corruption is another major problem contributing to Jamaica's indebtedness.

3.11 The Economic Impact of Corruption

The World Bank (2011) noted that crime in Jamaica was most destructive to its economic and social structure, as it robs the country of its potential to grow, creates instability, retards human capital, propels migration of the most skilled workers, and discourages investment (p. 12). They estimated the cost of bribery alone to be over US$1 trillion worldwide. They also believed that per capita incomes could be potentially increased by a "400% governance dividend" by simply curtailing crime and corruption. They concluded that corruption deters investments and job creation, as it increases operating costs by an estimated 20 percent (Kaufmann/WB 2013, 1). Therefore, if corruption and crime can be curtailed, Jamaica's per capita GDP could increase to well over US$20,000.

Per capita GDP remains a very useful indicator for standardized comparisons of governance and development across countries (Hall and Jones 1999; Easterly and Levine 2003). As can be seen from Table 3.4 below, even during the COVID-19 pandemic when economies globally were ravaged, Barbados and Singapore still maintained per capita GDP levels that were multiples of Jamaica's US$5,369 and $4,665 for 2019 and 2010 respectively.

Table 3.4 – Comparative Per Capita GDP (Current US$)

YEAR	JAMAICA	BARBADOS	SINGAPORE
2011	5,111.466	16,453.353	53,890.429
2012	5,209.859	16,249.674	55,546.489
2013	4,989.734	16,451.279	59,967.426
2014	4,834.284	16,489.072	57,562.531
2015	4,907.927	16,524.90	55,646.619
2016	4,843.75	16,900.048	56,848.175
2017	5,070.1	17,391.669	61,176.456
2018	5,359.994	17,745.255	66,679.046
2019	5,369.498	18,148.498	65,640.708
2020	4,664.529	15,191.164	59,797.752

Source: World Bank – World National Accounts Data (2021)

Let's take a look at Jamaica's World Governance Indicator rankings, in comparison to the two reference countries – Barbados and Singapore.

3.12 Comparators – Jamaica, Barbados, and Singapore

The World Bank not only provides assessments, critiques, and loans to member countries, it also provides useful, sound, empirically tested World Governance Indicators (WGIs) that can be used to compare the quality of governance across countries.

Jamaica's WGI 'Control of Corruption' scores, for example, were below 50% for 10 out of the 12 years of assessment up to 2010, while Barbados' scores were consistently above 86%. In Singapore's case, early legislation was enacted to discourage state capture and corruption, with the sanctions being quite severe (Lee 2000; Heilbrunn 2004).

Singapore is, therefore, seen as one of the least corrupt countries in the world, with WGI scores consistently above 96%. As Table 3.5 below shows, five (5) of the six (6) WGI global

Chapter 3: Jamaica's Political Economy 1930s to Present – with Barbados and Singapore as Comparators

governance scores for Jamaica were well below those of the two comparators in 2010.

Table 3.5 World Governance Indicators (2010)

Indicator /Country	Voice & Accountability	Political Stability	Government Efficiency	Regulatory Quality	Rule of Law	Control of Corruption
Jamaica	60.19	32.08	62.68	59.81	37.44	44.98
Barbados	88.63	87.74	89.00	66.99	82.94	89.47
Singapore	37.44	89.62	100.00	98.56	93.36	98.56

Source: World Bank/KKZ (govindicators.org)

Levels of Political Stability, Control of Corruption, and Regulatory Quality have also been empirically proven to influence indebtedness (see Williams and Siddique 2005, and; Jalles 2011). Though international lending agencies will stipulate their terms and conditions, it is the quality of governance, and the integrity of policymakers, that will determine how effectively funds are utilized, and debts repaid. This is as true for Jamaica, as it is for any other country, including the comparators, Barbados and Singapore.

Table 3.6 World Governance Indicators (2019)

Indicator /Country	Voice & Accountability	Political Stability	Government Effectiveness	Regulatory Quality	Rule of Law	Control of Corruption
Jamaica	68.5	59.5	70.7	62.0	44.2	54.30
Barbados	86.2	80.0	73.6	66.8	63.9	88.5
Singapore	39.4	97.6	100.00	100.0	96.6	99.5

Source: World Bank/KKZ (govindicators.org) – Accessed Aug. 17, 2021

As the 2019 WGI scores for all three countries in Table 3.6 clearly show, Jamaica's scores have improved somewhat. Yet they were still well below those of Singapore, and; even in the case of Barbados' slightly declining scores, Jamaica remained at the lowest level of the three (3) comparators.

Chapter 3: Jamaica's Political Economy 1930s to Present – with Barbados and Singapore as Comparators

Barbados

Barbados is located in the Lesser Antilles and is the easternmost island in the Caribbean. It has a landmass of 430 km², and a population of approximately 300,000. The economy which was mainly dependent on agriculture is now 80% dependent on services. During the 1960s Barbados diversified into light manufacturing, off-shore financial services, and upscale tourism (Downes 2001, 35). Barbados Central Bank Governor Worrel reported that further diversification was planned, in order to recover from the 2007/08 global recession (pers. comm. 2012).

Like Jamaica, Barbados has faced major public debt challenges. Craigwell et al. reported that a large portion of Barbados' public debt was borrowed from London in the 1950s and 1960s, for infrastructural projects (1988, 137). Subsequently, the Government skewed borrowing to the domestic market.

During the 1970s oil crisis, Barbados focused on attracting international business including offshore financial services, as a key strategy for expanding GDP and enhancing development (ILO 1999, 33-4). By 2010, Barbados had a per capita GDP of US$15,035 (current US), and a Debt-to-GDP ratio of 97%.

Length of Tenure - Barbados

The Democratic League of Barbados was formed by Charles Duncan O'Neal in 1924. The Barbados Progressive League led by Grantley Adams was then founded on March 31, 1938, and; later renamed the Barbados Labour Party (BLP). They won five seats in the House of Assembly in 1940, and the election of 1946. By 1954 Grantley Adams (BLP) became Barbados' first Premier.

In 1955, Errol Barrow broke away from the BLP and formed the Democratic Labour Party (DLP). The BLP again won the 1956 election. The Barrow-led DLP then won the 1961 election, and led Barbados into independence from Britain on 30 November 1966, when the Barbados Independence Order (Constitution) was presented. Barrow continued, as Prime Minister from 1966 to 1976.

Grantley Adams died in 1971 and was succeeded by his son Tom, who led the BLP to election victory over the DLP in 1976. He won a second term in the 1981 election, but died in 1985. He was succeeded by Bernard St. John, who lost to the Errol Barrow-led DLP in 1986. Barrow died in 1987 and was succeeded by Lloyd Sandiford. The BLP, led by Owen Arthur, won the 1994, 1999, and 2003 elections. He was defeated by David Thompson of the DLP in 2008. Thompson died in 2010 and was succeeded, without much rancour, by Freundel Stewart, who received his own mandate in 2013.

At the general election of May 2018 Mia Amor Mottley QC, of the Barbados Labour Party defeated Freudnel Stewart by a landslide, becoming the first female Prime Minister of Barbados. PM Mottley was no political neophyte, as she entered the political arena in Barbados in 1994, as one of the youngest Ministers of Government, and was later named Attorney General, and then Leader of the Opposition, prior to winning the 2018 elections. Her victory resulted in a clean sweep of all parliamentary seats in favour of the BLP. She is seen as a highly respected, visionary leader, across the Caribbean region.

Singapore

Singapore is a former British base, located in south-eastern Asia, between Malaysia and Indonesia. It has a landmass of 728 km^2, and a population of just over 5.7 million. It was founded as a British colony in 1819 and occupied from 1942 to 1945 by the Japanese. Singapore was a part of the Malayan Federation from 1963 until August 9, 1965, when it gained independence from Britain.

Up to 2014, the largest component of Singapore's public debt was Singapore Government Securities (SGS), which were mainly issued to support the Central Provident Fund (CPF). The CPF is a

Chapter 3: Jamaica's Political Economy 1930s to Present – with Barbados and Singapore as Comparators

pension fund that was set up by the British, prior to Singapore's Independence, to which employer and employee each contributed 5%, to be drawn down by the employee at age fifty-five. By 1968, Singaporean workers were also allowed to use their accumulated CPF savings to finance down payments on homes, and service mortgages over 20 years. Lee (2000) noted that the CPF had set a firm foundation for Singapore's socio-economic development.

As with Barbados, the government of Singapore saw the importance of maintaining a high savings rate. Singapore's savings rate was raised from 5% in 1955 to 25% by 1984, with the main objectives being to boost the CPF, enhance development, encourage homeownership, and ensure that future generations would not have to bear the welfare cost of the present one (Lee 2000, 95; 970). The national savings rate is an indicator or measure of the amount of income saved by businesses, households, and the government. As the IMF (2021) noted, this is a useful source of funding, to mobilize domestic investments.

Whereas Stone (1985) and Panton (1993) have suggested that Jamaican policymakers met the social needs of the people by welfare distribution through clientelism, Lee Kuan Yew said the leaders of Singapore avoided the welfare-state approach, by focusing on asset acquisition, enhancement, and human capital development, to increase productivity, as they saw welfare as being inimical to self-reliance (2000, 103-4).

They also sought to maintain interest rates above the inflation rates, to avoid erosion of savings. Revenues to meet recurrent and capital expenditures were mainly raised through consumption taxes. He also reported that Singapore had generally maintained a budget surplus, "except for the years 1985 to 1987 when we were in recession" (Lee 2000, 106). Monetary stability and prudent fiscal management boosted savings, investment, and productivity, which Lee felt were prerequisites for success. Singapore's economy, like Barbados and Jamaica, is driven by manufacturing, tourism, and services. They also depend heavily on the importation of consumer goods and raw materials for the manufacturing sector.

Chapter 3: Jamaica's Political Economy 1930s to Present – with Barbados and Singapore as Comparators

Singapore does, however, have the advantage of greater economic diversification (see Chapter 6).

Like Jamaica and Barbados, Singapore had its own challenges during the 1970s oil crisis. Yet, Lee reported that "There was belt-tightening but no hardship" (2000, 63). This was a pragmatic approach, compared to Jamaica's decision to borrow from the Soviet Union and others. Singapore's investment attractiveness is enhanced by an international image of good governance. Their 2010 per capita GDP was US$41,122 (current); while their Debt/GDP was 99%. Up to the completion of this study, they had not borrowed externally since the early 1990s.

Length of Tenure - Singapore

Lee Kuan Yew was President of Singapore from 1959 to 1990, and up to 2013 he still provided oversight. Goh Chok Tong succeeded him and led Singapore for fourteen (14) years, before handing over leadership to Lee Kuan Yew's son Lee Hsien Loong, who has been Prime Minister since 2004, and; President since May 2011. The opposition Workers Party (WP) of Singapore won an unprecedented six (6) Parliamentary seats in the 2011 elections, demonstrating increasing democracy. Lee Kuan Yew died in March 2015.

The most recent general election in Singapore was held in July 2020, with the People's Action Party (PAP) which has been in power since Independence winning 83 seats, and the Workers Party (WP) 10 seats.

As we review the comparator countries – Jamaica, Barbados, and Singapore, and the role of governance in managing their public debt, an ageing population poses a challenge for all three (3). This is important, as the governments of all three countries have current and future pension obligations that will affect the fiscal accounts.

3.13 Comparative Population Ageing and Pension Obligations

An ageing population poses a significant potential liquidity risk for all three (3) countries. Up to 2020, the percentage of the population over 55 years old was 24%, 22%, and 23% for Jamaica, Barbados, and Singapore respectively. The challenge is even greater when percentage of the population over 65 is examined (see figure 3.3).

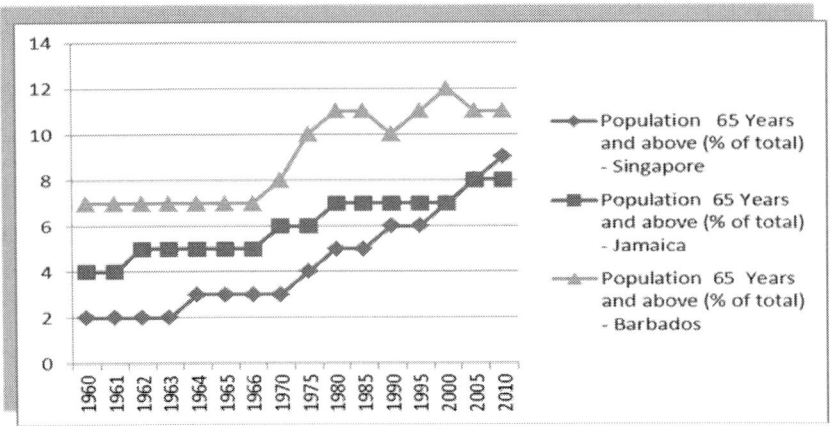

Figure 3.3 Comparative Population 65 Years and Over (World Bank data)

Though Singapore had a slightly slower rate of ageing than Jamaica and Barbados up to the mid-2000s, its rate of ageing was on the increase. This could lead to depletion of a large portion of the Central Providence Fund (CPF) investments, and the National Insurance Scheme (NIS) of Jamaica and Barbados, even as the respective governments seek to meet debt obligations from the same fiscal resources.

Between 2003 and 2006 pension reforms in Barbados led to significant increases in the surpluses of the NIS. However, by 2010 the fund had a 61% exposure to government securities (GOB 2012, 7), increasing the level of risk in the portfolio.

The CPF also has significant exposure to government securities. It is, therefore, the macroeconomic policies chosen over

Chapter 3: Jamaica's Political Economy 1930s to Present – with Barbados and Singapore as Comparators

the foreseeable future that will determine the viability of these funds.

3.14 Macroeconomic Policy Choice - Monetary and Fiscal

Monetary policy includes strategies by the government aimed at influencing an expansion or contraction in spending, through money supply, interest rates, and inflation control; while fiscal policy is aimed at using government expenditure and revenues to manage aggregate demand. "Among the factors that influence the cost competitiveness of Jamaican goods and services, none have wider application or deeper impact than the monetary and fiscal policies which determine: the exchange rate, inflation, and; interest rates" (Seaga 2004, 188). Jamaica, Barbados, and Singapore have employed different monetary and fiscal policy tools since independence.

Jamaica

Jamaica's monetary policy is implemented through the Bank of Jamaica (BOJ), and; fiscal policy through the Ministry of Finance and the Public Service. The BOJ came into operation in 1961, with responsibility for the issuance and redemption of currency, regulation, and supervision of the banking system, implementation of monetary policy to control inflation, and maintenance of stability in foreign exchange markets.

The BOJ Act states that Jamaica's monetary policy is aimed at regulating growth in money supply and credit, with due consideration to expected revenues required to finance the country's economic activities, while targeting price stability. These monetary policy operations are implemented through the regulation of:

- Cash Reserve Requirement - funds held so banks can meet liabilities;

- Discount Rates – the interest rate charged to financial institutions, and;
- Open Market Operations – the issuance of Certificates of Deposit, and; the purchase or sale of other government securities.

"Fiscal policy, on a whole, is geared towards having an impact on demand in the long run, with monetary policy assisting in the short run by maintaining price stability" (Scarlett 2010, 4). Successful macroeconomic policy management requires effective coordination.

Recognizing the importance of this, and the Central Bank's key role in the governance process, two senior financial sector technocrats were asked (in separate interviews) if they had received sufficient support and resources to successfully implement the monetary policies necessary for economic stability, to enhance Jamaica's debt management strategies. The first said:

> Yes, in so far as having honed our methodology, I think we have the resources to do it. The kind of support that we need is really about fiscal policy, which is quite dominant in Jamaica. Where we see ourselves going in the future does require the practice of fiscal responsibility, if monetary policy is to focus on inflation targeting. So internally I think we are properly staffed. We have the requisite framework to go forward. The kind of support that we need is perhaps some legislative changes to grant more autonomy, and we need fiscal support in terms of the policy environment. (pers. comm.)

The second said:

> Somewhat. I would say mostly 'yes'. The caveat here though is that you really can't sustain successful monetary policy if your fiscal accounts are out of kilter. It doesn't matter how wonderful the Central Bank is and how well trained its people are, or how much they know about monetary policy, it is not going to be successful unless there is effective fiscal management; not just from the point of view of managing the deficit, but also in terms of allocating resources consistent with achieving specific outputs and outcomes. (pers. comm.)

Chapter 3: Jamaica's Political Economy 1930s to Present – with Barbados and Singapore as Comparators

These responses cohere with the views of Kwon et al (2006) who observed that in countries like Jamaica with very high levels of debt, simple money-based stabilization will be ineffective without fiscal consolidation (p. 22). Both responses reinforce the need for effective coordination of fiscal and monetary policies and greater fiscal discipline.

Indiscipline in policy implementation can be costly, as was demonstrated in 1998. The Finance Minister clearly outlined that monetary policy was focused on attaining single-digit inflation and alleviating the pressure in the foreign exchange market, to moderate the impact of the fallout from the financial sector (FINSAC) crisis (Davies 1998). Yet, he reported that an amount of eleven billion dollars (J$11B) that was set aside to support this policy, was transferred from the account of the Ministry of Finance at the BOJ, to provide overdraft facilities for Century National, Eagle Commercial, and Workers Bank (Davies 1998, 230-4). All three banks subsequently collapsed.

An IMF Technical Financial Assistance programme had to then be crafted for 1998/99. Minister Davies later conceded that inconsistencies often arose, as various interest groups sought to lobby for the focus to be placed on their sector or operations.

Other governance decisions have also undermined the BOJ's effectiveness in achieving monetary policy objectives. Section 37, of the BOJ Act states that the Government of Jamaica can borrow a maximum of 40% of its estimated expenditure, in any given year; or a percentage the House of Representatives may approve.

Yet, Minister Davies' report, that up to 1992 Ministries and Departments could have drawn "cheques on their expenditure clearing accounts held at the BOJ, as the Central Bank would honour these cheques regardless of whether there were adequate resources or not in the accounts" (2004, 36), repeated government-related losses on the books of the BOJ, coupled with excessive borrowing, provided evidence of policy abuse and indiscipline.

These poor governance decisions, which were accompanied by rapid currency depreciation and an aggressive monetary policy stance, resulted in deposit rates well above 35%, exacerbating Jamaica's debt problem.

Barbados

Barbados' monetary policy has been focused mainly on exchange rate stability, interest and inflation rate controls. As a result, the Government of Barbados was able to maintain monetary stability and outperformed countries whose policies have yielded to currency depreciation (Blackman 1995). Barbados' focus remains on managing interest rates, supported by adjustments in reserve requirements, discount rate, and moral suasion (Moore and Skeete 2010, 3).

Unlike Jamaica, up to 2014, Barbados had placed little emphasis on using Open Market Operations as an inflation control mechanism. As former Technical Advisor at the IMF, and Barbados Central Bank Governor Dr DeLisle Worrel (1994) emphasized, "Open market operations may not be used to alter economic fundamentals, but they may usefully accommodate seasonality and short-term effects" (p 251). When asked in 2012 if he still held that opinion, his response was:

> Certainly! That is clear from the experiences of our countries. I would think that that is as true of Jamaica, Trinidad, Guyana [and] anyone, as it is of Barbados. The reasons are obvious. This is an era where both firms and households have on-going relationships outside of the country. That provides everyone with access to foreign exchange. So if you try to make monetary policy specifically for the domestic space, and if that is out of line with the interest rates that are on offer abroad, then funds are going to move one way or another. They are either going to move in, if your interest rates are very high people see opportunities to take advantage; or if your interest rates are not high enough, they are going to move out. (pers. comm. 2012)

The high level of social capital in Barbados has also engendered trust and enhanced their government's ability to employ moral suasion to aid in debt management (Osei 2002; Henry 2013). Onis (1995) emphasized that active consent and cooperation build trust, and; where these are absent, constant budget deficits and high inflation may result (p. 103).

Though Barbados now faced fiscal challenges on account of the global recession (and more recently, the global pandemic) they have implemented measures aimed at curbing excessive spending, reducing budget deficits, and ending financing of the fiscal deficit by the central bank (IMF 2014 p.10).

Singapore

The Monetary Authority of Singapore (MAS) is the regulator of the financial sector and the central bank, with responsibility for monetary policy. Singapore's exchange rate based monetary policy is implemented by buying and selling US dollars in the foreign exchange market, through foreign exchange swaps, inter-bank loans, and the sale, purchase or repurchase of government securities (Parrado 2004, 4). These economic choices have contributed to low inflation and sustained growth; while high savings rate gave the authorities room to manoeuvre (Parrado 2004, 5).

As stated earlier, the savings rate has been cited as an important factor for domestic investments. The industrialization programmes of each country have been financed by a variety of sources. These issues are discussed in the next segment.

3.15 Industrialization Strategies

Jamaica

In the 1950s Premier Bustamante invited the World Bank, British industrialists, and American consultants, to help determine Jamaica's industrial development requirements, and promote foreign direct investment through import substitution (Panton 1993). The main objectives of import substitution industrialization

Chapter 3: Jamaica's Political Economy 1930s to Present – with Barbados and Singapore as Comparators

(ISI) were to diversify the economy, and create an absorption source for Jamaica's surplus labour.

By 1963 primary products (agricultural produce, raw materials, etc.) contributed £31.6 million (13%) to Jamaica's Gross Domestic Product (GDP). From 1965 to 1969, poor planning and drought curtailed the output of the agricultural sector. As a result, its contribution to GDP fell to 9% by 1969 (ESSJ 1965-1975). Imports and unemployment then increased rapidly.

The bauxite and tourism sectors then became the main contributors to GDP (ESSJ/PIOJ multiple copies). Subsequently, more than $69 billion was spent on food imports (2010); while agriculture's contribution to GDP fell to 5.5% (Hussey-Whyte 2011). Mr Seaga who had vociferously opposed PM Manley's ideas on import-substitution argued in favour of diversification through manufacturing. He expanded on this when he became Prime Minister in 1980. However, as Best and Levitt posited, Jamaica's policy-making was too theoretical and lacked sensitivity to the features and realities of the Caribbean (1968, 406). This showed up in the Caribbean Basin Initiative (CBI) industrialization thrust. The assembly-line manufacturing system promulgated by Adam Smith's theory was introduced, and (807) Free Zone workers paid on a piece-work basis, expecting that this would increase efficiency and productivity. Instead, workers complained of meagre minimum wages and substandard working conditions. This drew the attention of Member of Parliament (MP) Princess Lawes, who asked her colleague Labour Minister J.A.G Smith to investigate the complaints (1986). Though he reported that the conditions of work were satisfactory, subsequent investigations proved otherwise.

Bear in mind that 1987 was the year that Jamaica experienced an eight percent (8%) growth in Gross Domestic Product, largely on account of the Free Zone operations. As James (1988) reported:

Chapter 3: Jamaica's Political Economy 1930s to Present – with Barbados and Singapore as Comparators

> Shipments from the Free Zone in 1986 were valued at US$69.7 million, with earnings by the Jamaican economy totalling US$14.21 million. Free Zone officials said shipments last year were about US$100 million, with earnings by the Jamaican economy totalling US$20 million. (p.1)

The investors subsequently left Jamaica without notice, leaving the Free Zone workers with no recourse to receive their severance pay. The workers were made poorer; while the debt incurred to prepare the Garment Free Zone facilities expanded. In an effort to utilize the facilities and reduce unemployment, PM Seaga sought to enter into a similar agreement with Canada, but failed.

Potter et al. (2004) later argued that the Caribbean Basin Initiative (CBI) was a US AID policy aimed at opening up Caribbean markets to US exports, accessing cheap labour, subsidized factory space, duty waivers of 10 to 15 years, and unhindered repatriation of profits, resulting in negative trade balances in favour of the United States.

Imports, driven mainly by Informal Commercial Importers (ICIs) then increased rapidly. This excessive demand for foreign exchange to finance large volumes of imports worsened Jamaica's current account deficit, which averaged 11.2% from 1981 to 1985, and; reached 21% by 2008, as exports declined and imports of consumer goods increased (World Bank data). Meanwhile, the exchange rate moved from J$1.78/US$1 in 1981 to J$80.47/US$1 by 2008.

The World Bank (2011) posited that it was the expansionary fiscal policies and lack of competitiveness in the 1970s that led to Jamaica's adoption of an import substitution strategy, which worked against it, in contrast to countries like Barbados that continued to pursue a private-sector led growth strategy.

Chapter 3: Jamaica's Political Economy 1930s to Present – with Barbados and Singapore as Comparators

Barbados

Barbados' early development policies also included import substitution, promotion of foreign direct investment (FDI), and export of primary product; alongside a major strategic push for human capital development (Barbados Economic Survey 1964-1986; Downes 2002).

As import substitution was unable to generate adequate levels of employment in Barbados' small domestic market, the authorities expanded their focus to include export manufacturing of chemicals and garments from the 1960s to 1970s, electronics in the 1980s, and technology in the 1990s. Their financial services sector continues to expand.

Singapore

Vietor and Thompson reported that, after unsuccessfully pursuing an import substitution strategy from 1959 to 1965, the government of Singapore focused on bettering its neighbours at attracting foreign direct investment (FDI), and; developing to First World status (2008, 3). While Singapore has always been constrained by limited land space and has had no notable contribution from agriculture since 2006, manufacturing contributed 22% to GDP by 2010. This triples that of Barbados and more than doubles that of Jamaica.

Chapter 3: Jamaica's Political Economy 1930s to Present – with Barbados and Singapore as Comparators

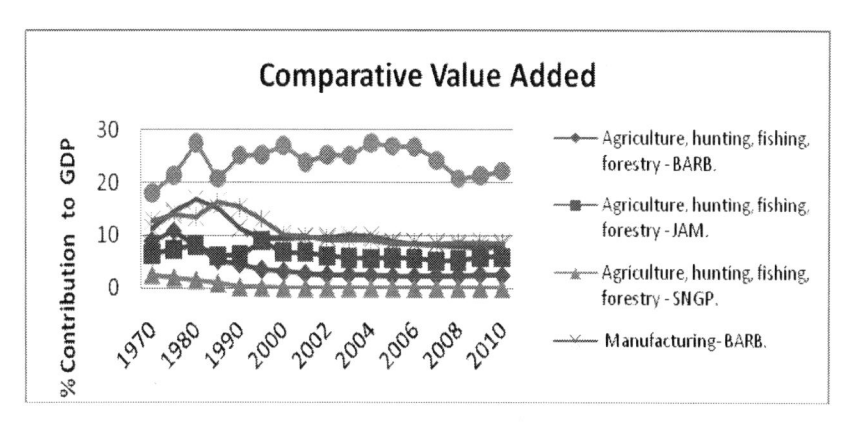

Figure 3.4 Singapore: Comparative Contributions from Agriculture and Manufacturing UN 2011

In reviewing Singapore's development and growth strategy, Lee reported that they made sure not to misuse the trust of the people through corruption and poor governance, as they needed this support to make maximum use of the country's limited natural assets (2000, 7). During the formative years, Lee travelled extensively to observe various models of development in Asia, Europe, North America, and the Caribbean. Reporting on his 1975 visit to Jamaica, he said:

> [P]rime Minister Michael Manley, a light skinned West Indian, presided with panache and spoke with great eloquence. But I found his views quixotic. He advocated a "redistribution of the world's wealth." His country was a well-endowed island of 2000 square miles, with several mountains in the center, where coffee and other subtropical crops were grown. They had beautiful holiday resorts built by Americans as winter homes. Theirs was a relaxed culture. The people were full of song and dance, spoke eloquently, danced vigorously, and drank copiously. Hard work they left behind with slavery. (Lee 2000, 364)

Lee reported that in contrast, Singapore set out to establish high standards in security, health, education, telecommunication, transportation, and services, and; to be a supply source of entrepreneurs, engineers, managers, and other professionals in the region. The Export Development Board (EDB) became a one-stop

Chapter 3: Jamaica's Political Economy 1930s to Present – with Barbados and Singapore as Comparators

agency to simplify the investment process. They also used fiscal incentives and training to drive export promotion and FDI, with equity participation from European, American, and Japanese Multi-national Corporations (Lee 2000, 57). Former PM Manley indicated his awareness of this strategy when he said:

> I have never failed to be surprised at how superficially people talk about things like the economic miracles of South Korea, or Taiwan, Hong Kong and Singapore, and will attribute it to a thousand factors like culture and don't attribute it to one of the most critical other factors which is the massive investment that those countries have made in training. Huge unending investments in training, in foreign universities in America all over the place and everything they can build themselves. And I see training as perhaps the most difficult problem we are going to face between now and the 21st Century. (1988, 322)

He also noted that Singapore, with a population of 2.6 million at the time, had 18,000 people in science and technology at the tertiary level; while Jamaica with a similar population of 2.5 million had only 1800 pursuing similar studies (p. 316). He said this gave Singaporeans a 'master disposition' in the economy of the world, and; called on Parliament to note that "[S]ocial opportunity, Human Resource Development and the chance to participate, are all aspects of one phenomenal development" (p. 324).

Twenty-seven (27) years later, and forty years after Lee's visit, Jamaica's policymakers are still inviting dialogue to identify the key success factors to help Jamaica achieve sustainable growth and development, and curtail indebtedness. He emphasized that development and productivity were paramount, and could be achieved by hard-working people and a government of integrity (Lee 2000, 57-8).

Chapter 3: Jamaica's Political Economy 1930s to Present – with Barbados and Singapore as Comparators

3.16 Rationale for Using Barbados and Singapore as Comparators

These former British colonies – Barbados and Singapore have been chosen as comparators, due to their similarities to Jamaica (open, small island states), period of Independence from Britain, post-independence experiences, and challenges faced. All three countries:

- Gained independence from Britain in the 1960s: Jamaica 1962, Singapore 1965, and Barbados 1966.
- Adopted a Westminster Parliamentary system, with similar Common Law provisions, including Constitutional protection of property rights.
- Have multi-ethnic populations, and the accompanying governance challenges.
- Seceded from regional groupings: Jamaica and Barbados sought membership in the West Indies Federation, and seceded after a referendum in 1961/2. In 1963 Singapore merged with Malaya to form Malaysia, but seceded by August 1965, due to conflicts, and;
- Are small, open, export-driven, import-dependent economies, with most of their raw material being imported.

Context is important in this analysis, and so it is noted that Singapore has had a more authoritarian form of government, while Barbados and Jamaica have had democratic forms since Independence. So that, the level of democracy and freedom of dissent that citizens have in Barbados and Jamaica has not been observed as openly in Singapore. Additionally, though all three Parliaments are based on the British Westminster model, Singapore's Republican system, in the context of Asia, differs somewhat, from the Monarchical system within which Jamaica and Barbados operate.

Since August 2021, Barbados Prime Minister the Hon. Mia Mottley has started dialogue with the citizens of Barbados to

Chapter 3: Jamaica's Political Economy 1930s to Present – with Barbados and Singapore as Comparators

amend their constitution to remove the Queen of England as Head of State, nominate a President, and move to make Barbados a republic by November 30, 2021 (Caricom Today, 2021).

This publication also highlights other distinct differences in outcomes between the comparators, such as:

- Development, and macroeconomic policies pursued.
- Political ethos, and; level of social capital.
- Fiscal policy stance, and;
- Global perception of governance, and human development (recall WGIs discussed, and UN/HDI reports cited).

As Henry and Miller (2008) noted, former colonies of Britain, inheriting political, legal, and economic institutions that were almost identical, have experienced outcomes that were starkly different (p.2). Table 3.7 summarizes some of these outcomes, from a 2010 World Economic Forum (WEF) assessment of the perception of governance and fiscal management in the three countries, with '1' being the highest ranking.

Table 3.7 Comparative Rankings – JA, BD, and SG

INDICES Ranked	JAMAICA	BARBADOS	SINGAPORE
Global Competitiveness Index	95	43	3
Public Trust of Politicians	107	19	2
Ethics	89	22	1
Judicial Independence	51	19	21
Government Efficiency	90	16	1
Favouritism in Decision-making	116	31	3
Wastefulness of Govt. Spending	98	18	1
Transparency: Policy-Making	64	21	1
Quality of Educational System	98	15	1
Health and Primary Education	102	41	3
Brain Drain	98	29	4

Source: WEF (2010) – rank from 139 countries (with 1 being the highest)

Much has been shared anecdotally within and outside the Jamaican Parliament, about how Jamaica has performed, in

Chapter 3: Jamaica's Political Economy 1930s to Present – with Barbados and Singapore as Comparators

comparison to Barbados and Singapore. An empirical analysis of this nature is very useful in aiding in closing some gaps in the body of knowledge, of how governance contributes to indebtedness and poor macroeconomic performance in small developing countries like these.

Note carefully, Jamaica's paltry scores, compared to Barbados and Singapore. Many inferences relating to the global perception of governance in Jamaica, and the comparator countries may be drawn from the data in Table 3.7. This could easily take us into the second volume to this publication.

Conclusion

This chapter has reviewed the literature and explored relevant socio-political and historical issues relating to governance, public debt, the economy, and global perception of the quality of governance in Jamaica, Barbados, and Singapore since Independence. It has shown how the quality of governance, reflected through leadership styles, culture, political ideology, policy choices, frequent changes of political administration leading to the abandonment of projects and programmes, and questionable fiscal decisions, have contributed to debt accumulation in Jamaica, and had a deleterious impact on growth and development.

This publication is comprised of seven (7) chapters. The preceding chapters provided a background to the study, locating it in a body of theoretical and empirical works related to macroeconomic management, institutional economics, governance, and fiscal management, with a focus on government's role and fiscal responsibility. This was followed by a discussion of policies pursued, governance indicators, and outcomes for the three countries.

Chapter One introduced relevant works of early economists like Smith, Keynes, and Nurkse, and; the more contemporary works of Coase, North, Kaufmann, Kraay Zoida-Lobaton, Acemoglu et al, Henry and Miller, Sachs, and others. It presented

Chapter 3: Jamaica's Political Economy 1930s to Present – with Barbados and Singapore as Comparators

the conceptual framework and philosophical position taken in the study, and; highlights how governance indicators have been used in examining macroeconomic performance, and global perceptions of various aspects of governance.

Chapter Two presented a survey of the literature relating to macroeconomic management, with particular focus on New Institutional Economics (NIE), Plantation Economy models, Development Economics, Governance, Political Economy, and Public Finance.

Chapter Three looked at the political economy of governance in Jamaica, and presented a brief overview of the comparators Barbados and Singapore.

Chapters Four and Five will provide a review of public debt accumulation in Jamaica, with some international case studies on public debt experiences, to garner lessons for Jamaica.

Chapter Six will fuse the previous discussions and provides an in-depth review of the findings from the aggregate data analysis, elite (key informant) interviews, and surveys, to show the relationship between governance in Jamaica and the accumulation of public debt since Independence in 1962.

Chapter Seven - The Conclusion will present a review of the original research questions, summarizing the findings, and showing how they inform the relevant literature. This will conclude **Volume I** of this publication.

Volume II will contain additional policy implications, and recommendations applicable to improving the channels through which governance impacts public debt in small developing countries like Jamaica, and; lessons in good governance for nation-states.

Notwithstanding the size and characteristics of the countries highlighted in this study, given the governance, and political challenges that we have witnessed in recent years in developed countries like the United States of America, Britain, and others in recent years, there is no doubt that there are many lessons in good governance and fiscal management from this publication, to be

Chapter 3: Jamaica's Political Economy 1930s to Present – with Barbados and Singapore as Comparators

garnered by policymakers and technocrats of developing (emerging market) countries, and developed (first world) countries alike.

Chapter 4

ANTECEDENTS AND FACTORS CONTRIBUTING TO PUBLIC DEBT ACCUMULATION IN JAMAICA

4.1 Introduction

The central question asked was,

How has the character of governance in post-independent Jamaica contributed to the country's indebtedness from 1962 to 2010?

As with the earlier discourse, this chapter will highlight the role played by those in governance with regards to the origin, and accumulation of Jamaica's public debt.

The publication has so far, unequivocally established that governance is integral to debt management, and economic performance, recognizing that the outcomes in different countries are influenced by the character, or quality of governance exercised, the institutions created, and the effectiveness with which transaction costs are managed.

This chapter shows that public debt in Jamaica increased exponentially from 1962 to 2010, without commensurate national gains, in terms of economic growth, high-quality infrastructure, or sustained development.

It also briefly reviews in some select case studies, strategies employed in other countries and regions, including Barbados, Singapore, South Korea, and the European Union, to glean lessons from their experiences for Jamaica, and other countries that will seek to extract the lessons from this publication, and the volume to follow.

Chapter 4: Antecedents and Factors Contributing to Public Debt Accumulation in Jamaica

4.2.1 Jamaica's Public Debt: Components

Jamaica's public Debt-to-GDP was 130% in December 2010. This consisted of:
- **Domestic Debt**: Treasury Bills (T-bills), Local Registered Stock, Bonds, Commercial Bank, BOJ, and Other Loans, JDX Benchmark Notes, Consumer Price Indexed Bonds, and Other Notes, and;
- **External Debt**: IBRD/World Bank, IDB, IMF, Inter-Government, USAID, EDC, Bonds, Commercial Banks, Other Commercial credit (BOJ 2011).

This was a wide range of securities and credit facilities, for a small, open, export-dependent country like Jamaica. This made it even more difficult to meet debt service obligations, given the multiple costs of capital, range of terms and conditions, with some loans requiring the borrower to use the creditor's manpower and equipment.

The main focus in this first segment is on Treasury Bills, as they provide the indicative rate from the central bank to the financial sector. These have contributed greatly to debt accumulation in Jamaica, throughout the 1980s and 1990s. They are also common debt securities, with generic features that allow for global comparisons. Treasury bill rates are often seen as the indicative, 'risk-free' rate of return, or 'Short-term Government Debt Yield' (econstats.com), and; can provide a fair indication of interest rate trends over time.

Figure 4.1 below, shows trends in T-bill rates between Jamaica, Barbados, Singapore, and a select group of countries that have featured prominently in past and present debt crises.

Chapter 4: Antecedents and Factors Contributing to Public Debt Accumulation in Jamaica

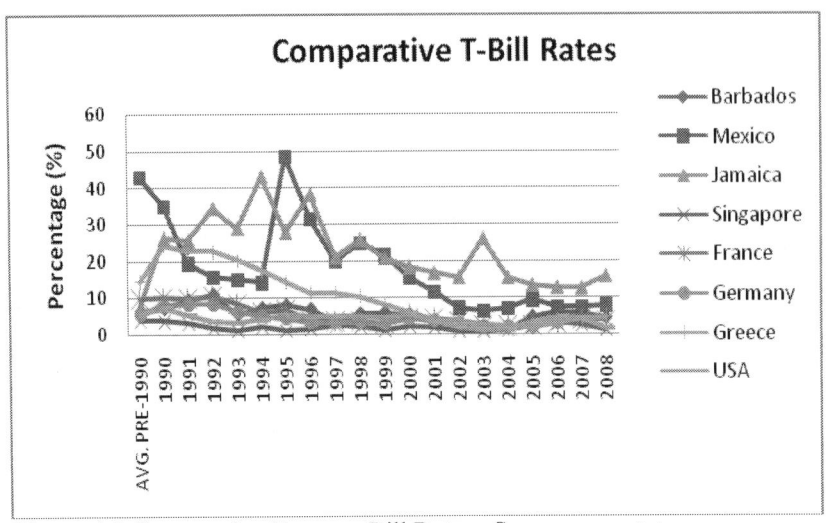

Figure 4.1 Comparative Treasury Bill Rates - Source: econstats.com

Note how the T-bill rates for Jamaica, Greece, and Mexico trended higher than the others; while Germany and France (key European Union members) trended low and closely over the same period. Most rates peaked in the 1990s, which was classified by the World Bank as "a decade of macroeconomic crises and turbulence in emerging markets" (2005, 243). Observe also, how relatively stable Singapore's and Barbados' rates were after 1990.

Jamaica, Mexico, and Greece appeared as outliers, with higher than average T-bill rates up to the mid-1990s. By 2008 T-bill rates were significantly reduced, though Jamaica's remained high. More recently the USA, Greece, and Barbados have been faced with debt management challenges, exacerbated by a prolonged global recession. Still, Jamaica's T-bill rates remained well above these and all others since 1996/7. Meanwhile, Mexico's T-bill rate declined from a pre-1990 average of 43%, to below 8% by 2008.

Treasury Bills have been used in Jamaica to support both fiscal and monetary policy objectives to: (i) provide a source of funding to meet government's short-term budgetary obligations; (ii) set benchmark rates for the financial sector; (iii) and control liquidity of financial institutions. Though there are advantages of

Chapter 4: Antecedents and Factors Contributing to Public Debt
Accumulation in Jamaica

using T-bills for these purposes, they can cause undue market segmentation, and significant fluctuations in the volumes of a government's interest obligation, during a planning period. A government that is too heavily dependent on the use of T-bills will have difficulty meeting its debt service obligations (interest and principal payments) over the medium-, to long term, due to the short tenure and rapid maturity of these instruments. In Singapore's case, "limited reliance on central bank paper to mop up liquidity has avoided segmentation of the public debt market" (IMF 2008, 12).

4.3 Impact of IMF T-bill Recommendation on Jamaica's Debt

The IMF has contributed to Jamaica's indebtedness, by encouraging the excessive use of T-bills as a monetary policy tool. In 1977 Finance Minister Coore presented a resolution for authorization to borrow J$200 million by issuing Treasury Bills. By 1979 the limit was increased to J$300 million. As part of the April 1981 three-year Extended Fund Facility (EFF) arrangement, the IMF then recommended a further T-bill issuance of J$115 million to $140 million per month to help mop up liquidity (GOJ 1981, 13). This policy recommendation, and the willingness of the government to continue to employ this tool well after ending its IMF borrowing relationship, demonstrate the gravity of the governance problem, which contributed to further accumulation of public debt.

The returns paid by the Government of Jamaica, encouraged investments in government paper, to the detriment of the real sectors of the economy. The government, in turn, capitalized on the demand. Of the J$491 million of T-bills issued in 1983, more than 85% was held by commercial banks, and; 15% by the Bank of Jamaica (BOJ) and other Government bodies (BOJ reports). Between 1984 and 1994 the limit was increased from $750 million to $7.5 billion. Treasury bill rates peaked at 49% by 1993, and fell

Chapter 4: Antecedents and Factors Contributing to Public Debt Accumulation in Jamaica

to 29% in 1994 when Minister Davies proposed another increase from $7.5 billion to $12 billion. By 1995, rates escalated to 43%, just before the FINSAC crisis.

The Government of Jamaica (GOJ) was eventually mandated by the IMF in 2010 to reduce interest cost through the Jamaica Debt Exchange (JDX). "Yields on GOJ 6-month Treasury Bills moved from a high of 10.49% at the end of financial year 2009/10 to 6.63% in March 2011" (GOJ 2011, 20). There was no evidence in the Hansard of Parliament, or Ministry Papers reviewed, to show that policymakers had properly or thoroughly evaluated the impact of this 1981 IMF Treasury Bill recommendation on Jamaica's debt accumulation. Having established this, it is important to briefly discuss the role and purpose of two of Jamaica's largest providers of loan funds – The international financial institutions (IFIs) - The World Bank and the IMF.

International Financial Institutions, and Jamaica's Public Debt

4.4   The Role of the World Bank and IMF

The World Bank (WB) was expected to provide funding for reconstruction after World War II (IMF 2007, 66). When the United States Government intervened with the Marshall Plan, there was no longer a need for this (Burnside and Dollar 2004, 19). The World Bank then turned its focus to funding infrastructural projects, particularly in developing countries. Its main mandate is now to promote long-term economic development, and the eradication of poverty through technical and financial assistance (IMF 2007).

World Bank loans are long-term and usually aimed at reforming specific sectors of the economy, through projects in health, education, community development, and environmental protection (World Bank 2011). Nanda (2006) also reported that the World Bank is now focused on good governance from an economic perspective, particularly with regards to how development assistance is used. Transparency, Accountability, Observation of the Rule of Law, and Efficiency were highlighted as being of paramount importance to the Bank's governance and development thrust (p. 105).

4.5 The International Monetary Fund (IMF)

The IMF's objective at formation was to facilitate the movement of financial resources among and between member countries, for international trade, by maintaining exchange rate stability (Dijkstra and Hermes 2003). It now focuses on macroeconomic support, and; sees itself as providing a public good, to protect financial stability worldwide (Dijkstra 2008); encourage monetary cooperation internationally; provide technical advice and policy guidance to strengthen economies; provide loans, and craft programmes to eliminate Balance of Payment (BOP) challenges (IMF 2011).

IMF loans are usually short to medium term. Their short-term BOP support is provided through Stand-By Arrangement (SBA) loans, and; medium-term support, through their Extended Fund Facility (EFF) loans. These are the main facilities that Jamaica has accessed since establishing a borrowing relationship with the IMF.

More recently, on account of the global pandemic, the IMF has introduced new facilities, one of which the Government of Jamaica has accessed. On May 15, 2020, the IMF announced that it had approved a US$520 million disbursement under its Rapid Financing Instrument, to "meet the urgent balance of payment needs stemming from the COVID-19 pandemic..." (IMF 2020).

Chapter 4: Antecedents and Factors Contributing to Public Debt Accumulation in Jamaica

1960s-1970s: Early Borrowing Relationships; Failed IMF Tests

On February 22, 1962, MP Florizel Glasspole presented a Bill authorizing the issuance of National Savings Bonds, to encourage investment by small savers, and aid Jamaica's development. He urged frugality and noted that Jamaica neither had enough capital nor accumulated savings, to carry out the required development work.

Opposition Spokesman Sangster countered that the PNP administration was financially weak, and seeking to siphon off what little funds were left, as it desperately required money that no one else was willing to lend. Member Lightbourne concurred, arguing that many of the schemes on which the Government had spent large sums of money had neither met with public approval nor were properly prioritized (1962, 51; 327).

Premier Manley defended the proposal and argued that investment could be expanded through capital expenditure by the government (Keynesian view). He dared anyone to say that the PNP Government should stop building roads, hospitals, schools, health centres, and other social amenities, and; emphasized that the growth of capital formation propelled by the PNP from 1956 to 1962 had exceeded anything that any economist would have thought possible. This was an emphasis on Fixed Capital Formation. Figure 4.2 shows the peaks in Gross Fixed Capital Formation (GFCF) during every PNP administration.

Chapter 4: Antecedents and Factors Contributing to Public Debt Accumulation in Jamaica

Gross Fixed Capital Formation - Ja % of GDP

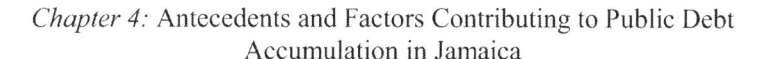

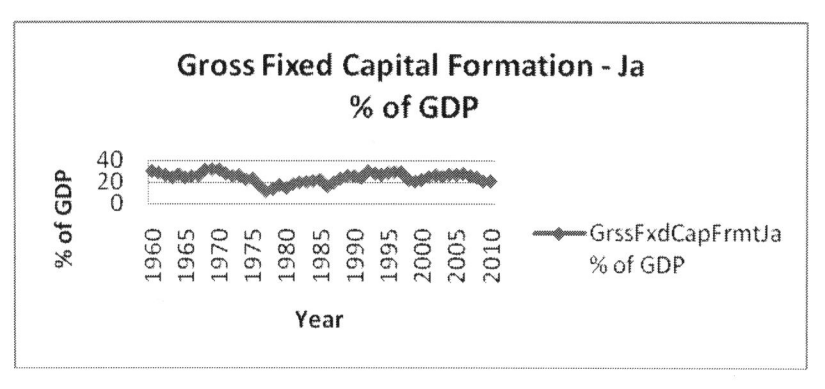

[Graph showing GFCF as % of GDP from 1960 to 2010, fluctuating roughly between 20 and 40]

Figure 4.2 GFCF as % of GDP 1960-2010 - Source: WB Database

While infrastructural development is important, the empirical and statistical evidence showed that it has neither generated sustained economic growth nor driven competitiveness through greater technical capabilities of Jamaica's human capital.

A month later, Minister Arnett proposed an amendment to the 'Canadian and United States of America Loan Law', to permit Jamaica to borrow outside the USA and Canada, for the first time. MP Sangster opposed, on account of impending elections, saying the PNP's majority would pass the Law "and run us into some more debt, on top of debt with which they have saddled us in the last seven years – some of which were completely unnecessary because that money that has been borrowed on behalf of this country has been wasted" (1962, 868).

Yet, weeks later, when the JLP won the 1962 election, Minister Sangster presented a resolution for Parliament to approve the Loans (National Savings Bonds) Regulations, which he had vociferously opposed. He then stated that:

> [I]f we look at the debt situation as of 31st March, we find that the total debt is £37,865,592 ... one of the things it is interesting to note, is that ten years ago, on the 31st March 1952, the total debt was £14.5 million, and; five years ago, on the 31st March 1957, the debt was £20.4 million. Today, over the ten year period, it is £37.86 million. (Sangster 1962, 6)

This was an increase in total debt of 41% from 1952 to 1957

and 86% from 1957 to 1962, even before Independence. The debt included T-bills of £5.6 million held by commercial banks, and long-term debts of £32 million, owed to stock and bondholders in Jamaica, the USA and the UK. This was close to the full year's Recurrent Revenue, with total debt charges outstanding being £2.96 million at 8% (Sangster 1962). Jamaica's debt expansion had begun in earnest!

By February 1963 when Jamaica received membership in the IMF and World Bank/International Bank for Reconstruction and Development (WB/IBRD), Minister Sangster presented an amendment to the Government's Securities Law, to permit the issuance of securities through the London Market, and to assure overseas lenders that in the event of a Judgement "of a competent Court of Jurisdiction in the United Kingdom, the moneys would be automatically paid out of the Consolidated Fund" (p. 324). He emphasized that Jamaica always paid its debts, and; accused the PNP administration of borrowing and spending recklessly, from large Customs revenues, while leaving "a debt of £700,000 with regard to Jamaica Woolens" on the books (p. 327). Opposition Leader Norman Manley conceded that this was due to a case of poor judgement that was being investigated.

Jamaica then obtained its first World Bank loan of US$5.5 million, in 1965, for a Highway project. Subsequently, loans were accessed for family planning, landslide risk reduction, agricultural credit, debt management, fiscal sustainability, education, and public sector reform projects, some of which are still incomplete. By 1968 Jamaica's public debt expanded to £107.7 million. Then came the oil crisis.

In the first six months of 1973, the price of crude oil moved from US$6 to US$36 per barrel. Like many oil-dependent countries, Jamaica approached the IMF and World Bank for debt financing to meet its Balance of Payment (BOP) obligations (Manley 1982; Levitt 1991; Seaga 2009). However, as Wei and Wu (2000a) argued "countries that experience a BOP crisis are often criticised for having either too much short-term borrowing or too much borrowing in a hard currency" (p. 486). Both cases applied to Jamaica.

PM Manley applied a bauxite levy to cushion the impact of mounting fiscal challenges. This netted J$164 million in 1973 (ESSJ 1974). Stone (1985) noted that Manley took comfort in knowing that he was able to take on the capitalists and successfully apply this levy. Girvan et al (1988) then reported that the Manley administration later engaged in the redistribution of wealth and nationalization of assets, resulting in greater fiscal challenges.

The high levels of public expenditure, declining foreign exchange revenues from tourism and agriculture, and increasing oil and other commodity prices, led to a foreign exchange crisis, and; loan talks with the IMF. The following statement made by Manley is quite instructive in this regard:

> During the latter part of 1976, there had been talks with the IMF in which representatives of the Fund had stated the view that Jamaica should devalue its currency by 40% and take various other corrective measures including sharp cut-backs in budgetary expenditure. Obviously, this could not have been done in the middle of an election campaign and it was agreed that the matter would be discussed immediately after the election if we were still in government. (1982, 151)

Jamaica's public debt passed the J$1 billion mark by 1976. When the administration accessed the first IMF loan of US$74.6 million in July 1977, they continued focusing on heavy social service expenditure, infrastructure projects, and expansion of the public sector. This was contrary to the conditions of the agreement, which required reforms in "areas of income policy, fiscal policy, balance of payments, exchange controls and exchange rate policy", and limited use of money creation to finance the budget (Coore 1977, 2). The IMF was not pleased.

In his frustration, PM Manley tried to find a way to break ties with what he termed, "pro-United States neo-colonialism and to develop a foreign policy consistent with self-respect and the exercise of sovereignty" (Stone 1985, 287). This approach

Chapter 4: Antecedents and Factors Contributing to Public Debt Accumulation in Jamaica

overshadowed the policies, through a drastic move to the radical left. The government eventually implemented exchange controls, with limited room to expand credit, control inflation, or reduce the pressure on the BOP accounts (Stone 1985).

Shortly after, there was a significant increase in loans offered and taken, as OPEC made windfall gains from inflated oil prices. Subsequently, interest rates on the global market increased dramatically, resulting in a quadrupling of external debt service costs. Jamaica then faced both an exchange rate shortage and a Balance of Payment crisis.

Though hikes in oil prices contributed to these challenges, geopolitical issues were also relevant. Prime Minister Manley's steadfast focus on the socialist agenda resulted in severe hardships. He sought help from members of the non-aligned movement, but this failed to stimulate the economy.

By December 1977 Jamaica failed the IMF test. The following January the agreement was cancelled. As Lewis (1994) noted, "governments of mixed economies coming into power on a wave of popular frustration, always run straight onto the rocks of the balance of payments and have to reverse themselves (for example France in 1936, and 1981; Britain in 1945; Jamaica in 1976)" (pp. xxxviii-xxxix).

In response to the challenges, the Manley administration attempted to create an Emergency Production Plan (EPP), to mitigate the impact of the foreign exchange crisis, through self-reliance. Panton (1993) noted that upon realizing that economic development without the IMF would have been catastrophic, they halted this plan, and eventually signed a new Extended Fund Facility (EFF) Agreement in 1978.

The EFF was originally introduced in 1974, to provide three to four years medium-term loans to member countries whose economies were perceived to be experiencing Balance of Payments (BOP) problems, and distortions in production and trade (IMF 2007). Such problems are deemed to be inherently structural,

Chapter 4: Antecedents and Factors Contributing to Public Debt
Accumulation in Jamaica

requiring a longer time-frame than Stand-by Arrangement, for effective adjustments. Manley later lamented that:

> The 1978 IMF agreement was like the moment when a jet, having just landed, puts those mighty engines in reverse to achieve the quickest possible stop on the runway. By the second half of 1978, the jet was in reverse with a vengeance. ...Throughout 1978 and into 1979, the experience with the IMF was harrowing. ...I certainly spent many harrowing hours at the time considering resigning either on behalf of the government or personally. In the end I rejected both and stayed on. It may have been my biggest personal mistake. (1982, 166)

Jamaica again failed the June 1979 test. As the administration contemplated another break with the IMF, Manley reported that more than 2000 PNP delegates participated in almost thirty hours of deliberation, though "No one felt that the present strategies could work, although few could voice their concerns in terms of standard economic jargon" (1982, 183). As a senior technocrat interviewed for this study noted, "Government over time has allowed too much meddling from non-elected interest groups and individuals in policy formulation. I think this has retarded policy decisions" (pers. comm. 2011).

4.6.2 More Failed IMF Tests; New Creditors: 1980

On February 5, 1980, Finance Minister Bell reported that Jamaica's foreign exchange problem had been worsened by high energy cost, low productivity, excessive imports, negative growth, lack of investor confidence, and political instability. Expenditure had to be curtailed through cuts in wages and salaries, food subsidies, and a Special Employment Programme, to reduce the deficits. Financing was to be provided by a tax package of J$10 to $15 million, and J$214 million savings from a Venezuelan Caribbean Oil facility. The IMF was also asked to provide a 'holding arrangement' loan of J$142 million. The World Bank was to provide J$30 million; while commercial banks would finance seven-eighths (7/8th) of the amortization payments, with interest

Chapter 4: Antecedents and Factors Contributing to Public Debt
Accumulation in Jamaica

rates ranging from 13% to 18% (Bell 1980, 75-105). This debt was quite expensive, as Jamaica's pre-1990 average T-bill rate was only 7.8% (recall figure 4.1 above).

Minister Bell was replaced by Minister Hugh Small, who reported in May 1980 that the Government would end negotiations with the IMF; while the international commercial banks had agreed to hold Jamaica's syndicated debts and maintain the deferral of the refinancing scheme. He also reported that the IDB would possibly provide foreign exchange loans; while the World Bank would examine Jamaica's economic programmes.

Jamaica then obtained an OPEC Special Fund loan of US$7 million, for BOP support, and US$3 million for project financing. Loans were also reportedly accessed for BOP support from Libya (US$50 million); Netherlands (US$25 million), and; Sweden (US$2 million). Germany was to provide an import financing loan (US$8 million), while, Norway, Canada, and the US agreed to participate as a Donor Country group (Small 1980, 19). Together, these accounted for an increase of almost 30% in Jamaica's debt, between 1979 and 1980.

While Minister, Small accused Mr Seaga of contacting overseas governments and members of international banking circles, seeking to discourage investment and assistance to Jamaica, he conceded that this was not the only cause of Jamaica's problems, as politicians needed to be frank and honest about where they went wrong in the 1970s (p. 19).

Mr Seaga contended that the government should be blamed, and; referred to a contingent of PNP representatives who had gone overseas to seek loan financing, as 'the government's travelling money begging team'. He argued that from 1972 to 1980 they had obtained J$368 million from additional taxes, which was twenty times as much as all previous Governments since 1944; yet, for the first time, loans were being used to finance recurrent expenditure, including salaries and travelling. He also listed several other sources which had provided J$10.724 billion to the Manley administration, including J$2.7 billion from money printed by the

Bank of Jamaica (seignorage), un-backed resources of J$660 million, J$1.212 billion from the Capital Development Fund, extra credit to the public sector of J$760 million, J$22 million from the Sugar Authority, and an additional J$5 million which he termed 'bonanza funds' (Seaga 1980, 28).

PM Manley called the 1980 election shortly after, again promising to break ties with the IMF. Bertram succinctly captured the situation as follows:

> The signing of an agreement with the International Monetary Fund in April 1977 signalled the resurgence of capital in no uncertain manner. For the next three years anti-communist hysteria which frightened the owners of capital and resulted in further deterioration of the economy, sealed the electoral fate of the PNP. (1995, 79)

4.7 Large Loan Inflows - More Failed IMF Tests: 1980s

When PM Seaga won the 1980 elections, he took responsibility for the Finance portfolio and established a new relationship with the IMF. This was buoyed by a strong bond with President Ronald Reagan of the United States of America, and Prime Minister Margaret Thatcher of Britain, both of whom continued to encourage economic liberalization. That alliance opened doors for almost US$400 million of loan funds to Jamaica from April 1981 to June 1984. Combine these with the IMF's recommended T-bill issuance of J$115 million to $140 million per month, to obtain a true picture of the gravity of these governance decisions, which have contributed to Jamaica's public debt accumulation.

As the debt crisis worsened, the need for improved fiscal controls became paramount. Stabilization and Structural Adjustment policies stipulated by the IMF and World Bank were some of the earliest conditions presented to address this.

Entities considered inefficient were recommended for privatization, to minimize the role of government, and expand that of the private sector. By 1981 there was also a major focus on

Chapter 4: Antecedents and Factors Contributing to Public Debt Accumulation in Jamaica

export-oriented production, with further expansion in tourism, agriculture, financial services, and telecoms.

Jamaica obtained the second IMF Extended Fund Facility of US$336 million in April 1981. Targets were set to reduce the fiscal deficit from 15% to 7.4% of GDP; increase the NIR to US$283 million; depreciate the Jamaican dollar, and; liberalize imports. Note that a depreciating currency (J$/US$) results in greater indebtedness, for that portion of the debt (external debt) that is denominated and payable in foreign currencies such as, for example, the United States dollar.

The NIR targets were not met. The actual balances ranged between -$532.2 million and -$808.7 million from 1980 to 1983, and; remained negative from 1984 to 1992 (PIOJ/ESSJ multiple copies), suggesting that the growth that was recorded from the foreign direct investment (FDI), benefited overseas investors more so, than Jamaica. Consequently, funds flowed predominantly outwards.

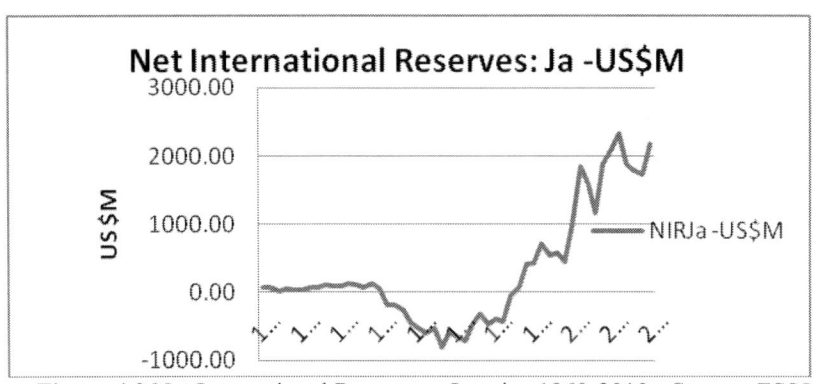

Figure 4.3 Net International Reserves - Jamaica 1960-2010 - Source: ESSJ

Neither was the fiscal balance target of 7.4% achieved. Outturns for the period 1962 to 2010 are graphed in figure 4.4.

Chapter 4: Antecedents and Factors Contributing to Public Debt
Accumulation in Jamaica

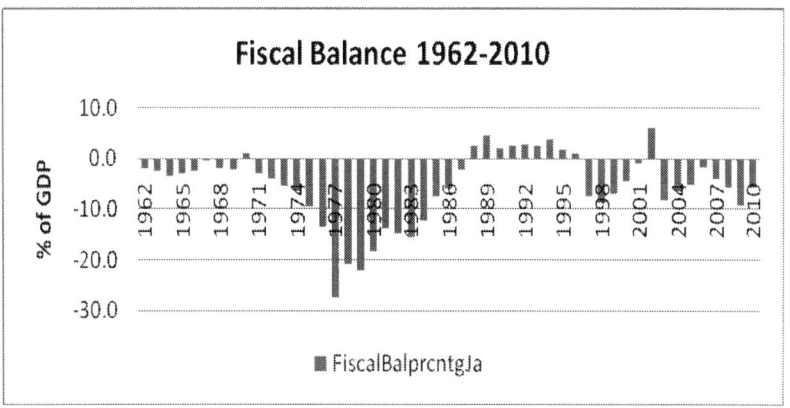

Figure 4.4 Fiscal Balances 1962-2010 (data from STATIN, and; King et al. 2008)

By 1984, Jamaica's Debt-to-GDP reached the historical peak of **212%**. The Seaga administration failed to meet the performance criteria outlined by the IMF, and the three-year EFF was interrupted, but not cancelled. A new one-year Stand-by Arrangement was signed on June 22, 1984 (ESSJ 1985, 2.5). After repeated rescheduling of loans between 1980 and 1985, multi-year rescheduling then began in 1985, to allow time to improve Jamaica's debt service capacity.

However, as Ricardo (1955) argued, a country is neither distressed by the repayment of interest nor relieved by exoneration from debt. Rather, a country finds itself in a penurious state, through lack of fiscal discipline and excessive borrowing (p. 251). Consequently, from 1985 to 1988, "the excess of repayments and interest over the disbursement of new loans amounted to [US] $891 million" (Levitt 1991, 20). Levitt also pointed out that from 1986, outflows exceeded inflows, at an average rate of 12% of GNP. Total external debt moved from US$1,867 million in 1980 to US$4,038 million by 1989; while external debt servicing costs continued to increase, as seen in figure 4.5 below.

Chapter 4: Antecedents and Factors Contributing to Public Debt Accumulation in Jamaica

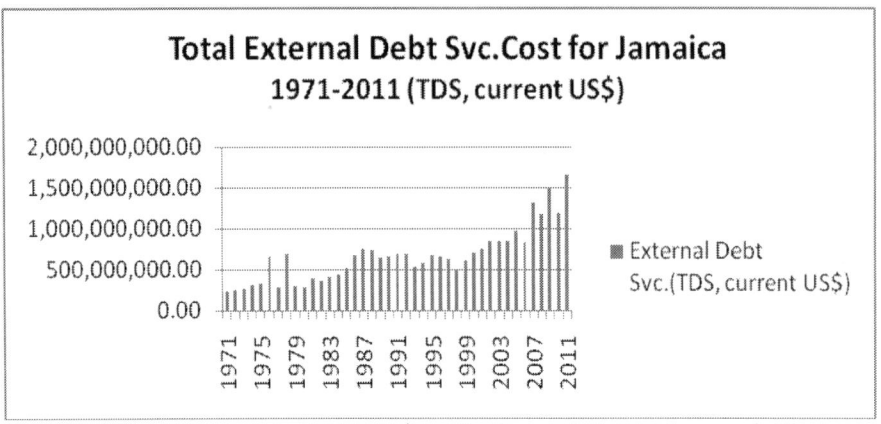

Figure 4.5 External Debt Service (US$) - Jamaica 1971-2011 (WB databank)

Oil prices fell significantly by 1986, leading to reduced cash flows from OPEC sources. This was worsened by a further reversal in Jamaica's windfall gains from the bauxite levy. Girvan et al. (1998) noted that during the period 1986 to 1988 there was a sharp IMF-sponsored deflationary adjustment, aimed at rapid closure of the fiscal deficit, and sharp reductions in real wages. As a result "The second half of the 1980s saw a reduction in net multilateral flows, a further increase in reliance on bilateral donors, on a rapidly escalating burden of debt service...Jamaica was locked in a debt trap" (Levitt 1991, 18).

Constant devaluations worsened the Balance of Payment problem. The Seaga administration launched a programme to convert Jamaica's long-term commercial bank debt to equity in July 1987, to stimulate and encourage equity investments in Jamaican enterprises by foreigners, and; to reduce the external debt burden. The hotel industry and export processing zones (EPZ) were the main areas identified to stimulate growth in foreign exchange earnings. US$4 million was also earmarked to be converted for social sector projects. A debt-for-nature swap led to the creation of a Trust Fund. Robinson (1998) noted, however, that this relief was modest. The government continued to borrow heavily from commercial banks, the IMF, and others, leading to an even greater dependence on debt financing, as economic

Chapter 4: Antecedents and Factors Contributing to Public Debt Accumulation in Jamaica

challenges increased. Unemployment rates ranged from 21% to 28% between 1980 and 1987, falling to 18% in 1989 (ESSJ 1980-1991).

Jamaica's public debt expanded from $5.663 billion in 1980 to $35.389 billion by 1989 (MOFP data), even as the Seaga administration continued the liberalization thrust. Ranis (2004) noted that efforts to open up an economy would be unsustainable and lead to inflation and Balance of Payments (BOP) challenges if external forces encouraged governments to increase spending through deficit budgets and expansion of money supply.

Dijkstra later noted that "the US and, to a lesser extent, other rich countries, that pushed for the expansion towards market opening and market oriented reforms" also contributed to Jamaica's debt expansion (2008, 16). The problem was exacerbated when President Reagan decided to increase interest rates, to boost funds flowing into the US, to offset their budget deficits (Reifer and Sudler 1996). This further increased Jamaica's outstanding debt obligations (Levitt 1991; Potter et al. 2004). Klak posited that "wasted windfall loans and political thinking that seek industrialization through foreign investment, led to governmental insolvency by the 1980s" (1993, 6).

While PM Seaga initially embraced the IMF's stipulations, including currency devaluation, and the removal of import restrictions, Jamaica's trade balances remained unfavourable throughout most of his tenure, as shown in figure 4.6.

He reported in my interview with him, that he strongly objected when the IMF demanded a more rapid devaluation of the Jamaican dollar (pers. comm. 2011). Growing disenchantment led to PM Seaga's defeat in the 1989 election.

Chapter 4: Antecedents and Factors Contributing to Public Debt Accumulation in Jamaica

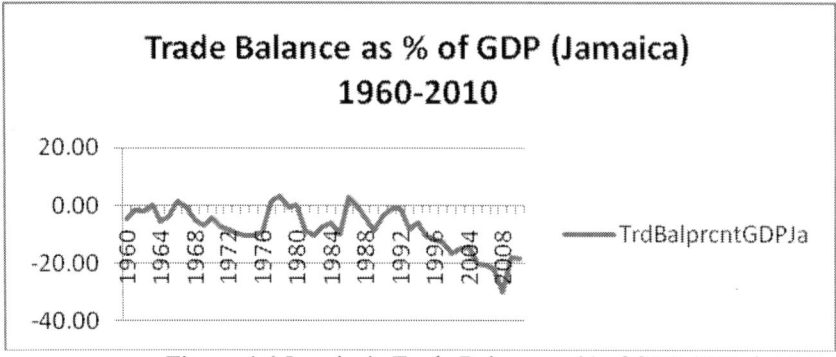

Figure 4.6 Jamaica's Trade Balance as % of GDP (WB data)

4.8 The New Manley Regime and the IMF: 1989

Prime Minister Michael Manley's Finance Minister Mullings notified Parliament in 1989 that reported losses at the BOJ were due in part to "the cost of using monetary tools to balance the demand for foreign exchange and to maintain stability in the domestic financial system" (p. 62). He introduced new revenue measures; increased the cash reserve ratio; reinstated the liquid assets requirements of banks, and; announced another devaluation of the Jamaican dollar, as stipulated by the IMF. Still, large Treasury Bill (T-bill) issuances, coupled with devaluations, further increased Jamaica's debt service obligations and expanded the public debt.

Shortly after, Industry Minister Claude Clarke reported that subsidies had to be removed from several consumer goods, to honour the agreement with the multilaterals who were asked to permit a phased reduction of the J$395 million deficit, to allow for the restoration of health, and educational services to reasonable levels for the very poor (1989, 67). Those measures had a severe impact on the vulnerable (Stone 1985; Levitt 1991). This gave credence to an observation made by Angresano (2007) that some perceived the IMF and World Bank to be neo-colonial in their approach, with insufficient attention being placed on poverty reduction (p. 43).

Chapter 4: Antecedents and Factors Contributing to Public Debt Accumulation in Jamaica

Finance Minister Mullings supported Industry Minister Clarke's point, noting that the first IMF agreement, coupled with eight (8) years of Structural Adjustment had led to a deterioration of the economy, reflected in high budget deficits, foreign exchange shortage, expanding Balance of Payments and trade deficits, and a general decline in per capita incomes. He also emphasized that while US$108 million had been borrowed from the IMF, "Our sense of national self-respect dictates that we cannot continue forever in the stranglehold of lenders" (1989, 75). Minister Small succeeded Minister Mullings.

By June 1989 Deputy Prime Minister P.J. Patterson in his role as Minister of Development, Planning, and Production, introduced a Five Year Development Plan, formulated by thirty-five (35) task forces, with 'global features' prescribed by the Medium Term Economic programme of the World Bank and IMF. He emphasized that tourism, agriculture, minerals, and services were identified as key export sectors to enhance Jamaica's foreign exchange inflows, and; announced that a J$1.6 billion line of credit would be made available to the private sector. The Government of Jamaica again decided to seek assistance from the IMF.

4.9 1990-1997: Borrowing Again; Ending the IMF Relationship; FINSAC Crisis

The IMF approved Jamaica's eight loan programme, a 15-month Stand-By Arrangement, on March 23, 1990. At year-end, external public debt stood at US$4.15 billion, with debt service payments at 30% of GDP. By 1991 NIR was $426 million; Debt-to-GDP 178.1%, and; inflation peaked at 80.2%.

Finance Minister Small then presented a resolution to Parliament for the approval of another Extended Fund Facility (EFF) loan of US$153 million, subject to prior actions. He pointed out that while the prolonged dependence on multilateral and bilateral sources left Jamaica suffering from 'adjustment fatigue',

Chapter 4: Antecedents and Factors Contributing to Public Debt Accumulation in Jamaica

donor countries such as the USA, Japan, and the European Economic Community (EEC) were suffering 'aid fatigue'. He also emphasized that twelve years was a very long time for Jamaica to deal with the IMF and "their harsh prescriptions" (Small 1991, 19). He then announced the government's intention to phase out the use of Certificates of Deposits (CDs) as a tool to contain liquidity, due to the impact of compound interest on the cost of Jamaica's public debt. They (CDs) were later re-introduced under Minister Patterson. Total recorded disbursements from the IMF to Jamaica up to 1992, exceeded US$761 million (Hillarie 2000).

By 1993 Prime Minister Patterson conceded that during the PNP administration of 1974 to 1980 the economy performed badly with a positive trade balance only achieved in 1978 when unemployment was at 24.2%. In his opinion, many of the hardships faced resulted from Jamaica's appetite for consumption being greater than its production was able to support. He added that:

> Our position is that whilst we are grateful for the assistance provided by these loans, the experience with those adjustment loans is teaching this country an important lesson. The lesson is that we can only be free to determine appropriate economic policies as a Sovereign Government, by increasing production and increasing our rate of domestic savings. (Patterson 1993, 1870)

To date, this has not been achieved. High interest rates and heavy borrowing increased Jamaica's debt obligations exponentially throughout the 1990s. By 1994 Mr Seaga noted that though the PNP said external debt had been reduced, the domestic debt continued to grow out of control, and was being serviced at forty-five to sixty percent (45 to 60%) interest. He emphasized that "If it continues in that rate of geometrical progression, we will be meeting here one day to decide when next to meet because there is no money to spend. All you are dealing with after that is paying salaries and paying debts" (p. 457). Figure 4.7 shows comparative (WB) deposit rates between Jamaica, Barbados, and Singapore from 1980 to 2010.

Chapter 4: Antecedents and Factors Contributing to Public Debt
Accumulation in Jamaica

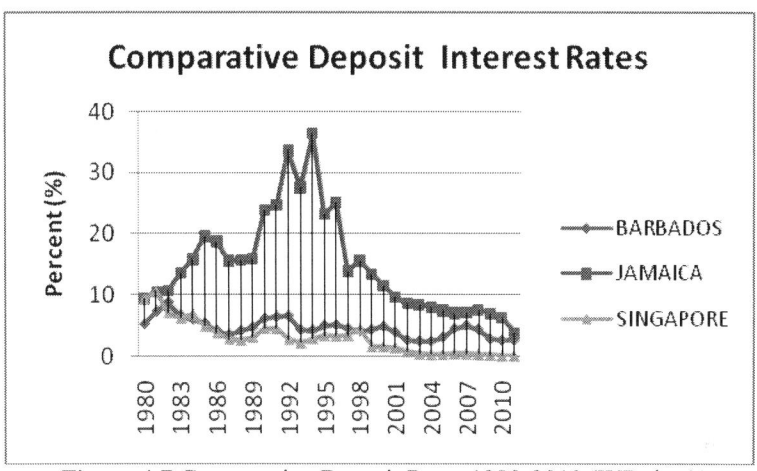

Figure 4.7 Comparative Deposit Rates 1980-2010 (WB data)

The Patterson administration defended the high interest rate regime, as a means of mopping up liquidity and curbing inflation. A further decision by the Government to grant inflationary wage increases for public sector employees worsened the public debt challenges. Still, in 1995, the Government made an early repayment on a US$50 million medium-term loan, and; announced that it would not seek recourse to IMF financing, once the EFF had expired. That borrowing relationship officially ended, when Minister Davies noted that:

> [T]his administration has on occasions been forced to accept loans from multilateral institutions, loans with conditionality with which we disagreed, but we took it simply because we needed the foreign exchange to bolster the position of the Bank of Jamaica so that we could pay our debts on time. (1995, 202)

He then reported that Jamaica would retain full membership in the IMF, but not as a borrower. In 1996 he noted that since the EFF ended in 1995, Jamaica's only financial relationship with the IMF related to repayment of prior debts, "most of which were incurred by the previous JLP administration" (p. 325). He reported that the obligations to the IMF were reduced from US$380 million

Chapter 4: Antecedents and Factors Contributing to Public Debt Accumulation in Jamaica

in 1989 to US$125 million by 1996. Subsequently, there was a more radical restructuring of the debt portfolio from external to domestic debt. By 1997 the country was again in a crisis, which the government sought to address through the Financial Sector Adjustment Company (FINSAC).

4.10 FINSAC: 1997-2000s

Close to the end of the Cold War in the mid-1990s, shifts in geopolitical and ideological perspectives led to expectations of a more collaborative approach to public administration and finance. Prime Minister Patterson called on parliamentarians to take "very seriously, the mission of improving the quality of governance" (1999, 39), emphasizing the importance of equity, honesty, transparency, and accountability in governance. However, Meeks (2001) noted that even as the Patterson administration sought to be more communicative with the Jamaican populace, the financial sector collapse of 1997 pushed all this into oblivion, as:

> In their place has emerged the silhouette of a largely unimaginative regime, one that is presiding over a decade without any real growth and that, in deciding to underwrite the profligacy of the banking sector, has placed an enormous yoke of debt around its own neck, as well as around the necks of this and future generations of the country's citizens. (p. 12)

Jamaica's financial sector collapsed, costing the country more than US$140 million.

4.10.1 Intervention, Rehabilitation, and Divestment
A Three-Pronged Approach

FINSAC was established in January 1997, to rebuild confidence in Jamaica's financial sector. The high interest rate regime of the 1990s, and weak regulations were identified as major contributory factors to the 1996/97 financial 'meltdown'. Returns on government securities ranged from 35% to 50%; while interest on

Chapter 4: Antecedents and Factors Contributing to Public Debt
Accumulation in Jamaica

loans and overdrafts peaked above 60%.

Opposition Spokesman (Shadow Minister) on Finance Audley Shaw later told Parliament that J$6.75 billion of liquidity support that was promised for FINSAC was not provided; while $5.6 billion of debt that should have been paid, was rescheduled. He pointed out that this accounted for 5.3% of GDP, taking the fiscal deficit to 9.9%, and not 4.6% as reported by Minister Davies (2000).

In response, Minister Davies reported that assets associated with FINSAC should have been disposed of, paid into the Consolidated Fund, and the funds disbursed to FINSAC. However, the assets were sold and funds utilized immediately, as he felt that there was too much bureaucracy involved. This effectively bypassed the regulatory procedures required for transparency and good governance.

4.10.2 The FINSAC Intervention

By February 2000 Minister Davies reported that FINSAC had total debts of J$108 billion, $38 billion of which was owed to government agencies, and $70 billion to third parties, including the National Commercial Bank (NCB) and Union Bank, who were to receive interest-bearing FINSAC notes. He said the FINSAC debt would be liquidated over time, while the balance owed would just have to be written off, leaving $74 billion of non-performing loans on the books.

Two debt collection options were explored. The first was to employ an aggressive collection strategy; the second was to sell the portfolio to the most suitable interested buyer. A quick winding up of FINSAC and access to cash flow were the Minister's stated priority considerations. The first option was seen as problematic and time-consuming, so Minister Davies proposed that J$0.30 in the dollar could be collected, using the second option. FINSAC reportedly had J$20 billion worth of assets. The other J$50 billion was being sought as loans from the IDB and the World Bank, to wind up, pay interest on FINSAC notes, help recapitalize the institutions, and retire some of the notes issued.

Prime Minister Patterson then emphasized that Jamaica had no plans to return to the IMF, who decided on the economic model, imposed conditionalities and "set exams that we have to sit quarterly and they determine whether we pass or fail with the resulting national trauma" (2000, 4). An IMF Staff Monitored Programme (SMP) was agreed, to enable regular evaluation of targets achieved, and; to indicate to the international capital market that the country's economic programme was credible and worth supporting.

By August 2000 Minister Davies announced that FINSAC's cost had increased to J$130 billion, $50 billion of which would be cancelled. Seventy-eight billion dollars ($78 B) was to be taken on to the books of the Government, as part of the restructuring cost. Interest cost was calculated at J$9 billion (3% of GDP), and the FINSAC bonds held by Central Government were later converted to Local Registered Stock (Davies 2000).

FINSAC first intervened in the Eagle Group of Companies, followed by thirteen (13) financial institutions, having more than 200 subsidiaries and associated companies. Minister Davies reported that 1.5 million accounts, 570,000 insurance policies valued at J$175 million, and pension funds in insurance companies, valued at J$19 billion were protected (2001). As Laeven and Valencia noted, "a large component of the financial problems was in the insurance sector, whose restructuring cost reached 11 percent of GDP" (2008, 24).

4.10.3 Financial Sector Rehabilitation, and; Divestments

By April 2001 Jamaica borrowed US$325 million from the multilaterals, to help solve the FINSAC problem (Davies 2001, 627). The government then assumed all associated contingent liabilities (IMF/WB 2002). Thirteen of fifteen hotels were sold (divested), with negotiations initiated to dispose of the other two.

Chapter 4: Antecedents and Factors Contributing to Public Debt
Accumulation in Jamaica

Mr. Shaw emphasized that mismanagement on the part of the government had led to the demise of the financial sector; while persons engaged by the Government to carry out the FINSAC restructuring exercise, later obtained senior positions in the very companies they had restructured. He also noted that there was a major shift in Jamaica's external debt profile from 1996 to 2001, where costly short-term bonds accounted for 28% of Jamaica's external debt, in comparison to 3% in 1996/97; while the less costly bonds had declined by 25%. Total external debt increased by 23%, between 2000 and 2001. Shaw also observed that there was a high level of indiscipline with regards to money supply, where targets were set at around 10% and increased as high as 40%, while high interest rates were used to prevent a rapid devaluation of the Jamaican dollar. Debt service cost accounted for 62% of Jamaica's total budget in 2001 (Shaw 2001).

By February 2002, Dr Davies reported that the remaining FINSAC debt of J$19.5 billion would be retired by J$6.2 billion, J$1.9 billion, and J$2.6 billion from the sale of the JPS, Life of Jamaica and the government's seventy-five percent (75%) share of NCB, J$7.7 billion from the World Bank and IDB, and J$1.2 billion from government and other sources. Mr Shaw objected.

Minister Davies admitted that the financial sector crisis, and the attempts at resolution, would continue to affect future budgets, as almost one-third (1/3) of Jamaica's public debt was due to FINSAC alone (2002, 51). He also conceded that had FINSAC not been on the books, Jamaica's debt stock would have remained stable from 2001 to 2002.

By March 2002 interest payments increased significantly, in tandem with the conversion of FINSAC bonds to Local Registered Stock (Davies 2002, 3). Still, he emphasized that his administration would have done it all over again, to prevent social disorder. The government had to absorb FINSAC costs of 35 to 40% of GDP (MOFP 2002). By April 2002, J$75 billion, or 36% of the budget was earmarked for amortization payments, and $60 billion, or 29% for interest. Minister Davies proposed to finance

Chapter 4: Antecedents and Factors Contributing to Public Debt Accumulation in Jamaica

this, in part, by additional loans of J$58.3 billion from the domestic market and US$61.1 billion from the external market. He said that more than 70% of the $58.3 billion was to be used for domestic debt amortization; $26.1 billion was to pay down the external debt; with $6.1 billion from the domestic borrowings, earmarked to help clear off due debts.

There was still a fiscal gap of J$17.6 billion, which he proposed to close by selling the Jamaica Grande hotel, remaining shares of the JPS, Cable and Wireless, and another cellular license. Mr Shaw retorted that while less than 20% of the budgets of Barbados and Trinidad and Tobago needed to be set aside for servicing debt, "We are in a position where we are borrowing money just to repay the money we borrowed in the past" (2002, 116-7). He, like the IDB (2005, 190), argued that it would take many generations to pay off the FINSAC debt.

Where funds were recouped, the revenues have reportedly benefited the collectors more so, than the people of Jamaica, as Prime Minister Golding reported:

> The Government sold the FINSAC debts for an initial payment of [US] $23 million and thereafter it was entitled to a percentage of whatever is recovered. Up to the end of January, the debt collectors had recovered a total of $122 million dollars, after you take out $6 million for operating expenses. So they have collected $122 million net, from which they have paid over to government its share of that $122 million which is $30 million. So they have been left with $92 million ... for themselves. (2008, 3)

A FINSAC Commission of Enquiry established in 2008, met in September 2009, with many recriminations. Still, at May 2015 the J$100 million Commission had not submitted a report. A former Central Banker put the FINSAC issue into perspective as follows:

Chapter 4: Antecedents and Factors Contributing to Public Debt Accumulation in Jamaica

> There was also reform of financial legislation in the early 1990s which left too many loopholes for people who were not prudent to exploit. Again that was a democratic reform process. So you are reforming legislation and you call all the people who were to be regulated to testify about what the regulations should be. Some people would say you are 'calling the foxes to help you design the hen house'. Of course, they objected to everything which would restrict imprudent behaviour, so loopholes were left. That inadequate legislation in the early 1990s had to later be reformed after the financial sector meltdown in 1997/1998, reflecting that what was done 6 to 7 years earlier was woefully inadequate. The process was not properly done and the people who were to be regulated had an equal say in how the regulations should be designed. (pers. comm. 2012)

He concluded that the financial meltdown was, therefore, due to: loose macroeconomic policies; inter and intra-company lending; insurance companies using short-term investments from clients to finance fixed asset investments, and; the resolution of financial institutions, by an arbitrary 'good bank, bad bank' approach, using FINSAC notes, and later government paper as underlying securities; while high inflation masked the inefficiencies and nepotism within financial institutions.

Kwon et al. (2006) later observed that Jamaica's chronic indebtedness was due to off-budget obligations and FINSAC (p. 19). The World Bank (2011) emphasized that FINSAC which cost Jamaica 40% of GDP, stymied growth and significantly increased the country's public debt, due to the hasty liberalization of the financial sector; inadequate regulations influenced by sector interest groups; poor governance; arbitrary reserve requirements, and; mismatching of short-term funds with long-term investments (p. 57).

I asked a former Prime Minister in an interview for this publication, what he would have done differently. He stated that avoiding the process would have led to incalculable costs, though a great impediment to economic success and growth in Jamaica "has been what resulted in the necessity to create FINSAC and the huge debt which accrued to the public sector as a result of seeking to fulfil that obligation" (pers. comm. 2011).

Jamaica's debt problem was also worsened by exponential increases in the debt ceiling.

4.11 Raising the Debt Ceiling - FINSAC Obligations Dominate

The debt ceiling is to be set at the time when the government agrees to raise a loan and brought to the books when authorized (GOJ Constitution 1962). Policymakers increased Jamaica's debt ceiling from £25 million in 1964 to £50 million in 1967, through the Loan Act of 1964. More than eighteen (18) subsequent amendments were made, including one for J$15.5 billion in 1985. A subsequent increase to $60 billion in 1993 was to meet a $24 billion debt obligation from BOJ losses (recall earlier discussions), pay public sector salaries, and provide a cushion for loans over the ensuing three years (Small 1993).

Another amendment in 2001 raised the limit from J$170 billion to $400 billion, to meet FINSAC obligations, estimated then, at 35% of GDP (Davies 2001). By 2007 the Government again increased the borrowing limit to $700 billion; then to $920 billion by 2008, when the stock of debt stood at one trillion dollars. Minister Shaw said this increase was to facilitate payments of interest accrued on FINSAC debts, and meet obligations relating to Air Jamaica, Sugar Company of Jamaica (SCJ), Clarendon Alumina Production (CAP), and other expenditures. Projected expenditure on debt servicing was $3.2 billion.

The government then absorbed $16.7 billion of Sugar Company of Jamaica (SCJ) debts, while facing additional costs of more than $8 billion for Highway 2000/NROCC (Shaw 2008). The US$100 million global bonds issued to assist in financing this project were indexed to inflation, making the debt even more expensive.

The 2007/08 global recession resulted in even more severe challenges, as inflows from remittances and tourism declined. By the end of 2009, the debt service payments were so high that

Chapter 4: Antecedents and Factors Contributing to Public Debt
Accumulation in Jamaica

investors and financial commentators began discussing the possibility of a default.

The IMF continued to provide technical assistance through the Staff Monitored Programme (SMP) –an informal agreement between the IMF and a member country's authorities for the IMF to monitor the country's economic programmes, and Article 4 Consultations. In desperation, Jamaica revived its borrowing relationship with the IMF and obtained a Stand-by Arrangement loan in 2010. This agreement came with a mandate to reduce debt service obligations through a debt exchange – the Jamaica Debt Exchange (JDX); strengthen fiscal consolidation to reduce government deficits and debt accumulation; reduce the Debt-to-GDP ratio to 100 % by 2016, and; cut the public sector wage bill to 9% of GDP. Inflation fell from 16.8% in 2007 to 11.7% by 2010. Still, recommended public sector reforms to reduce the public sector wage bill to 9% of GDP have remained outstanding since the 1978 IMF agreements (see Ministry Paper 17/1979, 6).

This piecemeal approach has led to mixed results. The Golding-led JLP administration failed to implement all the provisions of the IMF agreement and lost the December 2011 election, after Prime Minister Bruce Golding's sudden resignation in October 2011. As noted earlier, the then Education Minister Andrew Holness took the reins of leadership of both the JLP and the country, as Prime Minister. When he sought to obtain his own mandate, he lost to Prime Minister Portia Simpson-Miller, who was able to withstand bitter internal elections to gain leadership of the PNP just before the elections.

The Simpson-Miller administration, with Dr. Peter Phillips (one of her former rivals in the PNP's internal leadership elections), as Finance Minister, promised to have an IMF agreement in place soon after that election. Meanwhile, the Net International Reserves (NIR) fell from US$2.171 billion in 2011 to US$823 million by April 2013, when the exchange rate reached J$101 to US$1, and the debt stood at J$1.8 trillion. Recall that movements in exchange rates increase the level and cost of external and currency-denominated domestic debt. A four-year Extended Fund Facility (EFF) was eventually signed in May 2013, after a second debt exchange, the National Debt Exchange (NDX) was successfully implemented.

4.11.1 Finance Ministers' Perspectives of International Financial Institutions

Jamaica's relationship with the International Financial Institutions (IFIs) has been influenced by divergent ideological perspectives of national leaders – Prime Ministers and Finance Ministers, in particular.

Opposition Spokesman (Shadow Minister) on Finance Omar Davies argued in 2008 that, whereas Jamaica had in the past benefited from technical assistance from the World Bank, IDB, and IMF, their technicians had no special expertise "in designing appropriate social and economic policies to run our country more than ours" (p. 2).

He posited that the differences his administration had with the multilaterals were common to both the JLP and PNP, as "former Prime Minister Seaga, in the 80s, was so dissatisfied with the policies being laid down by the multilaterals that he demanded a tripartite review" as their policies had failed Jamaica (2008, 2). He emphasized that Jamaica ended its borrowing relationship with the IMF, largely on account of its use of devaluation as a main methodology for dealing with the debt problem. He also took issue with their faith in the free market system, and the use of cross-conditionalities.

On the other hand, Minister Shaw argued that "we must subject ourselves to cross-conditionalities, not just between the World Bank, IDB and IMF ... [but] to everybody, all of our stakeholders" (2008, 3), as this would assist the Government in being more accountable and prudent in its operations.

Chapter 4: Antecedents and Factors Contributing to Public Debt
Accumulation in Jamaica

By 2012 the IMF adopted a more receptive approach, with its Managing Director Madame Christine Lagarde urging her team to devise programmes with sensitivity to the needs of individual countries, in a timely and flexible manner, ensuring that the focus remained on growth and austerity measures, over targets; with fiscal adjustments being made at a pace conducive to the achievement of objectives (p. 4). She emphasized that these reforms were the most significant governance changes in the history of the IMF (p. 7). Consistent with this approach and for the first time in Jamaica's borrowing relationship, the IMF agreed to permit US$90 million of the US$932.2 million being borrowed through the 2013 four-year EFF, to be used for budgetary support.

Jamaica was subsequently successful in eight (8) reviews up to June 2015. While some economic stability has returned, a piecemeal approach to the required structural reforms (public sector pension and tax) continues to be taken, even as lack of competitiveness and high levels of debt remain as major hindrances to sustainable development in Jamaica.

The COVID19 pandemic that has been raging since late 2019 to the time of publication of this book (2021), has exacerbated the problem, as the Jamaican economy is heavily dependent on tourism, a sector that has been most severely affected by restrictions in travel, and economic challenges globally.

4.12 Public Debt Administration

Jamaica

Before 1998 the Bank of Jamaica (BOJ) and the Ministry of Finance shared debt management responsibilities. In 1998 a Debt Management Unit (DMU) was created in the Ministry of Finance, to synchronize debt management and fiscal policy. This included strategy formulation, borrowing, registration, recording, monitoring, and making payments associated with Government securities. The BOJ retained responsibility for external debt

Chapter 4: Antecedents and Factors Contributing to Public Debt Accumulation in Jamaica

payments, periodic secondary trades to enhance liquidity, and primary issues, including Treasury Bills (IMF/WB 2002).

Jamaica's stated debt management objectives were to access adequate financing for the Government of Jamaica, at minimum costs, while maintaining public debt at sustainable levels over the medium term (IMF/World Bank 2002, 152). However, 'adequate' and 'sustainable' were vague, and did not address the institutional controls required for prudence, effectiveness and efficiency. Consequently, there was repeated rescheduling, through two debt exchanges.

Kraay and Nehru (2003), and Dijkstra (2008) have suggested that the risk of a country running into major arrears, requiring rescheduling or amendments depended on: (1) The debt burden it carried; (2) the type and quality of institutions and policies being pursued. These are influenced by the legislative provisions and constraints guiding the sovereign's debt management strategy, and their public sector borrowing requirements (PSBR).

Jamaica's PSBR is outlined by the Ministry of Finance at the beginning of a financial year when the budget and debt management strategies are presented. Section 119 of the Jamaican Constitution states that Jamaica's public debt is charged on the Consolidated Fund – an account into which all revenues of Jamaica are paid (S. 114). This debt includes interest, sinking fund payments, and redemption monies associated with it (p. 64).

Repayment of public debt takes priority as a statutory expense without the need for Parliamentary approval (Constitution of Jamaica S. 119). During our examination of the records, there were more than twenty-eight (28) pieces of legislation in Jamaica relating to the regulation, issuance, and administration of public debt. These included the Treasury Bill Act; General Loan and Stock Law; Local Registered Stock Law; Debentures (Local) Law; Land Bonds Act; Loan Equity Investment Bonds Act; Financial Administration and Audit Act; Loans National Development Bonds Act, and; Loans National Savings Bond Act. The Loan Act of 1964 outlined the legal framework within which Jamaica could

Chapter 4: Antecedents and Factors Contributing to Public Debt
Accumulation in Jamaica

borrow to finance Capital Expenditure programmes, including types of creditors and financial instruments.

Loans from the World Bank, IDB, and the IMF, are governed by other legislation. Much of Jamaica's public debt legislation was adopted from the colonial system, which gave excessive powers to the Minister of Finance and local authorities, without the requisite institutional controls to ensure probity. This has contributed to Jamaica's debt accumulation.

The GOJ was mandated by the IMF in 2010, to improve the debt management process, by consolidating these laws. A Public Debt Management Bill was tabled in Parliament and passed in November 2012 for this purpose. The GOJ later presented a Fiscal Rule (commitment) to the IMF in March 2014, with the main stated aims being to: (1) improve transparency; (2) consolidate gains from structural reforms, and; (3) reduce public debt to 60% of GDP by 2025/26. Discussions with technicians in the Debt Management Unit (MOFP) revealed that this was central to Jamaica's current fiscal strategy.

Barbados

The Central Bank of Barbados handles the floating of government securities, while the Treasury Department handles the issuing of T-bills. The Barbados Ministry of Finance (as in Jamaica) handles the general administration of public debt. The legislation governing debt management in Barbados include the Savings Bond Act 1980, Treasury-Bill and Tax Certificate Act 1987, Special Loans Act/Special Loan (Amendment) Act 1977-1993, External Loans Act 94D, and the Local Loans Act 1988. As at March 2010, Barbados' public debt consisted "mainly of bonds and debentures, issued both locally and internationally, loans from international financial institutions, and borrowing under financial lease arrangements" (GOB 2011, viii). Less than 10% of Barbados' external debt was owed to multilaterals (IMF 2011).

However, the country faced fiscal challenges brought on, in part, by a "severe slowdown in tourism triggered by a protracted recession" (IMF 2014, 10), and worsened by the impact of the COVD19 pandemic, on this tourism-dependent economy.

Still, the government and people of Barbados have historically demonstrated the political will to make tough decisions to improve economic performance (Henry 2013). The IMF (2014) reported that the Barbados government had decided to address its public debt challenges through a 15% reduction in the civil service (3500 posts), "further downsizing by attrition of about 500 positions per year until 2018/19, wage cuts for elected and appointed officials, and a two-year nominal wage freeze, among other measures" (p. 7).

Yet, Barbados managed to maintain high savings rates, with their 2013 Deposit of Financial Institutions to GDP being three times the Caribbean's average, at 120%; while credit to the private sector exceeded the Caribbean average by almost 10 percent. Capital Account legislation in Barbados prevents unauthorized large capital outflows (IMF 2014). "A new interest rate policy was instituted in 2013 ... Under this policy, the CBB absorbed about 44 percent of T-bills issued in the first 11 months of 2013 and short-term interest rates fell by about 50 basis points" (IMF 2014, 6).

Singapore

Singapore's Constitution allows the President to provide strict oversight over fiscal affairs. This has helped to prevent abuse of fiscal authority. They borrow through Singapore Government Securities issued by the Monetary Authority of Singapore (MAS). Their debt issues are regulated by the Government Securities Act which covers bonds and Treasury Bills (T-bills) through the Local Treasury Bills Act, Public Securities Association (PSA), International Securities Market Association (ISMA), and Global Master Repurchase Agreement (GRMA), for trading repurchase instruments (GOS 2011).

Chapter 4: Antecedents and Factors Contributing to Public Debt Accumulation in Jamaica

Singapore minimizes T-bill usage and incorporates exchange rate management into its debt management strategy. T-bill ceilings are authorized by a resolution of Parliament (as in Jamaica and Barbados) but must be approved by the President, who also has constitutional authority as head of state to block the Government from drawing down past reserves it did not accumulate (GOS 2012).

Singapore's external debt was minuscule up to the 1990s; while domestic debt, acquired mainly through the Central Provident Fund, is comprised of Singapore Government Securities, and Special Singapore Government Securities (GOS 2011, 3). As of July 2011, the ceilings for Singapore's Government Securities and T-bills were SG $320 billion, and SG $60 billion respectively. Public debt outstanding was SG $354 billion, or 108% of GDP (GOS 2011).

It is also instructive to look at issues relating to public debt and governance, from the experiences of other countries globally, with which Jamaica has had bilateral relationships. Each should be read only as a mini case study, with debt management lessons for Jamaica, and other countries that may face public debt challenges.

4.13 GLOBAL CASES – with Debt Management Lessons

Japan and China – with Reference to the USA, Germany, South Korea, and Singapore

Japan's public debt became unsustainable around 1932 due to "loss of fiscal discipline because of the military's effective veto over budget processes and because of the absence of pressure for sound fiscal policy from international financial markets" (Shizume 2007, 32).

According to Nurkse, "It is instructive to consider the contrast between China and Japan, where 80% of China's foreign capital came from investment, while most of Japan's was obtained through external public debt" (1953, 90). He noted that Japan subsequently took a strategic decision to assign 12 to 17% of its national income to capital formation (recall Gross Fixed Capital Formation discussed earlier).

By 2002, the IMF/WB noted that debt management policies in Japan were aimed at providing stability to finance fiscal needs, and; curtail medium to long-term cost of debt, to avoid unduly burdening tax-payers (p. 163).

Not long after the 2011 Tsunami and earthquake, Japan's manufacturing sector rebounded. Still, its public Debt-to-GDP remained high, at 214% in 2012 (WB data). So, though Japan had invested heavily in resilient infrastructure, the level of borrowing, and risk exposure in its debt portfolio posed challenges.

Vinals (2012) reported that Japan also faced a potential risk of contagion from Europe and the USA on account of the 2007/08 global recession, as "bank holding of government bonds could rise to about one-third of banks' total assets in five years' time, tying banks ever closer to the sovereign and potentially weakening financial stability should interest rates rise" (p. 1). Vinals saw macro-prudential vigilance and fiscal consolidation as possible solutions to the problem.

As in the case of Japan, the investment portfolios of Jamaica's financial institutions, and the NIS in Barbados, were highly exposed to sovereign debt, increasing their vulnerability to default risk.

Though investments in China were mainly for the export market, China was seen as the pariah of the east, on account of political repressions which climaxed in the June 1989 Tiananmen Square massacre, which delayed political reform and economic advancement (Todaro 1997, 230). However, by 2012 the IMF's Lagarde praised China's remarkable transformation, in becoming the world's largest economy in thirty years. As China continues to expand its global investments, and strengthen diplomatic relations through trade and infrastructural development assistance, it has now become a net lender.

Chapter 4: Antecedents and Factors Contributing to Public Debt Accumulation in Jamaica

Meanwhile, Japan is still in the company of Germany and France, among the seven largest countries globally, in terms of GDP. The capital stocks of both Germany and Japan were ravaged during World War II, yet they have recovered. Now, "both Japan and Germany save and invest a higher fraction of their output than does the United States" (Mankiw 2010, 200). Like Singapore, Japan now owes most of its public debt to its citizens. Still, Heckman (2011) believed Japan could learn valuable debt management lessons from South Korea, whose total public debt in 2010 was 23% of GDP, while Japan's was over 200%.

As Nurkse pointed out, "the reason why even in the United States the people save nothing is not that they cannot afford to save, or do not want to, but that they live in an environment which makes them want new consumption goods even more" (1953, 2). Sixty-eight years later, and this statement still holds great relevance. The USA had its credit rating downgraded on August 5, 2011, as a result of its spiralling debt.

As reported by the IMF (2021) Japan's General Government Gross Debt-to-GDP for 2020 was 256.5%. That of China was 69.6%, while that of the USA was 132.8%.

According to the Office of Management and Budget and Federal Reserve Bank (OMBFed) of St. Louis (2021), the US Total Public Debt as a percentage of GDP was 127.65% as at Q1 2021 (first quarter). In dollar value, the public debt of the United States of America was US$28.133 trillion as at the first quarter of 2021.

Finance Minister Dr. Nigel Clarke reported on March 9, 2021, that Jamaica's Debt-to-GDP had increased by 16 points to 110%, largely due to the impact of COVID19 on economic performance (Clarke, 2021). This was nine (9) days before the World Bank reported that they had agreed to provide US$150 Million (J$22,950,000,000) "for a Resilient COVID-19 Recovery in Jamaica" (World Bank, 2021).

South Korea

The Asian financial crisis of 1997-98 occurred in tandem with Jamaica's FINSAC crisis. The Asian crisis was blamed on foreign currency shortages and inadequately developed financial markets. Several Asian countries, including South Korea (Asia's 4th largest economy), turned to the IMF for assistance in December 1997.

They were told to reduce the current account deficit to 1% of GDP; cap inflation at 5%; build reserves to greater than eight weeks of imports; restructure failed banks, remove government guaranteeing of bank deposits, replace this with a deposit insurance scheme; open up securities market, and; ease restrictions on dismissal policy, to allow for equity with international standards (IMF 1997; Nanto 1998). These were very similar conditionalities to those presented in Jamaica's IMF agreements. South Korea made the critical adjustments, without much resistance.

Consequently, South Korea which was well below the radar of economic growth in 1965, was able to expand its economy and increase per capita income from US$1,100 in 1960 (Todaro 1997) to US$15,500 by 2008 (WB data). The significant expansion of South Korea's manufacturing sector and export markets have also contributed to this success. Some have argued that South Korea has benefited from United States aid, as it has been of geopolitical importance since 1945, based on its strategic location in relation to North Korea.

Others like Angresano (2007) have argued that South Korea "adopted only four or five of the ten elements advocated by the [Washington] Consensus" (p. 52). Yet, it was subsequently named among the UN (2010) top ten countries on the income and non-income dimensions of development – including health, and education. As Ducote noted, "the quality of governance becomes a critical factor in explaining development" (2007, 1).

Nanto (2009) pointed out that though South Korea was severely impacted by the Asian crisis and had to borrow US$58 billion from the IMF in December 2007, it showed resilience and

Chapter 4: Antecedents and Factors Contributing to Public Debt Accumulation in Jamaica

subsequently experienced economic growth of 3% to 6% per annum (p. 82). The Economist (2011) also noted that, South Korea was the only country that transformed itself from being a major aid recipient to significant wealth in one generation (p. 1). From 1990 to 2010 South Korea's average government debt was 18.6% (Trading Economics, 2013). In 2020, South Korea's General Government Gross Debt as a percent of GDP was 53.2%, even in the midst of a global pandemic (IMF 2021).

Like China, South Korea has changed from a planned to a mixed economy since the late 1990s. They now spend more than any other rich country (except America) on tertiary education, with the government spending 5% of GDP, and citizens 2.8% (Economist 2011). In terms of governance, the question remains, who should be responsible for human capital development, and; how does this impact development?

> For Rosenstein-Rodan, the 'skilling' of labour was the first task of industrialization, but one that had to be undertaken by the state, because it does not pay firms to train potentially mobile workers. By contrast, TW Schultz raised the question of individuals' and families' own investment in what he called human capital – a stock of skills that could be deployed to earn future income (Toye 2006, 25).

Todaro (1997) argued that such major structural changes require a radical shift in mind set, institutions, and belief systems (p. 110). Similarly, Kuznets (1971) had emphasized that if a country is to optimize the benefits of new technology [including up-skilled labour], they must be flexible and willing to embrace institutional, ideological, and attitudinal changes. Japan, South Korea, Singapore, and China have all demonstrate the capacity to do this. The lessons to be learned from these countries are:

1. Frugality and fiscal discipline can reduce indebtedness;
2. A public/private partnership in education and training can spur GDP growth, and reduce the need for debt financing, and;

3. Country-specific adjustments to economic modelling and strategy can be effective in curtailing public debt (Angresano 2007).

South Korea, like Singapore, has a pension system with sufficient liquidity to meet its short-term pay outs (OECD 2013). However, as is the case in Jamaica, Singapore, and Barbados, an ageing population in South Korea can pose fiscal challenges over the long term.

The European Union (EU)

Like the Caribbean, Latin America, and Asia, countries in Europe have been faced with debt management challenges. This was not always so. Nurkse (1953) noted that "Loans to governmental authorities (central, state and municipal) accounted for over half of French and German foreign investment outstanding in 1914. Britain's 30% of investment outstanding consisted of Government bonds" (p. 90).

The EU was formed out of the 1957 Treaty of Rome. By 1993 this agreement permitted free regional movement of labour, goods, services, and capital. Germany, France, Italy, and Belgium are members of the EU. Marano (1999) examined the process of debt management in these four (4) countries, using a simulation model, to evaluate how the effect of fiscal policy on debt and deficits, could impact economic growth.

Though these countries are members of a Union, their fiscal policies are crafted and implemented at the national level. Monetary policies in the EU were focused on reducing inflation in the 1990s, while fiscal policies were directed at increasing tax revenues and reducing public expenditure.

The Maastricht Treaty, and later the Stability and Growth Pact of the European Union, required members to decrease their deficits until a balanced budget was attained (Marano, 1999, 591). This Treaty, Pact, and the Ecofin Council, also outlined constraints aimed at achieving prudent management of public finances and debt in the EU (previously the European Monetary Union - EMU). The Inter-institutional Agreements (IIA) of 1993-1999, and 2000-2006 provided a financial framework to guide the process. According to Marano (1999) these constraints have collectively included procedures stipulating that:

- The ratio of government deficit and Debt-to-GDP, should decline "substantially and continuously" (p. 5); or be exceptional and temporary.
- Information should be passed to the European Commission every 1st of March and September, accounting for the government's deficit in excess of investment expenditure, and; the member state's economic and budgetary status over the medium-term (p. 5).
- Thresholds were also set for the primary surplus, deficits, and public debt.

Debt-to-GDP was expected to stabilize at a ratio of 60%, with a fiscal deficit of 3%. The Stability and Growth Pact defined 'sound government finances' as a situation where each member state aims to achieve a budget balance or surplus over the medium term (p. 5). Countries, whose financial positions were found to be outside the deficit and debt targets in March, would be liable to face sanctions in December, including the conversion of a portion, or all, their non-interest bearing deposits, for distribution among member states.

The European System of Integrated Economic Accounts allowed for revenues from privatization to be used for debt reduction, but not deficit; while dividends from robust growth should be used to balance the budget, and not to adjust the fiscal position. Some have argued that a number of EU members including Spain and Italy have not obeyed the rules set out in previous pacts. Subsequently, a new treaty referred to as the Fiscal Compact was crafted in March 2012.[1]

The IMF (2012) noted that the crisis in the EU resulted from mispriced risks, weak prudential frameworks, and large imbalances in the private and public sector, worsened by the recession (p. 3). They also argued that bad fiscal policies derailed the efforts, through a high level of market integration, and cross-border lending; while regulatory supervision was mainly carried out at the national level. Ultimately, there was no effective regional oversight.

By September 2012 the IMF's Christine Lagarde reminded Euro area leaders to fulfil their promise to implement a single supervisory system and allow for the banks to be capitalized directly through the European Stability Mechanism. She noted that the EU needed fiscal amendments and structural reforms to achieve stability and recover.

Even as Britain prepares to make its exit from the European Union, there are profound lessons for Jamaica from the EU's debt management experience: A focus on economic growth through improvements in fiscal policy and restraint, are more effective and lasting, than simply adjusting the primary surplus or targeting "stabilization of the economy over the cycle" (Marano 1999, 24).

Argentina

Argentina ranked 11th in the world in terms of income per capita in the 1870s. Yet, between 1965 and 1990 it was ranked below the 50th (Smith 1997). Facing a debt of over US$195 billion in 2001, the authorities in Argentina declared that it was just too big to be repaid. "In December 2001, after four years of deepening recession and mounting social unrest, Argentina's government collapsed and ceased all debt payments" (Hornbeck 2004, 1). Debt-to-GDP increased from 47.4% in 1999 to over 150% by 2002.

---

[1] BBC News – broadcast in Jamaica on March 2, 2012 at 12:38 pm

Chapter 4: Antecedents and Factors Contributing to Public Debt Accumulation in Jamaica

Hornbeck (2004) noted that when the IMF decided to grant Argentina an Extended Fund Facility (EFF) in 1998, IMF staff raised strong objections (p. 38). Before Argentina's default, the IMF facilitated most of its demands, resulting in major challenges, and a crisis of confidence in international capital markets. They later conceded that they had "erred in the pre-crisis period by facilitating Argentina's weak policies for too long, after recognizing that the level of political instability was inimical to the fiscal discipline required" (IMF 2004, 3).

They saw Argentina's challenges as being mainly due to prolonged hyperinflation, poor fiscal controls, unsustainable debt levels, and a convertibility regime in which the peso was pegged to the United States dollar. They recommended reforms in social security, the labour market, financial sector, exchange rate, and fiscal adjustments.

In highlighting the lessons learned, the IMF (2004) noted that: (i) The exchange rate regime chosen must be consistent with policies and constraints, and; (ii) Risks must be thoroughly evaluated and rules clearly outlined to establish if and when financial support is to be made available.

Mexico

Mexico also faced a debt crisis in 1982. They made changes to their economic structure, moving from a focus on import substitution to a more liberalized economic model, aided by NAFTA since 1994. They took steps to pass their Fiscal Responsibility Law in 2006and successfully turned the economy around (GOM 2012).

In highlighting the differences in approaches taken by Argentina and Mexico, Jamaica's Opposition Spokesman (Shadow Minister) on Finance Audley Shaw (2001) noted that the President of Mexico recognized that short-term disjointed measures would have been inadequate to address the severe debt crisis, and so he embarked on a strategy to meet with all creditors and stakeholders

Chapter 4: Antecedents and Factors Contributing to Public Debt Accumulation in Jamaica

to renegotiate the country's debt. He concluded that Jamaica also needed to take such "a radical, dramatic, bold approach to reducing our public debt" (2001, 684). Improved governance made the difference in Mexico.

Castro et al. (2009) noted that Mexico's transformation was supported at the highest level, and; included reforms enabled by "(i) institutionalizing the links between strategic planning and the budget process, (ii) the launch of a performance-based budgeting initiative, and (iii) the introduction of planning and evaluation tools at the program level" (p. 4). They were also aided in this, by the United States and the IMF, through a US$50 billion emergency financial assistance package (Villarreal 2010). By March 2012, Mexico's Debt-to-GDP was below 40%.

Like Barbados, Mexico's debt management, fiscal and monetary policies are now coordinated using similar assumptions, with the Central Bank representing the government in key economic areas (GOM 2012). Debt limits and strategies must also be approved by the Mexican Congress (IMF 2002).

The key lessons to be learned from Mexico are: (i) There are significant benefits to coordinating the planning and budgeting process, with monetary and fiscal policies, and; (ii) High-level policy support is required to improve governance, and instil fiscal discipline, to strengthen institutional controls and reduce indebtedness.

Debt Forgiveness data from the World Bank showed that between 1990 and 2007, Jamaica received large volumes of concessions and grant funding (US$613 million) to help fix its debt problem. Mexico on the other hand is recorded to have received only US$1.3 million, and Argentina US$16.62 million.

Additionally, under President Bush's Enterprise of the Americas Initiative US$217 million (and later US$94 million) of debt owed by Jamaica to the USAID were written off up to 1991 (Small 1992). The Netherlands (2003) also reported that they forgave 43% of the debt owed by Jamaica to them, rescheduled 57%, and granted Jamaica US$1,249 million of debt relief since

Chapter 4: Antecedents and Factors Contributing to Public Debt Accumulation in Jamaica

1990. Yet, Jamaica's public debt continued to expand exponentially.

Today's interconnected world presents an opportunity to improve governance and debt management, through greater transparency in fiscal operations. This is essential if the GOJ is to obtain stakeholder support to fulfil its stated mandate to improve fiscal discipline and reduce indebtedness (GOJ 2014, Part 1).

Conclusion

This chapter looked broadly at public debt accumulation, and debt management strategies employed in Jamaica since Independence. It also reviewed the role of the IMF and the World Bank in the strategies employed, with a special focus on the use of Treasury Bills (T-bills) as a dominant policy tool that has contributed significantly to increasing indebtedness.

The Chapter also used mini case studies of countries globally in Asia, Latin American, North American, the Caribbean, and the European Union, to review their debt management strategies, and glean lessons for good governance over a country's fiscal resources. We have seen how strategic policy coordination and commitment on the part of policymakers to implement required structural reforms, can, as in the cases of Barbados, South Korea, and Mexico, contribute to curtailing indebtedness.

While there were conflicts with some aspects of the structural reforms laid out in Jamaica's IMF agreements, there is abundant evidence from the borrowing experiences of these countries, that debtor countries' governments had the authority and some autonomy to adjust some policy prescriptions to suit their circumstances, while making key structural changes to reduce indebtedness (IMF 2004; IDB 2005, 3; Henry 2013, 34-42; Angresano 2007).

The remaining chapters will present further findings from this study, with specific answers to other research questions posed. The

Chapter 4: Antecedents and Factors Contributing to Public Debt
Accumulation in Jamaica

final chapter provides a summary of the study. Volume II will present additional policy implications and recommendations.

Chapter 5

FINDINGS - PUBLIC DEBT AND GOVERNANCE IN JAMAICA

5.1 Introduction

The central question that is being answered throughout this publication is:

How has the character of governance in post-independent Jamaica contributed to the country's indebtedness from 1962 to 2010?

Using the global governance indicators discussed earlier as a measure of the overall perception of governance in countries examined globally, one may conclude that Jamaica has an image of poor governance (see WGI 1996-2012; WEF 2010).

This is worsened by the fact that large portions of funds borrowed for development programmes and projects, accompanied by massive grants and concessions received, have not significantly enhanced development.

Up to the mid-2000s (2010/2011), this problem was further aggravated by rapidly accumulating debt, and increasing debt service payments, due in part to profligacy, continuous currency devaluation, haphazard policy formulation, and unconstrained borrowing. Jamaica entered Independence with a 'legacy' of debt, which expanded (in percentage of dollar value) during each political term. Percentage increases in public debt per administrative term were as follows:

Chapter 5: Findings – Public Debt and Governance in Jamaica

- **86%**: 1957 to 1962 (PM N. Manley)
- **270%**: 1963 to 1971 (PMs Bustamante/Sangster/Shearer)
- **743%**: 1972 to 1979 (PM M. Manley)
- **525%**: 1980 to 1989 (PM Seaga)
- **2191%**: 1990 to 2007 (PMs M. Manley/Patterson/Simpson-Miller)
- **64.5%**: 2007 to 2011 (PM Golding)

This publication presents evidence to support the argument that since 1962, governance decisions in Jamaica have contributed significantly to the country's indebtedness. It is a country Case Study of Jamaica, and so Barbados and Singapore are presented mainly as comparators. Four research questions were posed to answer the central question.

5.2 Public Debt and Governance in Jamaica

Question 1: *What is the extent of Jamaica's indebtedness, and; how has this been influenced by; or influenced, development-related governance decisions?*

Jamaica was one of the most highly indebted countries globally, with a Debt-to-GDP ratio of 129% in 2010. This reached 149.4% by 2013 (Phillips 2014). Total public debt increased from $1.81 billion in 1977 to $1.520 trillion by 2010. As of March 31, 2013, it was $1.88 trillion. It is now well over $2 trillion, with contingent liabilities.

Table 5.1 Changes in Public Debt, by Political Admin. (J$B)

Year of New Admin	1977	1980	1989	1998	2007	2011
Public Debt (J$B)	1.81	5.66	35.39	242.89	990.8	1630
Increase in Debt (J$B) over previous period	1.42	3.85	29.73	207.5	747.9	639.2
Party in Power	**PNP**	**PNP**	**JLP**	**PNP**	**PNP**	**JLP**

Source: data - Ministry of Finance ($); Electoral Office of Jamaica (yr.)

Chapter 5: Findings – Public Debt and Governance in Jamaica

Structure and Maturity Profile of Jamaica's Public Debt – The Jamaica Debt Exchange –

In 1994 Jamaica's Finance Minister Dr. Omar Davies highlighted the importance of extending the tenures of government securities, to reduce the interest cost across the debt portfolio. This was eventually carried out on a large scale 16 years later, through the Jamaica Debt Exchange (JDX) initiative, a joint effort between investors, financial institutions, and the Ministry of Finance, mandated by the IMF in 2010.

Its main objective was to reduce the high debt service costs and extend maturities on the domestic debt. The total debt service cost was approximately 112% of revenues for ten years; with interest accounting for 65% (Shaw 2010, 6).

Post-Jamaica Debt Exchange (JDX) - Domestic Debt

After the Jamaica Debt Exchange, 86.4% of the remaining J$813.8 billion of domestic debt was denominated in Jamaican dollars, and 13.3% in US dollars. Sixty percent carried a fixed-rate of interest, while 40% was variable. The government's variable rate instruments are re-priced, on the basis of Jamaica's six-month T-bill auctions; while fixed rates are set for the life/tenure of the security.

Fixed rates on local currency debt enhance medium-term planning, though this can pose a problem in an environment where interest rates are trending downwards. A subsequent examination of the maturity profile and structure of the debt showed that after the JDX in 2011, there was still a bunching of approximately J$400 billion of domestic debt maturities - payable in one to five years, even after the tenure extensions. Written authorization was received from P. Gray of JMMB to use the images in Figures 5.1 and 5.3 to present this graphically.

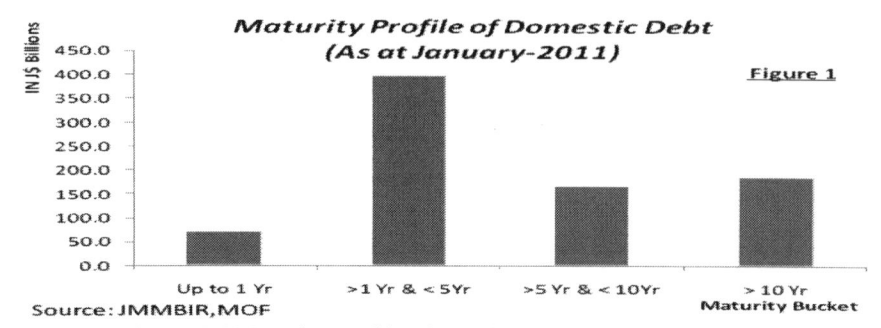

Chapter 5: Findings – Public Debt and Governance in Jamaica

Figure 5.1 Maturity Profile of Jamaica's Domestic Public Debt

A second debt exchange – the National Debt Exchange (NDX), was carried out in 2013 to address some of these anomalies. Upon completion of the NDX, the maturity profile of Jamaica's domestic debt reflected a shift towards the longer end of the curve (yields that are usually ten years or longer). See Table 5.2 below.

Table 5.2 Pre and Post-NDX Maturity Profile of Jamaica's Domestic Debt

PERIOD	FY 2011/12	Proportion	FY 2012/13	Proportion	Change
	J$ M	%	J$ M	%	J$ M
Up to 1 Year	109,121.30	12	63,897.60	6.3	-45,223.70
> 1 - 5 Years	399,936.40	43.8	171,602.90	17.0	-228,333.50
> 5- 10 Years	175,240.00	19.2	313,656.60	31.1	138,416.60
>10 Years	228,344.70	25	459,191.50	45.6	230,846.80
TOTAL	**912,642.30**	**100**	**1,008,348.60**	**100**	**95,706.20**

Source: MOFP Medium-Term Debt Management Strategy 2013-16: Tab 11, p.25

Table 5.2 and Figure 5.2 show that after two debt exchanges, maturities will still almost double for securities due in 5 to 10 years, and; beyond 10 years.

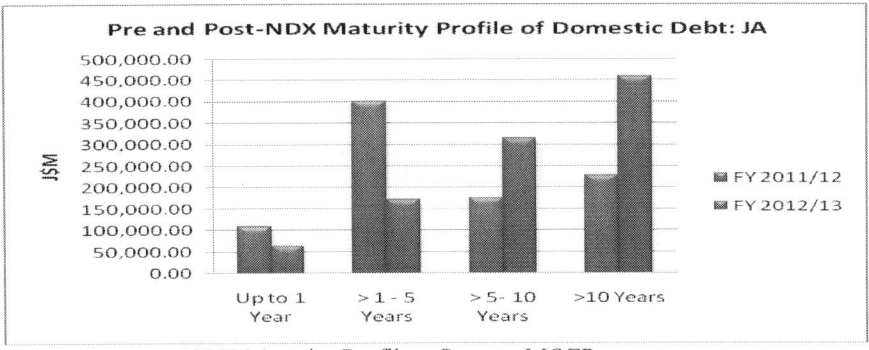

Chapter 5: Findings – Public Debt and Governance in Jamaica

Figure 5.2 Post-NDX Maturity Profile – Source: MOFP

Foreign currency denominated (external) debt poses an even greater challenge, due to currency risk from devaluation, high interest rate premium, and timing of payments. The IMF/World Bank (2002) also observed that the foreign exchange risk in Jamaica's domestic debt portfolio was significantly increased by the issuance of US dollar instruments (p. 156).

External Debt

Jamaica's external public Debt-to-GDP was close to 50% from 2001 to 2008. By 2010 it increased to 61.4%. As at January 2011, 81.9% of the country's external debt was denominated in US dollars, and 13.88% in Euro (MOFP 2011); with 74.7% carrying a fixed interest rate, and 25.3% being variable.

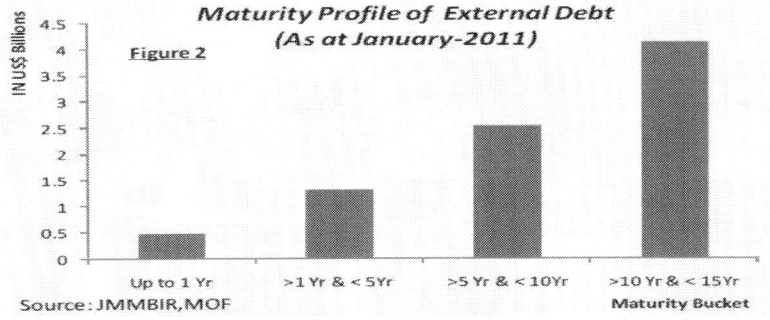

Figure 5.3 Maturity Profile of Jamaica's External Public Debt

Chapter 5: Findings – Public Debt and Governance in Jamaica

Though external debt was not included in the debt exchanges, there was a bunching of US$1.3 billion of external maturities due and payable in one to five years. We found that this would almost double every five years subsequently. When this coincides with the domestic debt maturities, Jamaica will face another crisis, if significant economic growth and new sources of revenue are not created.

Additionally, the IMF (2002) noted that countries with external Debt-to-GDP under 40% faced only a two to five percent (2-5%) likelihood of a debt crisis; while those above 40% were 15 to 20% more likely to face a crisis. Table 5.3 shows Jamaica's external debt position since 1962.

Table 5.3 Jamaica's External Public Debt-to-GDP (%) 1962-2011

1962-1971	1972-1981	1982-1991	1992-2001	2002-2011
7.9	8.9	75.2	94.4	47.3
8.1	10.3	139.5	100.0	46.8
8.9	12.6	156.1	75.6	50.9
9.1	13.6	152.9	67.6	50.0
9.6	16.4	128.0	47.5	49.4
9.6	16.4	120.6	45.5	48.6
10.7	31.6	102.9	43.0	48.7
10.2	31.3	101.9	36.3	54.15
8.9	63.0	101.0	39.9	61.4
8.6	69.6	158.9	46.9	57.7

Source: STATIN; MOFP – Jamaica

Jamaica has experienced recurrent crises since Independence, with external Debt-to-GDP exceeding 100% for 10 of the 12 years, between 1982 and 1993. It was well over 40% for 30 of the 32 years from 1980 to 2010/2011.

After the NDX, there was a major shift in the currency composition of the debt portfolio from Euro to US dollars, even as Jamaica's external debt stock "increased by $54,659.1 million due mainly to a 13.3% depreciation in the Jamaica dollar relative to the US dollar" (MOFP, 2013, 13).

Chapter 5: Findings – Public Debt and Governance in Jamaica

Table 5.4 Currency Composition of JA. External Debt (%)

CURRENCY	2008/09	2009/10	2010/11	2011/12	2012/13
US Dollar	81.9	79.2	82.4	86.8	89.9
Euro	13.0	16.1	13.6	9.3	5.7
Japanese Yen	2.8	2.6	2.1	1.9	1.5
Chinese Yuan	0.0	1.1	1.2	1.4	1.5
Pound Sterling	0.6	0.6	0.4	0.3	0.2
Other	1.7	0.5	0.3	0.3	1.3
Total	100	100	100	100	100

Source: MOFP (2013/14)

Jamaica's external debt was not included in the NDX, and so, the concerns regarding the clustering of maturities is worsened by these higher US$ obligations, and the rapid currency depreciation (J$115.70/US$1 by Feb. 2015, and; J$153/US$1 by 2021).

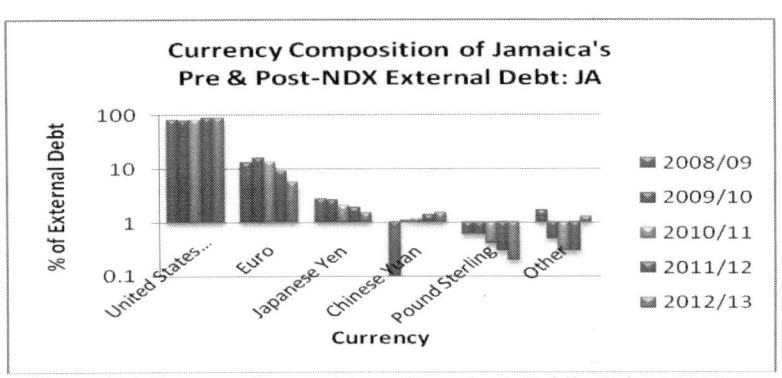

Figure 5.4 Currency Composition of Jamaica's Public Debt: MOFP

After the submission of my research finding to the UWI, the GOJ subsequently conducted a buyback of global bonds that were coming due in 2022, 2025, and 2028, totalling US$1 billion. I have no idea who, if anyone, shared my findings with the authorities, though they were readily accessible. The GOJ then issued new bonds, through a reopening of global bonds coming due in 2045 (IMF 2020, 19). This maturity extension provides a respite, and extends the repayments over a longer time frame, though there was no clear indication if the very high 2022 coupon rates or terms were varied/adjusted.

Chapter 5: Findings – Public Debt and Governance in Jamaica

Debt and Development-Related Governance Decisions – Part I

Up to 2010/2011 Jamaica had one of the poorest records of macroeconomic management in the Caribbean region, resulting in high levels of debt since the 1970s. This has led to limited expenditure on social services to spur growth (Payne and Sutton 2007).

The government of Jamaica allocates funds for recurrent and capital expenditure to ministries, departments, and agencies, through its annual budget. Since 'percent' brings quantitative data to a common size, Jamaica's budget data were converted to percentages for these analyses. This study is mainly focused on recurrent expenditure, as this has had a greater direct impact, than capital expenditure, on citizens' daily interactions with public sector social service providers.

Capital expenditure is analyzed separately, as Gross Fixed Capital Formation (GFCF). Table 5.5 below outlines total public debt, and percentage allocations to the key development-related Ministries of Education, Health, and National Security, from 1962 to 2010/2011.

Table 5.5 Debt and Recurrent Social Service Expenditure as % of Total at 5-year Intervals

YEAR	Total **Public Debt in J$ M**	Recurrent **Education** budget as % of Total Expenditure	Recurrent **Health** budget as a % of Total Expenditure	Recurrent **National Security** budget as % of Total Expenditure
1962-63	**75.76**	13.6	11.2	13.6
1970-71	**275.90**	10.4	8.3	4.8
1975-76	**705.39**	14.2	7.2	5.5
1980-81	**5,662.90**	14.6	8.2	6.8
1985-86	**26,144.60**	8.5	5.3	6.1
1990-91	**43,242.59**	9.2	5.2	5.2
1995-96	**196,967.62**	8.2	3.4	4.7
2000-01	**341,195.79**	10.4	4.2	10.4
2005-06	**827,253.89**	9.8	3.9	4.9
2010-11	**1,570,400.00**	14	6.3	7.5

Source: Ministry of Finance; & ESSJ: National Budgets 1962-2012.
Percentages are calculated

Chapter 5: Findings – Public Debt and Governance in Jamaica

Between 1962 and the first IMF loan agreement in 1977/78, recurrent allocation to Education as a percentage of Total expenditure was between 10% and 16%, and; Health between 6% and 11%. This declined to 5.3% for Education and 2.9% for Health, by the end of the Seaga administration in 1989. From 1990 to 2006 Education received between 4.9% and 13.5%, and; Health 4.4% to 5.2%. Allocation to Education then increased from 11% in 2007 to 14% by 2010, and; Health from 5.3% to 6.3%, when the JLP took a policy decision to offer free health care and education, to keep an election promise. A further analysis was done to see which social service was most severely affected by increasing indebtedness.

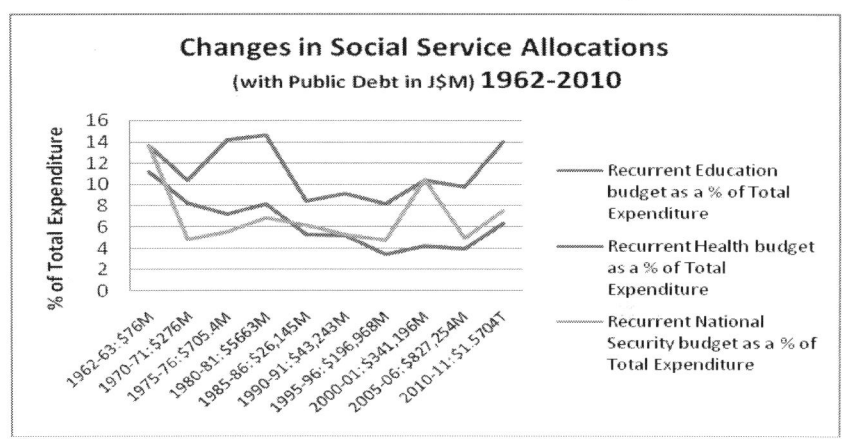

Figure 5.5 Changes in Social Service Allocations, with Debt
Data Source: MOFP

Figure 5.5 above shows that, of the three social services examined, allocation to Health showed the greatest decline, relative to increases in public debt. This was followed by allocations to National Security. National Security was included in the study, as crime continues to be a major problem hindering Jamaica's development. This study shows that at the pinnacle of Jamaica's debt expansion, and during every financial crisis, these allocations declined significantly. Meanwhile, the government continued to finance several capital projects, many of which have

Chapter 5: Findings – Public Debt and Governance in Jamaica

proven to be infeasible; while large sums which were borrowed, and allocated to education, yielded dismal results, due to inadequate planning, lack of real (grassroots) stakeholder engagement, and inadequate (if any) cost-benefit analyses.

Further Qualitative and Quantitative Findings

As Davies (1984) emphasized, the budget is the main guide to the nation's socio-economic policy. He discussed Jamaica's fiscal performance from 1974 to 1983, and concluded that Jamaica's debt service obligation was the chief contributory factor to the growth of public sector expenditure, resulting in "reduction in the provision of the most basic social services" (p. 27).

This was borne out in the Government of Jamaica's 1978 five year plan, in which there were "decreasing levels of expenditure in health and education" (Panton 1993, 134). The IDB (2005) also reported that since the 1980s there were minimal if any, improvements in education, and health (p. 1). Though politicians emphasized the importance of education and training, to economic growth and development, the lack of strategic expenditure in these areas has continued to impede development. Figure 5.6 is a graphic representation of the allocation trends.

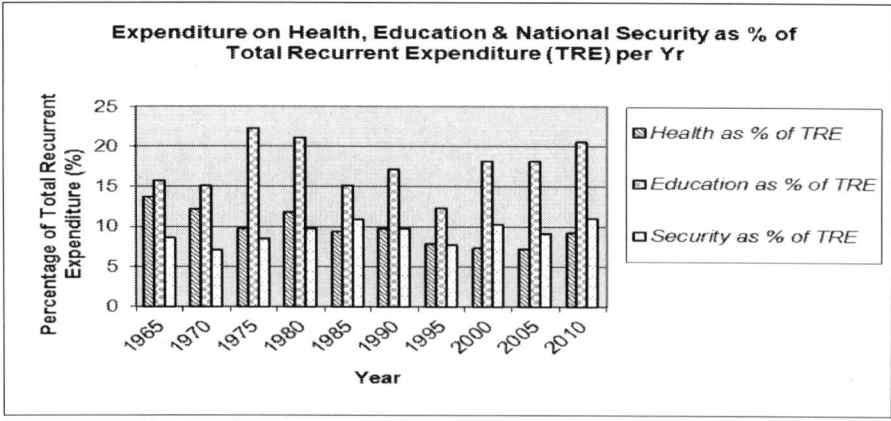

Figure 5.6 Changes in Allocated Recurrent Expenditure on Social Services 1965-2010 (MOFP)

Chapter 5: Findings – Public Debt and Governance in Jamaica

Note how sharply allocations to Education and Health fell during the mid-1980s when Jamaica's public debt peaked at 212% - with external public debt ranging from 101 to 159% between 1983 and 1991.

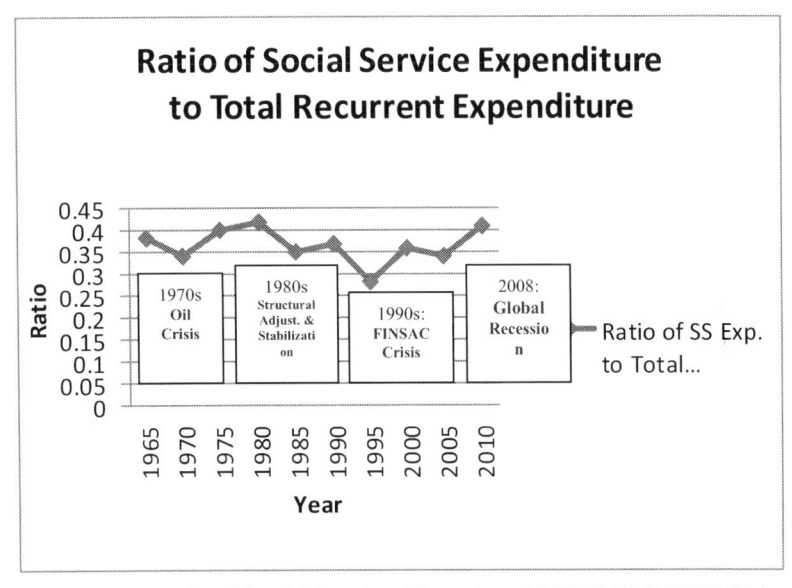

Figure 5.7 Ratio of Social Service Allocations 1965-2010 (MOFP JA.)

Allocations to all three social services again fell sharply during the FINSAC crisis during the mid-1990s. Two decades later, the Planning Institute of Jamaica (PIOJ) reported that debt servicing, and public sector wages were still curtailing the government's ability to focus on these development-related areas (2009, 7).

The 3% to 9% of Jamaica's budget which was allocated annually to Health between 1962 and 2010 was grossly inadequate, as borne out by increasing complaints from public health, and other medical personnel about limited resources, defective equipment, and increased patient loads (pers. comm.).

Chapter 5: Findings – Public Debt and Governance in Jamaica

Linking the Qualitative and Quantitative

While this publication is written in simple language to meet the needs of readers at all levels, including students, it was important, while eliminating complex technical aspects of the study, to share some basic statistical findings, to demonstrate the gravity of the debt problem, contributory factors, and their impact on the provision of social services which are essential to the wellbeing and development of a nation.

There was a significant and strong negative correlation between all forms of public debt as a percentage of GDP in Jamaica, and Allocation to Health as a percentage of Total Recurrent Expenditure, from 1960 to 2010. This suggests that, as seen in the data and graphs presented earlier, as Debt-to-GDP levels increased, the Government of Jamaica's allocation to Health was likely to decrease.

The greatest negative impacts on health allocation, therefore, were likely to be from increases in Total and Domestic public Debt-to-GDP (%). The relationship between allocation to health, and External public Debt-to-GDP (%) was also significant.

King (2000), like Payne and Sutton (2007), felt that Jamaica's declining social infrastructure had contributed significantly to the country's economic stagnation. The PIOJ concurred, reporting that inadequate staffing and equipment in health centres, were negatively affecting Jamaica's economic performance and development (2009, 17). Similarly, Johnston and Montecino (2011) observed that expenditure on education and social infrastructure had not increased in line with increases in interest payments on debt, and; this was inimical to productivity, growth, and human capital development (p. 4).

Public Debt, Social Services, and Productivity

Recall from the development and growth literature discussed in Chapter 2, that investment in human capital and technology, through effective institutions is expected to drive growth.

Chapter 5: Findings – Public Debt and Governance in Jamaica

Though the IDB noted that Jamaica had made some progress in education, gender equity, and health care in the 1990s, they concluded that high debt levels had slowed progress towards achieving the important Millennium Development Goals (2005, 23). Not much progress was made up to 2011 (see Table 5.6 below).

Table 5.6 Jamaica's Human Development Indicators - Results, & Targets to 2030

OUTCOME INDICATORS	Baseline 2007 or most current	Proposed Targets 2012	Proposed Targets 2015	Proposed Targets 2030	COMMENTS
Human Development Index	0.736	0.745	≥ 0.754	≥ 0.800	**Score in 2000: 0.737.** A minimum high human development score is 0.80.
Life Expectancy at Birth	72	72.8	73.4	76.4	Based on comparable levels in Caribbean countries in the High Development range of the HDI. Standard - 2 years per decade.
Adult Literacy Rate (15+ yr.)	85.8%	89.7%	≥91.6%	≥98.3%	Targets are based on regional literacy rate projections for 2015 by UNESCO, and; average literacy rates for Caribbean countries with high HDI.
% of population with tertiary certification (24+y/o)	10.10%	12%	18.7%	37%	The proposed targets are set to match the percentage in **Barbados** by 2012 and to be at the level of top ten OECD countries by 2030.
% of labour force certified (14+ yr.)	18.7%	50%	60%	90%	Locally set target by the taskforce on Labour Market. HEART Trust/NTA had targeted increasing the % of labour force certified, to 50% by 2008-10.

Source: GOJ (2011) 'Vision 2030', combined from Tables 7 & 11 (pp. 56 & 76)

Debt and Development-Related Governance Decisions – Part II

The preceding segment has shown that governance decisions related to public debt accumulation in Jamaica have indeed affected budget allocations to key social services required to spur economic growth and development, particularly from the mid-1970s onward.

Chapter 5: Findings – Public Debt and Governance in Jamaica

It was also important to determine if any other development-related governance decisions may have contributed to increasing the level of public debt. To examine this, thirty-six (36) **macroeconomic** and **social** variables were entered into SPSS for analysis, using data from the World Bank, IMF, Ministry of Finance, Central Bank, Economic and Social Surveys, the BOJ, and STATIN from 1962-2010. The researcher first ran frequencies to examine whether there were outliers that needed to be excluded, before creating a multiple-regression model. The initial model had Total Public Debt-to-GDP (%), as the dependent variable (TPD), and proxy of **indebtedness**, and; fifteen (15) predictor (independent) variables entered as proxies for **development-related governance decisions**.

i. Allocation to Education as % of Total Recurrent Expenditure [ALLED]– investment in human capital development
ii. Allocation to Health as % of Total Recurrent Expenditure– investment in physical quality of labour
iii. Allocation to National Security as % of Total Recurrent Expenditure [ALLNS]– investment in risk reduction, and strengthening the rule of law
iv. Out of Pocket Health Expenditure as % of Total Health Expenditure – shortfall in government's expenditure to improve the physical quality of labour
v. Health Expenditure per capita – to test any association with 'Allocation to Health'
vi. Gross Fixed Capital Formation as % of GDP [GFCF] – investment in physical capital for growth & development
vii. Unemployment – idle labour capacity
viii. Inflation [INFRAT]– effectiveness in liquidity management
ix. Exchange Rate [EXRAT]– level of monetary discipline exercised to enhance competitiveness
x. Crude Birth Rate % - labour replenishment rate
xi. Crude Death rate % - labour attrition rate
xii. Life Expectancy at Birth [LEB]– expected usefulness of labour as a factor of production
xiii. Percentage of Population over 65 y/o – indicator of quality of life
xiv. WGI Political Stability – as indicated in theory, political instability impacts indebtedness
xv. Population size – available labour pool

Chapter 5: Findings – Public Debt and Governance in Jamaica

Result: There was a statistically significant association between Total Public Debt-to-GDP (%), and Gross Fixed Capital Formation (GFCF %), Allocations to Education, and National Security, Exchange Rate (J$ to US$1), and Inflation Rate, from 1962 to 2010. See additional policy implications and additional recommendations in **Volume II** of this publication (to come).

Bear in mind that major cost overruns, and high annual maintenance and staffing costs were/are associated with the projects and programmes discussed in Question #2 below.

5.3 Some Governance Decisions and Their Impact on Debt Expansion

Question 2: *What role has governance played in fostering the build-up of debt in Jamaica?*

Good governance is responsive, accountable, consensus-oriented, participatory, effective and efficient, equitable and inclusive, transparent and follows the rule of law (UNESCAP 2009). These all have a bearing on the fiscal impact of governance, which is the main focus in answering this question.

Qualitative Findings – Costly Governance Decisions

1. The Reform of Secondary Education (ROSE) Project - US$8.8 M

The Patterson administration entered into an agreement on May 07, 1993 to obtain a loan of US$32 million from the World Bank to:

i. Improve quality and access to education, for grade 7 to 9 students;
ii. Strengthen the Ministry of Education's capacity, and;
iii. Improve the provision of social services.

Chapter 5: Findings – Public Debt and Governance in Jamaica

At that time Jamaica was 1% behind the Caribbean region in Mathematics, and 4% behind in English. There were two phases – **ROSE 1** 'completed' in September 2002, and; ROSE 2 was to have been completed in 2010.

Three years into the **ROSE 2** phase, Opposition Leader Seaga reported that 30% to 40% of grade six students entering high school were still functionally illiterate; while pass rates in English and Mathematics were 27% and 25% respectively, placing Jamaica at 17 out of 17 countries in the Caribbean region (2004). He argued that lip service without action was at the base of the problem that was preventing education from being the real priority on Jamaica's development agenda.

The results were still dismal after five years when Dr Peter Phillips told Parliament that 37% of students in traditional secondary schools had failed English, while 60% failed Mathematics (confirmed by data accessed from the MOE for this study). The failure rates in non-traditional and technical schools were in the 80th percentile for English and 90th for Mathematics (2009).

Though Prime Minister Patterson emphasized that productivity, access, equity, and quality were to be improved (2003, 256), seven years later the World Bank still identified "(i) uneven quality of primary and secondary education; (ii) youth at risk; (iii) inadequate access to upper secondary education by the poor; (iv) constraints in education finance, and; (v) constraints in institutional capacity" (2010, 11) as major challenges with the **ROSE** programme.

Consequently, the World Bank rated this GOJ's ROSE project as '**Moderately Unsatisfactory**', due to inadequate risk assessment and mitigation measures; unrealistic estimation of loan obligations and ability to counter-finance the project, and; tardiness in getting rid of the obstacles that prevented the steady flow of funds (WB 2010). An agreement was, therefore, reached with the World Bank to cancel US$23.2 million of the loan. They concluded that efforts were being duplicated, as secondary school students were just learning what they should have learned at the

Chapter 5: Findings – Public Debt and Governance in Jamaica

primary level. Seventeen (17) years after the loan was taken, the results remained dismal, while the public debt expanded.

By 2011 the World Bank noted that the level of human capital in Jamaica's labour force was low due to the poor quality of education and training. They concluded that "existing quality indicators put Jamaica below the Caribbean region average" (p. 8).

More than seventy percent (70%) of respondents to the island-wide survey for this study identified human capital development and training as important factors that should be addressed by the government, to increase productivity, and reduce Jamaica's indebtedness. Still, the profligate expenditure continued through the Career Advancement Programme (CAP).

2. The Career Advancement Programme - J$390.8 M

Even as the ROSE programme failed under the PNP administration, the JLP administration introduced the Career Advancement Programme (CAP) in December 2009. This was targeted at 2000 Jamaican students between 16 and 18 years, who had left the secondary system without qualification. The initial estimated cost was J$82 million.

Yet, according to Reid (2013), "during the 2010-2011 financial year, $390.8 million was pumped into the programme, but only two students were certified competent after assessments were conducted." Again, hundreds of millions of dollars were wasted, as Jamaica's debt expanded to record levels.

3. By-Passing Parliamentary Procedures and Oversight

Jamaica's policymakers have also repeatedly bypassed institutional controls put in place for transparency and prudent fiscal management, at great cost to the economy. A few instances relating to excessive public debt accumulation, and an increasing fiscal burden include:

- Disposal of FINSAC assets (see Chapter 4);

- Bear Stearns' underwriting of expensive long-term fixed-rate global bond issuance of US$200M, at 9%;
- Sale of FINSAC debts for $23M; collectors made $92M; (see earlier discourse in this publication from Golding and Davies on the FINSAC issue).

4. Government Guarantees

A review of GOJ Ministry Papers and the Parliamentary Hansard (1962-2010) also showed that more than 300 debt-related Government Guarantees were approved by Parliament, to secure loans for projects, public sector bodies, and other entities (see Appendices). These have contributed significantly to increasing public debt in Jamaica (IMF/WB 2002, 40).

One senior technocrat confirmed that the public debt figures are also often understated, by using Government Guarantees to carry the debt through departments, and agencies of government (pers. comm. 2012). As discussed earlier, constitutionally, debt has the first claim on Jamaica's fiscal resources. So, excessive use of Government Guarantees to support loss-making entities, increases debt service obligations, default risk, and reduces the fiscal space required for vital development programmes.

5. Deferred Financing

Deferred Financing is an arrangement in which the government engages a service provider to complete a project, and be paid at a later date. This has also served to expand Jamaica's public debt, as the deferred obligation must be paid in the future, even as other public debt obligations continue to expand.

In 2001 Opposition Spokesman (Shadow Minister) of Finance Audley Shaw complained that the Patterson administration was attempting to disguise the debt obligation from the IMF's Staff Monitored Programme (SMP), through Deferred Financing arrangement for road construction, bridges, etc. that would be payable in five years. He indicated that the interest cost on the

Chapter 5: Findings – Public Debt and Governance in Jamaica

J\$9.5 billion debt was 29% - and twice as high as borrowing on the domestic market.

Dr Davies did not deny this, but argued instead, that Deferred Financing was also used by the Seaga Administration in the 1980s. He pointed out that his administration took corrective action then, by amending the Financial Administration and Audit (FAA) Act to empower the Minister of Finance to enter into Deferred Financing arrangements; with a proviso that "no credit arrangement shall be entered into without prior approval of the Minister" (2001, 919), and; that upon delivery of the good or service, the amount due is to be charged to an appropriation account, and carried as a liability on the Consolidated Fund.

One may ask, why was this authority vested in the Minister, and not Parliament, when the FAA Act clearly states that "No payments by way of loans or advances shall be made from the Consolidated Fund without the prior approval of the House of Representatives" (S14B (1) Laws of Jamaica 1999, 19-20)?

Some projects under Deferred Financing arrangements were also reportedly omitted from the estimates of expenditure (Reynolds 2011; Jamaica Observer 2011). This was contrary to Section 2b (4) of the FAA Act which states that liabilities created through Deferred Financing "shall form part of the public debt" (Laws of Jamaica 1999, 30). Incremental deferral of liabilities of this nature, therefore, leads to an understatement of the public debt. Additionally, creditors must be compensated for payment delays. Applying the principle of time-value of money, funds paid at the time the obligation is created, ceteris paribus, yields more equitable benefits, than those deferred.

Minister Davies also argued that Deferred Financing: (i) allowed the Government to deal with urgent works, without having to access public funding immediately (2001). The accounting concepts of 'prudence' and 'substance over form' reinforces Section 2(b) of the FAA Act, suggesting that provisions should be made for all liabilities that are known, with the details or material facts relating to a transaction of material value, being reflected in the books, including details on how they affect the entity, in this case, the economy.

The World Bank/IDB (2006) confirmed that numerous legislation, Deferred Financing, and letters of undertaking being used to finance public investments, were negatively affecting the debt management process, and placing unnecessary pressure on future budgets (p. iv).

They also referenced the Auditor General's 2003/04 report, in which six (6) loans totalling US$6 million were entered into with private and public sector entities, using Letters of Undertaking and Comfort Letters, that did not differ significantly from Government Guarantees.

The report stated that "[T]his method of financing has been discontinued unless there is Parliamentary Approval" (WB/IDB 2006, iii). Unfortunately, it was not discontinued, as, by January 26, 2010, Minister Shaw presented a Bill entitled 'An ACT to Amend the FAA Act (S. 24)':

> [T]o repeal those sections which were amended to facilitate an agreement for deferred financing arrangements to include a transitional provision to address any deferred financing arrangements that were outstanding ...[and] to satisfy a commitment that was given by me as Minister of Finance, to the Cabinet, and to Parliament, not to utilize any further deferred financing arrangements and to fulfil conditions agreed to in financing agreements for debt reduction and growth enhancement between the Government of Jamaica and other lending agencies. (Shaw 2010, 6)

During the December 2011 pre-election debate, Dr Peter Phillips accused Mr Shaw of using Deferred Financing for an eleven billion (J$11B) expense for Jamaica Urban Transit Company (JUTC) buses. This was neither refuted by Mr Shaw nor his counterparts. These 'creative' methods of increasing the debt, like the arbitrary expenditure of borrowed funds for educational programmes, speak to poor governance, and profligacy in fiscal management in Jamaica.

Chapter 5: Findings – Public Debt and Governance in Jamaica

6. Use of Petro Caribé Funds

The Governments of Jamaica and Venezuela entered into the Petro Caribé Agreement on June 29, 2005, for Venezuela to supply petroleum products and crude oil to Jamaica (GOJ 2006). Forty percent of each payment made by Petrojam was to be converted to a 25-year loan, with a grace period of two years, when the price per barrel of oil was between US$50 and US$100, and; 35%, when the price was below US$50. The interest rate was 2% per annum; with the agreement being renewed annually.

The Cabinet decided on January 16, 2006, to use proceeds from the Petro Caribé fund to reduce the overall cost of domestic debt; reduce the cost of energy through alternative sources; upgrade and expand infrastructure; social programmes targeted at the vulnerable, and; modernization of sectors that could expand economic development, through earning or saving foreign exchange (GOJ 2006).

Unfortunately, the Petro Caribé Fund, like the National Housing Trust (NHT), was repeatedly tapped by the Government for budgetary support, unrelated to their mandates (see GOJ 2014c, 37); while funds were disbursed to distressed entities like the Sugar Company of Jamaica, Air Jamaica, and US$12 million to the Government (Shaw 2008, 4). These governance decisions were clearly contrary to prudent fiscal management. There were also irregularities in the fiscal management of the related Jamaica Develop Infrastructure Programme (JDIP), according to the Auditor General (2011).

7. The Jamaica Development Infrastructure Programme

On June 29, 2010, Minister Shaw presented a Government Guarantee for a fifteen (15) year 6% loan of US$340 million, from the EXIM Bank of China, to finance road improvement and rehabilitation works, costing US$400 million. Jamaica was required to find 15%. The loan was to be serviced from a Road Maintenance Fund (RMF) created by the Patterson administration in 1999, to accumulate revenues from a 31% tax on petrol. At that time, the JLP was accused of instigating what is now known as the **'1999 gas riots'**, which resulted in death and mayhem, and a rolling back of the tax, by 50%.

Yet, by April 2009 the Golding-led JLP administration increased the burden on taxpayers by adding a Special Consumption Tax (SCT) of J$8.75 more per litre on fuel. He promised that 20% of this tax would be used for road maintenance. This was to be increased to 35% in 2010 and 50% in 2011 – totalling J$3 billion.

Minister Shaw reported that J$4.8 billion was collected through this SCT, with $960 million being set aside for road maintenance. By March 2011 he reported that $1.7 billion had been transferred from the SCT to the Road Maintenance Fund (RMF). However, a November 2011 Auditor General's (AG) investigation found that:

- The amount transferred was really $667.186 million, and; $761.6 million directly to the National Works Agency (NWA);
- Waivers totalling J$1.25 billion was granted to three importers, from May 2009 to June 2010;
- There was no evidence that there was consultation or prior approval by the relevant ministries and agencies;
- SCT funds were used to pay outstanding debts of the NWA, and;
- The projected cash flows from the Road Maintenance Fund (RMF) could only service the first two years of the fifteen years loan.

The Auditor General concluded that these findings indicated "instances of breaches of the Road Maintenance Fund Act and failure by the Ministry of Transport and Works to observe the wishes of Parliament" (AG 2011, 12). Still, the SCT was again increased in 2015, even as the high cost of energy continues to undermine Jamaica's economic development, while roads constructed and 'repaired' up to 2021, have been repeatedly

Chapter 5: Findings – Public Debt and Governance in Jamaica

undermined, eroded, or destroyed after periods of moderate to heavy rainfall lasting for less than twenty-four hours.

8. Wasteful Expenditure on Energy

The high cost of energy has been increasing the cost of doing business in Jamaica, and; contributed to Jamaica's indebtedness for decades. Meanwhile, politicians have continued to make repeated commitments to address this problem, while expending large sums of money on energy projects, without achieving the touted cost-reduction objectives.

This started as early as 1983 when Utilities Minister Pearnel Charles presented a proposal to purchase a power generating barge from the USA for US$6.8 million. This required a US$1.8 million deposit, with US$900,000 paid upfront for training and support services. This barge was reportedly taken from Guam in the Pacific, and; was reportedly capable of producing only 10 of its 25 megawatts of power-generating capacity.

The persons trained were reportedly unable to improve the condition or efficiency of the barge, though US$400,000 had been spent to replace tubes and other parts of the boiler. The project failed, resulting in a significant economic cost to Jamaica (Hansard 1983/84).

The profligacy continued as the JLP and PNP administrations are reported to have collectively spent US$2.8 million out of a budgeted US$5.4 million from 2007 to 2012, on a Liquefied Natural Gas (LNG) project, which was later scrapped, and the oversight committee dissolved (Thompson 2012). A new bidding process was botched and again delayed in 2014, while Jamaica's energy costs soared, and debt obligations expanded.

9. Misuse of Capital Development Fund (CDF)

The Capital Development Fund (CDF) was built up from the bauxite levy introduced by Prime Minister Michael Manley, to finance capital projects in Jamaica. On October 2, 1980, Minister

Chapter 5: Findings – Public Debt and Governance in Jamaica

Small presented a resolution to transfer J$80 million from the CDF to the Consolidated Fund (the government's main account) to meet recurrent expenditure - contrary to the CDF's originally stated purpose. This was repeated for decades until in 2008 Prime Minister Bruce Golding admitted how awkward it was to use the CDF for ventures other than special capital projects in "those communities that generate the bauxite" (p. 3). A senior bauxite executive interviewed, expressed similar sentiments, saying:

> Something I have always put forward is that just a small portion of the levy should go back into the communities where there is active mining, and that doesn't happen. Ten cents of each dollar for instance, that we contribute back into our mining area would make a huge difference to schools, to roads, to water supply, to housing in the areas. (pers. comm. 2011)

The executive concluded that successive administrations have not managed the CDF effectively, leading to poor community development.

10. Profligacy in Agriculture - Spring Plains Wastage

Jamaica has thousands of acres of arable land, and could easily be a net exporter of agricultural produce. Yet, major financial losses have been incurred by the government of Jamaica on failed projects, including the six hundred (600) acre Spring Plains project, embarked on to replace sugarcane and banana with winter vegetables (Seaga 1983).

The project lasted for three (3) years and was abandoned, after incurring losses totalling $48 million, due to inadequacies in planning, management, and crop choice (Ahmed 2001, 9).

11. More Profligacy in Agriculture - Sugar Company of Jamaica

Similarly costly was the Sugar Company of Jamaica (SCJ) which was purchased by the Government of Jamaica (GOJ) in 1998.

Chapter 5: Findings – Public Debt and Governance in Jamaica

From March 1998 to February 2001, "approximately $5.7 billion was advanced to or on behalf of the SCJ. …there was considerable debt outstanding, statutory deductions not paid, [and] a variety of trade creditors were owed funds" (Davies 2002, 2).

By 2007, Mr Shaw reported that that the SCJ debts grew by approximately J$2 billion per year, to reach $21 billion by 2007. By 2009 Minister Tufton reported that the SCJ was bankrupt.

A Chinese company COMPLANT, then reportedly purchased the SCJ's assets of the Frome, Bernard Lodge, and Moneymusk Estates for US$9 million, with a fifty-year (renewable) lease of 18,000 hectares of land, at the very low price of US$35 per hectare [US$14.16/acre] (Gordon 2011).

The Government of Jamaica could have avoided this excessive Sugar Company of Jamaica (SCJ) debt burden, as divestment of the SCJ, and privatization of Air Jamaica had been placed before Parliament as early as 1994 (GOJ 1994). Why wasn't it divested? Yet, by 2011 Minister Shaw reported that CAP, Air Jamaica, and the SCJ were still costing the economy J$27 to $30 billion per year. From the time of SCJ's acquisition in 1998 to 2011, Jamaica's public debt increased from J$242.82 billion to J$1.63 trillion.

12. Clarendon Alumina Production (CAP): US$360 M Losses

The Clarendon Alumina Production Company (CAP) was formed in 1985, in response to the closure of the JAMALCO (formerly Alcoa) refinery. Alcoa later requested and became a partner of CAP. The GOJ decided on a fifty-fifty joint venture, and spent US$115 million on capital expansion, though the company was facing major financial challenges (Golding 2009). From 2000 to 2002 debts totalling US$190 million at 9.5% and 10.48% were incurred for CAP, to "assist the country's fiscal budget, fund the refinery and residue disposal lake expansion project, and undertake a capital sustaining project" (Shaw 2009, 5).

Minister Davies then presented a resolution for a US$200

Chapter 5: Findings – Public Debt and Governance in Jamaica

million Government Guarantee for CAP, saying the Board had submitted a proposal that would return the company to profitability (Ministry Paper 87/06). Bear Stearns was then engaged to arrange and underwrite this long-term fixed-rate facility to access the funds on the international markets. At the time CAP owed US$20 million to the Accountant General, and US$14 million to Jamaica Bauxite Mining.

As was the case with the disposal of the FINSAC assets, the normal process of tabling, and allowing Parliamentarians time to review this US$200 million contingent debt, was bypassed. Mr Shaw chided Minister Davies for this, and; the fixed price of under US$240 per ton at which the bauxite/alumina was presumably contracted. By December 2008 CAP's debt increased to US$504 million (Golding 2009). Yet, in January 2009 Minister Shaw presented a resolution to provide another Government Guarantee of US$127.7 million to be paid to Alcoa on behalf of CAP. He also reported that Jamaica had lost significant revenues, as the contracted fixed price was US$180 per ton, and not $240 as touted. Meanwhile, the London Metal Exchange price was US$491 per ton. He noted that as a consequence, CAP was costing the country an additional US$16 million per month. Prime Minister Golding added that CAP's interest alone, of US$2.35 million per month, was more than pension payments to government workers, or the cost of the police and justice system combined (2009).

Recall earlier discussion on the impact of debt on declining social service expenditure allocations by the government. Four major governance decisions led to these costs, and further debt accumulation:

- Poor borrowing decision by the government, as the profitability promised by Minister Davies never materialized, after the US$200 million 9% bond was issued;
- The fixed-price contract by the PNP, and; the forward sale ten-year contract (1986 to 1996) by the JLP which led to major losses when market prices increased to Jamaica's

Chapter 5: Findings – Public Debt and Governance in Jamaica

detriment (having contractually agreed to sell at a significantly lower price);
- The GOJ having to find its portion of the required funds for expansion, while simultaneously servicing CAP's debts, with little or no contribution from Alcoa.

Dr. Davies later accused the Seaga administration of carrying out the advanced sale of bauxite and alumina, arguing that Jamaica was indebted to Marc Rich, and others in the 1980s; while Prime Minister Manley chose not to disclose the full impact of this on the national debt (1998, 230-234). This was not refuted. Marc Rich, an alleged related party to Alcoa/CAP, reportedly benefited greatly from the largesse of successive Jamaican administrations. As Barclay and Girvan reported:

> In the early 1980s, he developed close ties to the then Prime Minister, Edward Seaga, loaning the country more than US$200 million, donating US$45,000 to send the country's track and field team to the 1984 Olympics and underwriting the cost of sending the bobsled team to the 1988 Winter Olympics (Tully, 1988; Juravich and Bronfenbrenner, 2000). In 1986, when the government re-opened the Jamalco plant, which was temporarily closed by Alcoa in 1985 during the protracted decline in the international aluminium industry, it entered into a ten-year agreement with Marc Rich whereby he purchased more than 4 million tons of alumina at less than one-half of the market rate (Juravich and Bronfenbrenner, 2000).
>
> Despite Prime Minister Michael Manley's promises to end his predecessor's ties to Marc Rich, he was forced to deepen them when he returned to office in 1989 (Mokhiber and Weissman, 2001). Faced with intense pressure from the IMF to raise more than US$50 million, Manley found it convenient to accept Rich's offer of US$50 million as a cash advance against future alumina production. (2008, 29)

By the time the JLP entered the 2009 Article IV Consultation with the IMF, losses from CAP and Air Jamaica were estimated at 3% of GDP. Jamaica's Gross value added to GDP from mining declined significantly over this period - 1990 to 2010 (see figure 5.8).

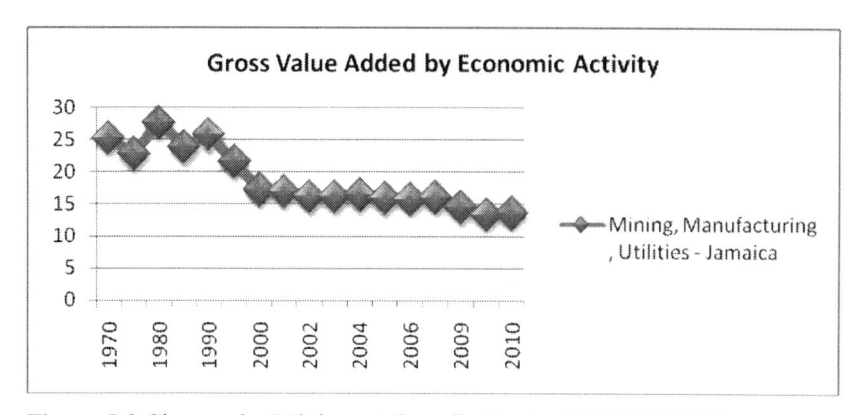

Chapter 5: Findings – Public Debt and Governance in Jamaica

Figure 5.8 Changes in (Mining…) Contribution to GDP (UN 2011)

CAP's estimated losses were US$360 million, that was US$185 million in 2007; with further losses of US$175 million which was expected up to 2012 (IMF 2011, 11).

13. AIR JAMAICA – Government Guarantees

Like CAP, Air Jamaica had been a drain on the public purse for many years. In 1994 its liabilities, excluding redundancy and termination payments, totalled J$2.12 billion; with total estimated cost of divestment being J$2.45 billion. Several Government Guarantees were later granted in Air Jamaica's favour, including one for US$101.8 million in June 2009, and another for $1.8 billion in December 2009 (at 22.51% and 19.04%) for global bonds issued through NCB (see Ministry Papers 51 and 121/09).

After several subsidies and significant losses before and after Sandals Resorts hotelier Butch Stewart took control of the airline, Air Jamaica was taken over by Caribbean Airlines of Trinidad and Tobago in 2010. By December its remaining debts reached J$10 billion per year (Shaw 2010, 4); with divestment costs estimated at J$14 billion by 2011 (Jackson, 2011).

Chapter 5: Findings – Public Debt and Governance in Jamaica

More Quantitative Findings

Jamaica reached its highest percentage of Debt-to-GDP during the 1980s, when large inflows of **external debt**, cause the country's debt to reach highest historical level of 212%. The majority of this was external debt, payable in foreign currency.

The next highest build-up was during the early 1990s, and 2000s, when FINSAC, followed by large global bond issues, and low foreign exchange (FEX) inflows, led to further borrowing to pay off old debt, and meet budgetary obligations (see figure 5.9 below).

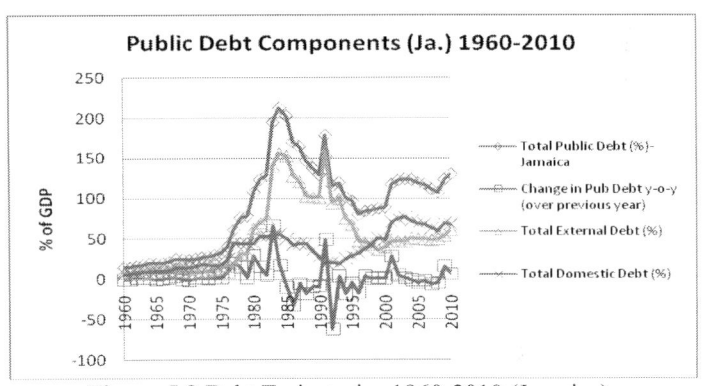

Figure 5.9 Debt Trajectories 1960-2010 (Jamaica)

To examine the role that government had played, through their style of governance, in fostering this build-up of debt, it was useful to examine some macro-economic and social (outcome) indicators of governance decisions in Jamaica, with the variables below, included in the initial model.

The dependent variable, External Debt-to-GDP (%), was deemed the best proxy for the dependent variable, "build-up of debt." The predictors (independent variables) for the "role of governance" were proxied by the following:

    i.   Population – available size of labour pool
    ii. Inflation Rate [INFRAT]– effectiveness of liquidity management

Chapter 5: Findings – Public Debt and Governance in Jamaica

    iii.   Unemployment Rate [UNEMP]– effectiveness in managing idle capacity
    iv.   Fiscal Balance % - efficiency in managing fiscal resources
    v.   Exports of Goods and Services as % of GDP [EXPRT] - as a measure of 'competitiveness'
    vi.   Allocation to Education % [ALLED] – investment in human capital development
    vii.   Allocation to National Security % [ALLNS]– investment in risk reduction, through crime-fighting capabilities, and strengthening the rule of law
    viii.   Life Expectancy at Birth [LEB]- expected usefulness of labour, as a factor of production

The choice of variables for this model was influenced by the theory (Acemoglu et al 2003; Henry and Miller 2008; Williams and Siddique 2005, and; Jalles 2011), findings from the Hansard (1962-2010), Economic and Social Survey of Jamaica (multiple copies), Bank of Jamaica, Auditor General, IMF, and World Bank reports. The predictors in the model were then examined for significance, resulting in a model which was created to test the relationships.

Result: There was a statistically significant association between External Public Debt as a % of GDP and Inflation Rate(%), Unemployment Rate(%), Life Expectancy at Birth, Allocation to Education(%), Allocation to National Security(%), and Exports of Goods and Services(%), from 1962 to 2010. See policy implications and additional recommendations in **Volume II** of this publication (to come).

GROSS FIXED CAPITAL FORMATION
– Expenditure on Infrastructural Projects –

Since Independence, Jamaica's investment in fixed capital has changed in line with the economic strategies, and political ethos of the times:
- 1960-1979 Structural Change - Industrialization thrust;
- 1980 to 1989 Free Market/Liberalism - under IMF/WB austerity;

Chapter 5: Findings – Public Debt and Governance in Jamaica

- 1990 to 2000s Keynesian – large debt-financed infrastructural projects.

Table 5.7 GFCF as a percentage of GDP - Averaged by Decade

	1960-69	1970-79	1980-89	1990-99	2000-08
Jamaica (%)	27.7	21.6	20.1	26.9	28.9
Ranking	7	67	96	37	20
# of countries ranked	76	113	153	181	177

Source: World Bank (2011, 51) – extracted from Table 1.9

The infrastructural works, for which funds were borrowed, form part of Jamaica's Gross Fixed Capital Formation (GFCF). Jamaica's GFCF increased from just over J$300 million in the 1970s to $690 million by 1980; $8.36 billion by 1990, and; almost $100 billion by the year 2000 (ESSJ).

Much of the infrastructural expenditure in the 1980s was geared at facilitating foreign direct investments (FDI), particularly for the garment free zones.

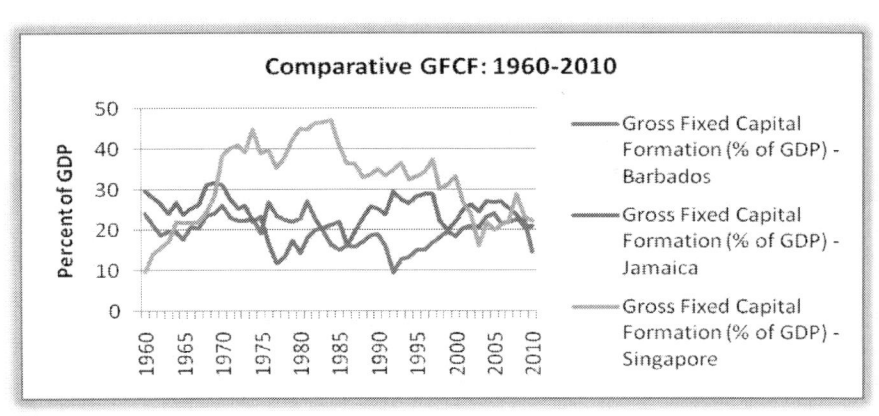

Figure 5.10 Comparative Gross Fixed Capital Formation to GDP 1960-2010 (WB)

Jamaica's GFCF exceeded those of Singapore and Barbados from the early to late 1960s, and; again from 2000 to around 2007. Yet, both countries have surpassed Jamaica on most measures of development from the mid-1970s to the present. During the 1960s to 1970s Jamaica's capital expenditure was focused on building schools, hospitals, and infrastructure geared at human capital, and

Chapter 5: Findings – Public Debt and Governance in Jamaica

economic development. During the 1980s there was a significant focus on expanding infrastructure for garment Free Zones. From the 1990s onward the emphasis was on the construction of highways, stadia, an airport, a cruise-shipping port, and other capital projects. In 2010 $231.5 billion was spent on GFCF (ESSJ).

The combined cost for the subset of capital projects and programmes discussed in this publication, which have featured prominently in international reports, Parliamentary debates, and public discourse on Jamaica's indebtedness, totalled more than **J$530 billion**, including debt and accumulated interest to maturity on global bonds issued to finance them.

Examination of these projects and programmes was not in the initial research plan. However, I spent over five (5) months in the Library of Parliament at Gordon House in Jamaica, dedicated to reviewing governance decisions in the Hansards and Ministry Papers, these programmes and projects above were prominent in the discourse during a majority of the Parliamentary sittings from as early as 1962.

Concurrently, discrepancies highlighted in reports from the Office of the Contractor General, Auditor General, IMF, World Bank, other multilateral partners to the GOJ, and local studies (dissertations), relating to some of these projects and programmes, made it difficult, and morally untenable, to exclude them.

Subsequent rapid deterioration of infrastructure, and recurring annual losses incurred from many of them, demonstrate a level of arbitrariness in the Jamaican government's borrowing and expenditure decisions. To aggravate the problem, major overruns on several of the externally financed projects, and rapid devaluation of the Jamaican dollar, further expanded Jamaica's public debt (OCG reports multiple copies).

As Nurkes (1953) pointed out, it may be advantageous for a government to access external loan funding for capital expenditure, if they are used for economic development in the domestic sphere, within a well-thought-out and executed programme. This has not generally been the case in Jamaica.

Chapter 5: Findings – Public Debt and Governance in Jamaica

Several of these projects and programmes which have been, and still are operating at significant losses, have been deemed infeasible, or have not yielded the touted benefits to Jamaica including the:

- US$51.7M Montego Bay Convention Center.
- US$30M Trelawny Multi-Purpose Stadium (Golding 2009).
- J$248M Sligoville Stadium (extensively damaged).
- US$300M Ian Flemming International Airport (Thame 2011).
- INTEC/Net-Serv $1.3B to $3.9B (Paulwell 2001, 1-2; Samuda 2002).
- US$393M HW2000 Phase1 (Shaw, 2002).
- J$13.2B HW2000 Phase 2 (Thame 2006).
- US$122M Falmouth Cruise Shipping Pier (Pinnock 2012).
- US$65.4M Palisadoes Shoreline project.

The two stadia which were built for Cricket World Cup 2007 have not been used much thereafter; while millions of dollars are still being spent on staffing and maintenance. When this researcher visited the sites to take photographs for this study in 2012 and 2013, some 'workers' were simply present, but not occupied.

This was totally unlike the 1950s and very early 1960s when infrastructural development (GFCF) was centred on creating a strong industrial base. This included the construction of schools, colleges, hospitals, and transportation infrastructure, to develop Jamaica's technical and human capital, to meet labour and industry demands. The results were seen in the levels of economic growth during that period.

The High Cost of Arbitrary Borrowing

As the governance decisions discussed have shown, successive administrations (PNP and JLP) have demonstrated a proclivity to arbitrarily borrow, often, without a defined strategic plan for utilizing the inflows, resulting in recurrent losses. This has contributed to Jamaica's rapid public debt accumulation.

Chapter 5: Findings – Public Debt and Governance in Jamaica

To aggravate the governance and public debt problem, leaders of both the JLP and PNP have demonstrated a tendency to borrow, then celebrate the large amounts they were able to borrow, particularly overseas, while Jamaica's public debt increased to unsustainable levels. For example, when Mr Shaw complained that the stock of debt had increased between 12 and 13 fold from 1989 to 2001, Dr Davies justified his latest borrowing by gloating that it was the Canadian Imperial Bank of Commerce (CIBC) that had approached and offered his administration a loan of US$75 million, which they just accepted. An additional US$100 million was accessed shortly thereafter, through a local private placement (2001).

By December 2001 he again celebrated the first Security and Exchange Commission (SEC) endorsed, twenty-year GOJ global bond, issued to access an additional US$250 million, at 11.625%, saying it would provide a "broader distribution of GOJ bonds and faster access to the markets in the future" (p. 3). He took pride in noting that this was the longest tenure ever launched on the international capital market by any administration in Jamaica.

Bear in mind that governments issuing global bonds can choose to offer bonds of shorter tenures, with a callable feature, to better monitor changes in the marketplace, and take advantage of downward movements in interest rates. Rapid currency depreciation of more than 130% since the issuance of that global bond in 2001, has significantly increased the debt service cost of these bonds, which the Minister said was to "reduce the demand by the Ministry of Finance for financing on the domestic market, thus assisting in reduction in interest rates" (Davies 2001, 3).

Domestic interest rates fell below 7% by March 2012, while this 11.625% debt must be repaid in US dollars, up to the year 2022. There was a subsequent extension of the maturity date on these bonds. However, there was no clear indication I the coupon rate of 11.625% was adjusted. Meanwhile Oppenheimer (2014) had reported that coupon (interest) rates on Barbados' 2019, 2021, 2022, and 2035 global bonds were close to 7%.

Chapter 5: Findings – Public Debt and Governance in Jamaica

No sustainable development-related plan was outlined for the funds borrowed. The Prospectus simply stated that the US$250 million was borrowed for "general budgetary purposes and to finance existing debt" (GOJ 2001, 6). Opposition Member Samuda argued against using the funds for housekeeping matters, rather than paying out existing debt. Dr Davies conceded that his plan had been changed, and; funds expected from the World Bank would have been used to pay out the FINSAC notes, Local Registered Stock (LRS), and the National Commercial Bank (NCB).

The dialogue between the political parties in Parliament presented debt acquisition as though it were a conquest. Minister Davies later conceded that "[W]e have also taken on more debt than we had anticipated because of the greater than projected response from the International Capital Market" (2002, 3). This arbitrary debt accumulation continued in 2011 when Minister Shaw said his reason for taking on J$11 billion of un-programmed debt during the global recession, was because of "the low interest and the deal that was available" (Shaw 2011). When interest rates fell significantly after the recession, Jamaica was left with these high-cost debts, due and payable up to, and beyond 2022.

Conclusion

The character of governance in Jamaica, as demonstrated by the findings presented, has resulted in rapid debt accumulation, without a commensurate improvement in macroeconomic performance. Additionally, unstable inflation and rapid currency devaluation (at times prescribed in loan agreements) have not enhanced export competitiveness, but instead, have made US$ denominated domestic, external, and inflation-indexed debts very expensive and unpredictable. These poor governance decisions have increased debt levels, and depleted funds required to drive human capital development and growth. Consistent with the findings presented, the World Bank noted that:

Chapter 5: Findings – Public Debt and Governance in Jamaica

> Jamaica performs very poorly on many dimensions of governance. Jamaica's most evident and severe problem is its crime environment, which erodes social stability and casts doubt on the rule of law. In addition, Jamaica also performs poorly on its legal system…. Businessmen also perceive corruption to be particularly serious in Jamaica owing to lack of transparency. (WB 2011, 24)

Greater prudence and stronger institutional controls are required to enhance the quality of governance in Jamaica. This can help to deter a Minister or the Cabinet, from incurring additional debt, by wantonly by-passing legislative provisions, amending laws to satisfy a political objective and fast-tracking programmes without probity.

Chapter Six provides answers to Questions 3 and 4, examining Jamaica's debt, economic performance, and global governance ratings, against those of its comparators, Barbados and Singapore. Chapter Seven concludes.

Chapter 6

FURTHER FINDINGS: Comparators – Jamaica, Barbados, and Singapore

6.1 Introduction

A popular question in the development literature is: Why do some countries experience consistent levels of economic growth while others do not? Economic growth - the denominator - is as essential in reducing a country's Debt-to-GDP ratio, as is the level of debt - the numerator.

This chapter looks at this and other indicators and presents a comparative analysis of three former British colonies – Jamaica, Barbados, and Singapore, which faced similar conditions at independence but have experienced vastly different economic and social outcomes. Let's examine Jamaica's performance in relation to the comparator countries.

6.2 Debt and Economic Performance

Question 3: *How do Jamaica's public debt and economic performance compare to that of Barbados and Singapore?*

At Independence in 1962, Jamaica was ahead of Barbados and Singapore in terms of currency value (exchange rate), economic openness, level of industrialization, and per capita GDP. Jamaica now has much higher levels of external debt than both, and; lags behind them on most economic, development, and global governance indicators.

Chapter 6: Further Findings – Comparators: Jamaica, Barbados, and Singapore

Comparative Public Debt

Table 6.1 Total Public Debt-to-GDP (%) Indicators

INDICATOR	Jamaica	Barbados	Singapore
Debt-to-GDP % (2010)	130.00	97.00	99.00
Mean Debt-to-GDP % (1960-2010)	89.47	47.21	69.22
Standard Deviation of Debt-to-GDP%	55.88	25.57	24.43
External Debt as % of GDP 2010	61.30	30.70	Insignificant

Source: National Authorities; World Bank; Abbas et al (2010); IMF (2010; 2014)

Jamaica also had the highest Total Debt as a percentage of GDP, and Mean Debt, of all three countries from 1960 to 2010 (see figs. 6.1-6.3).

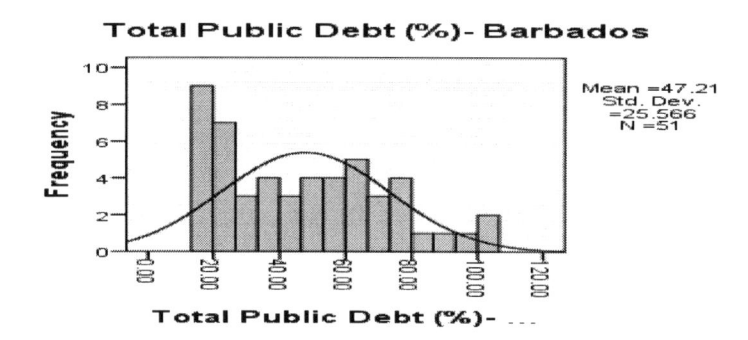

Figure 6.1 Barbados' Total Public Debt 1960-2010

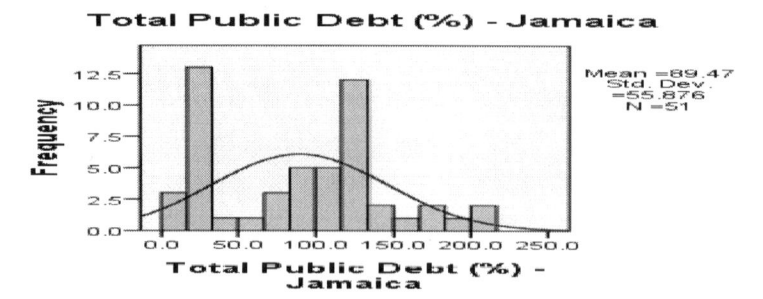

Figure 6.2 Jamaica's Total Public Debt 1960-2010

Chapter 6: Further Findings – Comparators: Jamaica, Barbados, and Singapore

Total Public Debt (%) - Singapore

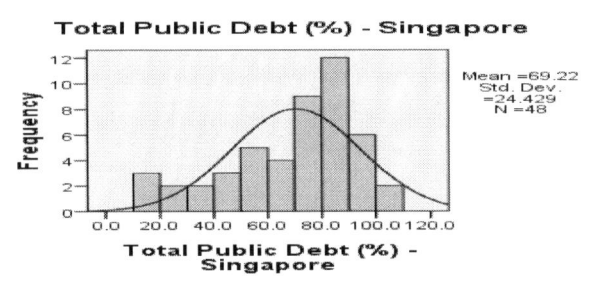

Mean =69.22
Std. Dev. =24.429
N =48

Figure 6.3 Singapore's Total Public Debt 1960-2010

As small, open, export-dependent, countries, all three faced similar economic challenges over the period being reviewed. Yet, there was much more volatility in Jamaica's total public Debt-to-GDP (%) levels, as seen in the standard deviation of debt, showing that Jamaica borrowed in a more erratic fashion.

Table 6.2 Comparative Public Debt-to-GDP (%) - 5 Yrs

	JAMAICA	BARBADOS	SINGAPORE
1965	19.5	22.83	17.6
1970	23.6	16.10	48.2
1975	32.2	25.76	52.5
1980	107.4	28.50	72.3
1985	202.7	45.50	82.7
1990	128.7	54.00	71.1
1995	96.9	66.30	70.1
2000	88.6	64.30	82.6
2005	119.1	77.60	95.8
2010	130	97	99.1

Source: National Authorities; World Bank; Abbas et al (2010); IMF (2010; 2014)

A deeper examination of the data showed that Barbados and Singapore also borrowed less, on average, than Jamaica, in relation to their national income (GDP) from 1980 to 2010 (see Table 6.2 and Figure 6.4).

Chapter 6: Further Findings – Comparators: Jamaica, Barbados, and Singapore

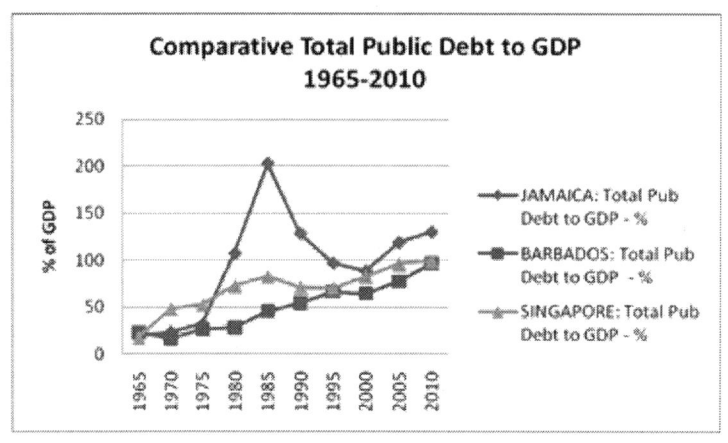

Figure 6.4 Comparative Total Public Debt-to-GDP (%)
Data Source: World Bank; Abbas et al; IMF

The Jamaican authorities had set a Debt-to-GDP target of 100% by 2016 (GOJ 2014). Barbados, on the other hand, had set a Debt-to-GDP target of 85% by 2018/19 (IMF 2014). Neither Singapore nor the IMF provided projections for Debt-to-GDP for that country.

Debt Structure - JAMAICA

For many years, International Financial Institutions, and analysts had focused mainly on Jamaica's external debt. During the mid-1990s the Jamaican authorities ended their borrowing relationship with the IMF, and skewed borrowings to the domestic market, offering returns in excess of 40% to attract lenders. Domestic debt as a percentage of GDP then increased from 19% in 1991 to 77% by 2003.

As investments in Government paper became more attractive than in the real sector, GDP growth slowed. Concurrently, Jamaica's external debt that had expanded exponentially during the 1980s to early 1990s, decreased from 159% to 47% from 1991 to 2003. This decline in external debt masked the real public debt

Chapter 6: Further Findings – Comparators: Jamaica, Barbados, and Singapore

challenge, and; caused the burgeoning high-priced domestic debt to remain 'under the radar' until the FINSAC crisis.

Note the transition point in Figure 6.5. This highlights the need for local and international stakeholders to place a greater focus on Total Debt-to-GDP, in order to recognize the early warning signs of a potential crisis.

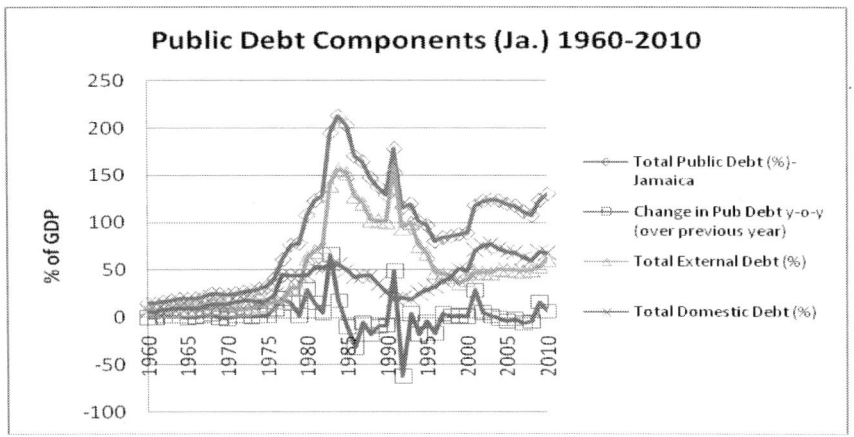

Figure 6.5 Public Debt-to-GDP (%) Components 1960-2010
Data Source: World Bank; Abbas et al; IMF

Debt Structure - BARBADOS

Bennett (1988) noted that though Jamaica and Barbados faced increased indebtedness and significant capital flight in the 1970s, Barbados "performed very well during the period from 1976 to 1980" (pp. 57-8). However, "[e]xcessive borrowing from the Central Bank (i.e. money creation) in 1981-82 and 1989-91 was partially responsible for the deterioration in the international reserves of the country and thus, the need to borrow from the ... IMF in 1982 and 1991" (ECLAC 2001, 42).

Barbados' external debt peaked above 25% in 1991. See Figure 6.6 which shows change in year-over-year (at 5 year intervals), that is, previous five year's Debt/GDP (%) - current years 5 year's Debt/GDP (%). External debt then declined

Chapter 6: Further Findings – Comparators: Jamaica, Barbados, and Singapore

substantially until 2000/01. It then fluctuated between 24% and 30%; while domestic debt has increased from 33% in 1991 to 72% by 2010.

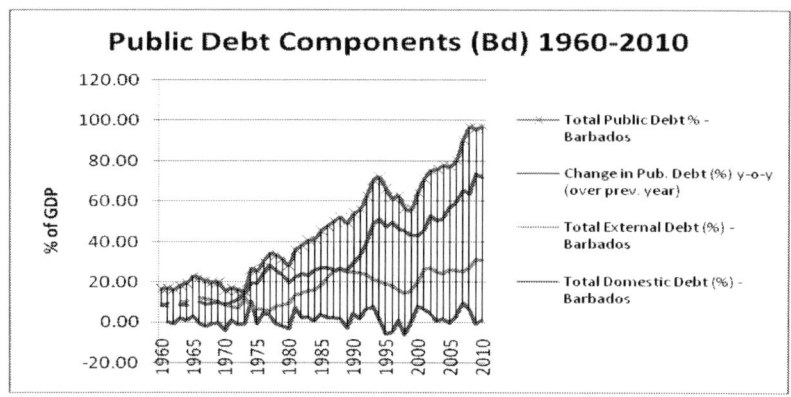

Figure 6.6 Total Public Debt-to-GDP (%) Barbados-1960-2010
Data Source: World Bank; Abbas et al; IMF

Unlike Jamaica, Barbados' "[e]xternal debt is mostly long-term and has a favourable amortization profile; while domestic debt is held by relatively stable investors, including the domestic financial system and the National Insurance Scheme" (IMF 2011, 18).

When the IMF recommended stabilization measures, the authorities and people of Barbados implemented the required structural reforms and cauterized the debt. Osei noted that the latter process worked effectively thrice in Barbados, but not in Jamaica, possibly due to "the nature of politics and the immediate circumstances of each country prior to the introduction of the policy, political culture, vibrancy of trade unions, policy style and state capacities for policy management" (2002, 1).

Chapter 6: Further Findings – Comparators: Jamaica, Barbados, and Singapore

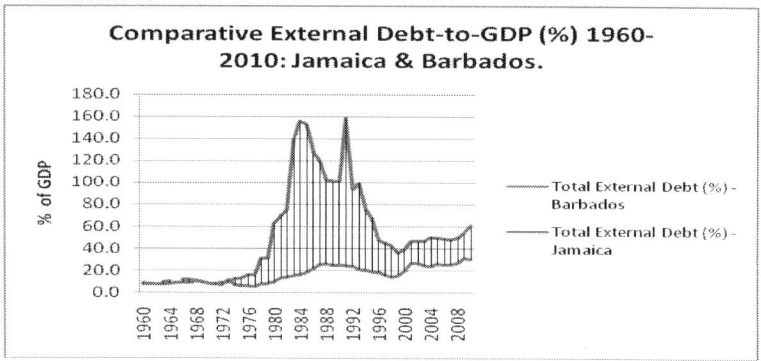

Figure 6.7 Comparative Ext. Debt-to-GDP (%):1960-2010
Data Source: World Bank; Abbas et al; IMF

Barbados' external Debt-to-GDP was low and declining, at 31% in 2010, compared to 62% for Jamaica.

Debt Structure - SINGAPORE

Singapore's debt structure is somewhat different from those of Jamaica and Barbados, as its domestic debt (mainly accessed through the Central Providence Fund or CPF that was introduced by Lee Kuan Yew) is approximately equivalent to its total debt. "Singapore does not borrow to spend...Proceeds from Singapore government's borrowing are invested" (SG 2011, 6).

Singapore Registered Stocks and Bonds account for the largest portion of their domestic debt; followed by Treasury Bills and Advance Deposits. Consequently, only Total Debt as a percentage of GDP is shown in Figure 6.8 below.

The Accountant General's Department of Singapore (2019) reported that the country's public debt (Total outstanding Government Borrowing) was S$562 billion, comprised of Singapore Saving Bonds (SSB), Treasury Bills (T-bills), Singapore Government Securities (SSG) Bonds, and Special Singapore Government Securities (SSGS).

Chapter 6: Further Findings – Comparators: Jamaica, Barbados, and Singapore

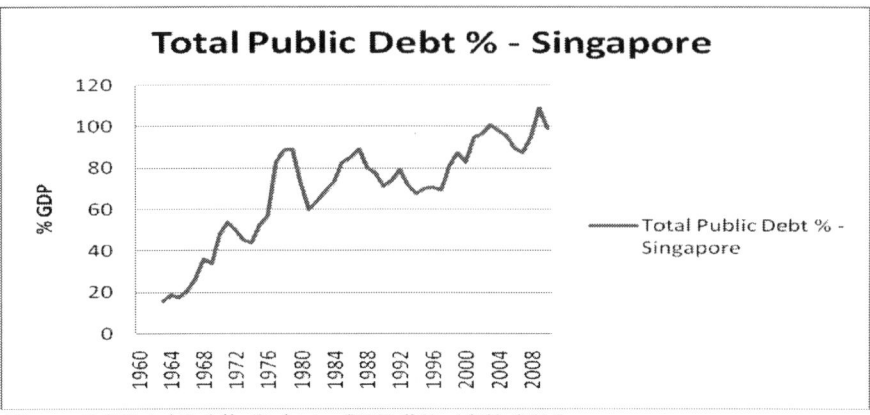

Figure 6.8 Total Public Debt-to-GDP (%): 1960-2010
Data Source: World Bank; Abbas et al; IMF

During the 1980s to early 1990s, the government of Singapore borrowed from the United Kingdom Special Aid Fund, World Bank (IBRD), Asian Development Bank, and others. Up to 2010, they had not borrowed externally since 1994 (SG 2011).

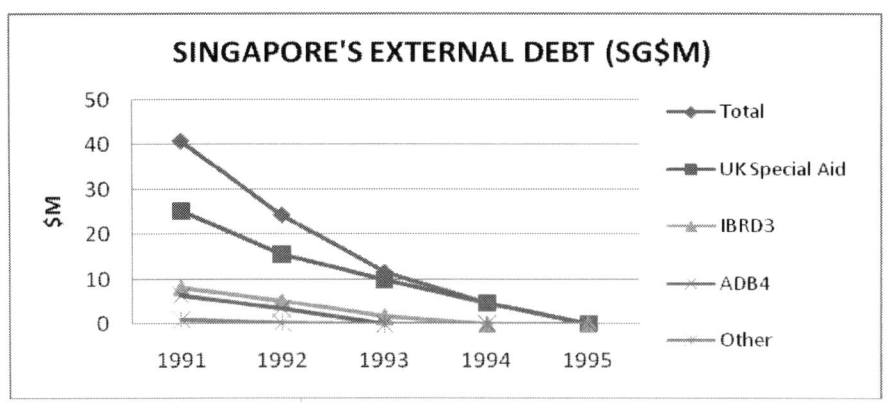

Figure 6.9 Singapore's External Public Debt – Components
Data Source: Acc. Gen. and MAS Singapore

Comparative Economic and Human Development Indicators

Barbados and Singapore had long been lauded as protoypes for good governance among developing countries. Former Finance Minister Shaw considered Singapore a major economic power in

Chapter 6: Further Findings – Comparators: Jamaica, Barbados, and Singapore

the world, due to its quality of government and human development (1994, 103).

Then Finance Minister Phillips concurred, noting that compared to "other countries that started out independence at a lower point on the development scale, Jamaica has underperformed ... compared to countries like Singapore, which came to explore Jamaica as the model they wanted to follow" (2009, 3). The findings give credence to these views.

Table 6.3 Comparative Indicators Prior to, and Post-Independence

Indicator	JAMAICA 1960	JAMAICA 2010	BARBADOS 1960	BARBADOS 2010	SINGAPORE 1960	SINGAPORE 2010
Total Debt-to-GDP (%)	23.6	130	16.1	97	48.2	99
Per Capita GDP (current US$)	429	**5,274**	379	**15,035**	395	**41,122**
Average Life Expectancy	68	73	68	77	68	81
Exchange Rate (LCU to US$)	0.77	85.86	1.71	2.00	3.06	1.36

Source: World Bank; National statistical offices; Abbas et al (2010)

Prior to independence, Singapore had the highest Total Debt-to-GDP (%), and Barbados the lowest. At the end of our review period in 2010, Jamaica's Debt-to-GDP was more than 30% higher than both. The quality of governance (political, economic, and administrative decisions) is reflected in these results.

This is in part due to the comparative volatility of Jamaica's borrowing strategy (type of securities, frequency, and timing of maturities), rapid currency devaluations, high interest costs, and profligacy.

a) Per Capita GDP

The World Bank has concluded that good governance is critical to development, as observed by differences in per capita income, which has been deemed a reliable predictor of infant mortality, poverty, and illiteracy (Grindle 2010).

Chapter 6: Further Findings – Comparators: Jamaica, Barbados, and Singapore

In 1960 Jamaica was ahead of Barbados and Singapore in terms of development, as represented by per capita GDP of (US) $429, $379, and $395 respectively. By 2010 Singapore's per capita GDP was 8 times that of Jamaica, and Barbados 3 times (see table 6.3 and figure 6.10).

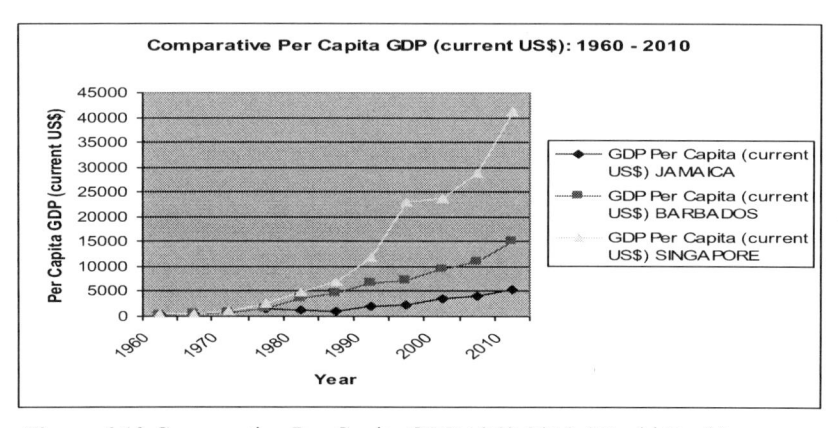

Figure 6.10 Comparative Per Capita GDP 1960-2010 (World Bank)

The significant take-off point between the three countries was around 1974/5, even while all three were facing high inflation and the world oil crisis. The macroeconomic strategies and institutional controls they employed in adversity (see Chapters 4 and 5) have resulted in the outcomes we now discuss.

b) Average Life Expectancy and Health Expenditure per Capita

Singapore and Barbados have allocated significant portions of their annual expenditure budget to areas targeted at development and growth (Lee 2000; ECLAC 2001; Downes 2004, 40).

Figure 6.11 shows comparative per capita Health expenditure for the three countries.

Chapter 6: Further Findings – Comparators: Jamaica, Barbados, and Singapore

Health Expenditure Per Capita (Current US$)

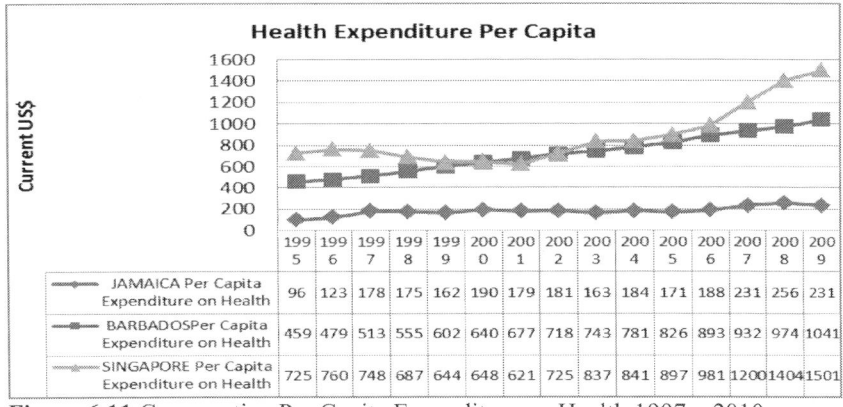

	1995	1996	1997	1998	1999	2000	2001	2002	2003	2004	2005	2006	2007	2008	2009
JAMAICA Per Capita Expenditure on Health	96	123	178	175	162	190	179	181	163	184	171	188	231	256	231
BARBADOS Per Capita Expenditure on Health	459	479	513	555	602	640	677	718	743	781	826	893	932	974	1041
SINGAPORE Per Capita Expenditure on Health	725	760	748	687	644	648	621	725	837	841	897	981	1200	1404	1501

Figure 6.11 Comparative Per Capita Expenditure on Health 1997 – 2010
Data Source: World Bank

Note how closely Barbados' Health expenditures trended with Singapore's from 1999 to 2006; while Jamaica's figures were well below the levels of both. According to the UN (2010), quality and ease of access to social services enhance life expectancy at birth, and by extension, development. This view led to a further examination of comparative Average Life Expectancy at birth, between the three countries.

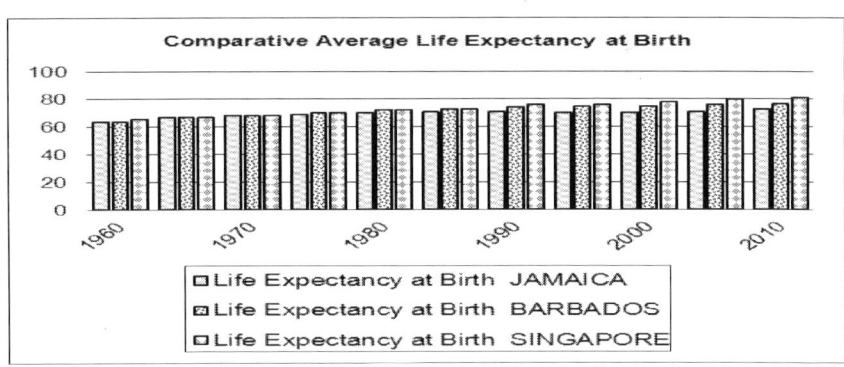

Figure 6.12 Comparative Average Life Expectancy 1960-2010 (WB)

Consistent with Expenditure on Health, Life Expectancy at birth increased by only 9 years for Jamaica, compared to 13 years for Barbados, and 15 years for Singapore, between 1960 and 2010. A healthy, well-educated population is likely to be more productive.

Chapter 6: Further Findings – Comparators: Jamaica, Barbados, and Singapore

c) The Outcomes - Productivity

Productivity outcomes reflect differences in the quality and impact of governance, through the development strategies employed by the government. Blavy (2006) analyzed panel data for 35 emerging economies and concluded that "low productivity is shown to be robustly associated with high levels of public debt" (p. 23). Productivity levels impact growth; while "[s]ustained growth ensures stability, which encourages investments and creates wealth" (Lee 2000, 106).

This symbiosis is inescapable, as sustained economic growth requires appropriate infrastructural development and the efficient deployment of capital and labour. A country's productivity level is measured by the amount of output for a given level of input. If we use 'GDP per Person Employed' as a proxy for productivity, we see from Figure 6.13, that both Singapore and Barbados have been significantly more productive than Jamaica over the period reviewed.

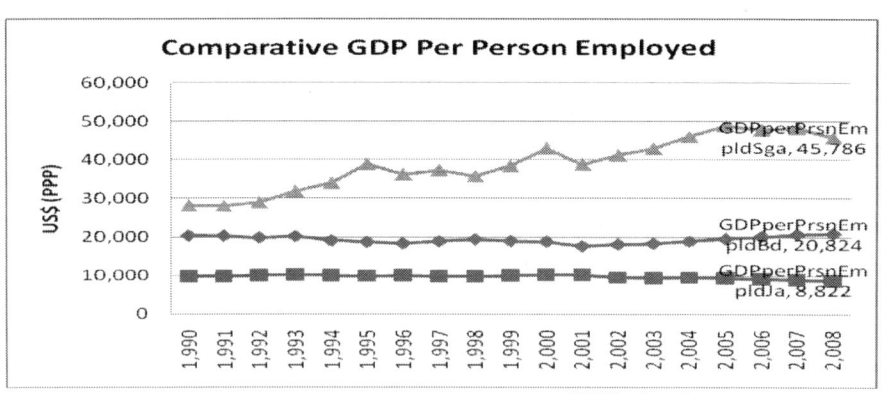

Figure 6.13 Comparative GDP per Person Employed (WB data)

Jamaica showed slight improvements between 1995 and 2001, averaging US$10,000 (PPP); then declined by over 16% to around US$8,800 (PPP) by 2008. Barbados on the other hand averaged US$20,000 up to 1993, declined by approximately 12% from 1994 to 2005, then increased to almost US$21,000 by 2008. Singapore

Chapter 6: Further Findings – Comparators: Jamaica, Barbados, and Singapore

averaged just under US$30,000 up to 1992, fluctuated between US$32,000 and $36,000 from 1993 to 1998; then increased consistently to well over US$45,000 by 2008.

Kuznets (1971) found that high rates of growth in Total Factor Productivity (TFP) were characteristic of almost every developed country he studied; so that productivity drives development.

Islam (1995), Hall and Jones (1999), and Easterly and Levine (2003) also found that TFP had a statistically significant impact on national income [GDP]. In fact, Klenow and Rodriguez-Clare (1997) concluded that roughly 90 percent of the differences in per capita GDP growth between countries were mainly due to differences in productivity levels.

Lucas (1988), Romer (1989), Greenwood, Herkowitz and Krusell (1997) all agreed that total factor productivity (TFP) can be attributed to factors such as investment-specific technical change.

Up to 2013, Jamaica continued to be dogged by low productivity levels, recurring budget deficits, high rates of unemployment, energy, and financial crises, resulting in repeated borrowing and exponential increases in public debt.

The current administration has stated that they are seeking to correct this through greater fiscal discipline, though they are yet to present a strategic plan to enhance human capital development and expansion of technological capacity to spur growth. Meanwhile, rapid currency depreciation continues to increase the interest rate risk in the debt portfolio.

d) Exchange Rate Decisions and Public Debt

The exchange rate bears a direct relationship to public debt. Rapid movements in exchange rates impact fiscal balances, through increased debt service obligations. Jamaica operates a floating exchange rate regime; while Barbados and Singapore operate fixed exchange rate regimes.

Chapter 6: Further Findings – Comparators: Jamaica, Barbados, and Singapore

Table 6.4 Comparative Exchange Rates

YEAR	JAMAICA	SINGAPORE	BARBADOS
1960	0.77	3.06	1.71
1965	0.77	3.06	1.71
1970	0.77	3.06	2.00
1975	0.91	2.49	2.02
1980	1.78	2.14	2.00
1985	5.50	2.11	2.00
1990	8.17	1.74	2.00
1995	39.80	1.41	2.00
2000	45.53	1.73	2.00
2005	64.58	1.66	2.00
2010	85.86	1.36	2.00

Source: BOJ; World Bank; MAS; & indexmundi.com

Jamaica

As table 6.4 shows, the policies and programmes of the Jamaican authorities have contributed to the depreciation of the currency by 9300% - from J$0.91 to US$1 in 1975, to $85.86 in 2010. By June 2015, the Jamaican dollar had depreciated by 12,670% (J$116.20 to US$1).

Bullock (2010) reported that since its transition from colonialism, Jamaica has operated several foreign exchange systems including sterling peg; US dollar peg; dual exchange rates; crawling peg; multiple exchange rates; auction; modified 'Dutch auction', and; an 'allocation' fixed-rate system. He concluded that "From the mid-1970s, however, exchange stems and stability have been negatively affected by an inability to sustain prudent fiscal management" (p. 1).

In 1985 PM Seaga reported that after several devaluations, US$210 million of foreign exchange reserves (NIR) in March 1972, was totally depleted, and replaced by a debt of US$554 million by 1980. The NIR remained negative throughout his tenure until he lost the 1989 election.

In less than twelve (12) weeks after taking office, the Manley administration announced a suspension of the foreign exchange Auction System and introduced a Fixed Exchange Rate System. By 1990, Acting PM Patterson replaced this with an Inter-Bank

Chapter 6: Further Findings – Comparators: Jamaica, Barbados, and Singapore

Foreign Exchange Trading System. This was the inception of the Bureaux de Change or Cambio system, where banks and later, authorized dealers could trade foreign exchange on their own accounts, instead of as agents of the Bank of Jamaica (central bank). Still, receipts had to be surrendered to the BOJ, who set the weighted average prevailing rate; while commercial banks surrendered a portion of their foreign exchange purchases.

Mr Seaga pleaded with the Manley/Patterson administration not to remove exchange controls in desperation; as it would lead to large outflows, while the country would require "more J-Dollars to service loans denominated in foreign exchange" (1991, 316-7). Still, the exchange rate was depreciated from J$21.57 to US$1 in 1991 to J$39.80 by 1995. Delong (2011), like Seaga, noted that borrowing in hard currency could be deleterious to developing countries' economies, as a depreciating currency makes foreign debt more expensive, and could lead to financial turbulence and vulnerabilities, with catastrophic consequences for growth and development (p. 2). Mr Seaga also lamented that the IMF sought to "use exchange rate adjustments to meet every problem in the economy", which was the basis of his dispute with them in 1985 (pers. comm. 2011).

Bullock (2010) concluded that Barbados' comparatively favourable macroeconomic performance relative to Jamaica was based on their commitment to fiscal prudence; which has helped to preserve the value of their currency (p. 1). The Jamaican dollar continues to depreciate rapidly, further expanding Jamaica's debt service obligations.

Barbados

Grenade and Lewis-Bynoe (2010) noted that "The early 1970s was a particularly challenging time for Caribbean countries" (p. 16). Nevertheless, Barbados pegged its exchange rate in 1975 to BD$2 to US$1, and has maintained that stable rate, through passive intervention in the foreign exchange markets (Worrell, Marshall and Smith 2000, 125).

When the IMF mandated Barbados to devalue their currency as a loan condition in 1991, they instead negotiated a tripartite agreement for a one-off wage cut of 9%, and; agreed to peg future wage increases to productivity (Osei 2002; Henry and Miller 2008). A fixed exchange rate has made Barbados' total debt service cost more predictable and manageable than Jamaica's.

Singapore

Singapore maintains a managed float exchange rate regime, operated within an undisclosed band; with its currency being valued against a basket of its major trading partners and competitors' currencies. Their exchange rates have been below SG $2.50 to US$1 since 1975. Like Barbados, this aids long-term planning.

The Exchange Rate and Debt

External and US dollar domestic debt obligations have increased exponentially in line with the rate of devaluation of the Jamaican dollar. As Mr Seaga argued, a pegged rate allows for a greater level of predictability and forward-planning, as the current floating exchange rate system leads to erratic movements in currency values, challenges in debt servicing, and economic decline. He emphasized that "Over the years, multiple devaluations of the currency have added greatly to the debt service burden. That was one of the reasons why I fought against any further devaluation after the mid-1980s and got the IMF to agree that we would peg the rate of exchange' (pers. comm. 2011).

However, Argentina's experience shows that a pegged exchange rate, in and of itself, does not necessarily improve a country's ability to maintain stability and control debt levels. Lack

Chapter 6: Further Findings – Comparators: Jamaica, Barbados, and Singapore

of fiscal discipline and political instability led to Argentina's crisis, and ultimately default on its sovereign debt (IMF 2004, 15).

All Finance Ministry executives interviewed for this study were of the opinion that fiscal discipline has enhanced exchange rate stability and economic performance in Barbados and Singapore. Hou (2003) emphasized that fiscal discipline contributes to sound governance, and is demonstrated by a government's ability to manage its financial operations seamlessly on a day to day basis, over the long term (p. 4).

Other Indicators

Table 6.5 Other Comparative Indicators (2010)

INDICES	JAMAICA	BARBADOS	SINGAPORE
Sov. Credit Rating (Standard & Poors)	CCC+	BB+	AAA
Average GDP Growth % (1962-2010)	1.7	2.4	8
Inflation (2010)	11.7	6	2.8

Sources: WB; IMF; GOB; MOFP; STATIN; National statistical offices; S&P (2012)

a) **Sovereign Credit Rating**

A country's credit rating provides a signal to investors and creditors as to the level of risk inherent in the country's debt. Jamaica's debt was deemed the riskiest of the three, and; classified colloquially, in securities markets, as 'junk bonds' by 2012, when its sovereign credit rating was downgraded by Standards and Poor's (S&P) from vulnerable B-, to CCC+.

Barbados' sovereign debt, which had a low investment-grade BBB-/A-3 rating prior, was downgraded to a speculative grade of BB+/B in 2012. In contrast, S&P accorded Singapore's an AAA high investment-grade credit rating in the same year.

Since the implementation of some of the stipulations of the IMF in its 2013 Extended Fund Facility Loan to Jamaica, by successive administrations, guided by the Economic Programme

Chapter 6: Further Findings – Comparators: Jamaica, Barbados, and Singapore

Oversight Committee (EPOC) there has been an attempt at exercising greater fiscal discipline (albeit with reports and ongoing investigations of corruption and profligacy still being rife).

In April 2020, Standard and Poor's "affirmed Jamaica's B+ long term foreign, and local currency credit ratings", but revised Jamaica's outlook from stable to negative (The Gleaner, 2020).

b) Gross Domestic Product (GDP) Growth – 1965-2010 Comparators: Jamaica, Barbados and Singapore

High levels of public debt, profligacy, low productivity, weak governance, and an appetite for ostentatious living, have been blamed for decades of low-to-no GDP growth in Jamaica. As Figure 6.14 shows, Jamaica's economic growth has been anaemic relative to Barbados and Singapore, particularly from 1972 to 1985/86, with an uptick in the early 1990s and subsequent declines from 1996 to 2010.

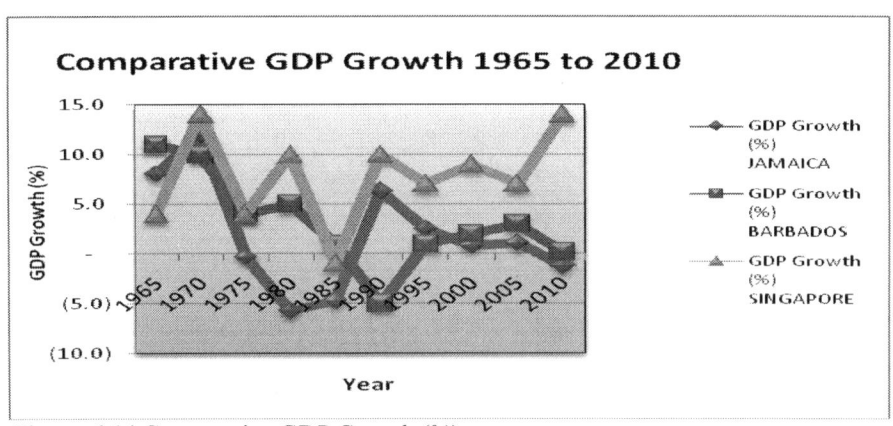

Figure 6.14 Comparative GDP Growth (%)
Data Source: WB; IMF; National statistical offices

A deeper examination of the key sectors contributing to the Gross Domestic Product of Jamaica, Barbados, and Singapore was also instructive. Data from the UN (2011) which was used to create the graphs in Figures 6.15 to 6.17 below, showed that Household Consumption Expenditure and imports were the dominant

Chapter 6: Further Findings – Comparators: Jamaica, Barbados, and Singapore

contributors to GDP in Jamaica from 1990 to 2010. Over the same period, imports consistently outstripped exports by 30% to 73% (Figure 6.15).

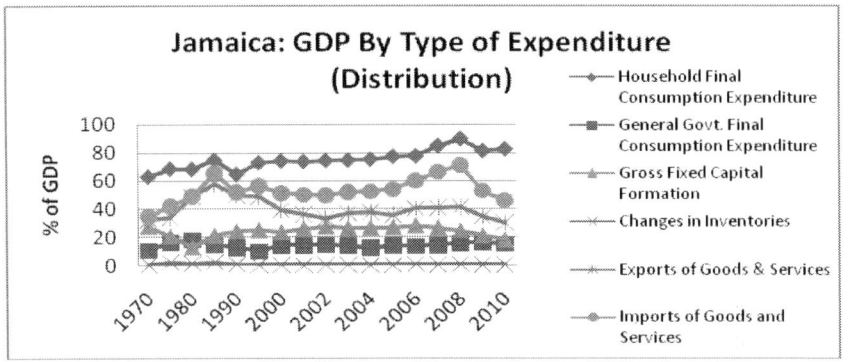

Figure 6.15 Percentage Contribution of Key Sectors to GDP – Jamaica
Data Source: UN 2011

This insatiable demand for imports, and corresponding growing demand for the US dollar, resulted in higher currency prices, increasing the cost of debt. Consequently, lack of competitiveness in exports has then contributed to a vicious cycle of unfavourable trade balances, low foreign exchange inflows, and large current account deficits.

Barbados

Successive administrations in Barbados have identified a low and stable exchange rate, and sound fiscal policies, as two of the key elements to drive their economic growth (GOB 1969-1972 Development Plan; Barrow 1965; Downes 2002; Grenade and Lewis-Bynoe 2010; Worrell 2012).

While Barbados, like Jamaica, is import-dependent, their ratio of export to import has been significantly more favourable than Jamaica's (Figure 6.16).

Chapter 6: Further Findings – Comparators: Jamaica, Barbados, and Singapore

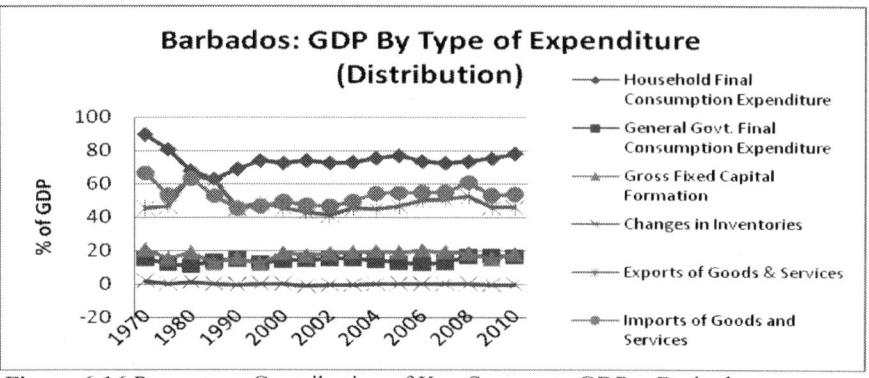

Figure 6.16 Percentage Contribution of Key Sectors to GDP – Barbados
Data Source: UN 2011

However, the potential for current account deficits can also be seen from the trajectory of the trend lines for imports and exports. Like Jamaica, Household Consumption Expenditure was dominant and has been the largest contributor to GDP in Barbados.

Singapore

Household and Government Consumption Expenditure in Singapore has shown a low, and consistent downward trend from 1970 to 2010; while exports continue to contribute significantly to GDP.

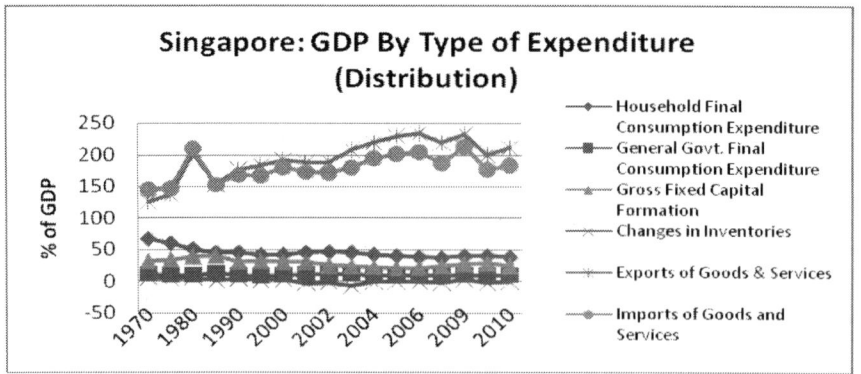

Figure 6.17 Percentage Contribution of Key Sectors to GDP – Singapore
Data Source: UN 2011

Chapter 6: Further Findings – Comparators: Jamaica, Barbados, and Singapore

Even at the peak of the recession (2008-2010), Singapore's exports continued to outstrip imports. While GDP growth is essential as the denominator in the Debt-to-GDP ratio, inflation must also be kept low, to minimize the nominal burden of debt.

c) Inflation

A prominent Caribbean Central Bank economist was asked what, in his opinion, was the main reason for Jamaica's current level of indebtedness. His response is below:

> A lot of it had to do with the huge inflationary episodes that you experienced for most of the decades of the 80s and 90s. And I think that sent up the nominal value of all obligations including your debt obligations, very rapidly. And that is a legacy which remains with you. So when you cure inflation you are left with this huge nominal burden and I think that will be an ongoing exercise which is going to be very difficult to rectify. As you know, even with the debt restructuring, the prospects of bringing that mountain of debt down is not going to be easy. The legacy of all those years of inflation is that it is very hard to secure debt at long term. (pers. comm. 2012)

Jamaica, Barbados, and Singapore all experienced significant spikes in inflation between 1971 and 1975, after the US abandoned gold parity, followed by the oil crisis (Worrell, Marshall and Smith 2000; Lee 2000). While inflation rates for Barbados and Singapore tapered from 1983 to 2010, Jamaica's rates increased rapidly up to 2010. Figure 6.18 shows that Barbados and Singapore consistently maintained single-digit inflation rates for more than 37 years from 1962 to 2010 - including periods of financial crises. Conversely, Jamaica's inflation rate peaked during every crisis period.

Chapter 6: Further Findings – Comparators: Jamaica, Barbados, and Singapore

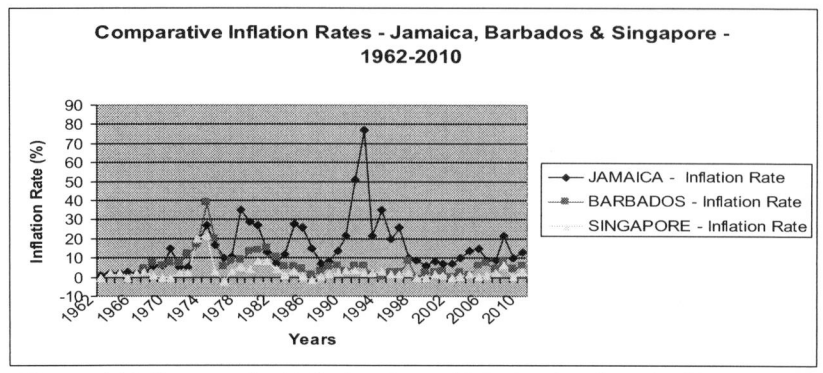

Figure 6.18 Comparative Inflation Rates (IMF; National Authorities)

Jamaica's inflation targets are set by the BOJ and approved by the Minister of Finance. A number of securities issued by the GOJ (J$37B at 2012/13) are indexed to inflation (GOJ 2014). This exacerbates the debt problem.

(d) Policy Focus and Outcomes

Jamaica

Jamaica's 2010/2011 monetary policy was focused on balancing currency stability and maintaining required levels of foreign reserves (BOJ 2010).

> **Result:** The currency depreciated by more than 10% per annum, while reserves fell from US$2.325 billion in 2006 to US$823 million in 2013 prior to IFI inflows.

Barbados

Barbados' monetary and fiscal policy included plans to keep inflation rates below interest rates, align fiscal and monetary policies, by reducing the fiscal deficit, maintaining reserves of over twenty-one weeks of imports, and allowing for flexibility in policy (GOB 2009).

Chapter 6: Further Findings – Comparators: Jamaica, Barbados, and Singapore

Result: Barbados' inflation outturn for 2010 was 5.8%, with a projection of 2% for 2014 (IMF 2014, 38). Coupon (interest) rates on its 2019, 2021, 2022, and 2035 global bonds were close to 7% (Oppenheimers, May 2014). Reserves increased from US$597 million in 2006 to $729 million by 2012 (IMF 2014, 38).

Singapore

Singapore's monetary policy was focused more on exchange rate management and inflation control, than on money supply or interest rates (MAS 2001, 2).

Result: "Over the past decade (2003-12), GDP growth and CPI inflation averaged 6.1 percent and 2.6 percent respectively. The exchange rate-centered monetary policy framework has been effective in terms of price stability and anchoring inflation expectations in the economy" (IMF 2013, 10).

Question 3, and Summary of Findings

The findings outlined in answering Question 3 provided a comparison of Jamaica's public debt and economic performance to those of Barbados and Singapore. The question asked was:

How do Jamaica's public debt and economic performance compare to that of Barbados and Singapore

The findings have shown that both Barbados and Singapore have outperformed Jamaica in terms of: (i) structure and composition of debt; (ii) economic growth; (iii) per capita GDP; (iv) productivity; (v) quality of sovereign credit; (vi) inflation; (vii) contribution of key sectors to GDP, and; (viii) exchange rate management.

An examination of the main sectors contributing to GDP

Chapter 6: Further Findings – Comparators: Jamaica, Barbados, and Singapore

showed that **Household Consumption Expenditure and Imports** were dominant for Jamaica and Barbados; while **Exports** contributed more to the economies of Singapore and Barbados than Jamaica. **Manufacturing** was the dominant contributor to Singapore's GDP; even as the contribution from Household Consumption and Government were low and trending downward (UN 2011).

The findings were consistent with relationships between governance, macroeconomic performance, and development highlighted in the literature, and economic development models discussed.

Question 4 delves further to examine comparative governance indicators.

6.3 Global Indicators of Governance

Question 4: *How does Jamaica rank against Barbados and Singapore, in terms of global indicators of governance?*

Comparative World Governance Indicators

Lack of transparency and accountability in governance are major challenges affecting fiscal management. Transparency International (TI) accorded Jamaica a ranking in transparency and good governance of 84 out of 132 countries in 2007, with the country at position 132 doing worst on this indicator (TI 2009). By 2010 Jamaica fell even further to 87 of 178.

Barbados was ranked much higher than Jamaica, at 17; while Singapore had the highest rank of 1.

At that time the Transparency International Corruption Perception Index (CPI) scored countries on a scale of 0 to 10, with countries scoring 10 perceived to have low levels of corruption, and those below 5 down to 0 perceived as being highly corrupt. Jamaica's CPI score was also low, at 3 out of 10 in that year. These

Chapter 6: Further Findings – Comparators: Jamaica, Barbados, and Singapore

scores reflected a broad perception of poor governance and high levels of corruption.

Though Singapore functioned mainly as an army base before independence, like Jamaica and Barbados it had a colonial past. However, unlike Jamaica, Barbados, and Singapore incorporated strong institutional controls (recall Chapter 2) within their governance systems (Acemoglu et al 2003; Henry 2013; Lee 2000).

On the other hand, weak governance institutions formed in post-colonial Jamaica were undermined by a clientelist-patronage political system (Stone and Brown 1981; Panton 1993), which has created an embedded culture of dependency between the 'governed' and 'governors'. This, in turn, has contributed to the resultant corruption, profligacy, economic underperformance, and rapid debt accumulation. Australia AID (2002) reiterated that corruption, profligacy, and lack of accountability, thwarts development (p. 5).

An examination of the very popular World Bank World Governance Indicators (WGIs) often referenced by researchers and policymakers globally, also showed that Jamaica's governance ratings were well below those of Barbados and Singapore. This was most pronounced in the areas of Control of Corruption, adherence to the Rule of Law, and Political Stability.

Chapter 6: Further Findings – Comparators: Jamaica, Barbados, and Singapore

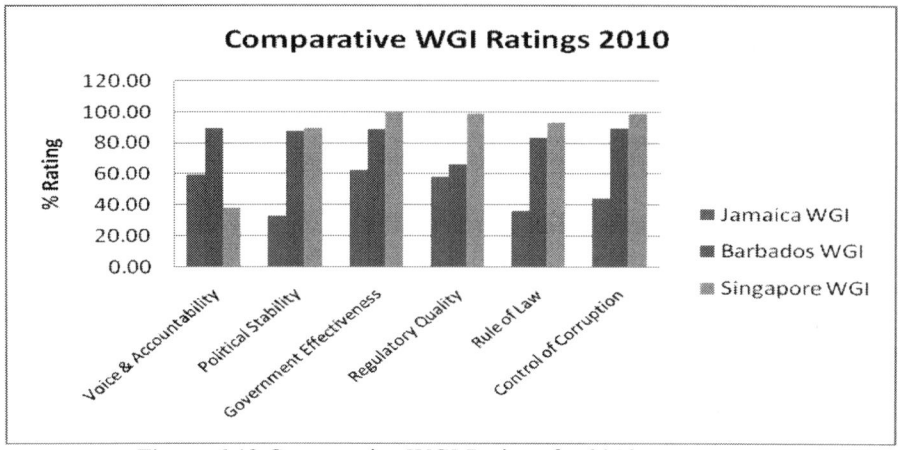

Figure 6.19 Comparative WGI Ratings for 2010

The institutional economics, development, and governance literature reviewed, have all clearly established that these are key areas that influence economic performance, indebtedness, and levels of investment in a country. Ozler and Tabellini also posited that political stability is a reliable determinant of external debt accumulation (1991, 1).

In 2021, the Corruption Perception Index (CPI) ranked countries on a scale from 0 to 100, with 100 being very clean, and 0 being highly corrupt. In its 2021 report, Singapore's CPI rank was 3, with a score of 85/100 (very clean). Barbados' rank was 29, with a score of 64/100 (clean). And, Jamaica's rank was 69, with a score of 44/100 – the most corrupt of the three countries in this study (Transparency International, 2021).

Some economists also feel that political instability increases the cost of external debt through premium rates charged for potential risk, and difficulty in attracting investments (see Chapter 2). This researcher learned from a June 2014 internship in the Debt Management Unit at the Ministry of Finance and the Public Service in Jamaica (MOFP) that issues relating to political stability risks are required to be included in the Prospectus Summaries for bonds being offered on the global capital markets.

Chapter 6: Further Findings – Comparators: Jamaica, Barbados, and Singapore

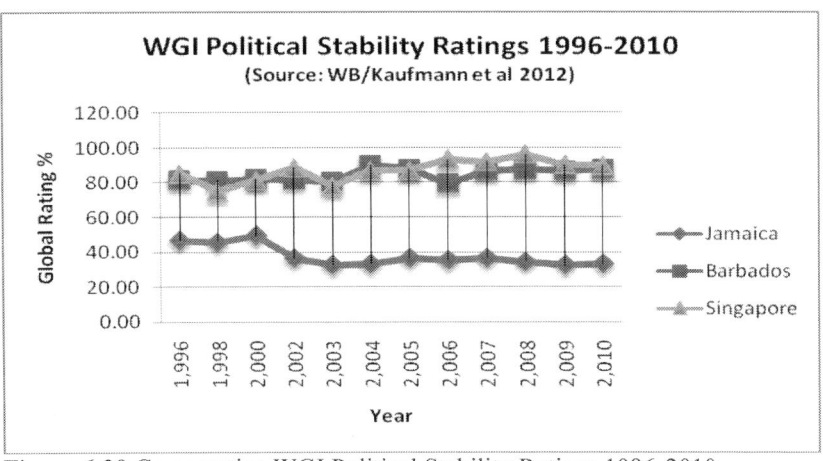

Figure 6.20 Comparative WGI Political Stability Ratings 1996-2010

As figure 6.20 above shows, Jamaica's scores on all governance indicators were below the 70th percentile; with three indicators being below the 50th. Poor governance is inherently linked to indebtedness and underdevelopment. A look at the trajectory of WGI ratings in Figures 6.21 to 6.23, for each country since the introduction of the indicators, is instructive.

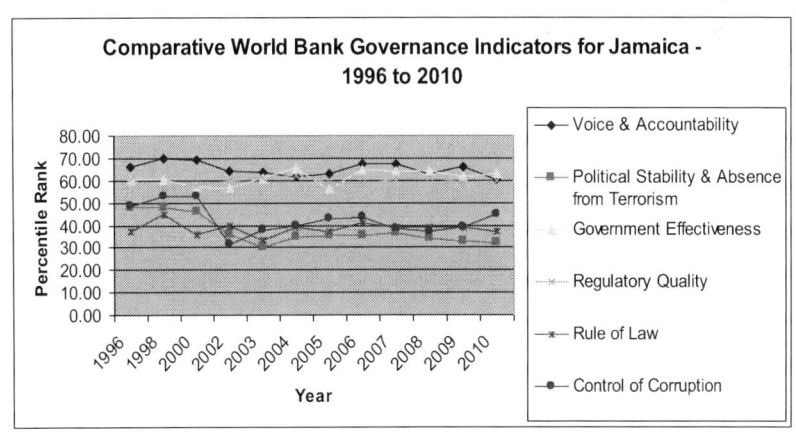

Figure 6.21 World Governance Indicators Ratings – Jamaica

The gains which were made in Government Effectiveness, Voice and Accountability in the 1990s have been eroded; while

Chapter 6: Further Findings – Comparators: Jamaica, Barbados, and Singapore

Regulatory Quality, Political Stability, and Absence from Terrorism are on a downward trajectory. Jamaica's ratings from 1996 to 2010 were also examined against those of Singapore and Barbados for a more thorough evaluation.

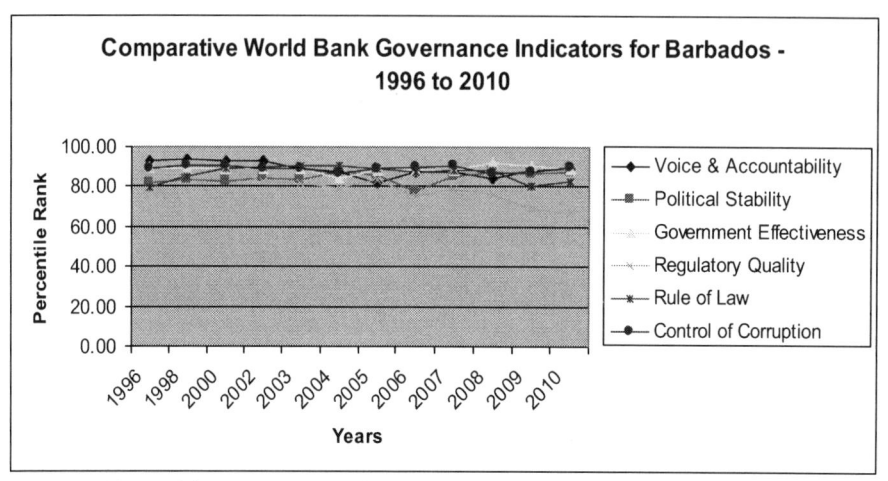

Figure 6.22 World Governance Indicators Ratings – Barbados

Barbados has done significantly better than Jamaica, on all six governance indicators, though Regulatory Quality was on a downward trajectory, falling below the 80th percentile since 2006. The related indicator of Government Effectiveness also declined marginally, between 2005 and 2010. Yet, Barbados remains well above the 80th percentile on all other indicators.

Chapter 6: Further Findings – Comparators: Jamaica, Barbados, and Singapore

Comparative World Bank Governance Indicators for Singapore - 1996 to 2010

- Voice & Accountability
- Political Stability
- Government Effectiveness
- Regulatory Quality
- Rule of Law
- Control of Corruption

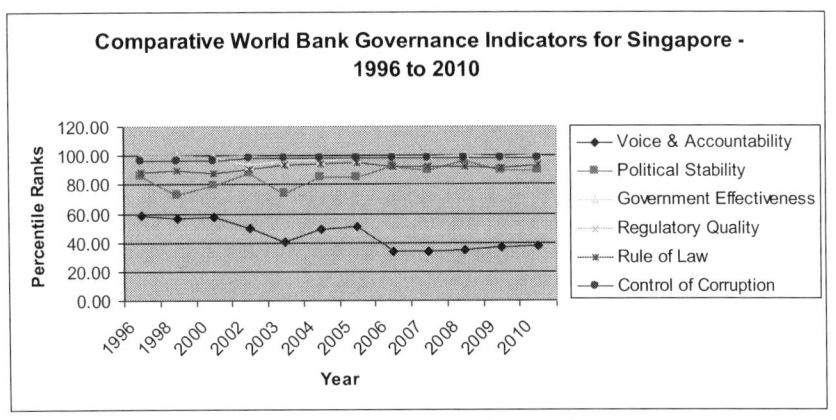

Figure 6.23 World Governance Indicators Ratings – Singapore

Singapore has ranked higher than Jamaica and Barbados on five of the six indicators; with scores above the 80th percentile on all but Voice and Accountability, for which they received scores below the 60th percentile. Jamaica had higher scores than Singapore, but lower than Barbados, here.

Still, the related perception of judicial independence in Singapore (21) is higher than Jamaica's (51) but lower than that of Barbados' (19). Figure 6.24 captures the 2010 'Voice and Accountability' rankings graphically, for all three countries.

Chapter 6: Further Findings – Comparators: Jamaica, Barbados, and Singapore

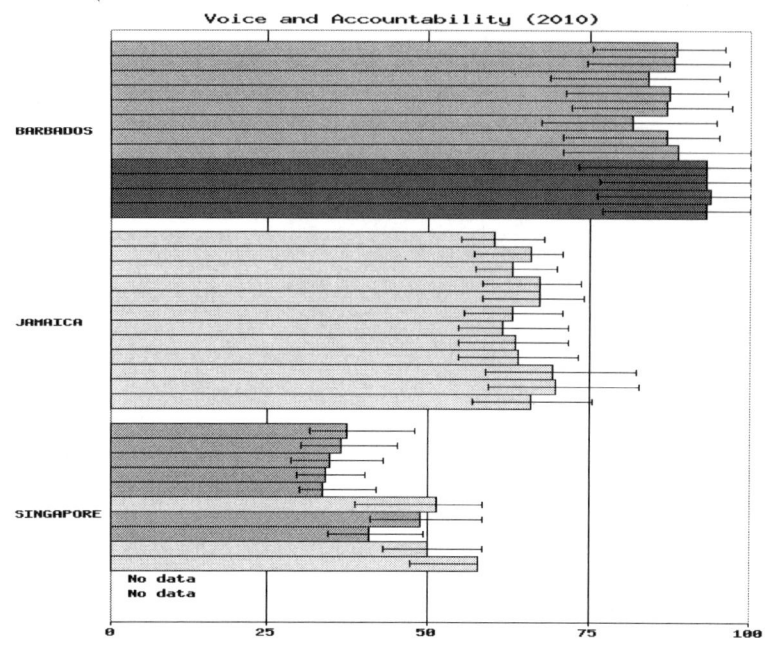

Figure 6.24 Comparative Ratings on Voice and Accountability
(Created by C. Smith using World Bank WGI facilities on Feb. 27, 2012)

A country that finds itself in the green zone is deemed to be in a favourable position. Countries in the yellow to orange zones are in an unfavourable position. At the end of 2010 Jamaica was in the yellow to orange zone on all six indicators, suggesting a global perception of poor governance.

Comparative Development Indicators

Voice and Accountability, Access to Information, and the ability to participate effectively in the governance process are fundamental to increasing the participation of citizens, in support of macroeconomic policy and debt management strategies. Some countries have sought to increase participation through affirmative action, or direct mandates. Barbados and Singapore have also out-performed Jamaica in these areas (see Table 6.6).

Chapter 6: Further Findings – Comparators: Jamaica, Barbados, and Singapore

Participation of Females in Parliament

Table 6.6 Comparative Development Indicators

INDICATOR	JAMAICA	BARBADOS	SINGAPORE
Female - Seats in Parliament (%)	13.60	13.70	24.50
Labour Force Participation rate (Male)	78.4	84.9	81.8
Labour Force Participation rate (Female)	62.2	76.5	60.6
HDI Rank	80	42	10

Source: UN, HDR (2010)

Though Singapore is generally perceived as a patriarchal society, they have significantly increased the proportion of female representatives in Parliament in just over a decade, relative to Jamaica and Barbados.

In 1997 only 3% of Singapore's Parliamentarians were female. By 2010 the proportion of female seats in Parliament in Jamaica, Barbados, and Singapore was 13.6%, 13.7%, and 24.5% respectively.

The proportion of females to males in Jamaica's Parliament has increased since the 2020 elections, moving to 28.571%. World Bank data (2021) also showed a substantial increase for Singapore up to 2020, though still below 30% (actual 29.474%). It is interesting to see Singapore, perceived as a patriarchal society, having a higher percentage of women in parliament than Jamaica.

Barbados is now led by a female Prime Minister and set to have a female President when the constitution is amended to make the country a republic in November 2021. Still, World Bank data showed that the proportion of women in parliament only moved from 16.667% in 2013 to 20% by 2020 (WB 2021).

Chapter 6: Further Findings – Comparators: Jamaica, Barbados, and Singapore

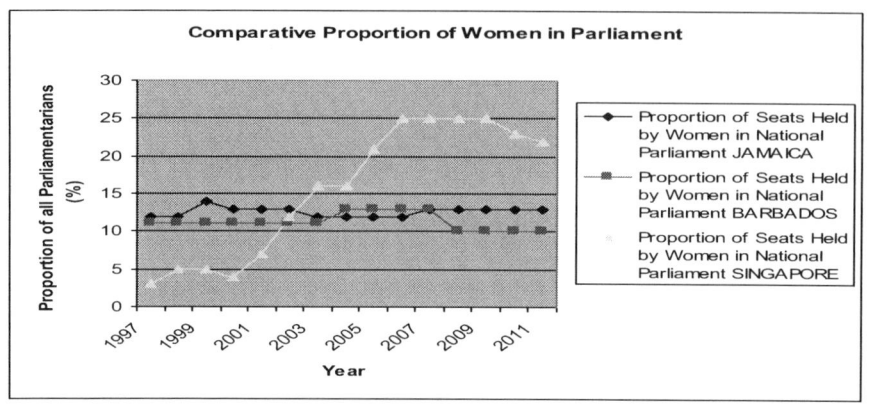

Figure 6.25 Comparative Proportion of Females in Parliament 1997-2010 (WB)

There is now a greater global thrust from the IMF, UN, and World Bank to increase the level of participation of women in governance, and; by the International Labour Organization (ILO) to improve gender equity in the labour force.

There was, however, a lower proportion of females participating in Singapore's labour force than in Barbados and Jamaica. Barbados had the highest rate at 76.5%. For 2019, the ratio of females to male in the labour force was 89.6%, 82.3%, and 81.1% for Barbados, Singapore, and Jamaica respectively (World Bank 2021).

6.4 Perspectives on the Quality of Governance in Jamaica

It is difficult to examine governance and its impact on public debt, without recognizing that politics is at the heart of governance, and so the voice of local citizens from all social classes must be heard.

The United Nations Economic and Social Commission for Asia and the Pacific's (UNESCAP's) eight characteristics of good governance discussed in Chapter 3, is the main area of focus for the ensuing segment, relating to findings from the elite interviews and local surveys conducted for this study. This is important because:

Chapter 6: Further Findings – Comparators: Jamaica, Barbados, and Singapore

i. Policymakers need to be made aware of how their stewardship is perceived both globally and locally;
ii. An understanding of local perceptions of governance can provide policymakers with useful information to increase social capital, in their efforts to reduce the country's indebtedness;
iii. They add robustness to the findings, by providing parallel comparisons (triangulation) for the global ratings discussed above.

1. Qualitative Findings – From Interviews, Hansard and Global Reports

You would recall from earlier throughout this publication (starting in Chapter 1) that good governance requires mutual accountability between stakeholders and policymakers (UNESCAP 2009). This, in turn, enhances public confidence (World Bank 2001, 40).

Over the last twenty-five (25) years, successive administrations in Jamaica have introduced various initiatives including the Matalon Committee of 1980, to identify ways of increasing accountability. These have had minimal effect, as borne out by the global and local evaluations.

Fifteen of the 18 key informants (elites – including former Prime Ministers, Finance Ministers, a bauxite company President, a cultural icon, technocrats from the and two Central Bank Governors from the Caribbean) interviewed, rated the character of governance in Jamaica from 1962 to 2010 on a scale of 1 (low) to 10 (high), based on the 8 governance characteristics from UNESCAP 2009, discussed in Chapter 1:

1. *Participation* ensures that the needs and interests of everyone are factored into the decision-making process.
2. *Effectiveness and Efficiency* are achieved when resources are used in a manner that yields the greatest benefit, at the

Chapter 6: Further Findings – Comparators: Jamaica, Barbados, and Singapore

least cost, to as many as possible; while sustaining natural resources and protecting the environment.
3. *Adherence to the Rule of Law* requires a fair legal framework, impartially enforced by an upright judiciary, and police force which recognizes and preserves human rights.
4. *Transparency* ensures that decisions taken are guided by rules and regulations, with clear, unambiguous, and precise information that is easily accessible to all.
5. *Responsiveness* requires that people are served in a timely manner.
6. *Consensus Orientation* is *achieved* when different interest groups are able to find a middle-ground so that the outcome serves everyone's best interest.
7. *Equity and Inclusiveness* suggest that everyone should feel a part of the governance process.
8. *Accountability* is achieved when public and private sector representatives are open and answerable to their stakeholders.

INTERVIEW FINDINGS

Accountability

The scores and comments from the interviews were as follows:
Accountability N=15; The **Mean** score was: 5.1 out 10; with only 47% giving a score above five (5). Comments:
- "Accountability is not yet a culture in Jamaica." Former PM
- "I think that from the PJ Patterson era we have become more accountable, and; from the Golding era, this has improved. I believe it's because the population [civil society] has demanded it." Former PM's widow
- "There appears to be no effective deterrence to administering public finances outside of the law. As for the politicians themselves, you hear stories about them not filing their Anti-corruption returns, and; they do it with impunity… The processes of accountability are very, very limited." Former Deputy Governor – Central Bank
- "We are not First World. There is a lot of finger-pointing and blaming and not taking responsibility or holding yourself accountable." Central Bank Executive

Chapter 6: Further Findings – Comparators: Jamaica, Barbados, and Singapore

- "The political directorate and parliamentarians, once they are elected, become metaphorically a law unto themselves, until the reckoning comes at the end of the electoral period and they either continue or are voted out. But only within recent times is there developing an ethos of accountability and with the growth of civil society bodies, these are being the vehicle to carry that." Professor
- "More recently special efforts have been made to deepen the levels of accountability. Institutions and laws have been passed which ensure that both Parliament and the public at large are able to judge the performance of Government under various heads." Former PM
- "There is the official picture of accountability which you would think is about 6, 7, or so, but in terms of the real nuts and bolts issues on the ground, it is lower" Senior Law Enforcement Specialist
- "One" Cultural icon

Effectiveness and Efficiency

The WB/IDB (2006) reported that inefficiency, lack of controls, and corruption were serious challenges affecting Jamaica's economic performance, worsened by multiple levels of oversight, and lack of effective enforcement mechanisms, "which result in a failure to address issues identified by various control bodies" (p. v). No significant improvements were made, as five years later, the World Economic Forum (WEF 2011) ranked Jamaica, Barbados, and Singapore at 90, 16 and 1 respectively, on Government Efficiency, with Singapore's ranking of '1' indicating the highest level of efficiency of the three. So with a score of 90, Jamaica was deemed highly inefficient. The interviewees' responses below are instructive.

Effectiveness and Efficiency N=16; The Mean score was: 3.9 out of 10; with 31% giving a score above five (5). Comments:

- "Having worked outside of Government and in Government, I don't know that we have been very effective or efficient at all. Too much money and time are wasted." Senior Public Sector Executive
- "The Government of Jamaica has not been efficient or effective in the use of its resources." Former PM
- "I can't give a global mark. I think there are areas we have been good at and areas we have been bad at." Former PM's widow

Chapter 6: Further Findings – Comparators: Jamaica, Barbados, and Singapore

- "Decisions have not necessarily always been driven by objective considerations. Sometimes they are subjective. Sometimes there are partisan and interest group issues which undermine the effectiveness of government." Former Deputy Governor – Central Bank
- "There are things that just don't get done and people who are left out." Central Bank Executive
- "It prompts in me, issues like the effectiveness of public policymaking, and the effectiveness of the implementation of those public policy determinations.... The issue seems to me over the past 40 years has been consistency and fixity of purpose in terms of implementation, and; not being side lined by what essentially amounts to political tribalism." President private sector organization
- "4" Former PM
- 'Governmental effectiveness and efficiency have been very low. Particularly with regards to implementation capability. The lag between policy decisions and actual implementation." Professor
- "The Parliament may have been more effective and more deliberate in different periods; but there has been a process, which to a large measure has been observed between 1962 to now." Former PM
- "Effectiveness and Efficiency – 4." Senior Government Official

High levels of bureaucracy and duplication of efforts in the public sector have also contributed to the wastage of public funds (Tindigarukayo and Chadwick 2003; NRCA 2004).

Responsibility splintering and excessive bureaucracy worsen the problem. The WB/IDB (2006) also found weak links between the priorities, planning, and budget of the government, as well as inefficiency and lapses in the monitoring of public expenditure. They recommended comprehensive reform of the legislation, and the drafting of the Public Debt and Public Guaranteed Debt Acts to address some of the anomalies.

Participation

Participation refers to the extent to which men, women, vulnerable members of society, and minorities are involved in the governance process, directly or through their elected representatives. This includes freedom of expression and involvement in organized bodies.

Chapter 6: Further Findings – Comparators: Jamaica, Barbados, and Singapore

Private Sector Participation

It is generally, the private holders of capital who drive innovation and entrepreneurship. The private sector is, therefore, important to the maintenance of economic, social, and political stability. If disgruntled, they can act in overt or covert ways, to weaken a government, whose stance, they believe, is inimical to their interest. For example, Jamaica's debt spiralled in the 1970s, when politically disgruntled members of the private sector reportedly removed large sums of money from their accounts in Jamaica (capital flight).

Seaga (2009) reported that this occurred because Mr Manley denounced private sector leaders as 'rapacious capitalists' steering "the country into a confrontation that widened the gap of understanding and deepened the class divide" (p. 225). Panton (1993) noted that, Manley recognized the economic implications of this, and subsequently appointed key private sector leaders to top positions in government. In reflection, Manley asked:

> Who says that 'deeds speak louder than words'? Our 'deeds' to the private sector were the most eloquent testimony to our sincerity with respect to the mixed economy. …It was obvious that the private sector chose to assume the worst, presumably because we were challenging the system in the pure form which they prefer. They were not prepared to accept the entirely honourable place which they were being offered in a modified system. (Manley 1982, 135-136)

Mr Seaga gained power shortly after. Though "the private sector continued to support the government's stated ideological position, sharp disagreements over strategy, tactics, and power relations reduced initial enthusiasm for the JLP into growing mistrust of the government's intentions" (Panton 1993, 86). He too lost favour with the private sector by 1989.

Subsequently, Prime Ministers Patterson and Golding openly engaged the expertise of the private sector, with top private sector executives (for example, from the large Grace Kennedy

Chapter 6: Further Findings – Comparators: Jamaica, Barbados, and Singapore

conglomerate) serving in the Senate, across PNP and JLP administrations.

By 2004 Minister Davies acknowledged the private sector as the catalysts driving the partnership for progress, leading to increased dialogue and consensus between the Government, Trade Unions and civil society, in an effort to find ways to collaborate, stimulate economic activity, and reduce the fiscal deficit.

By 2013 there was significantly greater direct private sector participation in governance, through the Economic Programme Oversight Committee (EPOC) formed to ensure probity, provide guidance, and ensure that Jamaica adhered to the IMF targets in the 2013 Extended Fund Facility (EFF) agreement. The elites interviewed gave the following scores, and shared their views on this aspect of governance.

Participation N=16; The **Mean** score was: 5.8 out of 10; with 62% of respondents giving a score above five (5). Comments:
- "I think we have made some strides in the 1970s, and; we continue to make an effort to broaden participation." Central Bank Executive
- "There really is no effective participatory democracy. …The richer people have access to the corridors of power." Former Central Banker
- "If you were to look at gender presence in governance institutions, the House of Representatives and the Senate, the House of Representatives has about 13% women over 50 years and the Senate is about 25%. That doubles it, but [the] standard target that has been set for good reason globally…. 30% is the standard for Parliament and we have not achieved that. I, therefore, regard this as an area of deficit." Professor
- "One would have wished that there would have been greater levels of civil participation, and; here I think the weakness is in Local Government and in enhancing the systems in enhancing community development." Former PM
- It has made political decision-making in Jamaica very inefficient because there is far too much consultation and attempts to please everybody." Senior Law Enforcement Specialist
- "I give them a pass on that one because of the maintaining of a decent democracy, comparatively speaking." Cultural icon

Though some attempts were made to increase participation, there was still a strong perception of inequity in

Chapter 6: Further Findings – Comparators: Jamaica, Barbados, and Singapore

governance. Both aspects of governance (participation, as well as equity and inclusiveness) are central to the real involvement of stakeholders. Participation from the grassroots level of the Jamaican society was, and still is, woefully low.

Equity and Inclusiveness

Equity and Inclusiveness N=16; The Mean score was: 4.6; with 25% giving a score above five (5). Comments:
- "I don't know if we have been those things either. The truth is, I think we have tried to be equitable and fair. We have amended some legislation and have done some of the right things in principle. I don't know if we have converted them into action." Senior Public Sector Executive
- "Successive administrations have prided themselves in being equitable and inclusive, though often it is on a partisan basis, through the exploitation of the vulnerabilities of the people, and perpetuating the cycle of poverty." Former PM
- "It depends on the subject matter. In terms of our social programmes, health etcetera, we have tried. However our business programmes have shut out some of the small business operators, so again it is a variable grade." Former PM's widow
- "Social exclusion of the growing inner cities and in particular young people, with respect to educational outcomes, in relation to lack of economic opportunities, has been one of the more striking deficits in our period since Independence." Professor
- "Perhaps in terms of equity and inclusiveness and consensus orientation we haven't been consistently good." Former PM
- "In terms of intent, it would really be around 8. However, in terms of action, it is around 6. They really preach a doctrine of equity and inclusion, but the ineffectiveness of the bureaucracy and all those other issues retard participation." Senior Law Enforcement Specialist

Following the Rule of Law

Good governance requires an impartial legal framework; protection of human rights; an independent judiciary, and; a police force that is fair and free from corruption (UNESCAP 2009).

Chapter 6: Further Findings – Comparators: Jamaica, Barbados, and Singapore

Following the Rule of Law N = 16; The Mean score was 5.4; with 50% of respondents giving a score above five (5). Comments:
- "The country is so disorderly." Senior Public Sector Executive
- "We have the mechanisms in place; though we have a 'bly culture' in Jamaica that works against this. There is no specificity and often too much vagueness." Former PM
- "From the legislative point of view we have achieved somewhat." Former PM's widow
- "We have a Parliamentary system defined by law." Former Finance Minister
- "They do not follow the rule of law, and; you do not have a system in place to actually have consequences. The incentive system for following the rule of law is very weak." Former Deputy Governor – Central Bank
- "This is an area where privilege can exempt you." Central Bank Executive
- "I think the government has failed the people in terms of managing just about everything - the economy, social services, crime… A typical example is squatting. It is badly managed." President of International company
- "Generally I have given them a passing grade but nothing too spectacular… with an issue like the whole 'Manatt Duddus Affair', JDIP contracts, LNG bids, all of these things have created a great deal of public controversy." President of Private Sector organization
- "What I have done is to give them an average, as there have been periods in which the scores would have been high and periods in which the scores would have been low." Former PM
- "Too often the impression is given, and there is substance in it that persons in the higher reaches of society, whether it is political, private or social, do not have the same law applied to them." Professor
- "I think in following the rule of law things have worked quite well." Former PM
- "This is a very dismal score." Senior Government Official
- The rule of law is respected and it is preserved… However, there are operational inefficiencies in the law enforcement and criminal justice system." Senior Law Enforcement Specialist
- "The actual persons in government [deserve] 1, because they are some of the main ones who breach the law." Cultural icon

Chapter 6: Further Findings – Comparators: Jamaica, Barbados, and Singapore

Corruption and the Rule of Law

Corruption has been identified as one of the main channels through which resources are diverted, thus, impeding development and growth (Heilbrunn 2004). Wei and Wu (2000a) also argued that "Corruption could lead to a financial crisis by weakening domestic financial supervision and damaging the quality of banks' and firms' balance sheets" (p. 489).

The impact of corruption on Jamaica's economic performance has been repeatedly highlighted by local and international observers including the World Bank, and the Office of the Contractor General. However, as Heilbrunn noted, the work of anti-corruption agencies can be undermined by a lack of independence from the political executive (2004, 1).

Osei (2007) found that several anti-corruption initiatives taken by the Jamaican Government were generally ineffective, as many were merely symbolic, and without commitment, while role conflicts, lack of appropriate levels of financing, weakness in enforcing the law, and; an overloaded justice system hindered anti-corruption initiatives.

These role conflicts have been clearly and publicly demonstrated, as the police, the Independent Commission of Investigations (INDECOM), and the Director of Public Prosecution (DPP) - all integral to upholding the rule of law in Jamaica - have publicly aired their disagreements, as to who had what authority to deal with allegations of corruption and abuse of state power (see Greenland 2012, F13). This often resulted in lack of convictions or major disagreements between these key organs of governance.

It has been argued that corruption can be stemmed by increasing accountability and transparency (IMF/World Bank 2002; IDB 2005). The introduction of the Offices of the Contractor General (OCG) and Auditor General (AG) in Jamaica was expected to address this. However, Jones, like Osei, argued that much of this type of action was simply political symbolism to "give the appearance that "something was being done," thereby helping to legitimize the conditions, practices, policy outputs, etc. which otherwise would be unacceptable" (1974, 11).

Osei (2007), like the OCG (2008-2012), has also argued that profligacy and corruption have seriously undermined growth and development in Jamaica, and increased indebtedness. The Jamaican authorities' reluctance to regulate unregistered financial institutions ('Ponzi schemes') in Jamaica has been presented as a case in point.

More Allegations of Corruption in Governance – 'Ponzi Schemes'

Less than ten years after the FINSAC crisis that was blamed on weak regulation, a plethora of unregulated financial institutions ('Ponzi schemes'), including Olint and Cash Plus, developed, and reportedly gained prominence in the corridors of power in Jamaica, as unsuspecting, naive investors were fleeced of millions of dollars (some borrowed).

Persons were lured into 'investing' and promised returns of up to 10% per month. There were many calls for the Government to intervene. The initial response of the Government of Jamaica was a series of radio and television advertisements telling persons to think before investing. When a crisis arose, PM Golding reported that:

> There was a concern that was expressed to me by the Minister, that he could not understand the inertia of the FID [Financial Investigations Division] in relation to alternative investment schemes. Because some of the players in the investment schemes, were persons of interest to the FID, and; yet not once, not in one instance, did they exercise any of the powers that reside within the FID, in support of the FSC and its investigations into the operations of alternative investment schemes. (Golding 2008, 4)

Investments continued, without "a reasonable dispatch of court processes which might well have advised investors and

Chapter 6: Further Findings – Comparators: Jamaica, Barbados, and Singapore

others interested, of their peril in respect of these matters" (Thwaites 2011, 6). One of the main players, David Smith of Olint Corporation and Locket International, was subsequently convicted of fraud in the Turks and Caicos Islands, and reportedly wanted in the United States, but not convicted in Jamaica. Inaction on the part of national leaders led to major losses to investors and the economy.

Interestingly, PM Golding stridently stated in 2011, that it was his understanding that David Smith made significant contributions to the PNP. However, later reports revealed that Smith had made contributions to both the JLP and PNP (Carvajal et al 2009, 11). This was also carried in a Newstalk 93 report in 2012 that raised questions about corruption, accountability, lack of political intervention, and failure to uphold the rule of law in Jamaica. After all that stridency, Golding later conceded that "I don't think any of us here is blameless in terms of failing to maintain a resolute position that ought to have been taken" (2011, 6).

As Small (1980) emphasized, "[T]he allegations of corruption are tied very closely to allegations of mismanagement" (p. 20). Dr Peter Phillips also asserted that the governance process was being brought into disrepute, as public officials continued to amass wealth, without evidence of income to prove that it was legitimately gained (2010). The problem persisted. In frustration, Contractor General Christie reported that "despite evidence of instances of corruption, no one is held accountable, no tough sanctions are imposed, and no remedial action is taken" (Gleaner 2011, 1).

Questionable fiscal decisions, as revealed by the famous 2003 speech by then Finance Minister Davies, dubbed 'Run Wid It', also led to allegations of profligacy and wanton public expenditure for political gain. When questioned, he was reported as saying "clearly it was more a suggestion that the decision to proceed had been beneficial to the PNP. Yes, I regret the statement, but then I don't know any political person who has not made a speech which he didn't regret" (Davies, as quoted in Moxam 2004). Many still

Chapter 6: Further Findings – Comparators: Jamaica, Barbados, and Singapore

use this to evaluate his fiscal attitude, and that of Jamaican politicians in general.

As Golding had argued in 1990, "a public perception exists out there that government's operation is characterized by waste and inefficiency and corruption, and I think there is much in what goes on in Government that provides justification for that view" (p. 49).

Lack of fiscal prudence, corruption, and cost overruns continued to tarnish Jamaica's image, widen the fiscal deficits and expand the public debt. In 2008 the OCG reported that:

- 1432 of the 9,264 contracts awarded were not approved by the Public Body's Procurement Committee;
- 39% were not awarded to registered contractors, and;
- 22.15% had undisclosed procurement methods.

Profligacy has also led to mistrust of politicians' motives in Jamaica. For example, in November 2009 PM Golding told Parliament that the Bank of Jamaica (BOJ) Governor was awarded a five-year salary and emolument package in May 2007, retroactive to August 2006. A house was reportedly procured for him at a cost of J$40.37 million. The Hansard recorded that the Governor presided over the meeting where the decision was made; then decided within a year that he did not wish to occupy it. Mr Golding reported that after the house was furnished for an additional J$11.33 million, he indicated an interest to purchase it for a lower price. Meanwhile, the BOJ reportedly paid a rental of J$2.5 million per annum plus a maintenance cost of J$5.9 million for another property he occupied.

When he "moved into his new house, the rental jumped from J$2.5 million a year to $10.8 million, and maintenance jumped from J$5.9 to $13 million" (Golding 2009, 4). He also reported that the Governor obtained loans totalling J$55.44 million from the BOJ, at five percent (5%) per annum, without collateral.

Chapter 6: Further Findings – Comparators: Jamaica, Barbados, and Singapore

The Auditor General confirmed that there was no evidence that these loans were approved by the BOJ's Board of Directors, or properly collateralized (2009, 5). Dr Davies argued that a title for a property was subsequently stamped in 2009 to register the government's lien for J$30 million of the loan. Mr Golding reasoned that the question of issuing a loan three years before receiving collateral should not arise against the Central Bank; even as the contract bypassed the normal prudential controls. As North (1991) argued, high transaction costs are incurred from weak institutional controls.

A new BOJ Governor was employed in 2010, receiving a similar package. Public trust began to wane on both sides, as Jamaica's governance image and the economy suffered from repeated allegations of profligacy and corruption relating to public officials.

Politicians' motives continued to be questioned, even as former JLP Member of Parliament Joseph Hibbert was alleged to have accepted bribes from Mabey and Johnson, in his capacity as Chief Technical Director, in the Ministry of Works. The UK Guardian (2009) reported that Hibbert received £100,000 as a kickback for the award of contracts worth £14 million. The matter was referred to the Director of Public Prosecution (DPP). When questions were raised in Parliament in 2010, no decisive action was taken. Mr Hibbert sat in Parliament well after the allegation, while the DPP reported that she was awaiting action by the police to proceed (Luton 2011). He died before any action was taken.

Another Member of Parliament, Kern Spencer was also reportedly implicated in a multi-million dollar fraud investigation relating to light bulbs subsidized by the Government of Cuba, for free distribution to Jamaicans. He, like Joseph Hibbert, sat in Parliament for an extended period of time, while the case was before the courts. The case was dismissed by the DPP in March 2014.

The BBC (2007) also reported that one Jamaican Prime Minister has also had to respond to allegations of corruption when the political party was alleged to have accepted J$31 million from Dutch oil lifting firm Trafigura Beheer prior to the 2007 elections. The Office of the Contractor General (OCG) argued that the agreement entered into by the Jamaican authorities with Good Works International LLC and Trafigura Beheer coincided with the timing of the 'gift' (2008). As the Contractor General noted, the absence of political will, and weaknesses in law enforcement bodies and anti-corruption institutions, create space for corruption to thrive (OCG 2011, 4). As Hobbes (1962) pointed out:

> [M]en are prone to violate the laws, three ways. First by presumption of false principles: as when men, from having observed how in all places, and in all ages, unjust actions have been authorized, by the force, and victories of those who have committed them, and; that potent men, breaking through the cobweb laws of their own country, the weaker sort, and those that failed in their enterprises, have been esteemed the only criminals. (1962, 219)

This suggests that laws will continue to be violated, and officials absolved of wrongdoing until punitive sanctions are applied to make an example of them.

As we continue to discuss the role of governance in managing public debt, and fiscal management overall, proposals for the tabling of legislation to prevent **corruption** through the electoral process have been taking an inordinately long time to be deliberated and passed in Jamaica's Parliament.

In 2011 Minister Andrew Holness highlighted a recommendation from the Electoral Commission, for political party registration and financing. Member Peter Bunting (former Minister of National Security, now Senator) concurred and introduced an Organization of American States (OAS) Draft Model Law as a possible prototype. This draft highlighted the potential danger of political parties receiving tainted contributions. Up to May 2015, the legislation required to enhance transparency in governance had still not been passed.

Chapter 6: Further Findings – Comparators: Jamaica, Barbados, and Singapore

Transparency

Transparency looks at the extent to which decisions are consistent with rules and regulations, openness in communication, and ease of access to information by those who will be impacted by the decisions (UNESCAP 2009).

Though Jamaica is a democracy, transparency through open communication has been a challenge, as the government tends to control the type and amount of information that is made available to the public, through the public sector bureaucracy, and its media channels. This has led to distrust.

When PM Patterson invited the Carter Center to help make Jamaica a model of transparency and good governance in 1998, they identified lack of access to information as a major hindrance. Subsequently, the Access to Information Act was passed in 2002. The Carter Center later reported that "Jamaica has established a new and more open form of governance and accomplished what many other countries are still attempting" (2006, 1).

Still, selective dissemination of information by the government and their agents continues to demonstrate that some of these gains may have been reversed (see JIS 2011; Director General, pers. comm. 2011).

Transparency in Governance N=15; The **Mean** score was: 5.2 out of 10; with 33% giving a score above five (5). Comments:
- "We still carry with us the old civil service culture, where everything is [a] secret." Senior Public Sector Executive
- "Elected officials today have a greater appreciation of the importance of transparency to politics and governance." Former PM
- "Generally government has not been transparent. You have the electoral cycle once every five years. In between, much of what happens in government is not really available as public information, in terms of how decisions are made, in terms of who benefits. In terms of how costs are distributed." Former Deputy Governor – Central Bank
- "Over the last 10 years a lot of effort has gone into making government more transparent." Central Bank Executive

Chapter 6: Further Findings – Comparators: Jamaica, Barbados, and Singapore

- "To the greatest extent to which they can simply embrace transparency is the better off we are going to be, going forward." President of Private sector organization
- '[T]here has been a degree of transparency that is worthy of positive note." Professor
- "[I]n terms of transparency, new mechanisms have been introduced, such as the whole question of dealing with the award of contracts, the creation of the Office of Contractor General ..." Former PM
- "I would say that we have improved, certainly over the last 20 to 25 years" Former Deputy Governor – Central Bank
- "To the extent that they have not been transparent, I think that is more linked to tradition. ...Information control is a key feature of large bureaucracies. But it is changing" Senior Law Enforcement Specialist
- "This is an average because it varied from administration to administration – 2." Cultural icon

Consensus Orientation

Good governance recognizes that the social, cultural and historical perspectives of stakeholders should be considered, to reach agreements on collective goals for sustainable development and growth (UNESCAP 2009).

Consensus Orientation N=16; The Mean score was: 4.9 out of 10; while 31% of respondents gave a score above five (5). Comments:
- "I think Michael Manley started that with Democratic Socialism, as much as some of us may not have liked it. But I think we have grown in that area." Former PM's widow
- "The way the political system is legally constructed is that it is based on the assumption that the electorate puts the decision-making power in the hands of a select number of a select group of persons. So consensus then is not legally required. ... but beyond that, I am not one that believed in the 'town-hall meeting'." Former Finance Minister
- "I think that's fairly strong. There is less of a dictatorial approach to policy-making, and a search for consensus." Central Bank Executive
- "Efforts have been made but these efforts have been largely ineffective. You have political tribalism, but perhaps even more pernicious is interest group politics. Interest group actually cuts across the political tribal divide. Interest groups who are buying political influence will buy political influence across the political divide." Former Deputy Governor – Central Bank

Chapter 6: Further Findings – Comparators: Jamaica, Barbados, and Singapore

- "It is instinctive in Jamaicans to want consensus. However, we have a culture and an institutional setting that makes it very, very difficult to achieve." Senior Government Official
- "[I]n a quest to achieve consensus on every important political decision, they usually overextend the debate and water down the process, so as to please everybody. And so what you end up with are policies which are ineffective." Senior Law Enforcement Specialist
- "[T]here are certain things that should have gone to a referendum that went through Parliament, and; I am sure constitutionally that they were wrong." Cultural icon

Responsiveness

Responsiveness N=16; The **Mean** score was 5.4, with 44% of elite respondents giving a score above five (5). Comments:

- "Government and political parties have been generally responsive. Their relevance depends on this." Former PM
- "We tend to do crisis management more than anything. We may be pushed to respond, rather than proactively responding." Former PM's widow
- "I think that's more like political awareness as opposed to ability. I think that every Councillor or MP would see him/herself as responsive or responsible; but as to their ability to respond, that is a function of resources." Central Bank Executive
- "This is related to the same factors [effectiveness and efficiency], as well as the reality that over time we have gotten ourselves into fiscal problems and debt. So apart from the issues of governance, the capacity to meet needs have been undermined by the unavailability of resources." Former Deputy Governor – Central Bank
- "Let's not belittle the degree to which we interpret responsiveness. I give it an 8 out of 10" Professor
- "When you assess the responsiveness of governance in Jamaica since Independence, the response to duty is very slow and unstructured; but the response to a threat or a challenge to their ability to govern is very swift. They are reactive." Senior Law Enforcement Specialist

The elites' ratings indicated that governance in Jamaica from 1962 to the twenty-first century, was perceived as being average to poor. These scores will be triangulated against those from the surveys and international reports and presented in this publication.

Chapter 6: Further Findings – Comparators: Jamaica, Barbados, and Singapore

SURVEY FINDINGS

One thousand (1000) Jamaicans island-wide and 60 MPs were targeted to participate in surveys to garner their perspectives on governance and debt management in Jamaica from 1962 to 2010.

STATIN's data showed that as at the end of 2011, 44.3% of the Jamaican population was under 25; 41.5% between 25 and 54 years, and; 3.1% between 55 and 59 years. At the end of the survey, similar age demographics were observed among respondents, as shown in figure 6.26. Twenty-one of the 810 respondents did not give their ages.

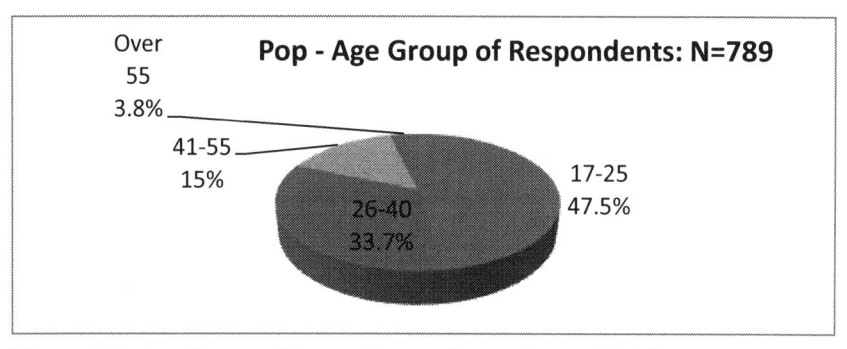

Pop - Age Group of Respondents: N=789

- Over 55: 3.8%
- 41-55: 15%
- 26-40: 33.7%
- 17-25: 47.5%

Figure 6.26 Age Group of Survey Respondents - General Public

Surveys provide a greater level of anonymity than elite interviews, and so, all respondents were asked to rate the character of governance in Jamaica on the same eight (8) characteristics that elites were asked to rate, and by political party (PNP and JLP).

Each of the eight (8) characteristics of good governance was first defined within the survey instrument (see Chapter 1, 1.4), to ensure consistent interpretation.

Each of the eight (8) characteristics was then set for rating, using a maximum score of ten (10) and a minimum of one (1). Five or fewer respondents gave scores of zero. Note that the higher the percentage of respondents giving a score **below** five (5), the worse the perception of the quality of governance, as it relates to that characteristic of governance being assessed.

Chapter 6: Further Findings – Comparators: Jamaica, Barbados, and Singapore

The difference between the **N value** (number of persons answering the question) and the **810** total respondents, accounts for those who did not respond to the question. The same applies to all 'characteristics' below. The findings are instructive.

Participation N=740-PNP; N=738-JLP; Mean ratings: 5.6 out of 10 for the PNP, and 5 for the JLP; with 50% of respondents giving the PNP a score above five (5); and 37% giving the JLP a score above five (5).

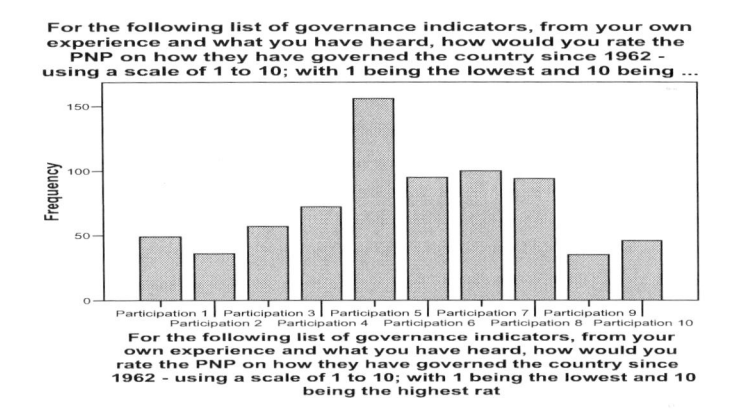

Figure 6.27 Public's Rating of **PNP - Participation**

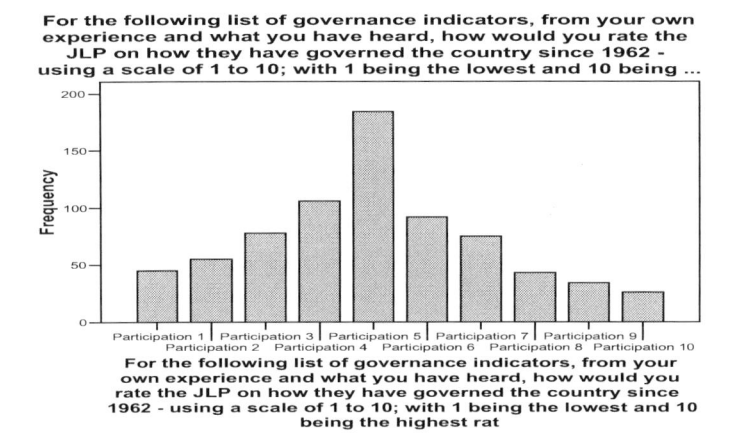

Figure 6.28 Public's Rating of **JLP - Participation**

Chapter 6: Further Findings – Comparators: Jamaica, Barbados, and Singapore

- 59% of all respondents reported that they had in fact participated in the governance process before.
- 87% of those who participated did so through the ballots, attending public meetings, signing petitions, and through demonstrations.
- 53% of those who did not participate said they just were not interested; 29% said they did not expect any results from participating; 18% were either unaware of the voting procedure or unable to vote at the time of an election.

The MPs were asked in their survey to state: (1) how actively each gender participated in governance at the constituency level; (2) if there were gender differences in the level and methods of participation, and; (3) the extent to which men and women were informed.

- 42% of MPs reported that men participated more actively than women.
- 51% said women participated more actively at the community and constituency levels.
- 44% said more men participated by directly interfacing with them. Women participated more as organizers.
- 72% felt that women were better informed than men.
- Less than 10% of either gender was perceived by the MPs to be poorly informed about issues relating to governance.

Effectiveness and Efficiency N=736-PNP; N=732-JLP

Both the PNP and JLP were rated 5 out of 10 (average) on this indicator; with 42% and 40% of respondents scoring the PNP and JLP respectively, above 5. Five respondents gave a score of zero.

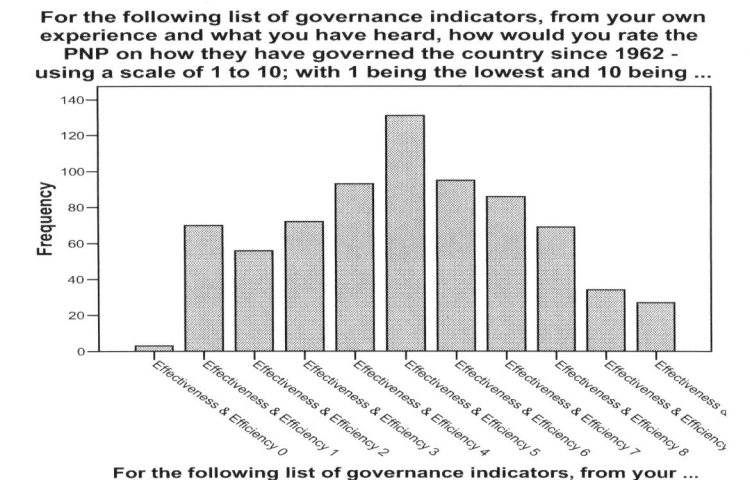

Chapter 6: Further Findings – Comparators: Jamaica, Barbados, and Singapore

Figure 6.29 Public's Rating of **PNP** on **Effectiveness and Efficiency**

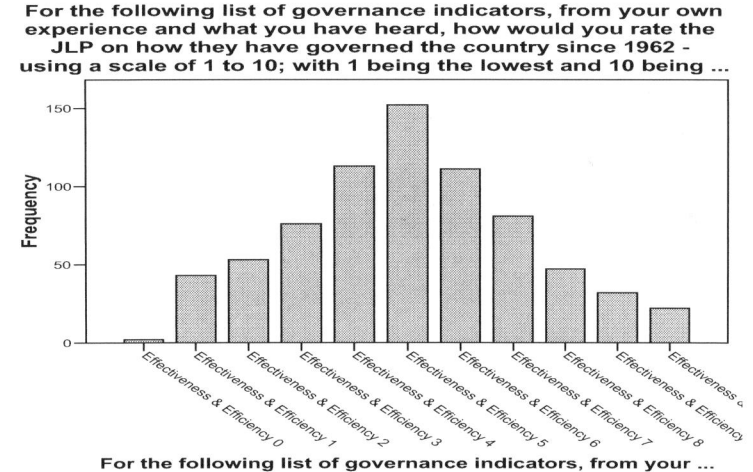

Figure 6.30 Public's Rating of **JLP** on **Effectiveness and Efficiency**

Cross-Referencing Perspectives of the Governors (Political Leaders) versus Governed (Citizens)

Both survey instruments were structured to allow for cross-referencing of the responses of MPs and the respondents from the

Chapter 6: Further Findings – Comparators: Jamaica, Barbados, and Singapore

general population island-wide, on the quality of governance and debt and economic management since 1962, so they could be analyzed from both perspectives. The results were as follows:

- 74% of the island-wide respondents felt that public sector institutions were not using the country's resources efficiently or effectively, to produce the best results. 93% of the MPs shared this view.

Following the Rule of Law N=735-PNP; N=729-JLP; The **Mean** score was: 4.98 for the PNP and 4.6 for the JLP; with 40% and 31% of respondents scoring the JLP and PNP respectively, above 5

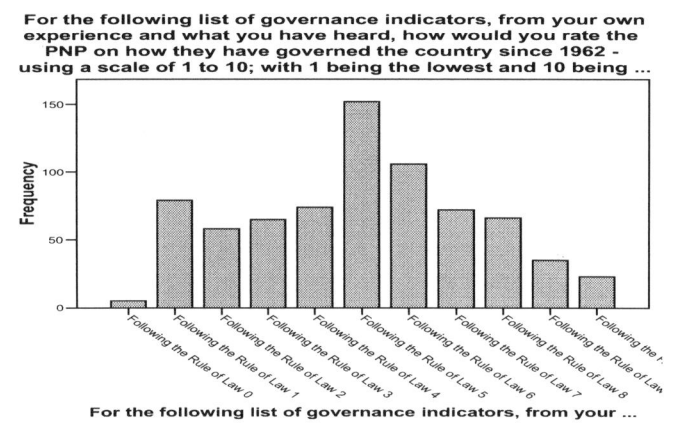

Figure 6.31 Public's Rating of **PNP** on **Following the Rule of Law**

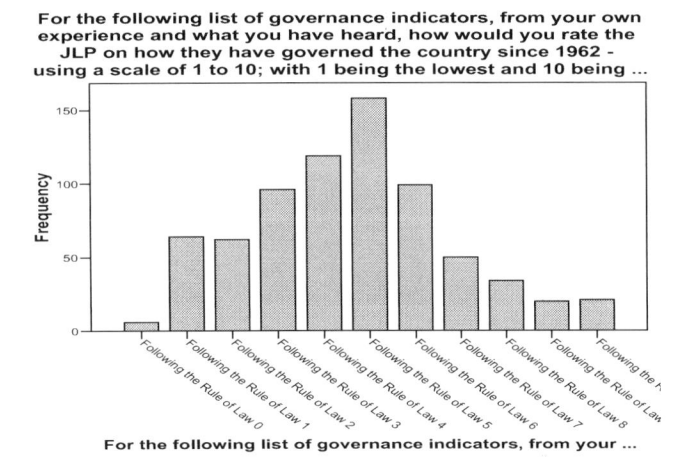

Chapter 6: Further Findings – Comparators: Jamaica, Barbados, and Singapore

Figure 6.32 Public's Rating of **JLP** on **Following Rule the of Law**

Given the findings discussed throughout this publication, it is clear that the extent to which the rule of law has been upheld in Jamaica during the forty-eight years under review is perceived as weak. Levitt (1991) argued that this resulted in violence and lawlessness in Jamaica in the 1970s and 1980s.

Similarly, Meeks noted that whether out of frustration with how slowly the 'wheels of justice' were turned, or other factors, Jamaicans have tended to demand and even participate in vigilante justice (2001). By 2006 Jamaica was described as the murder capital of the world (BBC). Former Security Minister Dr Peter Phillips blamed this lawlessness on the divisive nature of Jamaica's politics, saying:

> Jamaica's political culture is still much too divided and still too scarred by political tribalism. We need to do all that we can to prevent any division of the country along political lines, especially where the fight against crime is concerned. To do otherwise is a recipe for total failure… The truth is that administrations drawn from both parties over the years have not sustained an investment in law enforcement, commensurate with the increase in the levels of threat, faced by the Jamaican society. As a consequence, the signs of decay and obsolescence in our security apparatus are palpably evident. (2008, 3)

Chapter 6: Further Findings – Comparators: Jamaica, Barbados, and Singapore

With regards to the rule of law, political tribalism, instability, and Jamaica's overburdened courts, with its large backlog of cases awaiting trial over many years, have also negatively impacted the economy and hampered the work of the police.

Some law-enforcement officers have also been accused of extra-judicial killings and acts of corruption. In 2008 Prime Minister Golding emphasized that "If we can't rid the force of corruption, we will never be able to rid the country of crime" (p. 4).

- 95% of the respondents island-wide, and 76% of MPs, felt that corruption in the police force was a major problem. This was consistent with the responses of more than 70% of police officers surveyed island-wide for this study.
- 56% of respondents island-wide felt that members the legal system/framework had been impartial in their deliberations and decisions, while only 29% of the legislators (MPs) shared this view.
- Less than 20% of respondents island-wide felt that Government decisions were taken in a manner that followed rules and regulations; 76% of the MPs felt they did.
- 44% of the island-wide respondents felt that the judiciary was not independent; 86% of MPs felt that it was.

These were vastly differing views between the MPs and the citizenry on (i) the impartiality of Jamaica's legal framework; (ii) the extent to which government follows rules and regulations, and; (iii) the independence of the judiciary.

These are important areas of governance to be addressed if Jamaica is to build trust, social capital, and obtain citizens' support for the government's initiatives to cauterize the debt and crime problems.

Chapter 6: Further Findings – Comparators: Jamaica, Barbados, and Singapore

As PAHO (2010) noted, Jamaica's spiralling debt, fiscal indiscipline, and the major problem of crime was serving to stymie economic growth (p. 13). Crime impacts public debt and economic performance (Kaufmann/WB 2013).

Transparency N=737-PNP; N=724-JLP: The **Mean** score was: 4.7 for the PNP and 4.4 for the JLP. 34% scored the PNP above 5; with 27% for the JLP. Both the JLP and PNP were deemed to have done poorly on transparency.

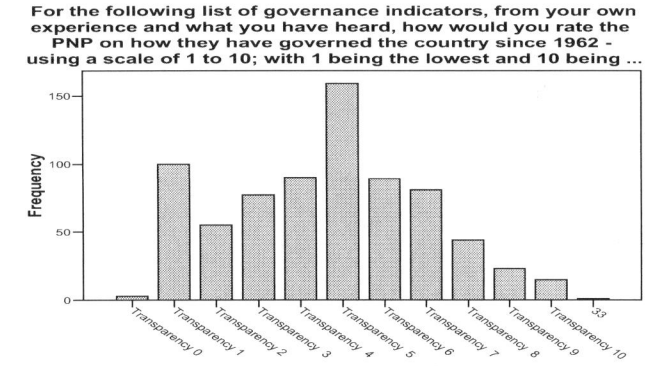

Figure 6.33 Public's Rating of **PNP** on **Transparency**

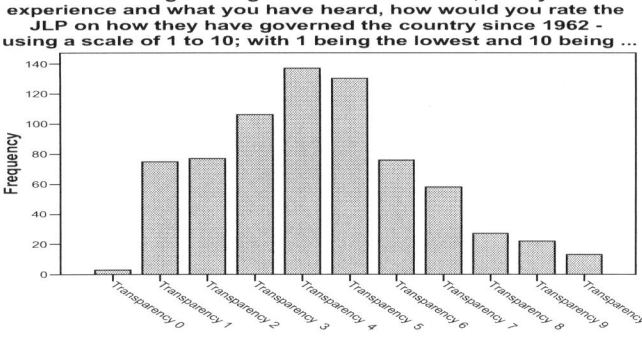

Figure 6.34 Public's Rating of **JLP** on **Transparency**

Chapter 6: Further Findings – Comparators: Jamaica, Barbados, and Singapore

Timely access to information is a key measure of transparency. While 92% of MPs felt that information provided by Central Government was available to those who were affected by it, only 55% of the respondents island-wide said they had easy and ready access to this information. Again, the Member of Parliaments' perception appeared incongruous with the citizens' views. Objectivity is at the foundation of good research, and so it was important to understand the factors which prevented citizens from accessing the information they needed from the government. We asked, and they answered:

- 12% said information was not provided even after they made the request;
- 22% said they were not aware of how to access the information.

Access to information can be improved by increasing the effectiveness and efficiency of the agents and channels of dissemination. Recall our report on the access to information project under PM Patterson. The speed and ease of access to information are outcomes or indicators of the government's responsiveness.

Responsiveness N=738- PNP; N=725-JLP; The **Mean** score was: 5.2 for the PNP and 4.7 for the JLP. The percentage of respondents scoring the parties above 5 was 45% for the PNP and 32% for the JLP.

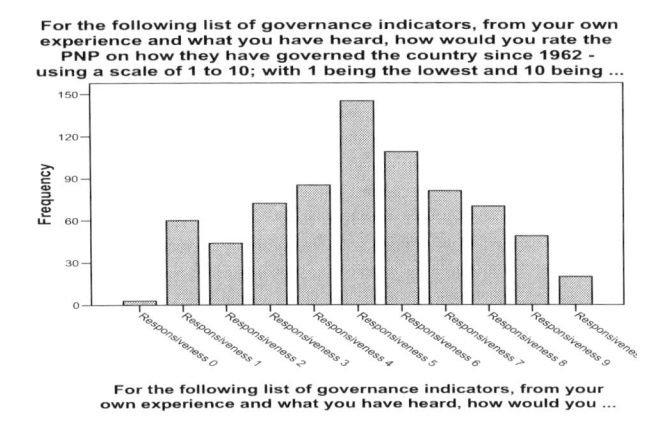

Chapter 6: Further Findings – Comparators: Jamaica, Barbados, and Singapore

Figure 6.35 Public's Rating of **PNP** on **Responsiveness**

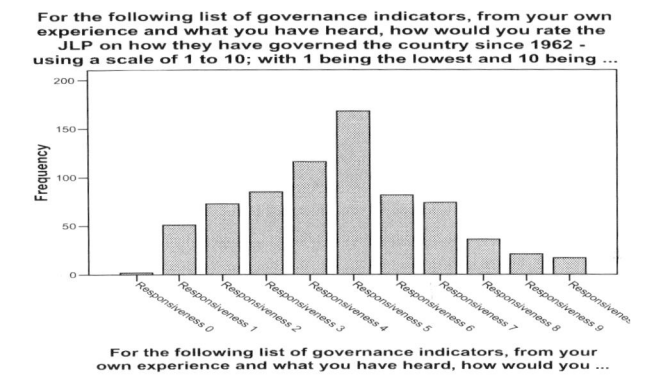

Figure 6.36 Public's Rating of **JLP - Responsiveness**

- Both groups (MPs 93%; Public 74%) generally felt that public services were provided within a reasonable timeframe. Still, the differential of almost 20% needs to be addressed.
- 74% of respondents felt that elected officials did not really listen to their concerns; while 84% felt that elected officials did not act upon their concerns.

Note that this 10% differential between officials listening and acting on the information they receive can contribute to a lack of trust, and stakeholder disengagement, while the GOJ seeks public

Chapter 6: Further Findings – Comparators: Jamaica, Barbados, and Singapore

support to achieve its economic objectives, including debt reduction targets. Osei (2002) emphasized that trust enabled the development of social capital and debt reduction in Barbados.

Consensus Orientation N=719-PNP; N=711-JLP; The Mean score was: 5.2 for the PNP and 4.8 for the JLP. The percentage of respondents scoring the parties above 5 was 43% for the PNP and 32% for the JLP.

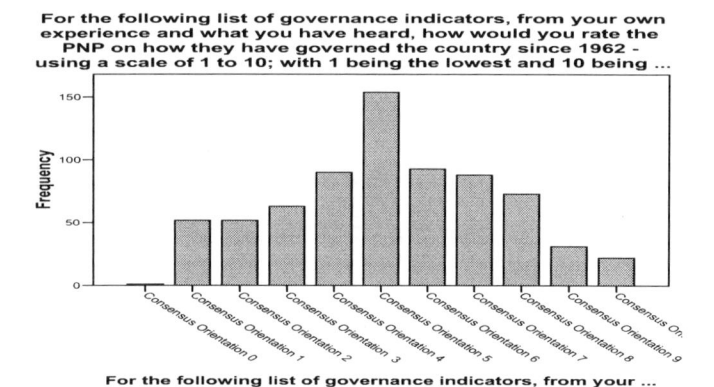

Figure 6.37 Public's Rating of **PNP** on **Consensus Orientation**

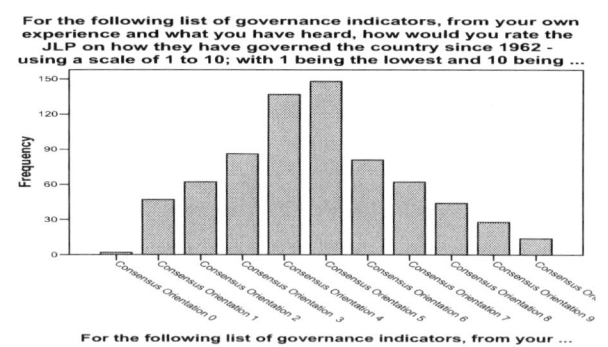

Figure 6.38 Public's Rating of **JLP** on **Consensus Orientation**

- While 93% of the MPs felt that the Government was making clear efforts to involve citizens, only

Chapter 6: Further Findings – Comparators: Jamaica, Barbados, and Singapore

59% of island-wide respondents/citizens shared this view.
- A further analysis using Crosstabs revealed that 51% of respondents who reported that they had never participated in the governance process, felt that the Jamaican Government rarely involved citizens in the decision-making process. Could this have been a disincentive affecting their participation?

Those who indicated that they had not participated in the governance process were fairly evenly distributed across age groups, with the distribution being slightly skewed towards those below 40 years old. This suggests that the youth respondents may have felt excluded.

- Only 36% of MPs felt that the Government generally took a long-term approach to determining what was required for sustainable development.
  - Thirteen percent (13%) of the respondents island-wide shared this view. This was a particularly significant finding.
- 11% of the MPs and 29% of the respondents island-wide felt that public officials rarely took a long-term approach to development.

The disparity in these perspectives (almost 3 to 1) sheds light on the findings in Chapter 5, outlining the lack of a strategic approach to development planning, and; supports the recommendation by Smith-Tennant (2009) that the people to be affected by the development, ought to be more involved in major expenditure development decisions. The resultant debt expansion from arbitrary development decisions including the Highway 2000 is instructive. UNESCAP (2009) also noted that the people must be

Chapter 6: Further Findings – Comparators: Jamaica, Barbados, and Singapore

involved, so that their social, cultural, and historical circumstances can be considered in the decision-making process.

- 72% of the MPs, and; 75% of respondents from the general public felt that the government clearly discussed and understood the cultural perspectives of their constituents.
- However, 24% of respondents island-wide felt that their social circumstances were neither clearly discussed nor understood by the government; 7% of MPs surveyed shared this view.

Equity and Inclusiveness N=730-PNP; N=727-JLP; The **Mean** score was: 5.2 for the PNP and 4.7 for the JLP. The percentage of respondents scoring the parties above 5 was 45% for the PNP and 34% for the JLP.

Equity and inclusiveness go to the heart of the quality of governance required to build social capital and obtain support for the government's debt management strategies.

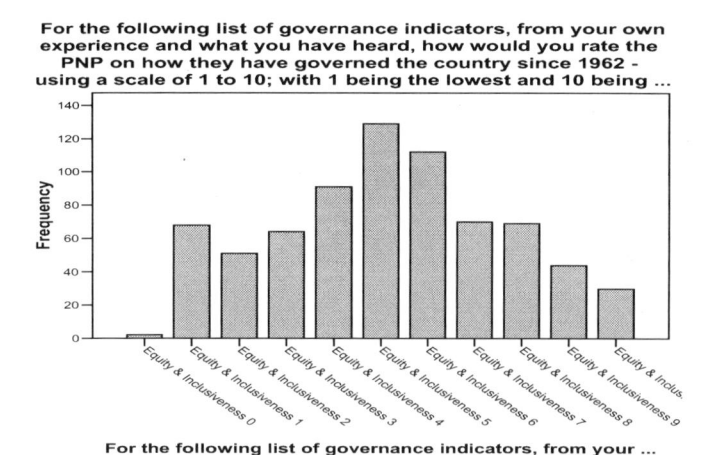

Figure 6.39 Public's Rating of **PNP** on **Equity and Inclusiveness**

Chapter 6: Further Findings – Comparators: Jamaica, Barbados, and Singapore

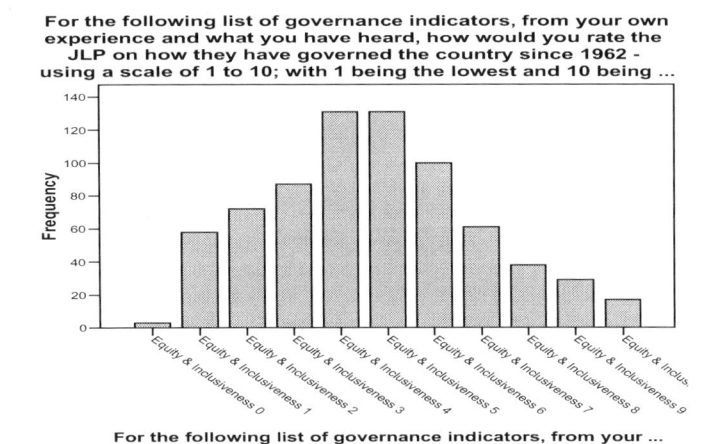

Figure 6.40 Public's Rating of **JLP** on **Equity and Inclusiveness**

- 82% of respondents island-wide did not feel that they had a stake in what the government was doing; 86% of MPs indicated an awareness of this perception.

There was also a general consensus among both groups that the youths, wards of the state, the disabled, and elderly were generally excluded from the mainstream of society, and the decision-making process. Again, a major issue of equity and inclusiveness arises in such circumstances.

Accountability N=737-PNP; N=727-JLP: The **Mean** score was: 4.7 for both the PNP and the JLP. The percentage of respondents scoring the political parties above 5 was 36% for the PNP and 34% for the JLP. This was one of two close scores between the two political parties (JLP and PNP, the other being **Effectiveness** and **Efficiency** (or lack thereof) in which they were both rated average, with a score of 5 out of 10.

Chapter 6: Further Findings – Comparators: Jamaica, Barbados, and Singapore

- 89% of MPs, and; 65% of members of the general public felt that private sector organizations were not generally held accountable to the public.

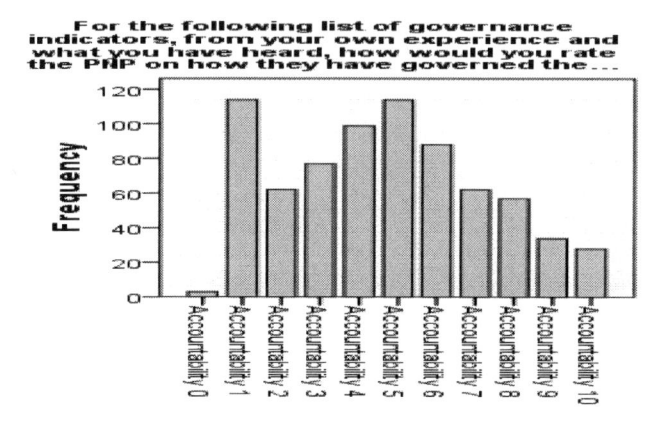

Figure 6.41 Public's Rating of **PNP** on **Accountability**

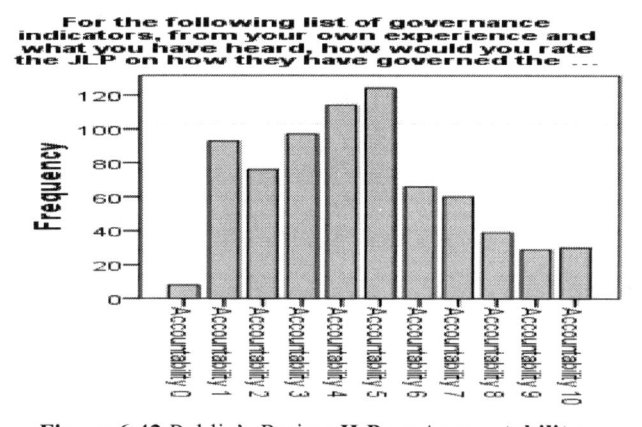

Figure 6.42 Public's Rating **JLP** on **Accountability**

Note the leftward skewing of both of these histograms towards the lower ratings. The interpretation is that both political parties were perceived as being weak in Accountability. The ratings from this study and related governance indicators are triangulated below, to see if there were any parallels. Congruence was observed

Chapter 6: Further Findings – Comparators: Jamaica, Barbados, and Singapore

in some of the scores/ratings from the elites' survey, those of the general public (citizens), and the global ratings of governance in Jamaica, with both political parties being perceived as weak in most areas of governance examined. The scores are presented graphically, in Table 6.7, and Figure 6.43 below.

6.5 TRIANGULATION SUMMARY

Table 6.7 Triangulation - Summary of Comparative Ratings

GOVRNANCE CHARACTERISTIC	Elites Rating	General Public Rating of PNP	General Public Rating of JLP	Global Rating
	Mean Score/10; & % above 5	Mean Score/10; & % above 5	Mean Score/10; & % above 5	Jamaica's Ranking (%)
Participation	5.80; 62%	5.60; 50%	5.00; 37%	n/a
Effectiveness and Efficiency/ Government Effectiveness	3.90; 31%	5.00; 42%	5.00; 40%	(WGI) 62.68
Following the Rule of Law/Rule of Law	5.40; 50%	4.98; 40%	4.60; 31%	(WGI) 37.44
Accountability/ Voice and Accountability	5.10; 47%	4.70; 36%	4.70; 34%	(WGI) 60.19
Regulatory Quality	n/a	n/a	n/a	(WGI)
Political Stability	n/a	n/a	n/a	(WGI)
Control of Corruption	n/a	n/a	n/a	(WGI)
Transparency	5.20; 33%	4.70; 34%	4.40; 27%	(CPI) 3.3
Responsiveness	5.40; 44%	5.20; 45%	4.70; 32%	n/a
Consensus-	4.94; 31%	5.20; 43%	4.80; 32%	n/a
Equity and Inclusiveness	4.60; 25%	5.20; 45%	4.70; 34%	n/a

Source: Interviews; Surveys; WGI - Kaufmann et al (2010); Transparency International CPI (2011)

Chapter 6: Further Findings – Comparators: Jamaica, Barbados, and Singapore

Perception of Governance in Jamaica (1962-2010) from Interviews and Surveys

	Partici pation	Effectiveness and Efficiency/	Following the Rule of Law/Rule of Law	Transparency	Responsiveness	Consensus Orientation	Equity and Inclusiveness	Voice and Accountability
Elite Rating - Overall	62	31	50	33	44	31	25	47
General Public - Rating PNP	50	42	40	34	45	43	45	36
General Public - Rating JLP	37	40	31	27	32	32	34	34

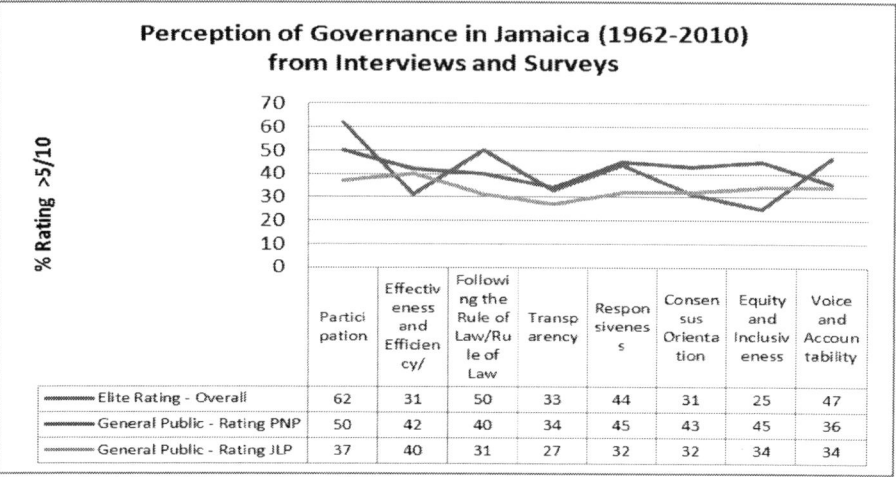

Figure 6.43 Local Perceptions of Governance Quality in Jamaica - Percentage of respondents giving score above 5/10; & Global Rating % from Table 6.7

From the trajectory of the trend lines in Figure 6.3 above, one is able to quickly see each group's perception of the quality of governance in Jamaica, on each of UNESCAP's eight characteristics of good governance discussed. We are also able to discern from the graph, particular areas of weakness, as well as the point of intersection where scores assigned were particularly close.

For the elites, governance in Jamaica was deemed weakest in the areas of Effectiveness and Efficiency, and Equity and Inclusiveness.

The general public saw the PNP as being weakest in Transparency and Accountability (compared to the other indicators of governance); while they saw the JLP's major weakness being in the areas of Following the Rule of Law, Transparency, and Accountability.

Though the trend line (curve) for the PNP's ratings is slightly above that of the JLP in some areas assessed, neither of the two political parties can take pride in these scores, as they were generally marginal, or below average.

Chapter 6: Further Findings – Comparators: Jamaica, Barbados, and Singapore

6.6 Subset of Key Governance Decisions Significantly Impacting Jamaica's Public Debt

We now have an understanding of how the quality of governance in Jamaica was perceived by elites interviewed, Members of Parliament and Jamaican citizens surveyed, Transparency International, The IMF, World Bank, and others, and how they believed this has contributed to the country's indebtedness.

It will be even more instructive to examine some key governance decisions that were made, and how these actually contributed to worsening the country's indebtedness, and prolonged economic stagnation.

Below is a subset of major projects and programmes relating to governance decisions associated with profligate expenditure in Jamaica, and efforts to contain their impact. They were selected, as they were very significant to the debt accumulated over several years (and touted attempts to correct the errors made). They have also contributed to the financial crisis that led up to the first major restructuring of Jamaica's public debt.

- **FINSAC** - cost more than 40% of Jamaica's GDP (World Bank 2011), inclusive of the NCB divestment.
- **Highway 2000** - perennially expanded Jamaica's public debt across its various phases, and administrations, and;
- **The JDX** - the first large-scale restructuring of Jamaica's public debt.

They were chosen because of their local and global relevance, having been highlighted in multiple global reports (WB, IMF, IDB, SEC, CaPRI, others). Below are the related survey findings relating to these subset of projects. The first question asked in this segment was: "Are you aware that Jamaica's public debt exceeded

Chapter 6: Further Findings – Comparators: Jamaica, Barbados, and Singapore

$1.5 Trillion in 2010?" Eight hundred of ten (810) of the targeted 1000 respondents answered this question.

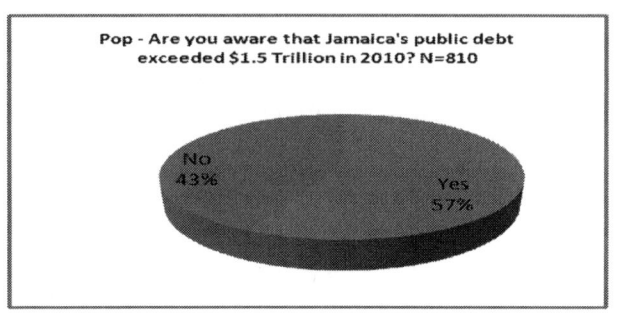

Figure 6.44 Public's Awareness of Level of Public Debt

Less than two-thirds (57%) of respondents were aware of the volume of Jamaica's public debt in 2010. This highlights the need for policymakers to communicate this more clearly, and engage the citizens more fully about the levels, and causes of Jamaica's indebtedness, as it is they (taxpayers) who will be required to contribute to the repayment of the debt.

This will make them more aware of the gravity of the country's liabilities, and their role in the process (including working to boost productivity levels in order to increase GDP, the denominator of the Debt-to-GDP ratio.

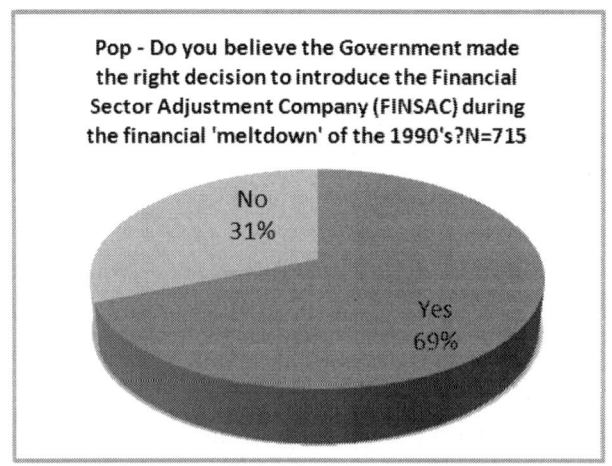

Figure 6.45 Respondents' Opinion on FINSAC

Chapter 6: Further Findings – Comparators: Jamaica, Barbados, and Singapore

31% of respondents believed the government did not make the right decision to introduce **FINSAC** during the financial 'meltdown'. Further probing was necessary to determine what options they perceived should have been considered.

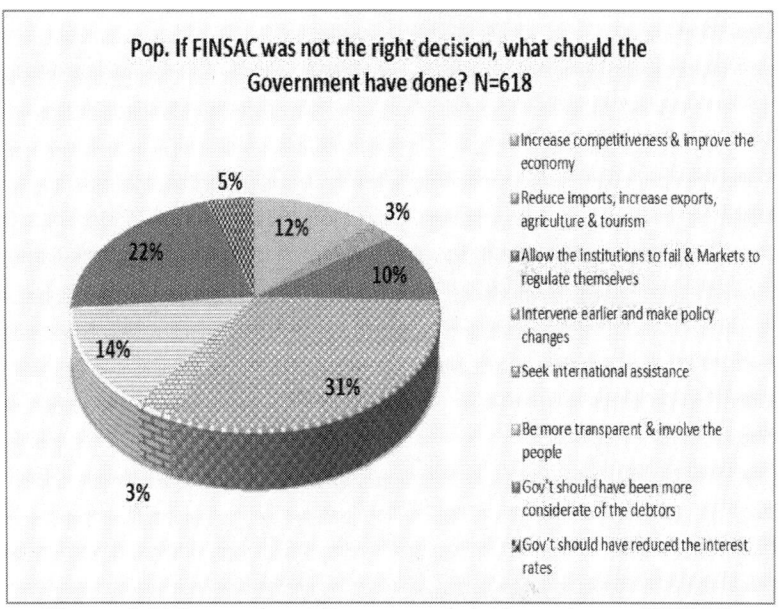

Figure 6.46 Respondents' Recommended Alternatives to FINSAC

36% of respondents felt that Government should have used policy measures (including interest rate reduction), or other strategic interventions, to avoid the need for FINSAC.

- Interestingly, the largest proportion of respondents (31%) believed the government should have intervened earlier, and made the required policy changes.

This is a very important finding. Governments and policymakers globally may benefit from recognizing how early interventions and the requisite policy adjustments can prevent financial crises and unnecessary accumulation of debt.

Chapter 6: Further Findings – Comparators: Jamaica, Barbados, and Singapore

Pop - Do you believe the Government made the right decision to take over debtors' assets and sell NCB during the financial 'meltdown' of the 1990's? N=685

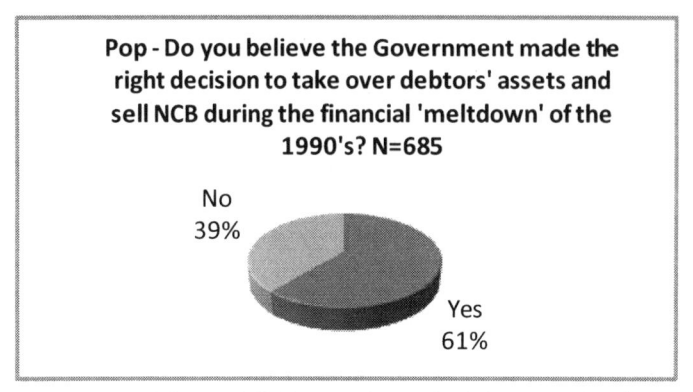

No 39%
Yes 61%

Figure 6.47 Respondents' Opinion on Sale of NCB

39% of respondents disapproved of the government's decision to take over debtors', and; the sale of the National Commercial Bank (NCB).

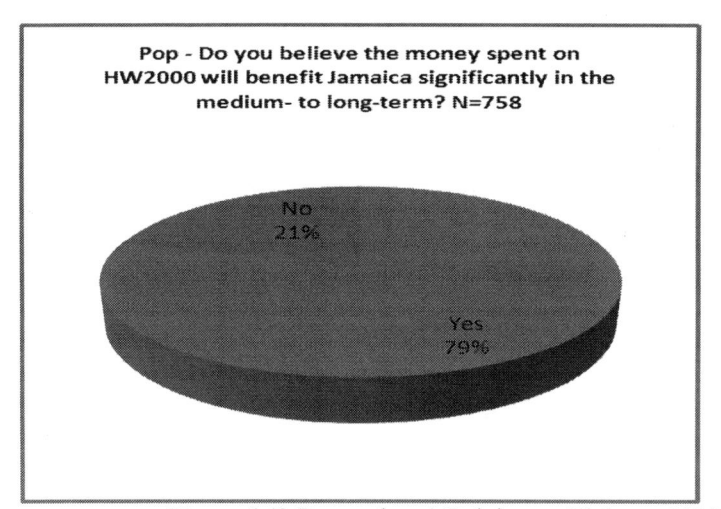

Pop - Do you believe the money spent on HW2000 will benefit Jamaica significantly in the medium- to long-term? N=758

No 21%
Yes 79%

Figure 6.48 Respondents' Opinion on Highway 2000

Though 79% of respondents felt that Highway 2000 (HW2000) would eventually benefit Jamaica, 34% of those who disagreed, believed the benefits would not accrue to Jamaicans, but to overseas investors.

Chapter 6: Further Findings – Comparators: Jamaica, Barbados, and Singapore

Pop - Why do you believe the Highway will not significantly benefit Jamaica in the medium-, to long-term? N=702

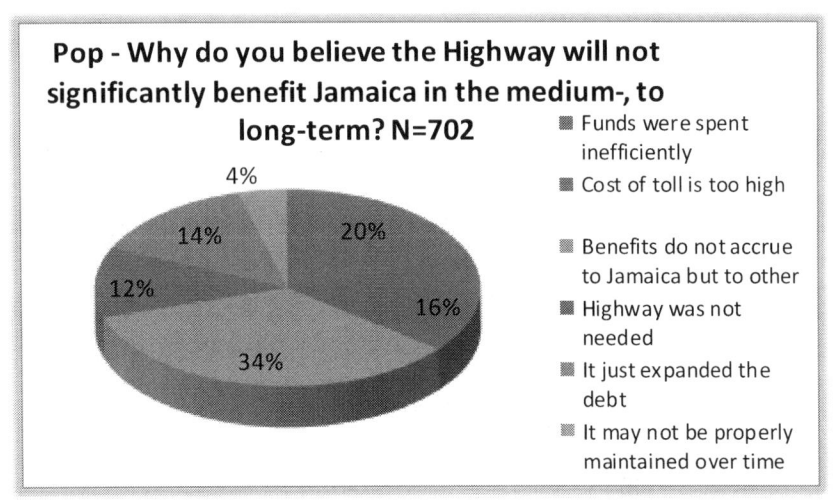

- Funds were spent inefficiently: 20%
- Cost of toll is too high: 16%
- Benefits do not accrue to Jamaica but to other: 34%
- Highway was not needed: 12%
- It just expanded the debt: 14%
- It may not be properly maintained over time: 4%

Figure 6.49 Respondents' Opinion on Why HW2000 May Not Benefit Jamaica

The cost of the toll fees, inefficiency in expenditure on the highway, and its impact on Jamaica's public debt were some of the reasons why respondents felt that HW2000 would not benefit Jamaica in the medium-, to long-term.

Pop - Do you believe the JDX will benefit Jamaica significantly in the short- to medium-term? N=688

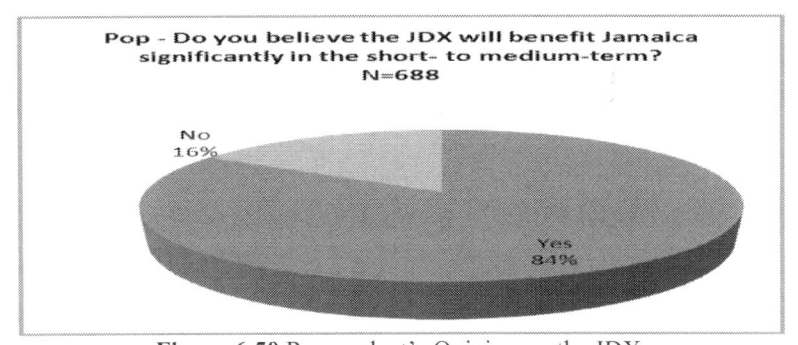

- No: 16%
- Yes: 84%

Figure 6.50 Respondent's Opinion on the JDX

84% of respondents believed that the Jamaica Debt Exchange (JDX) would benefit Jamaica in the short-, to medium-term.
- Unfortunately, as discussed earlier in this publication, the gains from the JDX were limited through poor maturity scheduling, leading to the need for a second debt exchange

– the National Debt Exchange (NDX) in 2013. This posed new challenges (see earlier discussion).

Conclusion

National leaders are expected to demonstrate the principles of good governance, by doing what is ethical and prudent to achieve sustainable development.

In highly indebted countries like Jamaica, these principles will guide the deliberation process, inform policy formulation and implementation, and guide political leaders and their opposition parliamentarians to go beyond what is politically expedient, to substantially reduce the country's indebtedness, and create an enabling environment for economic growth, and progress from households to firms, and ultimately, the economy.

The findings have so far shown that up to 2010, Barbados and Singapore created strong institutions and devised macroeconomic policies that have resulted in their achieving higher levels of economic growth, human capital development, lower levels of external debt, and a more favourable global perception of governance than Jamaica.

Most respondents, including elites, citizens in all fourteen (14) parishes across Jamaica, Members of Parliament (MPs), and even political leaders themselves, agreed that those in governance have done poorly in managing the country's resources, and its public debt.

The local and global perceptions of the character of governance, and the role of policymakers in managing Jamaica's public debt, ranged from average to poor; though gains were perceived to have been made in the area of Responsiveness.

The PNP's scores were slightly higher than the JLP's, in the areas of Participation, Responsiveness, Equity and Inclusiveness; while both political parties (JLP and PNP) were perceived to have done very poorly in the area of Transparency and Accountability in governance.

Chapter 6: Further Findings – Comparators: Jamaica, Barbados, and Singapore

Multiple studies cited throughout this publication, have highlighted that these weaknesses are symptomatic of corruption, profligacy, and state capture in government, leading to poor macroeconomic performance (Hellman and Kaufmann 2001; Camdessus 1997, v; Gray, Hellman and Ryterman 2004, 5; IMF/WB 2002).

When the responses of the citizens' (the governed) were cross-referenced against those of the Members of Parliament's (MPs – the 'governors'), there were divergences in how those who have governed and were in governance roles during the study, perceived their performance, relative to how citizens perceived and rated them.

Particular areas of concern for respondents were: lack of Equity and Inclusiveness, Transparency, Accountability, adherence to the Rule of law, access to information; and a lack of focus on sustainable development. Chapter Seven concludes this publication.

Chapter 7

CONCLUSION

Jamaica is much poorer than it should have been. This was not primarily the result of external factors, but rather, the consequence of a number of poor governance decisions. This pattern of failure can be broken by improving the quality of governance and correcting the weaknesses highlighted in these findings.

This publication has introduced you to (or reminded you of) several theoretical and empirical works relating to governance, and public debt management, with a wide focus on the economic implications of certain policy actions and models proposed by some of the most brilliant minds in economic development, governance, political science, and fiscal policy.

It reviewed the methodologies they employed and discussed the contributions and critiques associated with them. These included the classical works of Adam Smith, David Ricardo, John Maynard Keynes, Sir William Arthur Lewis, Simon Kuznets, Orville J. McDiarmid, Walt W. Rostow, and others.

Some looked at the government's role in macroeconomics, and debt management, while others presented economic models outlining how the government could facilitate development and growth, to minimize excessive accumulation of public debt. The latter is central to the Debt-to-GDP nexus.

The works of George Beckford, Lloyd Best, Kari P. Levitt, Carl Stone, Norman Girvan, James M. Buchanan, Daron Acemoglu et al, Douglass North, and others, have highlighted how obdurate retentions, and weak governance institutions, can affect macroeconomic performance, through interactions within the political economy, and the agencies created to manage the affairs of the State.

Those earlier works were extended upon, by the more contemporary works of economists and scholars like Todaro,

Chapter 7: Conclusion

Acemoglu et al, Chang, Fine, Kauffmann et al, Edwards and Tabellini, the World Bank and IMF, who examined how governance affects macroeconomic performance and indebtedness.

Though different ideological positions were taken, there was a consensus in the literature, that the quality of governance is affected by politics, culture, and the presence or absence of institutional controls.

Hence, the once popular purely orthodox stance is now being strongly contested by the heterodox approaches of economists like Todaro, Chang, and Toye. They have presented alternative strategies to the Washington Consensus, which have been successfully employed by developing countries in Latin America and Asia, to curtail indebtedness, achieve economic development and growth.

There was, however, a gap in the literature with regards to how governance contributes to indebtedness, and poor macroeconomic performance in small developing countries like Jamaica. This study contributes to closing that gap.

As Professor Edwin Jones reminded Jamaican Parliamentarians in 1993, "Governance is about the "politics of management" because it involves guiding society constructively and creatively to cope with development issues" (p. 1).

He emphasized that governance must be seen as an opportunity to find solutions to problems, and responses to the needs of society, through the implementation of sound economic and social policies, to create an environment that promotes equitable development, and participation of stakeholders. He outlined four requirements to achieve good governance:

i. capacity building for effective and efficient public management;
ii. rules and institutions to enhance the predictable and transparent conduct of private and public business;
iii. accountability for economic, financial, and political reform, and;
iv. Reliable information and incentive systems.

Chapter 7: Conclusion

These were important issues addressed throughout this study, on the Role of Governance in Managing Public Debt. The central question asked was:

How has the character of governance in post-independence Jamaica contributed to the country's indebtedness from 1962 to 2010?

This main research question was answered using a convergent Mixed Methods Research (MMR) design. In this research design, qualitative and quantitative data were collected and analyzed concurrently (within a similar timeframe.)

As outlined from Chapters One through Six, the data examined and analyzed, provided unequivocal evidence that the quality of governance in Jamaica from the country's Independence from Britain in 1962 to the twenty-first century has had a major impact on the country's indebtedness, and anaemic growth.

Jamaica's debt management strategy, public debt levels, economic performance, and quality of governance were juxtaposed against those of two of its counterparts – Barbados, and Singapore – that shared many similar characteristics to Jamaica at the time of their own independence.

The character of governance is reflected in the quality of economic, political and administrative decisions made by national leaders, and the resultant outcomes.

A subset of these decisions has been laid out for you in this publication. No other in-depth, empirical study of this nature was identified throughout the process of reviewing the literature and conducting the study.

While some decisions made by national leaders since independence were well-intentioned, many were driven by a political motive, and; some were clearly wasteful and profligate.

Leaders of both major political parties, formed out of union militancy and populism, thought it expedient to borrow and spend arbitrarily on poorly formulated social services, and infrastructural projects, which may have boosted their popularity and extended

Chapter 7: Conclusion

their tenure in power but served to expand the fiscal deficit and increase Jamaica's indebtedness. The impact of those decisions on debt accumulation, revealed a cost of more than **$530 billion**, for a subset of defunct or infeasible projects and programmes.

Though the GOJ has subsequently attempted and still has plans to further divest a number of these loss-making entities, some like the Montego Bay Conference Center and Ian Flynn airport are still on the books.

As the IDB (2007) noted, public debt can be a powerful tool to shape economic policy. If used efficiently the benefits can be tremendous. If not, it can inflict considerable harm (p. 1). This harm faced, is the albatross of debt that now hangs around the necks of current and future generations of Jamaicans. As Professor Edwin Jones emphatically stated:

"Governance is about the "politics of management" because it involves guiding society constructively and creatively to cope with development issues"

REFERENCES & APPENDICES

REFERENCES

Abbas, S.M. Ali, Nazim Belhocine, Asma El-Ganainy and Mark Horton. 2010. "A Historical Public Debt Database." Working Paper WP/10/245. Washington DC: IMF.

Abdellatif, Adel M. 2003. "Good Governance and its Relationship to Democracy and Economic Development." GF3/WS/IV-3/S1. Korea: Ministry of Justice.

Accountant-General Singapore. 2019. "Understanding Singapore Government's Borrowing and its Purposes." Accessed September 4, 2010. http://www.mof.gov.sg/docs/default-source/default-document-library/news-and-publications/featured-reports/understanding-singapore-govt-borrowing.pdf

Acemoglu, Daron, Simon Johnson, James Robinson, and Yunyong Thaichaoen . 2003. "Institutional Causes, Macroeconomic Symptoms: Volatility, Crises and Growth." Journal of Monetary Economics 50 (2003): 49-123. Accessed November 10, 2012. http://www.scholar.harvard.edu/jrobinson/files/jr_jmepublishedversion.

Afonso, Antonio. 1999. "Public Debt Neutrality and Private Consumption Some Evidence from the Euro Area." Portugal: Lisboa School of Economics and Management.

Ahmed, Belal. 2001. "The Impact of Globalization on the Caribbean Sugar and Banana Industries." Accessed February 5, 2010. http://www.caribbeanstudies.org.uk/papers/2001/olv2p1.pdf.

Aisen, Ari, and Francisco José Veiga. 2005. "The Political Economy of Seignorage." IMF Working Paper, WP 05/175. September 2005. Washington, DC: International Monetary Fund.

Alba, Richard. 2005. "Bilingualism Persists, But English Still Dominates." Washington DC: Migration Policy Institute.

Alesina, Alberto, and Roberto Perrotti. 1995. "Income Distribution, Political Instability and Investment." Discussion Paper, no. 751. New York: Columbia University Academic Commons.

Ali, A. 2001. "Political Instability, Policy Uncertainty and Economic Growth: An Empirical Investigation." Atlantic Economics Journal 29(1): 87-106.

Amany, El Anshansy and Marina-Selini Katsaiti. 2010. "Fiscal Performance and Growth: Do Institutions Matter?" Accessed January 26, 2014. http://economics.soc.uoc.gr/macro/docs/Year/2011/papers/paper_2_150

.Angresano, James. 2007. "Orthodox Economic Education, Ideology and Commercial Interests: Relationships that Inhibit Poverty Alleviation." Post-Autistic Economic Review, no. 44: 37-58.

Arrow, Kenneth J. 1987. "Reflections on the Essays." In Arrow and the Foundations of the Theory of Economic Policy. Edited by George Feiwel. NY: NYU Press, pp. 727-734.

Auditor General's Department of Jamaica (AG). 2011. "Report of the Road Maintenance Fund - November." Accessed January 14, 2012. http://www.auditorgeneral.gov.jm/files/u5/it.
___. 2008-2012. "Annual Report." Jamaica: Office of the Auditor General. Kingston, Jamaica.
AUSAID. 2002. Good Governance, Guiding Principles for Implementation. Canberra, Australia: Australian Agency for International Development. Accessed July 15, 2011. Accessed August 16, 2012. http://www.ausaid.gov.au/anrep/rep02/pdf/annualreport01_02.pdf.
Babbie, Earl. 2001. The Practice of Social Research. 9th edition. Belmont, CA: Wadsworth/Thompson Learning.
Bank for International Settlements (BIS). 2011. Interactions of Sovereign Debt Management with Monetary Conditions and Financial Stability. CGFS Papers No 42. Basle, Switzerland. Accessed June 5, 2012. http://www.bis.org/publ/cgfs42.pdf.
Bank of Jamaica (BOJ). 1962. "Report and Statement of Accounts for the Year Ended 31st December." Jamaica: United Printers Ltd.
Bank of Jamaica (BOJ). 2021. "BOJ Counter Rates". Accessed July 23, 2021. https://boj.org.jm/market/foreign-exchange/counter-rates/
___. 1970-1979. "Report and Statement of Accounts for the Year Ended 31st December." Jamaica: Bank of Jamaica.
___. 2006. "Statistical Digest." Jamaica: Bank of Jamaica.
___. 2009-2011. "Annual Report and Statement of Account for the Year Ended 31 December." Jamaica: Bank of Jamaica.
___. 2010-2012. Economic data. Accessed May 13, 2011. http://www.boj.org.jm/economic_data.php?report_id=78.
Baran, Paul. (1957) 1968. The Political Economy of Growth. NY: Modern Reader.
Barclay, Lou Anne and Norman Girvan. 2008. "Transnational Restructuring and the Jamaican Bauxite Industry: The Swinging Pendulum of Bargaining Power." Paper Presented at a Pre-Conference on the Global Economic History of Bauxite, Paris in September, 2008. Jamaica: University of the West Indies.
Barro, Robert. 1979. "On The Determinants of Public Debt." Journal of Political Economy, 87 (5): 940-71.
Barrow, Errol W. 1965. "Barbados Economic Survey: Summary." St. Michael, BD: Economic Planning Unit, Office of the Premier.
Barsky, Robert B., N. Gregory Mankiw and Stephen P. Zeldes. 1986. "Ricardian Consumers with Keynesian Propensities." The American Economic Review, Vol. 76, No. 4 (Sep., 1986): 676-91.
Bauer, P., and B. S. Yamey. 1957. Economic Analysis and Policy in Underdeveloped Countries. Chicago, Ill: Chicago University Press.
Beckford, George L. (1972) 1999. Persistent Poverty: Underdevelopment in Plantation Economies of the Third World. First published by Oxford University Press, and in 1983, 1988 by the author. Jamaica: The University of the West Indies Press.
Beckford, George, and Norman Girvan. 1989. Development in Suspense. Jamaica: Fredrick Ebert Stiftung.

Bennett, Karl. 1988. "External Debt, Capital Flight and Stabilization Policy – The Experiences of Barbados, Guyana, Jamaica and Trinidad and Tobago." Social and Economic Studies, 37 (4). Jamaica: Uni. Of the West Indies.

Bertram, Arnold. 1995. P. J. Patterson: A Mission to Perform. Jamaica: AB Associates and Supreme Printers and Publishers Ltd.

Best, Lloyd, and Kari Levitt. 1968. "Character of the Caribbean Economy." In Caribbean Freedom Economy and Society from Emancipation to Present. Edited by Hilary Beckles and Verene Shepherd: 405-20. Jamaica: Ian Randle.

Best, Lloyd. 2003. "Reflections on Reflections." In Independent Thought and Caribbean Freedom: Essays in Honour of Lloyd Best. Edited by Selwyn Ryan. St. Augustine. Trinidad and Tobago: Sir Arthur Lewis Institute of Economic Studies.

Best, Lloyd and Kari Polanyi Levitt. 2009. Essays on the Theory of Plantation Economy: A historical and institutional Approach to Caribbean Economic Development. Jamaica: University of the West Indies Press.

Bhagwati, Jagdish N. 1978. "Anatomy and Consequences of Exchange Control Regimes." Cambridge, MA: National Bureau of Economic Research. Accessed July 28, 2013. http://www.nber.org/chapters/c1024.pdf.

Blackman, Courtney N. 1995. "Financial Accounting for Central Banks – with Special Reference to CARICOM." In The Experience of Central Banking with Special Reference to the Caribbean. Edited by Ramesh Ramsara, 101-14. Jamaica: University of the West Indies.

Blavy, Rodolphe. 2006. "Public Debt and Productivity: The Difficult Quest for Growth in Jamaica." IMF Working Paper Series WP/06/235. Washington DC: International Monetary Fund.

Boothe, Paul and Bradford Reid. 1992. "Debt Management Objectives for a Small Open Economy." Journal of Money, Credit and Banking 24 (1).

British Broadcasting Corporation. 2009. Accessed April 16, 2011. http://news.bbc.co.uk/2/hi/americas/8159513.stm.

____. 2006. "Jamaica – 'murder capital of the world'." British Broadcasting Corporation. Accessed January 6, 2006. http://www.bbc.co.uk/caribbean/news/story/2006/01

____. 2007. "Jamaican Party Returns Gift." British Broadcasting Corporation, Accessed February 7. http://www.bbc.co.uk/caribbean/news/story/2007/02/070227_trafigura..

Bruntland Commission. 1987. "Our Common Future: Report of the World Commission on Environment and Development." UK: Oxford University.

Buchanan, James M. 1984. "The Moral Dimension of Debt Financing." In The Economics of Budget Deficits. Edited by Charles K. Rowley, William F. Shughart II and Robert D. Tollison. The Economics of Budget Deficit Vol. II. UK: Edward Elgar Publishing Ltd.

Buckley, Byron. 2006. "A Question of Leadership – Bruce vs. Portia Contrasting Strengths and Styles." Sunday Gleaner, November 26, 2006. Jamaica: Gleaner.

Buddan, Robert. 2009. "Nethersole and Sangster, Fathers of Financial Management." Sunday Gleaner, April 5. Jamaica: Gleaner.

Bullock, Colin. 2010. "It's Not an Easy Road Growing out of Debt." Sunday Gleaner, December 19. Jamaica: Gleaner.

___. 2010. "Exchange Rate Policy in Jamaica: A Search for Fiscal prudence and 'Reasonable Men." Abstract. Mona Business Review. Accessed May 2, 2011. http://173.203.89.141/openpublish/article/exchange-rate-policy.

Burnside, Craig and David Dollar. 2004. "Aid Policies, and Growth: Revisiting The Evidence." Working Paper No. 3251. Washington DC: World Bank.

Camdessus, Michel. 1997. IMF Managing Director. Accessed June 7, 2012. http://www.imf.org/external/pubs/ft/exrp/govern/govern.pdf.

Caribbean Development Bank. 2008. "The Caribbean Development Fund Act." Barbados: CDB.

___. 2013. "CDB in Jamaica – Real People, Real Development." Barbados: CDB.

Caricom Today. 2021. "Barbados Government Moving Ahead With Republic." Accessed August 24, 2021. http://today.caricom.org/2021/07/27/barbados-government-moving-ahead-with-republic/

Carter Center, The. 2006. "Observations of the Access to Information Act 2002." Accessed July 14, 2011. http://www.cartercenter.org/resources/pdfs/peace/americas/observations_amendments_jamaica2006.pdf.

Carvajal, Ana, Hunter Munroe, Catherine Pattillo and Brian Wynter. 2009. "Ponzi Schemes the Caribbean." IMF Working Paper WP 09/95. Washington DC: International Monetary Fund.

Castro, Manuel Fernando, Gladys Lopez-Acevedo, Gita Beker Busjeet, Ximena Fernandez Ordonez. 2009. "Mexico's M and E System: Scaling Up from the Sectoral to the National Level." ECD Working Paper No. 20. Washington, DC: World Bank.

Cayadi, Gundy, Barbara Kursten, Marc Weiss and Guang Yang. 2004. "Singapore's Economic Transformation." Czech Republic: Global Urban Development.

Central Bank of Barbados (CBB). 2007. "Functions of the Bank." Accessed March 31, 2012. http://www.centralbank.org.bb/WEBCBB.nsf/webp.

Central Intelligence Agency (CIA). 2013. "Singapore." In World Fact Book. Accessed April 7, 2013. https://www.cia.gov/library/publications..

Chami, Ralph, Adolfo Barajas, Thomas Cosimano, Connel Fullenkamp, Michael Gapen, and Peter Montiel. 2008. "Macroeconomic Consequences of Remittances." Occasional Paper 259. Washington, DC: International Monetary Fund.

Chang, Ha-Joon. 2002. Kicking Away the Ladder. Development Strategy in Historical Perspective. London: Anthem Press.

Chen, John-ren. 2007. "Goodbye Marx hello Confucius: Ideological paradigm Change in Economic Transition of PRC." Austria: University of Innsbruck.

Chenery, Hollis B. 1979. Structural Change and Development Policy. Baltimore, MD: John Hopkins University Press.

Chor Tik Te. 2009. "Compliance and Impact of Corporate Governance Best Practice Code on the Financial Performance of New Zealand Listed Companies. "Aukland NZ: Massey University.

Christie, Greg. 2011. "Overcoming the Problem of Corruption in Jamaica." Accessed November 2, 2012. http://www.cg.gov.jm/website_files/.

Clarke, Lavern. 2011. "Jamaica, IMF in Dance of Delays." Gleaner, October 7, 2011. Jamaica: Gleaner.

Clarke, Dr. Nigel [@drnigelclarkeja]. (2021, March 9). Although our nominal debt remained flat, due to the significant decrease in our GDP, because of COVID-19, Jamaica's debt-to-GDP ratio jumped a staggering 16 points, from 94% to a projected 110%. Accessed August 18, 2021. http://twitter.com/drnigelclarkeja/status/1369389110549417987?s=21

Collister, Keith. 2010. "Why Can't Jamaica Grow? Lessons from Barbados." Jamaica Observer, March 17, 2010.

Coase, Ronald. 1992. "The Institutional Structure of Production." American Economic Review 82 (4): 713-19.

Concise Encyclopaedia of Economics - Accessed December 28, 2010. http://ww.econlib.org.

Coore, David. 1977. "The IMF Agreement." Ministry Paper 28/1977. Jamaica: Houses of Parliament.

Cosenza, Elizabeth. 2007. "The Holy Grail of Corporate Governance Reform: Independence or Democracy?" Accessed March 15, 2012. http://www.law2.byu.edu/lawreview4/archives/2007/1/1COSENZA.FIN

Craigwell, Roland, Llewellyn Rock and Ronald Sealy. 1988. "On the Determinants of External Public Debt: The Case of Barbados." In Social and Economic Studies 37 (4). Jamaica: University of the West Indies, Mona.

Crotty, Michael. (1998) 2006. The Foundations of Social Research – Meanings and Perspectives in the Research Process. Australia: SAGE Pub.

Dal Bo, Ernesto and Martin Rossi. 2008. "Term Length and Political Performance." Accessed April 2, 2012. http://www.economia.uniandes.

Davies, Omar. 1984. An Analysis of Jamaica's Fiscal Budget." Jamaica: University of the West Indies.

Davis, Kevin, Angelina Fisher, Benedict Kingsbury and Sally Engle Merry. 2012. Governance by Indicators – Global Power Through Quantification and Rankings. UK: Oxford Press.

Delong, J. Bradford. 2011. What Have We Learned From the Financial Crises Of the 1990s?Accessed November 18, 2011. http://www.econ161.berkeley.edu/TotW/learned.html.

Dijkstra, Geske and Niels Hermes. 2003. "The Debt Crises, International Responses and Results of Debt Relief: Report of a literature survey and an economic analysis." The Hague: IOB.

Dijkstra, Geske. 2008. "Global Governance and Debt Relief – The Need for Policy Coherence and New Partnerships." Geneva Switzerland: EADI General Conference.

Domar, Evesey. 1946. "Capital Expansion, Rate of Growth, and Employment." Econometrica 14 (2): 137- 47.

___. 1957. Essays in the Theory of Economic Growth. New York: Oxford University Press.

Dooley, Michael P. 2000. "Debt Management and Crisis in Developing Countries." Journal of Development Economics, Vol. 63 (2000): 45-58.

Downes, Andrew S. (2002) 2004. "Economic Growth in a Small Developing Country: The Case of Barbados." Bridgetown, BD: University of the West Indies.

Downes, D. and Moore, W.R. 2007. "Does the Exchange Rate Regime Influence the Relationship between the Output Gap and Current Accounts." Applied Economics, 20(2): 227-40.

Ducote, Nicolas J. 2007. "World Governance Survey. Preliminary Analysis: Argentina." Buenas Aires, Argentina: Centro de Implementación de Políticas Públicas para la Equidad y el Crecimiento.

Easterly, Williams and Ross Levine. 2003. "Tropics, Germs and Crops: How Endowments Influence Economic Development." Cambridge, MA: National Bureau of Economic Research.

Eberstadt, Nicholas. 1989. "Missed Opportunities." Indianapolis, IND: Hudson Institute.

ECLAC. 2001. "Analysis of Economic and Social Development in Barbados: A Model for SIDS." Economic Commission for Latin America and the Caribbean, 22 June, 2001, LC/CAR/G. 652.

Economics Help. "Macroeconomics." Accessed April 12, 2011. http://www.economicshelp.org/macroeconomics/fiscal-policy.

Economics About. "Seignorage." Accessed February 10, 2010. http://economics.about.com/od/economicsglossary/g/seignorage.htm.

Econ Library.org. "Keynesian Economics." Accessed December 28, 2010. http://ww.econlib.org.

Economist Intelligence Unit (EIU). 2011. "Country Report 2010-2011." London: The Economist Group.

Economist. 2011. "What Do You Do When You Reach the Top?" Accessed December 27, 2012. http://www.economist.com/node/21538104.

___. 2011. "Who Were the Physiocrats?" Accessed January 23, 2014. http://www.economist.com/blogs/freeexchange/2013/10/economic

EconStats – a compilation of IMF, IFS data. Accessed March 15, 2012. http://www.econstats.com/ifs/NorGSc_Bar1_Y.htm.

Edie, Carlene. 2000. "Economic Performance, Leadership Crisis and Voting Bahaviour in the 1997 Jamaican Parliamentary Election." Journal of Social and Economic Studies, 49 (1) (March 2000). Jamaica: University of the West Indies.

Edwards, Sebastian and Guido Tabellini. 1991. "Explaining Fiscal Policies and Inflation in Developing Countries." NBER Working Paper No. 3493. Cambridge MA: National Bureau of Economic Research.

Electoral Commission of Jamaica. 2021. "Parliamentary Elections." Accessed August 24, 2021. http://ecj.com.jm/elections/election-results/parliamentary-elections

Encyclopedia Britannica. "Principles of Taxation." Accessed May 11, 2013. http://www.britannica.com/EBchecked/topic/584578/taxation/72010/Principles-of-taxation.

European Commission (EC). 2007. "Performance Measurement Report for Jamaica. Public Expenditure and Financial Accountability. Accessed June 10, 2011. http://ec.europa.eu/europeaid/what/economic-support/public-finance/documents/jamaica_pefa_report_2007_en.pdf.

Financial Sector Adjustment Committee (FINSAC). Accessed November 12, 2010. http://www.finsac.com/news/speeches/patrickhyltonthinktank.htm.

___ Fine, Ben. 2006. "New Growth Theory." In Rethinking Development Economics Edited by Ha Joon-Chang. London: Anthem Press.

FINSAC. Accessed November 12, 2010. http://www.finsac.com/news/speeches/patrickhyltonthinktank.htm.

Fitch Ratings. Full Rating Report – February 2011. Accessed May 19, 2012. http://www.fitchratings.cl/Upload/jamaica_2011.pdf.

Fitch Ratings. "Fitch Affirms Jamaica at 'B+' Outlook Stable." Fitch Rating Action Commentary – March 18, 2021. Accessed July 23, 2021. https://www.fitchratings.com/research/sovereigns/fitch-affirms-jamaica-at-b outlook-stable-18-03-2021

Foster, Patrick. 2006. "Portia Defends Her Constituency." Jamaica Observer. Accessed September 15, 2006. http://www.jamaicaobserver.com/news/112903.

Frederickson, H. G. and Kevin B. Smith. 2003. The Public Administration Theory Primer. Boulder, Colorado: Westview Press.

Girvan, Norman P, P.I. Gomes and Donald B. Sangster. 1983. Technology Policies for Small Developing Economies - A Study of the Caribbean. Jamaica: University of the West Indies.

Girvan, Norman, Rodriquez, Ennio, Sevilla, Mario A., Hatton, Miguel C. 1988. The Debt Problem of Small Peripheral Economies. Jamaica: United Coop Printers Ltd.

Gleaner, The. 2002. "Jamaica lagging in productivity – Experts say country lagging behind Barbados et al – Wages and labour costs named as factors." Gleaner, November 18, 2002. Jamaica: The Gleaner Co. Ltd.

___. 2008. "Spencer Not the First." Gleaner, February 27, 2008.

___. 2009. "S & P Downgrade Signals 'Deficiency' of Economic Team – Davies." Gleaner, August 7, 2009.

___. 2009. "Fitch Downgrades CAP – Says Investors Losing Confidence In Jamaica." Gleaner, November 28, 2009.

___. 2010. "FINSAC Commission of Enquiry." Gleaner, March 19, 2010.

___. 2011. "Deputy DPP Took Draft Request to UK." Gleaner, Nov. 1, 2011.

___. 2011. "OCG: Political Parties Should Debate Corruption." Accessed November 21, 2011. http://go-jamaica.com/news/read_article.

Global Forum on Transparency and Exchange of Information

(GFTEI). 2011. "Supplementary Peer Review Report, Phase 1, Legal and Regulatory Framework - BARBADOS." Accessed July 14, 2011. http://www.oecd.org/countries/barbados/50053228.pdf.

___. 2021. "Rating agency Standard and Poor's (S&P) today revised Jamaica's economic outlook from stable to negative." Accessed August 26, 2021. http://jamaica-gleaner.com/article/news/20200416/sp-revises-jas-outlook-stable-negative-reaffirms-b-rating

Gojamaica.com. 2011. "GOJ to Pay Billions to Highway 2000 Contractor." Accessed April 2, 2012. http://go-jamaica.com/news/read_article.

Gordon, Sabrina. 2011. "COMPLANT Employs SCJ as Agents." Gleaner, January 5, 2011. Jamaica: The Gleaner Co. Ltd.

Government of Barbados (GOB). 1964-1986. "Barbados Economic Survey." St. Michaels, BD: Economic Planning Unit, Office of the Prime Minister.

___. 1998. "The Laws of Barbados. The Guarantee of Loans (Companies) Act, Chapter 96 – L.R.O 1998." St. Michaels, BD: Government Printer.

___. 2009. "Draft Medium Term Development Strategy 2010-2014." Bridgetown, BD: Ministry of Economic Affairs, Empowerment, Innovation, Trade, Industry and Commerce.

___. 2010. "Barbados Economic Survey." St. Michaels, BD: Economic Planning Unit.

___. 2011. "Annual Reports and Financial Statements of the Accountant General for Financial Year 2010-2011." Accessed June, 10, 2012. http://treasury.gov.bb/sites/default/files/Financial%20Year%202010-2011%20Annual%20Accountant%20General%20Report.pdf

___. 2012. "Barbados Economic Review." St. Michaels, BD: Government of Barbados.

Government of Jamaica (GOJ). 1962. "JAMAICA: The Jamaica (Constitution) Order in Council 1962." Jamaica: Government Printing Office.

___. 1962-2010. "Estimates of Expenditure." Jamaica: Ministry of Finance.

___. 1962-2010. Ministry Papers outlining Government Guarantees. Jamaica: Houses of Parliament.

___. 1978. "Targets and Objectives of the Economic Programme for 1978-1980. Ministry Paper 10/1978. Jamaica: Houses of Parliament.

___. 1981. "Extended Fund Facility Arrangement with IMF." Ministry Paper 9/1981. Jamaica: Houses of Parliament.

___. 1983. Ministry Papers 32/1981; 34/1981; 35/1981, outlining Loans to Jamaica. Jamaica: Houses of Parliament.

___. 1988. "Going for Growth: The Medium Term Economic Progress Report." Ministry Paper 17/1988. Jamaica: Houses of Parliament.

___. 1999. "Financial Administration and Audit Act -1999." Jamaica: Ministry of Finance and Planning.

___. 2001. "Transaction Documents." Jamaica: Clifford Chance Rogers & Wells.

___. 2001. PROSPECTUS: 11.625% Notes Due 2022. Jamaica: Ministry of Finance and Planning.

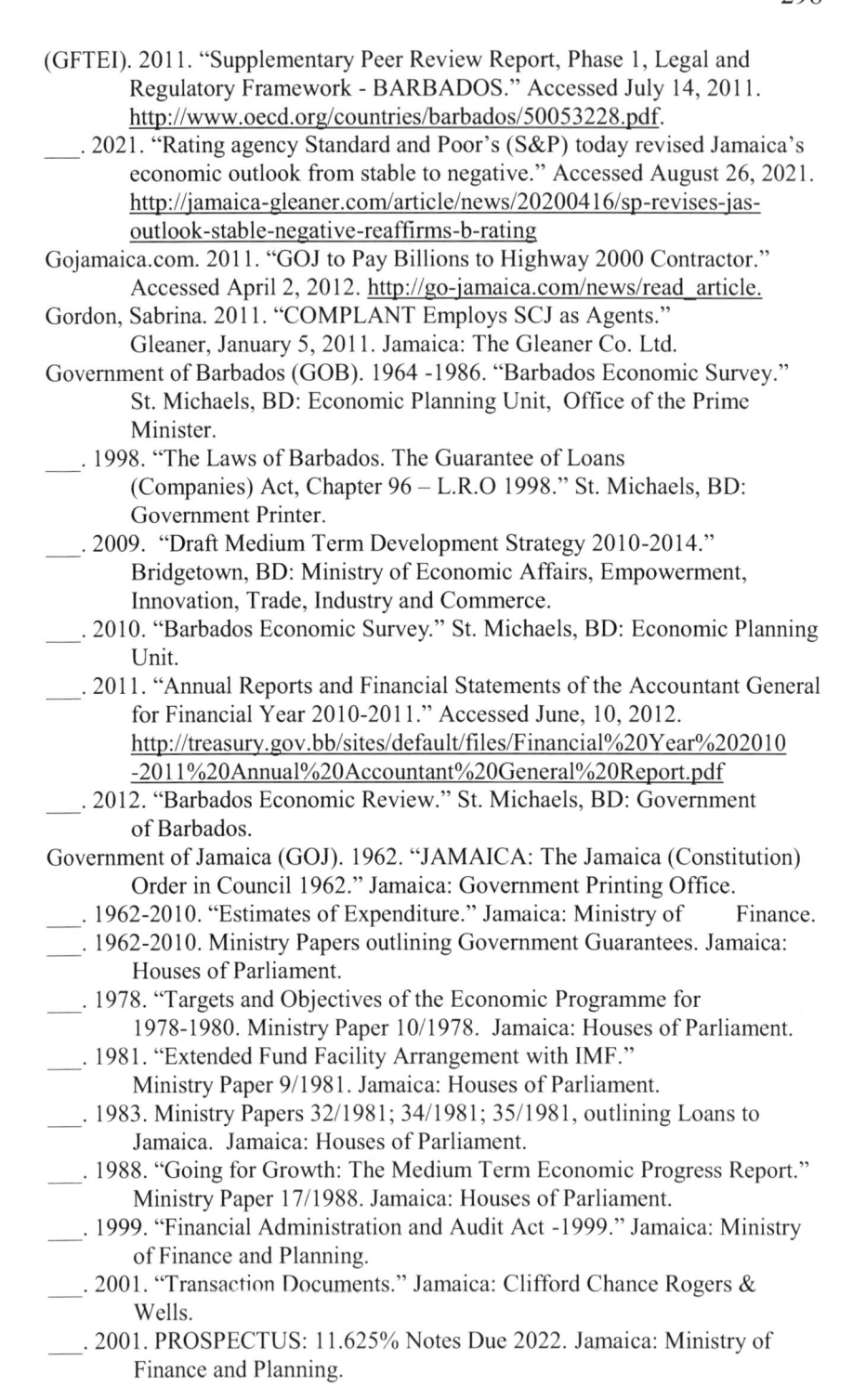

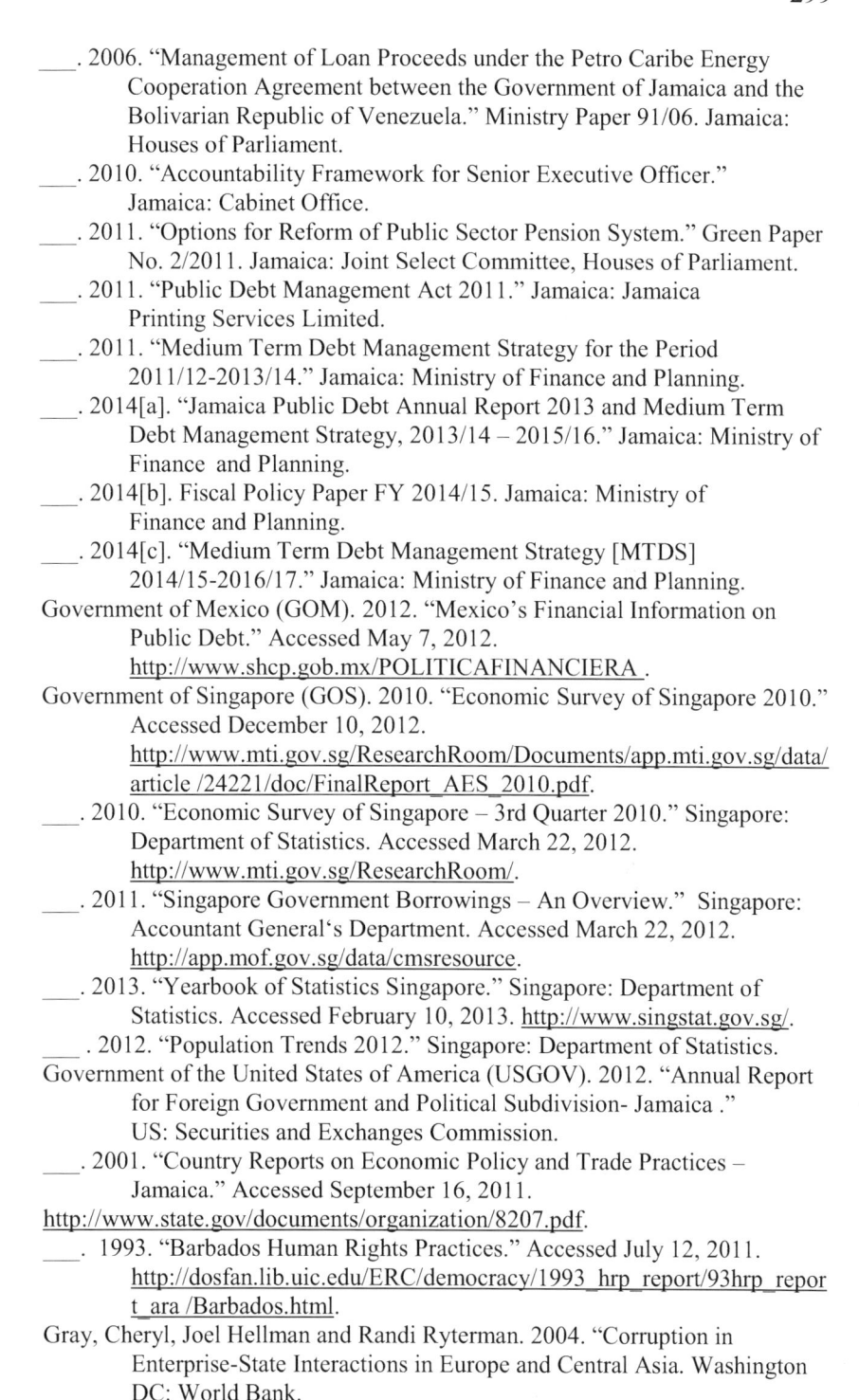

___. 2006. "Management of Loan Proceeds under the Petro Caribe Energy Cooperation Agreement between the Government of Jamaica and the Bolivarian Republic of Venezuela." Ministry Paper 91/06. Jamaica: Houses of Parliament.

___. 2010. "Accountability Framework for Senior Executive Officer." Jamaica: Cabinet Office.

___. 2011. "Options for Reform of Public Sector Pension System." Green Paper No. 2/2011. Jamaica: Joint Select Committee, Houses of Parliament.

___. 2011. "Public Debt Management Act 2011." Jamaica: Jamaica Printing Services Limited.

___. 2011. "Medium Term Debt Management Strategy for the Period 2011/12-2013/14." Jamaica: Ministry of Finance and Planning.

___. 2014[a]. "Jamaica Public Debt Annual Report 2013 and Medium Term Debt Management Strategy, 2013/14 – 2015/16." Jamaica: Ministry of Finance and Planning.

___. 2014[b]. Fiscal Policy Paper FY 2014/15. Jamaica: Ministry of Finance and Planning.

___. 2014[c]. "Medium Term Debt Management Strategy [MTDS] 2014/15-2016/17." Jamaica: Ministry of Finance and Planning.

Government of Mexico (GOM). 2012. "Mexico's Financial Information on Public Debt." Accessed May 7, 2012. http://www.shcp.gob.mx/POLITICAFINANCIERA .

Government of Singapore (GOS). 2010. "Economic Survey of Singapore 2010." Accessed December 10, 2012. http://www.mti.gov.sg/ResearchRoom/Documents/app.mti.gov.sg/data/article /24221/doc/FinalReport_AES_2010.pdf.

___. 2010. "Economic Survey of Singapore – 3rd Quarter 2010." Singapore: Department of Statistics. Accessed March 22, 2012. http://www.mti.gov.sg/ResearchRoom/.

___. 2011. "Singapore Government Borrowings – An Overview." Singapore: Accountant General's Department. Accessed March 22, 2012. http://app.mof.gov.sg/data/cmsresource.

___. 2013. "Yearbook of Statistics Singapore." Singapore: Department of Statistics. Accessed February 10, 2013. http://www.singstat.gov.sg/.

___. 2012. "Population Trends 2012." Singapore: Department of Statistics.

Government of the United States of America (USGOV). 2012. "Annual Report for Foreign Government and Political Subdivision- Jamaica ." US: Securities and Exchanges Commission.

___. 2001. "Country Reports on Economic Policy and Trade Practices – Jamaica." Accessed September 16, 2011.
http://www.state.gov/documents/organization/8207.pdf.

___. 1993. "Barbados Human Rights Practices." Accessed July 12, 2011. http://dosfan.lib.uic.edu/ERC/democracy/1993_hrp_report/93hrp_report_ara /Barbados.html.

Gray, Cheryl, Joel Hellman and Randi Ryterman. 2004. "Corruption in Enterprise-State Interactions in Europe and Central Asia. Washington DC: World Bank.

Greenland, Colin. 2012. "Forensics - Key to DPP vs. CG." Sunday Gleaner, May 20. Jamaica: The Gleaner Co. Ltd.

Greenwood, Jeremy, Zvi Herkowitz and Per Krusell. 1997. "Long-Run Implications of Investment-Specific Technological Change." American Economic Review, 87 (3): 342-62

Grenade, Kari and Denny Lewis-Bynoe. 2010. "Reflecting on Development Outcomes: A Comparative Analysis of Barbados and Guyana."Working Paper, 2010. Bridgetown, BD: Central Bank of Barbados.

Grindle, Merilee. 2005. "Good Enough Governance Revisited." A report for the Department for International Development (DFID). Boston, MA: Harvard.

___. 2010. "Good Governance: The Inflation of an Idea." Research Working Paper Series (RWP 10-023). Boston, MA: Harvard.

Guardian, U.K. 2009. "Mabey Johnson Foreign Bribery." Accessed November 1, 2011. http://www.guardian.co.uk/business/2009/sep/25.

Hall, Kenneth O., Dennis Benn. 2003. Governance in the Age of Globalization. Jamaica: Ian Randle.

Hall, Robert E. and Charles I. Jones. 1999. "The Productivity of Nations." Accessed December 21, 2010. http://elsa.berkeley.edu/~chad/ProdNat2.pdf.

Harrod, Roy F. 1939. "An Essay in Dynamic Theory." The Economic Journal 49 (193): 14-33. Accessed March 12, 2013. http://www.jstor.org/stable/2225181.

Heckman, Stephen. 2011. "South Korea could be model for Japan's Economic Development." Accessed July 30, 2011. http://www.japantoday.com/category/commentary/view.

Heilbrunn, John R. 2004. "Anti-Corruption Commissions Panacea or Real Medicine to Fight Corruption." Washington, DC: The World Bank Inst.

Hellman, Joel and Daniel Kaufmann. 2001. "Confronting the Challenge of State Capture in Transition Economies." Finance and Development, Sept. 2001, 38 (3). Washington, DC: International Monetary Fund.

Henry, Balford. 2013. "$29-B loan for JDIP clone." Jamaica Observer. Accessed June 5, 2013. http://www.jamaicaobserver.com/news.

Henry, Peter Blair and Conrad Miller. 2008. "Institutions versus Policies- A Tale of Two Islands." Working Paper 14604, December. Cambridge, MA: National Bureau of Economic Research.

Henry, Peter. 2013. Turnaround, Third World Lessons for First World Growth. New York: Basic Books.

Highway 2000. "About Us." Accessed September 28, 2011. http://www.h2kjamaica.com/web/index.php/about-h2k/.

Hilaire, Alvin. 2000. "Caribbean Approaches to Economic Stabilization." Working Paper – WP 00/73. Washington, DC: International Monetary Fund.

Hobbes, Thomas. 1962. Leviathan – Or the Matter of Forme and Power of a Commonwealth Ecclesiastical and Civil. Edited by Michael Oakeshott. New York: Collier Books.

Honourable Jamaica Houses of Representatives (Parliament). 2009. "Minutes." November 3. Jamaica: Gordon House.

Hornbeck, J. F. 2004. "Argentina's Sovereign Debt Restructuring." CRS Report for Congress RL32637. October 19. Washington, DC: The Library of Congress.

Hou, Yilin. 2003. "Public Administration: Challenges of Inequality and Exclusion." Georgia: International Association of Schools.

Hudson, Suzette and Robert Stennett. 2003. "Current Account Sustainability in Jamaica." Working Paper no. 02/11. Jamaica: Bank of Jamaica

Hussey-Whyte. 2011. "Montague Says Agriculture Should Contribute More to GDP." Jamaica Observer. Accessed September 16. http://www.jamaicaobserver.com/news/Montague-says.

Institute on Governance Canada. 2004. "Strengthening Social Policy." Accessed February 12, 2011. http://iog.ca/wp-content/uploads/2012/12/2004.

Inter-American Development Bank. 2005. "Country Programme Evaluation: 1990-2002." October 2005. Washington, DC: Inter-American Development Bank.

___. 2005. "Country Strategy with Barbados." Washington DC: Inter-American Development Bank.

___. 2006. "The Informal Sector in Jamaica." Washington DC: Inter-American Development Bank.

___. 2007. "Living With Debt. How to Limit the Risk of Sovereign Finance." In Economic and Social Progress in Latin America. Coordinated by Borensztein, Eduardo, Eduardo Levy and Yeyati Ugo Panizza. Accessed March 1, 2012. http://www.iadb.org/res/publications/pubfiles/pubITO-2007.pdf.

International Federation of Accountants (IFAC). 2009. "Evaluating and Improving Governance in Organizations." New York: IFAC. Accessed Feb. 8, 2014. http://www.ifac.org/sites/default/files/publications.

International Labour Organization (ILO). 1999. "Employment Policy in a Small Island Economy." Country Employment Policy Review, February 1999. Port of Spain TR: ILO, Caribbean.

International Monetary Fund (IMF). 1988. "World Economic Outlook." Washington DC: International Monetary Fund.

___. 1997. "IMF Stand-by Arrangement – Summary of Economic Programme. December 5, 1997. Washington, DC: International Monetary Fund.

___. 1990. "The Role of National Savings in the World Economy." Occasional Paper No. 67, March 19, 1990. Washington, DC: International Monetary Fund. Accessed August 17, 2020. http://www.elibrary.imf.org

___. 2002. "Assessing Sustainability." Washington, DC: International Monetary Fund.

___. 2004. "Evaluation Report – The IMF and Argentina 1991-2001." June 30. Washington DC: IMF Publication Services.

___. 2005. "Argentina Announces its Intention to Complete Early Repayment of its Entire Outstanding Obligation to the IMF." Press Release 05278. December 15. Washington DC: International Monetary Fund.

___. 2005. "Good Governance: The IMF's Role." Accessed March 19, 2012. http://www.imf.org/external/pubs/ft/exrp/gvern/govindex.htm.

___. 2007. "International Monetary Fund Handbook, Its Functions Policies and Operations." Edited by Bernhard Fritz-Krockow and Parmeshwar Ramlogan. Washington, DC: International Monetary Fund.

___. 2008. "IMF Country Report No. 08/198, Jamaica Selected Issues." Washington, DC: IMF. Accessed October 14, 2010. http://www.imf.org/external/pubs/ft/scr/2008/cr08198.pdf.

___. 2008. "IMF Country Report No. 08/280, Singapore: 2008 Article IV Consultation – Staff Report." Washington, DC: International Monetary Fund.

___. 2010. "IMF Revises up its Global Economic Forecast." Accessed April 21, 2011. http://blog-imfdirect.imf.org/2010/01/26.

___. 2010. "IMF Country Report No. 10/267, Jamaica 2009 Article IV Consultation and Request for a Stand-By Arrangement." Accessed January 3, 2011. http://www.imf.org/external/pubs/ft/scr/2010/cr10267.

___. 2010. "IMF Country Report 10/268, Jamaica: 2010 First Review of the Stand-By Arrangement." Accessed January 3, 2011. http://www.imf.org/external/pubs/ft/scr/2010/cr10268.

___. 2011. "IMF Country Report No. 11/49: Jamaica -Third Review under the Stand-By Arrangement." Accessed Feb. 15, 2011. http://www.imf.org/external/pubs/cat/longres.aspx?sk=24638.0 .

___. 2011. "Factsheet." The IMF and the World Bank. Accessed September 10, 2011. http://www.imf.org/external/np/exr/facts/imfwb.htm.

___. 2012. "IMF Country Report No. 12/7, Barbados 2011 Article IV Consultation." Washington, DC: International Monetary Fund.

___. 2012. "IMF Country Report No. 12/4, Singapore 2011 Article IV Consultation." Washington, DC: International Monetary Fund.

___.2012. "People's Republic of China 2012 Article IV Consultation." Washington, DC: International Monetary Fund.

___. 2012. "Growth Resumes, Dangers Remain." World Economic Outlook. Washington, DC: International Monetary Fund.

___. 2012. "World Economic and Financial Surveys." Accessed April 7, 2013. http://www.imf.org/external/pubs/ft/weo/2012/.

___. 2013. "Jamaica Request for an Extended Arrangement under the Extended Fund Facility." Washington, DC: International Monetary Fund.

___. 2013. "Transitions and Tensions." World Economic Outlook. Washington, DC: International Monetary Fund.

___. 2013. "Singapore: Report on the Observance of Standards and Codes." IMF Country Report # 13/326. Washington, DC: International Monetary Fund.

___. 2014. "Barbados Financial System Stability Assessment." IMF Country Report No. 14/53. Washington, DC: International Monetary Fund.

___. 2020. "Jamaica – Request for Repurchase Under Rapid Financing Instrument." IMF Country Report No. 20/167. Accessed Aug. 24, 2021.http://www.imf.org/~/media/Files/Publications/CR/2020/English/1JAMEA20200001.ashx

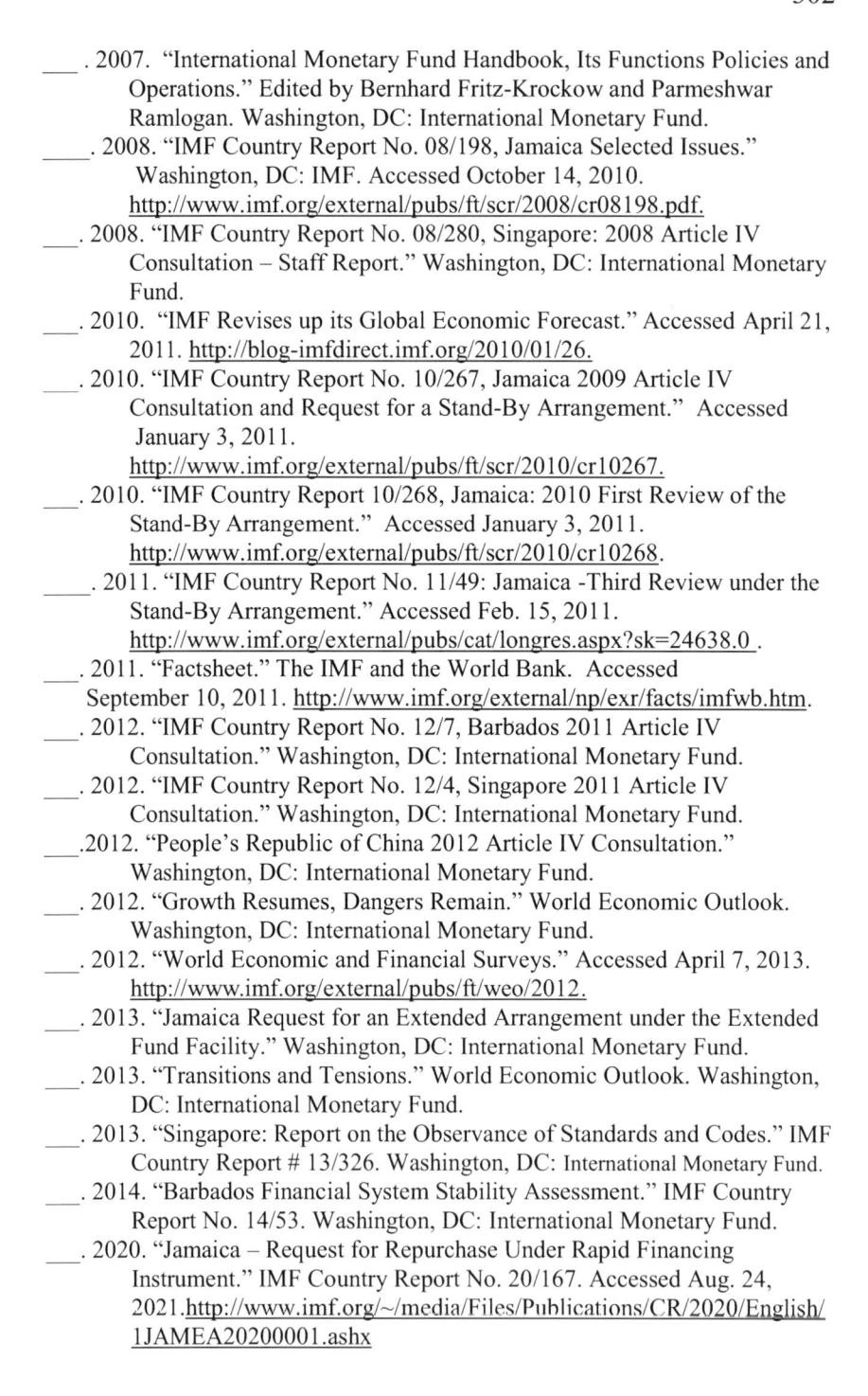

___. 2020. "IMF Executive Board Approves a US$520 Million Disbursement to Jamaica to Address the COVID-19 Pandemic." IMF Press Release No. 20/217. Accessed August 25, 2021. http://www.imf.org/en/News/Articles/2020/05/15/pr20217-jamaica-imf-executive-board-approves-disbursement-to-address-the-covid-19-pandemic?cid=em-COM-123-41597

___. 2021. IMF World Economic Outlook, April 2021. Washington DC:

___. 2021. International Monetary Fund Data Mapper. Accessed August 18, 2021. http://www.imf.org/external/datamapper/profile

International Monetary Fund/World Bank. 2002. "Guidelines for Public Debt Management: Accompanying Document." Approved by Sundararajan, V. and Kenneth G. Lay. November 21, 2002. Washington, DC: IMF.

Islam, Nazrul. 1995. "Growth Empirics. A Panel Data Approach." Quarterly Journal of Economics, November 1995, 110, pp. 1127-1170.

Jackson, Steven. 2011. "Air Jamaica Divestment Team Pats Itself on The Back." Gleaner, October 21, 2011. Jamaica: The Gleaner Co. Ltd.

Jalles, Joao Tovar. 2011. "The Impact of Democracy and Corruption on the Debt-Growth Relationship in Developing Countries." Journal of Economic Development, 41, Vol 36, no. 4 (December): 41-72.

Jamaica Information Service (JIS). 2011. "Jamaica Must Reverse Decline in Labour Productivity." Accessed November 23, 2011. http://www.jis.gov.jm/news/110-labour-social-security/9906-labour-jamaica-must-reverse-decline-in-labour-productivity-douglas

___. 2016. "'5 in 4' Growth Plan Will Benefit Poor and Vulnerable." Article written by Denise Dennis, November 9, 2010. Accessed August 24, 2021. http://jis.gov.jm/5-4-growth-plan-will-benefit-poor-vulnerable/

___. 2011. "Access to Information – Summary of the Act." Accessed July 14, 2011. http://www.jis.gov.jm/special_sections/ATI/default.html.

Jamaica Money Market Brokers Investment and Research (JMMBIR). 2010. "Monetary Policy Easing Continues." Market Call. November 18. Jamaica: Jamaica Money Market Brokers.

___. 2010. "BARBADOS – Murky Fiscal Waters Ahead." Market Call. Nov. 12. Jamaica: Jamaica Money Market Brokers.

Jamaica Observer. 2010. "Pressure Builds on PM." Jamaica: The Jamaica Observer Ltd. Accessed May 14, 2011. http://www.jamaicaobserver.com/news/Pressure--builds-on-PM_7611790.

___. 2011. "Cops Disciplined – 5 Sergeants, 17 Corporals Dismissed from JCF." Jamaica Observer, January 10, 2011.

___. 2011. "JP Targets New Markets for 2011." Jamaica Observer, March 02, 2011.

___. 2011. "Debate Battle." Jamaica Observer, December 16, 2011. Accessed May 8, 2012. http://www.jamaicaobserver.com/elections/news/Debate-Battle

James, Canute. 1988. "Government Probing Free Zone Working Conditions." Journal of Commerce, Apr. 05, 1988. Accessed August 24, 2021. http://www.joc.com/maritime-news/jamaican-government-probing-free-zone-working-conditions_19880405.html

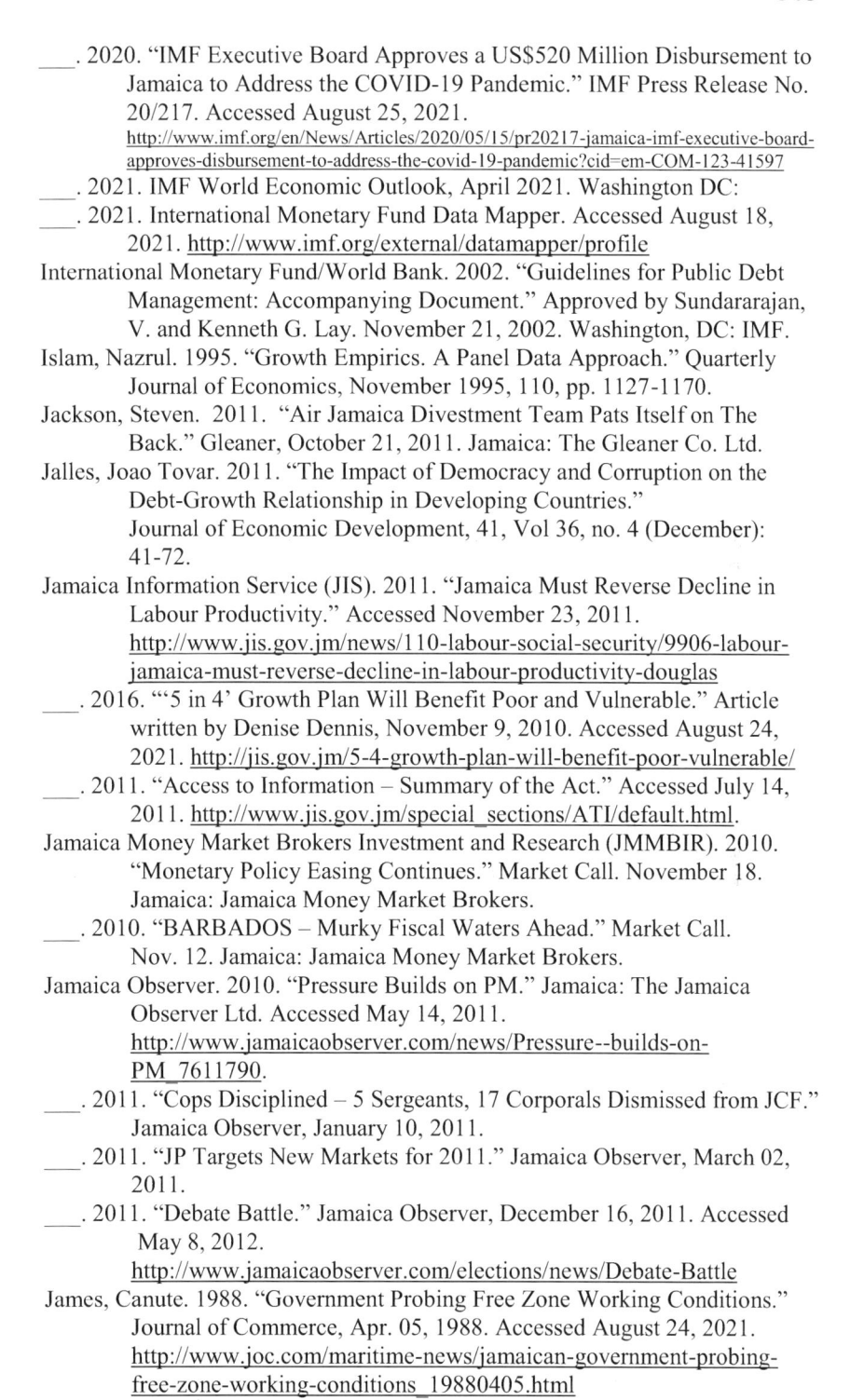

Johnston, Jake and Juan A. Montecino. 2011. "Jamaica: Macroeconomic Policy, Debt and the IMF. May 2011." Washington. DC: Center for Economic and Policy Research.

Jones, Edwin.1974. "Interest Group – Bureaucracy Interaction and Public Policy in Jamaica." Journal of Social and Behavioural Sciences, vol 20, no. 4. Ann Arbor, Michigan: Edward Brothers Inc.

___. 1981. "The Political Economy of Public Administration in Jamaica." In Perspectives on Jamaica in the 70's. Edited by Carl Stone and Aggrey Brown. Jamaica: Jamaica Publishing House.

___. 1993. "Demands of Governance in Contemporary Jamaica." Paper presented at a Seminar of PNP Parliamentarians. Wyndham, Rose Hall. Jamaica.

Juma, Calestous and Lee yee-Cheong. 2005. "Innovation: Applying Knowledge to Development." London: Earthscan.

Kappagoda, Nihal. 2002. "Institutional Framework for Public Sector Borrowing." Document no. 17. New York: United Nations Institute for Training and Research.

Karagiannis, Nikolaos, Anthony Clayton and Jessica M. Bailey. 2014. "Developmental Interventions in the Caribbean." Jamaica: University of the West Indies.

Kaufmann, Daniel. 2003. "Rethinking Governance: Empirical Lessons Challenge Orthodoxy." Washington, DC: The World Bank.

___. 2013. "Six Questions on the Cost of Corruption." Washington, DC: World Bank. Accessed April 16, 2011.http://go.worldbank.org/KQH743GKF1.

Kaufmann, Daniel, Aart Kraay and Massimo Mastruzzi. 2006. Governance Matters V: aggregate and individual governance indicators for 1996-2005." WPS 4012. Washington, DC: World Bank. Accessed January 10, 2011.
http://documents.worldbank.org/curated/en/2006/09/7088636.

Kaufmann, Daniel, Aart Kraay. 2007. "Where Are We, Where Should We Be Going?" October 2007. Washington DC: World Bank. Accessed March 7, 2011. http://info.worldbank.org/governance/wgi/pdf .

Kaufmann, Daniel, Aart Kraay, and Pablo Zoido-Lobaton. 2000. "Governance Matters: From Measurement to Action." Finance and Development, Vol. 37, no. 2.

Keynes, John M. 1936. The Treatise on Money. Basinstoke, London: Macmillan
Press Limited.

___. 1971. Collected Writings of John Maynard Keynes Volume VI- A Treatise On Money. London: Macmillan Press Limited.

Khan, Mushtaq H. 2007. "Governance, Economic Growth and Development Since the 1960s." Working Paper # 54. New York: United Nations.

Kimenyi, Mwangi S. 1990. "The Causal Relationship Between Revenues and Expenditures: A Developing Country Case Study. Journal of Public Finance and Public Choice, VIII, n. 1(April 1990). Dordrecht, Neth: Economia delle Scelte Pubbliche.

King, Damien and Latoya Richards. 2008. "Taking Responsibility: Jamaica's Debt." CaPRI Policy Paper W0801, March. Jamaica: Caribbean Policy Research Institute.

___. 2000. "The Evolution of Structural Adjustment and Stabilization Policy in Jamaica." Jamaica: University of the West Indies.

Kirkpatrick, Colin and David Tennant. 2002. "Responding to Financial Crisis: Better Off Without the IMF? The Case of Jamaica. Working Paper No. 38. Jamaica: Finance and Development Research Programme.

Klak, Thomas. 1993. "Recent Caribbean Industrialization Trends and their Impacts on Household Well-being." Accessed June 29, 2013. http://ufdcimages.uflib.ufl.edu/CA/00/40/01/36/00001/PDF.pdf.

Klenow, Peter J., and Andres Rodriquez-Clare. 1997b. "The Neoclassical Revival in Growth Economics: Has It Gone Too Far?" NBER Macroeconomics Annual 1997, Volume 12: 73-103.

K'nife, Kadamawe. 2007. Jamaica Governance, Planning and Economic Underperformance 1970-2000: Could Scenario Planning and Foresighting Provide a Basis For a More Sustainable Model Of Development. PhD diss., University of the West Indies.

Kraay, Aart and Vikram Nehru. 2003. "When Is External Debt Sustainable?" Washington, DC: The World Bank.

Krueger, Anne. 1978. "Liberalization Attempts and Consequences." Cambridge, MA: National Bureau of Economic Research.

Kuznets, Simon. 1971. "Modern Economic Growth: Rate, Structure and Spread." American Economic Review, 45 (1):1-28.

Kwon, Gohoon, Lavern McFarlane and Wayne Robinson. 2006. "Public Debt, Money Supply and Inflation. A Cross-Country Study and its Application to Jamaica." IMF WP/06/121. Washington, DC: IMF.

Lacey, A. R. 2000. A Dictionary of Philosophy. New York NY: Routledge.

Laeven, Luc and Fabian Valencia. 2008. Systemic Banking Crises: A New Database. IMF Working Paper WP/08/224. Accessed December 12, 2011. http://www.imf.org/external/pubs/ft/wp/2008/wp08224.pdf.

Lagarde, Christine. 2012. "China Development Forum 2012." Luncheon address by Christine Lagarde, IMF Managing Director in Beijing, China. Sunday, March 18. Washington, DC: International Monetary Fund.

___. 2012. "Promises to Keep: The Policy Actions Needed to Secure Global Recovery." Speech at the Petersons Institute for International Economics, Washington DC, September 24. Washington, DC: IMF.

___. 2014. "China's Youth, Global Leaders, Global Citizens." Speech at Tsinghua University, Beijing, China March 23, 2014. Washington DC: IMF.

Lal, Deepak K and H. Mynt. 1998. The Political Economy of Poverty, Equity and Growth: A Comparative Study. Oxford, UK: Oxford University Press.

Latin American Studies. 1999. "Jamaica Responds to Riot by Rolling back tax." Accessed November 1, 2011. http://www.latinamericanstudies.org/caribbean/responds.htm.

Laws of Jamaica (LOJ). 1999. "The Financial Administration and Audit Act." vol. IX. pp. 19- 20. Jamaica: Houses of Parliament.

Lawson, Tony. 1997. Economics and Reality. London: Routledge.
Le Franc, Elsie. 1999. "The Consequences of Structural Adjustment: A Review of the Jamaican Experience." Jamaica: Canoe Press.
Lee Hsien Loong. 1998. "The Asian Financial Crisis: Challenges to Business Management." Speech made on 30 July 1998, by DPM Lee Hsien Loong to IMD Alumni at the Shangri-La Hotel, Singapore. Accessed 30 Oct. 2012. http://stars.nhb.gov.sg/stars/public/
Lee Kuan Yew. 2000. From Third World to First, the Singapore Story 1965-2000. New York: Harper Collins Publishers.
Leedy, Paul. 1997. Practical Research, Planning and Design. New Jersey: Prentice Hall.
Levitt, Kari Polanyi. 1991. The Origins and Consequences of Jamaica's Debt Crisis, 1970-1990. Jamaica: Consortium Graduate School of Social Sciences, University of the West Indies.
___. 2000. The George Beckford Papers. Jamaica: Canoe Press.
Levi, Darrell. 1989. Michael Manley: The Making of a Leader. Jamaica: Heinemann Publishers (Caribbean) Ltd.
Lewis, W. Arthur. 1939. The 1930s Social Revolution. In Caribbean Freedom Economy and Society from Emancipation to Present. Edited by Hilary Beckles and Verene Shepherd. Jamaica: Ian Randle Publishers.
Lewis, W. Arthur. 1954. "Economic Development with Unlimited Supplies of Labour." Manchester School of Economics and Social Studies, 22: 139-191.
Lewis, W. Arthur. 1994. Sir Arthur Lewis Collected Papers 1941-1988, vol. 1. Edited by Patrick Emmanuel. St. Michael, BD: Institute of Social and Economic Research (Eastern Caribbean), University of the West Indies, Cave Hill.
Lim, Chong Yah. 2007. "Transformation in the Singapore Economy: Courses and Causes." In Singapore and Asia in a Globalized World. Singapore: World Scientific Publishing Co.
Lindahl, Erik. 1919. Just Taxation – A Positive Solution. Translated by Elizabeth Henderson. In R. A. Musgrave and A. T. Peacock, Classics in the Theory of Public Finance. London: McMillan
Linton, Latonya. 2021. "$31.1-Billion Infrastructure Programme to Drive Jobs, Economic Activity." Jamaica Information Service. Accessed July 23,2021. https://jis.gov.jm/31-1-billion-infrastructure-programme-to-drive-jobs-economic-activity/
Love 101. 2011. Interview with Damien and Dennis Chung. By Rev. Clinton Chisholm. On Morning Watch, December 7, 2011 at 7:54 am.
Lucas, Robert. 1988. "On the Mechanics of Economic Development." Journal of Monetary Economics, 22 (1988): 3-42.
Luton, Daraine. 2011. 'Jamaica Seeks Evidence From UK In Hibbert Case." Gleaner, July 6, 2014. Jamaica: The Gleaner Co. Ltd.
Mahmood, Sohail. 2001. "The Musharraf Regime and the Governance Crisis: A Case Study of the Government of Pakistan." New York: Nova Publishers.
Mankiw, N. Gregory. 2010. Macroeconomics. 7th Edition. New York: Worth Publishers.

Mankiw, N. Gregory, David Romer and David Weil. 1992. "A Contribution to The Empirics of Economic Growth." Quarterly Journal of Economics, 1-7 (2):402-37. Cambridge, Mass: Massachusetts Institute of Technology.

Manley, Michael. 1982. Struggle in the Periphery. London: Third World Media Limited.

Marano, Angelo. 1999. The Road to Sound Public Finances: Economic Growth vs. Primary Surplus. Milano Italy: Departimento di Economia e Produzione, Politechnico di Milan.

Martinussen, John. 1997. Society, State and Markets: A Guide to Competing Theories of Development. London: Zed Books Limited.

Marx, Karl. 1921. The Poverty of Philosophy. Stuttgart-Berlin.

___. 1967. Capital Vol. 1 – A Critical Analysis of Capitalist Production. Edited by Frederick Engels. New York: International Publishers Co. Inc.

Matthews, R. O. C. 1986. "The Economics of Institutions and the Sources of Economic Growth." Economics Journal, Vol. 96(4): 903-18

Maunder, Peter, Danny Myers, Nancy Wall, and Roger LeRoy Miller. 1991 Economics Explained. 2nd Edition. Hammersmith, London: Collins Educational Publishers.

Mauro, Paolo. 1995. "The Persistence of Corruption and Slow Economic Growth." Research Department. Washington, DC: IMF.

May, Erskine. 2004. Treatise on the Law, Privileges, Proceedings and Usage of Parliament, 23rd ed. UK: Lexix Nexis.

McDiarmid, Orville John. 1977. "Unskilled Labour for Development- Its Economic Cost." Washington, DC: The World Bank.

Meeks, Brian. 2001. "Reinventing the Jamaican Political System, in Reinventing Jamaica: A Conversation about the Renewal of a Diasporic Society." Souls, Fall, 2001, 3 (4).

Milas, Costas and Gabriella Legrenzi. 2002. "Multivariate Approach to the Growth of Governments." In Public Finance Review. 30 (1), January 2002: 56-76. Sage Publications.

Miller, Clyde Lee. 2013. "Cusanus, Nicolaus." The Stanford Encyclopedia of Philosophy (Summer 2013 Edition). Accessed Feb. 7, 2014. http://plato.stanford.edu/archives/sum2013/entries/cusanus/.

Ministry of Finance and Planning. 2006. "Debt Management Strategy FY 2006/07." Jamaica: Ministry of Finance and Planning.

___. 2010. "JDX Launch." Accessed September 05, 2010. http://www.mof.gov.jm/sites/default/files/JdX_Launch.

___. 2011. "Debt Management Strategy FY 2011/2012 – 2013/2014." April 28. Jamaica: Ministry of Finance and Planning.

Modigliani, Franco and Merton Miller. 1958. "The Cost of Capital, Corporation Finance and the Theory of Investment." Nashville, TN: The American Economic Review. 48 (June 1958):261-97.

Monetary Authority of Singapore. 2001. "Singapore's Exchange Rate Policy." Singapore: Monetary Authority of Singapore. February 2001.

Mongabay. Accessed May 6, 2012. http://www.mongabay.com/history/singapore.

Moore, Winston and Kevon Skeete. 2010. "The Implications of Monetary Policy Shocks for Government Debt Management in Barbados." Bridgetown, BD: Research Department, Central Bank of Barbados.

Moxam, Earl. 2004. "Omar Stakes His Claim." Gleaner, June 6, 2004. Accessed August 14, 2011. http://jamaica-gleaner.com/gleaner/20040606/cleisure/cleisure2.html.

Myers, John. 2008. "Uncertainty About $300m Banana Loan." Gleaner, September 17, 2008. Accessed November 10, 2011. http://jamaica-gleaner.com/gleaner/20080917/business/business6.html.

Nanda, Ved P. 2006. "The Good Governance Concept Revisited." In Annals of the American Academy of Political and Social Science, vol. 603 (January). Thousand Oaks. CA: SAGE Publishing.

Nanto, Dick. 1998. CRS Report for Congress, February 6, 1998. Washington, DC: The Library of Congress.

___. 2009. "The Global Financial Crisis – Analysis and Policy Implications." RL 34742, October 2, 2009. Washington, DC: Congressional Research Services. U.S. Congress. Accessed December 17, 2011. http://www.fas.org/sgp/crs/misc/RL34742.pdf.

National Resources Conservation Authority (NRCA). 2004. Accessed March 28, 2012. http://www.nrca.org/projects/Kingstonharbour/ComponentA.

Netherlands. 2003. "Results of International Debt Relief 1990-1999." IOB Evaluation NR 292. The Hague, Netherlands: Ministry of Foreign Affairs.

Newstallk 93 FM. 2012. Accessed May 9, 2012. http://www.newstalk.com.jm/index.php?module=Jamaican-News-Politics- online- Radio-stationandfunc=viewpubandtid=23andpid=873.

Ng, Francis and Alexander Yeats. 1997. "Good Governance and Trade Policy, Are They Keys to Africa's Global Integration and Growth?" Washington, DC: World Bank.

Niskanen, W.A. 1971. Bureaucracy and Representative Government. Chicago: Aldine.

North, Douglass. 1991. "Institutions." In Journal of Economic Perspectives, Vol. 5, No. 1 (Winter, 1991): 97-112.

___. 1990. "Institutions and a Transaction Cost Theory of Exchange." In Perspectives on Positive Political Economy. Edited by Alt, James E. and Kenneth Shepsle. UK: Cambridge Press.

Nurkse, Ragnar. 1953. Problems of Capital Formation in Underdeveloped Countries and Patterns of Trade and Development. New York: Oxford University Press.

Office of the Contractor General (OCG). 2008-2012. Annual Report. Jamaica: OCG.

___. 2012. "Open Statement by the OCG Regarding the Proposed Highway 2000 North South Link and the Container Trans-shipment Hub Project." Jamaica: OCG.

Office of Management and Budget and Federal Reserve Bank of St. Louis. 2021.'Federal Debt: Total Public Debt as Percent of Gross Domestic Product [GFDEGDQ188S]. Accessed August 19, 2021.

http://fred.stlouisfed.org/series/GFDEGDQ188S

Onis, Ziya. 1995. "The Limits of Neo-liberalism: Towards a Reformation of Development Theory." Journal of Economic Issues, 29 (1) (March).

Organization for Economic Co-operation and Development (OECD). 2013. "Annual Survey of Large Pension Funds and Public Pension Reserve Funds." Paris, France: OECD.

Osei, Philip D. 2002. "Disjointed Incrementalism, State Autonomy and Capacities and Social Policy in Jamaica." Paper Presented to SALISES Conference on Enabling Human and Economic Development. Jamaica: University of the West Indies.

___. 2002. "Tripartite Social Partnerships in Small States: Barbados and Jamaica in Comparative Perspective." Jamaica: University of the West Indies.

___. 2005. "Final Report to the National Advisory Council on Local Governance Reform in Jamaica." Jamaica: University of the West Indies.

___. 2007. "Corruption Scandals and Anti-Corruption Institution Building Interventions in Jamaica." In Corruption and Development: The Anti-Corruption Campaigns. Edited by Sarah Bracking. Basingstoke: Palgrave Macmillan.

Oxford Dictionaries Online. Oxford, UK : Oxford University Press. Accessed June 18, 2011. http://www.oxforddictionaries.com.

Ozler, Sule and Guido Tabellini. 1991. "External Debt and Political Instability." NBER Working Paper No. 3772. Cambridge, MA: National Bureau of Economic Research.

Pan American Health Organization (PAHO). 2010. "JAMAICA: PAHO/WHO Country Cooperation Strategy 2010-2015." Accessed January 8, 2012. http://www.who.int/countryfocus/cooperation_strategy/jamaica.

Pandeiros, Monica and Warren Benfield. 2010. "Productive Development Policies in Jamaica." IDB-WP128. Washington: Inter-American Dev. Bank.

Pantin, Denis. 1989. "Into the Valley of Debt: An Alternative Path to the IMF/World Bank Road in Trinidad and Tobago." St. Augustine TR: University of the West Indies, Department of Economics.

Panton, David. 1993. Jamaica's Michael Manley: The Great Transformation. Jamaica: Kingston Publishers.

Parrado, Eric. 2004. Singapore's Unique Monetary Policy: How Does it Work? IMF Working Paper 04/10. Washington, DC: IMF.

Patterson, Percival J. 1999. "Improving the Quality of Governance Through Public Sector Reform." Presentation to Parliament. Office of the Prime Minister. Jamaica: National Library of Jamaica.

Patton, M.Q. 2002. Qualitative Research and Evaluation Methods. Thousand Oaks, CA: Sage Publications.

Pattillo, C., H. Poirson and L. Ricci. 2002. External Debt and Growth. IMF Working Paper 02/69. Washington, DC: IMF.

Payne, Anthony and Paul Sutton. 2007. "Repositioning the Caribbean Within Globalization." Caribbean Paper No. 1, June 2007. Waterloo, Canada: The Center for International Governance Innovation.

Peters, Richard S. 1962. In Hobbes, Thomas, Leviatan – Or The Matter of

Forme and Power of a Commonwealth Ecclesiastical and Civil. Edited by Michael Oakeshott. New York: Collier Books.

Pinnock, Fritz. 2012. "Power Relations among Stakeholders and the Future of Cruise Tourism in the Caribbean." PhD dissertation, University of the West Indies.

Planning Institute of Jamaica (PIOJ). 1959-2010. Economic and Social Survey of Jamaica. Jamaica: PIOJ.

___. 1996. Economic Update and Outlook. Jamaica: PIOJ.

___. 2009. "PIOJ/Ministry of Foreign Affairs and Foreign Trade. Joint National Report of Jamaica on - Millennium Development Goals for the UN Economic and Social Council Annual Ministerial Review Geneva July 2009." Jamaica: PIOJ.

___. 2011. "VISION 2030 JAMAICA – National Development Plan." Jamaica: PIOJ.

Potter, Robert, David Barker, Dennis Conway, Thomas Klak. 2004. The Contemporary Caribbean. London: Pearson Education Ltd.

Private Sector Organization of Jamaica (PSOJ). 1996-1998. "Fiscal Policy." Jamaica: Private Sector Organization of Jamaica.

Przeworski, Adam and Fernando Limongi.1993. "Political Regimes and Economic Growth." Journal of Economic Perspectives, Vol. 7, no. 3 (Summer): 51-69.

Radio Jamaica Ltd. 2012. "Lottery Scammers Fleece Americans." Accessed May 3, 2012. http://rjrnewsonline.com/news/local/lottery-scammers-fleece-americans-300-million-us-annually.

___. 2013. "Development Expected in Completion of Report on FINSAC Enquiry." Accessed May 25, 2013. http://rjrnewsonline.com/local/developments-expected-in-completion-of-report-on-finsac-commission-of-enquiry.

Ranis, Gustav. 2004. "Arthur Lewis' Contribution to Development Thinking and Policy." Discussion Paper 891. New Haven CT: Yale University Economic Growth Center.

Reid, Tyrone. 2013. "When the CAP Won't Fit - Millions Spent, Many Students Still Incompetent; Outfit Gets New Teachers." Accessed March 5, 2013. http://jamaica-gleaner.com/gleaner/20130203/news/news1.html.

Reifer, Thomas and Jamie Sudler. 1996. "The Interstate System." In The Age of Transition: Trajectory of the World System. Edited by Terence Hopkins, and Immanuel Wallerstein. New Jersey: Zed Press.

Reinart, Carmen M., and Kenneth Rogoff. 2008. "This Time is Different: A Panoramic View of Eight Centuries of Financial Crises. BER Working Paper 13882. Cambridge, MA: National Bureau of Economic Research.

Reynolds, Jerome. 2011. "PNP Patriots Concerned about $11.3 Billion Bus Loan." Gleaner, December 16, 2011. Jamaica: The Gleaner Co. Ltd.

Ricardo, D. 1951. On Foreign Trade - Vol. 1. The Works and Correspondence of David Ricardo P. Edited by Sraffa and M.H. Dobb. Cambridge MA: Cambridge University Press.

___. (1955) 2002. The Principles of Political Economy and Taxation. London: J.M. Dent and Sons.

Rigobon R, and D. Rodrik. 2005. "Rule of Law, Democracy, Openness and Income: Estimating the Interrelationships." Economics of Transition 13(3): 533–64.

Robinson, Michelle. 1993. "Debt Relief, Principles and Practices, Jamaica's Experience." Paper presented to the Trade Union Educational Institute. Jamaica: University of the West Indies.

Robinson, Michelle. 1998. "Debt Management as Tool of Economic Development – Jamaica's Experience." Paper presented at Fourth Annual Meeting of NGO Working Group on the World Bank Latin America and the Caribbean.

Romer, Paul Michael. 1989. "Human Capital and Growth: Theory and Evidence." Working Paper, No. 3173. Cambridge, MA: National Bureau of Economic Research.

___. 1989. "What Determines the Rate of Growth and Technological Change?" Washington DC: World Bank Policy Planning and Research. PPR Working Paper Series, Issue 279.

Rodman, Peter W. 1968. "Development Administration: Obstacles, Theories and Implications for Planning." Paris, France: UNESCO.

Rodrik, Dani, Arvid Subramanian, and Franchesco Trebbi. 2004. "Institutions Rule: The Primacy of Institutions over Geography and Integration in Economic Development." Journal of Economic Growth 9 (2): 131-65.

Rosenstein-Rodan, Paul. 1943. "The Problem of Industrialization in Eastern and South Eastern Europe." Economic Journal, 53 (210/211):201-11.

Rostow, Walt W. 1971. "Politics and the Stages of Growth." Cambridge MA: Cambridge University Press.

Roubini, Nouriel and Jefferey D. Sachs. 1989. "Political and Economic Determinants of Budget Deficits in the Industrial Democracies." European Economic Review. (33): 903-38.

Rowley, Charles K, William F. Shughart II and Robert D. Tollison. 2002. The Economics of Budget Deficit Vol. II. UK: Edward Elgar Publishing Ltd.

Ryan, Selwyn. 2003. "Majoritarian and Consociational Systems of Governance: Paradigms in Conflicts." In Governance in the Age of Globalization. Edited by Kenneth O. Hall and Denis Benn. Jamaica: Ian Randle Publishers.

Sachs, Jeffrey. 2003. "Institutions Don't Rule: Direct Effects of Geography on Per Capita Income." Working Paper, No. 9490. Cambridge, MA: National Bureau of Economic Research.

Sachs Jeffrey and A. Warner, 1995b. "Natural Resource Abundance and Economic Growth." Working Paper, No. 5398. Cambridge, MA: National Bureau of Economic Research.

Saisana, Michaela, Paola Annoni and Michela Nardo. 2009. "A Robust Model to Measure Governance in African Countries." JRC Scientific and Technical Report. Accessed July 28, 2013. http://publications.jrc.ec.europa.eu/repository/bitstream.

Scarlett, Hubert G. 2010. "Tax Policy and Economic Growth in Jamaica." Jamaica: Bank of Jamaica.

Schumpeter, Joseph A.1939. Business Cycles: A Theoretical, Historical and

Statistical Analysis of the Capitalist Process. New York: McGraw Hill Book Company Inc.

Seaga, Edward. 2009. Edward Seaga: My Life and Leadership Vol. 1- Clash of Ideologies 1930-1980. Oxford, England: Macmillan Publishing Limited.

Seaga, Edward, Database Collection. Accessed March 6, 2013. http://www.macrodata.org/.

Shaw, Audley. 2011. Interview with Cliff Hughes. TVJ, on November 17, 2011.

___. 2011. Response to Dr. Phillips' question during Political Debate between Finance Minister Audley Shaw and Shadow Finance Ministers Peter Phillips. TVJ, on December 15.

Shepherd, Verene and Hilary Beckles. 2000. Caribbean Slavery in the Atlantic World- A Student Reader. Jamaica: Ian Randle.

Shizume, Masato. 2007. "Sustainability of Public Debt: Evidence from Pre-World War II Japan." Discussion Paper Series No. 201. Kobe, Japan: Kobe University.

Simpson-Miller, Portia. 2012. "Address by The Most Hon. Portia Simpson-Miller at Swearing In Ceremony on January 5, 2012." Jamaica: JIS. Accessed June 01. http://www.jis.gov.jm/news/leads-128/29531/.

Sirowy Larry, and Alex Inkeles. 1990. "The Effects of Democracy on Economic Growth and Inequality: A Review." Studies in Comparative International Development, 25(1):126–57.

Smith, Adam. (1776) 1981. An Inquiry into the Nature and Causes of the Wealth of the Nations. London: J.M. Dent and Sons.

Smith, Collette J-A. 2010. "Adjustments to Budget Too Pervasive." Letter to The Editor. October 1, 2010. Jamaica: The Gleaner Co. Ltd.

Smith, Stephen C. 1997. "Contributions of Alternative Approaches to Development – Korea and Argentina." In Economic Development, 6th Edition. Michale P. Todaro. Reading, MA: Addison-Wesley Longman.

Smith-Tennant, Sandria. N. 2009. The Role of Public Sector Projects in Facilitating Community Development: An Evaluation of Highway 2000. PhD diss., University of the West Indies.

Solow, Robert. 1956. "A Contribution to the Theory of Economic Growth." Quarterly Journal of Economics. Cambridge MA: The MIT Press, 70 (1): 65-94.

Standard and Poor's. 2012. "Barbados Ratings Lowered To 'BB+/B' From 'BBB-/A-3'; Outlook Stable." Accessed January 10, 2013. http://www.standardandpoors.com/prot/ratings/articles/en/us/?articleType=HTMLandassetID=1245337008175

STATIN (Statistical Institute of Jamaica). 1970-2006. "External Trade." Jamaica: Statistical Institute of Jamaica.

___. 1976. "National Income and Product 1969-2009." Jamaica: Statistical Institute of Jamaica.

___. 1998. "Statistical Yearbook of Jamaica." Jamaica: Statistical Institute of Jamaica.

___. 2004. "External Trade 1960 to 2004." Jamaica: Statistical Institute of Jamaica.

____. 2008. "Quarterly Gross Domestic Product October to December 2008." Jamaica: Statistical Institute of Jamaica.

____. 2009. "External Trade Statistical Bulletin January to December 2008." Jamaica: Statistical Institute of Jamaica.

____. 2010. "External Trade Statistical Bulletin January to March 2009." Jamaica: Statistical Institute of Jamaica.

Stiglitz, Joseph. 2002. "Capital Market Liberalization, Economic Growth and Instability: Risks without Rewards." In The Annals of the Academy of Political and Social Science, 579 (January): 219-48.

___. 2005. "What I Learned at the World Economic Crisis." In The Global Economy: 323-29. New York: Thomas Oatley Pearson Longman.

Stone, Carl and Aggrey Brown. 1981. Perspectives on Jamaica in the 70's. Edited by Carl Stone and Aggrey Brown. Jamaica: Jamaica Publishing House.

Stone, Carl. 1985. "Jamaica in Crisis: from Socialist to Capitalist Management." International Journal – The Caribbean. Vol. XL, no. 2. Ontario, Ca: Canadian Institute of International Affairs.

___. 1991. Rethinking Development: The Role of The State in Third World Development. In Rethinking Development. Edited by Judith Wedderburn. Consortium Graduate School of Social Sciences. Jamaica: University of the West Indies.

____. 1993. "Promoting Productivity through National Policies." In Caribbean Finance and Management. 8 (1 and 2) May 1993: 1-10. Jamaica: University of the West Indies.

Tellis, Winston. 1997. "Application of a Case Study Methodology." The Qualitative Report, Vol. 3(3), Sept. 1997.

Thame, Camilo. 2011. "Ian Fleming International Airport to Be Sold." Jamaica Observer, February 4, 2011. http://www.jamaicaobserver.com/business/Ian-Fleming-Int-l-airport.

Thomas, Clive Y. 1996. "A State of Disarray: Public Policy in the Caribbean." Bulletin of Eastern Caribbean Affairs, 21 (2), June. Bridgetown, BD: Institute of Social and Economic Research, University of the West Indies, Cave Hill.

Thomas, Clive. 2003. "Designing and Implementing Development Policy: The Shift to Holistic Approaches and Development Policy Frameworks." In Governance in the Age of Globalization. Edited by Kenneth O. Hall and Denis Benn. Jamaica: Ian Randle Publishers.

Thompson, McPherse. 2012. "LNG Project Lives." Gleaner, January 3, 2012. Jamaica: The Gleaner Co. Ltd.

Tindigarukayo, Jimmy and Sandra Chadwick. 2003. "Civil Service Reforms in Jamaica." Accessed April 2, 2012. http://mirror.undp.org/magnet/Docs/psreform/civil_service_reform.

Tiwari, Siddharth. 2013. "Staff Guidance Note for Public Debt Sustainability Analysis for market Access Countries." Washington, DC: International Monetary Fund.

Tobin, James. 1963. "An Essay on the Principles of Debt management." Cowles Foundation Paper 195. New Haven CT: Yale University. Accessed May 10, 2013. http://cowles.econ.yale.edu/P/cp/py1963.htm.

___. 1980. "Asset Accumulation and Economic Activity." Chicago: University of Chicago Press.

Todaro, Michael P. 1997. Economic Development. Reading, Mass: Addison-Wesley Longman Ltd.

Toye, John. 2006. "Changing perspectives in Development Economics." In Rethinking Development Economics. Edited by Ha Joon-Chang. London: Anthem Press.

Trading Economics. 2013. "South Korea Government Debt-to-GDP." Accessed January 7, 2013. http://www.tradingeconomics.com/south-korea/government-Debt-to-GDP.

Transparency International (TI). 2011. Corruption Perception Index 2002-2010. LAPOP report. Accessed March 9, 2011. http://www.vanderbilt.edu/lapop/.

___. 2012. "Corruption Perception Index 2010." Berlin, Germany: Transparency International.

___. 2021. "Corruption Perception Index 2010." Berlin, Germany: Transparency International. Accessed August 26, 2021. http://images.transparencycdn.org/images/CPI2020_Report_EN_0802-WEB-1_2021-02-08-103053.pdf

Tuckness, Alex. 2012. "Locke's Political Philosophy." The Stanford Encyclopaedia of Philosophy (Winter 2012 Edition). Accessed Feb. 7, 2014. http://plato.stanford.edu/archives/win2012/entries/locke-political/>.

United Nations. 1987. "Our Common Future." Report A/42/427, of the WCED, 4th August. New York: UN. http://www.un-documents.net/our-common-future.pdf.

___. 2007. "Public Governance Indicators: A Literature Review." New York: UN Department of Economic and Social Affairs.

___. 2008. "Declaration of Human Rights – Dignity and Justice for All." New York: United Nations.

___. 2011. "National Accounts Statistics." New York: United Nations Department of Economic and Social Affairs.

United Nations Development Programme (UNDP). 1997. "Governance for Sustainable Human Development." Policy Document. New York: UNDP.

___. 2010. "UNDP and Governance. Experiences and Lessons Learnt." Accessed July 2, 2010. http://mirror.undp.org/magnet/docs/gov/Lessons1.htm.

___. 1990-2013. "Human Development Report 2010." New York: Palgrave Macmillan.

United Nations Economic and Social Commission for Asia and the Pacific. 2009. "What is good Governance?" Accessed November 2, 2011. http://www.unescap.org/pdd/prs/ProjectActivities/Ongoing/gg.

United States Agency for International Development. 2005. "Democracy and Governance." Accessed February 12, 2011. http://www.usaid/gov/our_work/democracy_and_governance/.

United States Department of State (USDS). 2008. "Human Rights Report Barbados." Accessed May 14, 2012.

http://www.state.gov/g/drl/rls/hrrpt/2008/wha/119147.htm.

Vietor, Richard H. K, and Emily J. Thompson. 2008. "Singapore Inc." Harvard Business School 9-703-040 Rev: February 28, 2008. Boston, MA: Harvard.

Villarreal, M. Angeles. 2010. "NAFTA and the Mexican Economy." Federation of American Scientists. Washington, DC: Congressional Research Services. Accessed June 10, 2012. http://www.fas.org/sgp/crs/row/RL34733.pdf.

Vinals, Jose. 2012. "Transcript of a Press Conference on the International Monetary Fund's Global Financial Stability Report, October 10, 2012." Washington, DC: IMF. Accessed January 5, 2013. http://www.imf.org/external/np/tr/2012/tr101012.htm.

Virtue, Erica. 2012. "SEEING RED – NWC Unable to Collect Nearly $4b from 102 Communities. Gleaner, December 30, 2012. Jamaica: The Gleaner Co. Ltd.

Vranken, Jan, Pascal De Decker and Inge Van Nieuwenhuyze. 2002. "Social Inclusion, Urban Governance and Sustainability Towards a Conceptual Framework. Department of Sociology and Social Policy." March 2002. Antwerpen, Belgium: University of Antwerpen.

Wehrmeyer, W., A. Clayton and Ken Lum, 2002. "Foresighting for Development." Greener Management International. The Journal of Corporate Environmental Strategy and Practice 37: 24-36.

Wei, Shang-Jin, Yi Wu. 2000a. "Negative Alchemy? Corruption, Composition of Capital Flows and Currency Crises." Cambridge MA: National Bureau of Economic Research. Working Paper No. 8187. Accessed May 21, 2013. http://www.nber.org/papers/w8187.

Williams, Andrew and Abu Siddique. 2005. "The Use (and Abuse) of Governance Indicators in Economics: A Review." Economics of Governance (2008) 9:131-75.

Williams, Eric. 1970. From Columbus to Castro. The History of the Caribbean 1492-1969. New York: Random House.

Williamson, John. 1997. "The Washington Consensus Revisited." In Economic and Social Development into the XXI Century. Edited by L. Emmerij. Washington DC: Inter-American Development Bank.

Williamson, Oliver E. 2000. "The New Institutional Economics: Taking Stock, Looking Ahead." Journal of Economic Literature, Vol. 38, No. 3 (September 2000): 595-613.

World Bank. 1993. "Governance." Washington, DC: World Bank.

___. 2001. "Public Debt Management, Cash Management and Domestic Debt Market Development – Case Study of Tanzania." June 2001. Washington, DC: World Bank.

___. 2005. "Economic Growth in the 1990s – Learning From a Decade of Reform. Country Note F – Lessons and Controversies from Financial Crises in the 1990s." Washington, DC: World Bank.

___. 2010. "Implementation Completion and Results Report – Reform of Secondary Education Project II." Report No. ICR 00001238. Washington, DC: World Bank.

___. 2011. World Bank Reports on External projects. Accessed June 20, 2012.

http://web.worldbank.org/external/projects/main?p.K=104231andpiPK=73230andtheSitePK=40941andmenuPK=228424andProjectid=P071589.
___. 2011. "Toll Roads and Concessions." Accessed October 26, 2011. http://www.worldbank.org/transport/roads/toll_rds.htm#international.
___. 2011. "Jamaica Country Economic Memorandum – Unlocking Growth." Report No. 60374-JM, May 26, 2011. Washington, DC: World Bank.
___. 2021. "World Bank Provides US$150 Million for a Resilient COVID-19 Recovery in Jamaica." News Release 2021/125/LAC. Accessed August 24, 2010. http://www.worldbank.org/en/news/press-release/2021/03/18/world-bank-provides-us-150-million-for-a-resilient-covid-19-recovery-in-jamaica
___. 2021. World Bank IBRD – IDA National Accounts Data. "GDP growth (annual %) – Jamaica." Accessed August 24, 2021. http://data.worldbank.org/indicator/NY.GDP.MKTP.KD.ZG?locations=JM
___. 2021. World Bank National Accounts Data, and OECD National Accounts Data Files. "GDP per capita (current US$)." Accessed August 24, 2021. http://data.worldbank.org/indicator/NY.GDP.PCAP.CD?locations
___. 2021. World Bank IBRD – IDA Inter-Parliamentary Union. "Proportion of seats held by women in national parliaments (%)." Accessed August 26, 2021. http://data.worldbank.org/indicator/SG.GEN.PARL.ZS
World Bank/IDB. 2006. "Jamaica Joint Country Financial Accountability Assessment (CFAA) and Country Procurement Assessment (CPAR) Report 34962-JM, April 12, 2006." Washington, DC: World Bank.
World Bank Worldwide Governance Indicators. 2020. Geneva, Switzerland. Accessed Aug. 17, 2021. http://info.worldbank.org/governance/wgi/Home/Reports
World Economic Forum (WEF). 2010. Global Competitiveness Report. Edited By Klau Schwab. Geneva, Switzerland. Accessed Aug. 17, 2021. http://gcr.weforum.org/gcr20/.
World Health Organization (WHO). 1998. "Ageing: A Public Health Challenge." Accessed April 15, 2011. https://apps.who.int/inf-fs/en/fact135.html.
Worrell, D., D. Marshall, and N. Smith. 2000. The Political Economy of Exchange Rate Policy in the Caribbean. Working Paper R-401. Washington DC: IDB.
Worrel, DeLisle. 1994. "Open Market Operations in Small Developing Economies: The Barbados and Jamaican Experience." Presented at the Regional Programme of Monetary Studies Conference, Jamaica – November 23-26, 1994.
Yun-Han Chu. 2012. "Unravelling the Enigma of East Asian Economic Resiliency: The Case of Taiwan." Working Paper 44. Accessed April 2, 2012. http://jica-ri.jica.go.jp/publication/assets/JICA-RI_WP_No.44.
Zoli, Edda. 2005. "How Does Fiscal Policy Affect Monetary Policy in Emerging Market Countries?" BIS Working Paper No. 174. Basel, Switzerland: Bank for International Settlements Press and Communications CH-

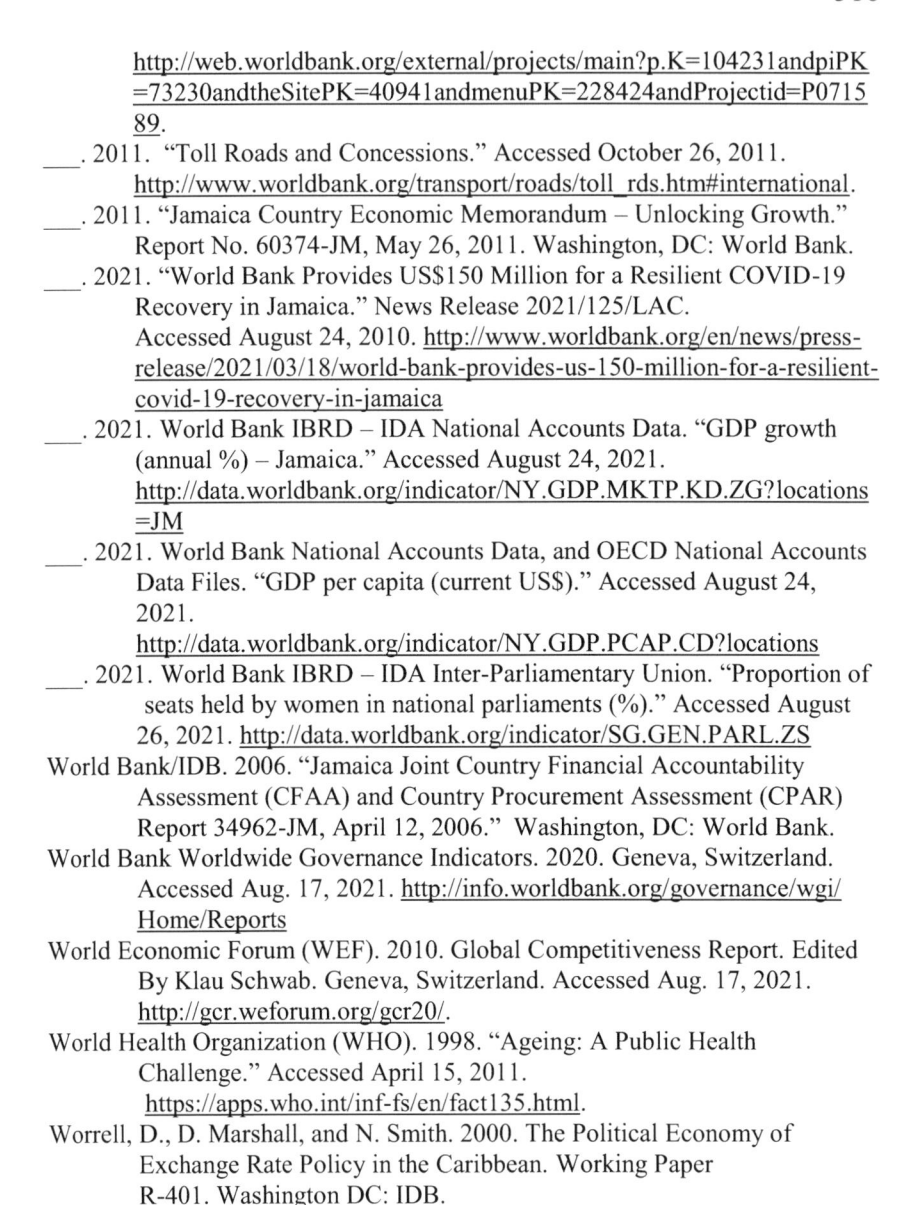

4002.

Jamaica Houses of Parliament. 1962-2010. Hansard Parliamentary Debates. Proceedings of the House of Representatives. Jamaica: Government Printing Office.

___. 2001. Barker, Alethia C. Governance. 4th December (unbound copies).
___. 2010. Baugh, Kenneth L. Governance. 13th July (unbound copies).
___. 1980. Bell, Eric. Debt. 5th February. Session 1979-1980, vol. 5, No. 3.
___. 1980. Debt. 5th January. Session 1979-1980, vol. 5, No. 3.
___. 1962. Federal Elections. Bustamante, Sir. Alexander. 6th March.
___. 1990. Charles, Pearnel. Tivoli Gardens. 6th June. Session 1990-1991, vol.16, No. 1.
___. 1989. Clarke, Claude. Economic Challenges. Session 1988-1989, vol. 14, No. 3.
___. 1977. Coore, David. IMF Agreement. Session 1977-1978, vol. 2, No. 3.
___. 2003. Dalley, Horace. Social Policy. 3rd April -30th July. Session 2002-2003, vol. 29, No. 1.
___. 1994. Davies, Omar. Economy and Inflation. 20th September 1994-13th December. Session 1994-1995, vol.20, No. 2.
___. 1995. Conditional Loans. 24th January-28th March. Session 1994-1995, vol.20, No. 3.
___. 1997. Jamaica Ending IMF Borrowing. 9th September-25th November. Session 1997-1998, vol. 23, No. 2.
___. 1998. Manley's Response to Debt Left by Seaga. 2nd April-28th July (unbound copies).
___. 2000. NIR – Balances Under Seaga. 20th April (unbound copies).
___. 2000. Speculation on FEX Rates. 6th April (unbound copies).
___. 2001. BOJ Hiking Interest Rates to Stabilize Market. 16th January-21st-March. Session 2000-2001, vol. 26, No. 3.
___. 2001. Commendation of Seaga. 29th March-17th July. Session 2001-2002, vol. 27, No. 1.
___. 2001. Impact of Debt on Social Service. 4th March -31st July. Session 2002-2003, vol. 28, No. 1.
___. 2001. Scenario Planning. 2nd October (unbound copies).
___. 2001. SCJ Debts. 4th December (unbound copies).
___. 2001. Celebrating SEC Endorsement. 18th December (unbound copies).
___. 2002. GOJ 2022 – Interest Cost. 6th February. (unbound copies).
___. 2002. FINSAC Interest Balloons. 20th March (unbound copies).
___. 2002. Post-FINSAC Risk Aversion. 4th April -31st July. Session 2002-2003, vol. 28, No. 1.
___. 2003. Auction System. 3rd April-30th July. Session 2002-2003, vol. 29, No.1.
___. 2004. Human Capital Development. 31st March-28th July. Session 2004-2005, vol. 30, No. 1.
___. 2005. Economic Model. 31st March-27th July. Session 2005-2006, vol.31, No. 1.
___. 2008. The IMF and Devaluation. 15th April (unbound copies).
___. 1962. Glasspole, Florizel. National Savings Bonds. 22nd February.

___. 1990. Golding, Bruce. Accountability. Session 1990-1991, vol. 16, No. 1.
___. 2008. FINSAC. 22nd April (unbound copies).
___. 2008. Charter of Fundamental Rights and Freedoms. 23rd April.
___. 2008. Money Missing from FID. 17th June (unbound copies).
___. 2008. Alternative Investment Schemes. 24th June (unbound copies).
___. 2009. Road Maintenance Fund. 5th May (unbound copies).
___. 2009. Ridding the JCF of Crime. 5th May (unbound copies).
___. 2009. BOJ Governor's Contract. 3rd November (unbound copies).
___. 2009. Private Sector Partnership. 30th November (unbound copies).
___. 2009. Trelawny Multi-purpose Stadium. 17 December 2009.
___. 2010. Cyber Crimes Bill. 10th February (unbound copies).
___. 2010. Tivoli Incursion. 22nd June.
___. 2011. Ponzi Schemes. 3th November.
___. 2008. Holness, Andrew. Governance. 20th May.
___. 2009. Deficiencies in Education. July.
___. 2009. Introduction of CAP Programme. December.
___. 2011. Campaign Financing. 2nd November.
___. 1986. Lawes, Princess. Free Zone Working Conditions. 24th September.
___. 1962. Lightbourne, Robert. Budget. Session 1962-1963, No. 1.
___. 1988. Manley, Michael. Link between Trained Manpower and Economic Growth. Session 1988-1989, vol. 15, No. 1.
___. 1961. Manley, Norman. West Indies Federation. 3rd August.
___. 1962. Budget, Debt, and; Dissolution of Parliament. 14th March.
___. 1988. Comparison between Jamaica and Singapore. Session 1988-1989 vol.15, no. 1
___. 1989. Mullings, Seymour. Private Sector-led Growth. Session 1988-1989, vol. 14, No. 3.
___. 1989. Loan for CAP and Halse Hall Bauxite Operation. Session 1989-1990, vol. 15, No. 3.
___. 2001. Paulwell, Phillip. INTEC/Net-Serv. 18th December (unbound copies).
___. 2008. Phillips, Peter. Jamaica's Divisive Political Culture. 10th June (unbound copies).
___. 2009. Comparing Jamaica to Singapore. 15th July (unbound copies).
___. 2010. Short Term Electoral Cycle Affecting Planning. 27th July (unbound copies).
___. 2014. Closing Budget Debate. 30th April.
___. 1990. Ramtallie, O.D. Regularizing Utilities in Garrison Constituencies. 6th June. Session 1990-1991, vol.16, No. 1.
___. 2002. Samuda, Karl. INTEC/Net-Serv. 22nd January (unbound copies).
___. 1962. Sangster, Donald Burns. Debt. Session 1961-1962, n. 4.
___. 1963. Government's Securities Law. Session 1962-1963, No. 1.
___. 1979. Seaga, Edward. Depletion of Foreign Exchange; Accountability. Session 1978-1979, vol. 4, No. 1.
___. 1979. Critique of Manley Regime. Session 1979-1980, vol. 5, No. 3.
___. 1980. Budget. Session 1980-1981, vol. 6, No. 1.
___. 1983. Treasury Bill as Monetary Policy Tool. Session 1983-1984, vol. 9, No. 3.

____. 1985. Devaluation and Structural Adjustment. 3rd July-26th March. Session 1985-1986 (insert).
____. 1986. Government Guarantee to Upgrade Inner City Kingston. 7th October.
____. 1991. Exchange Control. 25th April-15th August. Session 1991-1992, vol. 17, No. 1.
____. 1994. External Debt. 4th April-30th August. Session 1994-1995, vol.14, No. 1.
____. 1999. Fundamental Rights and Freedoms. Session 1999-2000, vol. 25, No.1.
____. 2000. Politicians' Responsibility. 18th April (unbound copies).
____. 2001. Trajectory of Growth in Jamaica. 29th March-17th July. Session 2001-2002, vol. 27, No. 1.
____. 2002. Offer to Advise Dr. Davies. 4th April-31st July. Session 2002-2003,
____. 2004. Monetary and Fiscal Policy Influences Competitiveness. 31st March-28th July. Session 2004-2005, vol. 30, No. 1.
____. 2005. Good Governance. 11th January-16th March. Session 2004-2005, vol. 30, No. 3.
____. 1995. Shaw, Audley. Economy. 20th September-13th December. Session 1994-1995, vol.20, No. 2.
____. 2000. FINSAC. 11th April 11 (unbound copies).
____. 2001. Reducing Interest Rates. 29th March-17th July. Session 2001-2002, vol. 27, No. 1.
____. 2001. 25th September (unbound copies).
____. 2001. PNP and Debt. 2nd October (unbound copies).
____. 2001. Demise of Financial Sector. 27th November (unbound copies).
____. 2001. Sugar Company (SCJ) Debts.18th December (unbound copies).
____. 2002. FINSAC. 12th March 12 (unbound copies).
____. 2002. Incessant Borrowing. 4th April-31st July. Session 2002-2003, vol. 28, No. 1.
____. 2005. Punitive Economic Policies. 31st March- 27th July. Session 2005-2006, vol. 31, No. 1.
____. 2006. Bear Stearns.
____. 2008. $140 B Cost of FINSAC. 19th February (unbound copies).
____. 2008. Capital Development Fund. 22nd April, and; 24th June.
____. 2008. FINSAC. 23rd April (unbound copies).
____. 2008. PetroCaribe Payments for CAP and Air Jamaica Debts. 28th October (unbound copies).
____. 2009. Clarendon Aluminium Production. 27th January (unbound copies).
____. 2009. Government Guarantee for NWC. 22nd July (unbound copies).
____. 2009. RCCL Costs. 16th September (unbound copies).
____. 2009. Working to Achieve Productivity. 17th December (unbound copies).
____. 2010. Amendment of Financial Administration and Audit Act. 26th January (unbound copies).
____. 2010. High Debt, Low Growth. 8th April (unbound copies).
____. 2010. Wanton Capital Expenditure. 29th June (unbound copies).
____. 2010. Stock of Debt. 14th December (unbound copies).
____. 2008. Simpson-Miller, Portia. Caring for the Poor. 17th April

___. 2010. Freeze on Tertiary Subsidy. 15th April (unbound copies).
___. 2010. Collective Responsibility. 1st June (unbound copies).
___. 1980. Corruption and Mismanagement. Small, Hugh. Session 1980-1981, vol. 6, No. 1.
___. 1992. Debt Financing Plan. Session 1992-1993, vol. 18, No. 1.
___. 1993. Economy. Session 1992-1993, vol. 18, No. 3.
___. 1993. Debt Ceiling. 14th July-28 July. Part 2 of 2, vol. 19, No. 1.
___. 2009. Spencer, Rudyard. Health Expenditure Cuts. 7th July (unbound copies).
___. 2011. Thwaites, Ronald. Ponzi Schemes. 30th November (unbound copies).
___. 2010. Tufton, Christopher. Sugar Company of Jamaica 10th February (unbound copies).
___. 1980. Vaz, Douglas. Capital Development Fund. Session 1980-1981, vol. 6, No. 2.

APPENDIX I

Photographs of Capital Project Discussed in This Publication
© CJAS

TRELAWNY MULTI-PURPOSE STADIUM

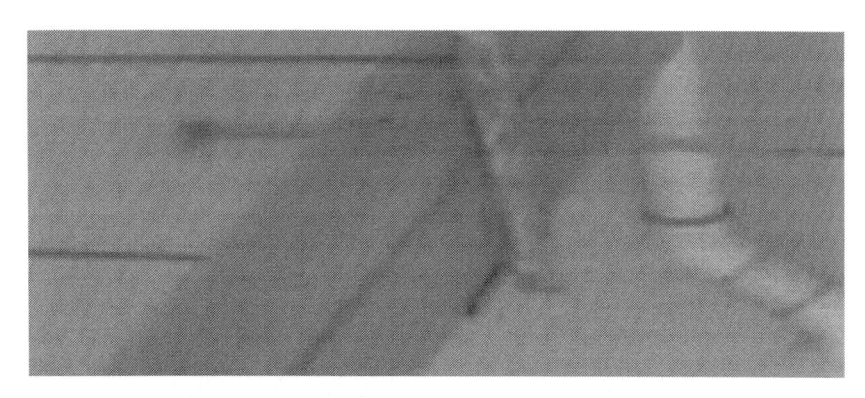

322

FALMOUTH CRUISE SHIP PIER - TRELAWNY

323

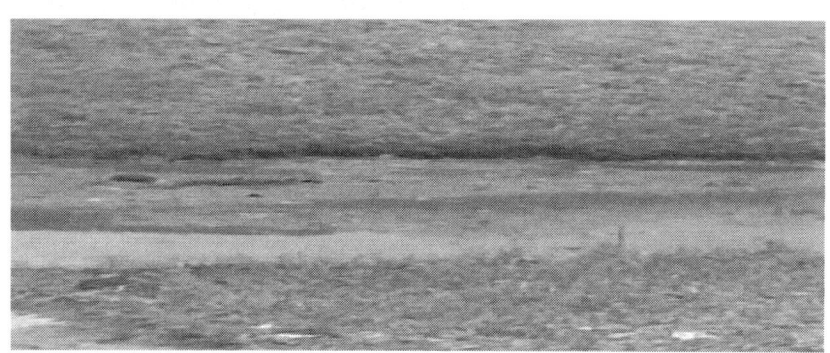

SLIGOVILLE STADIUM - ST. CATHERINE

PALISADOES SHORELINE PROJECT

APPENDIX II

Supplementary Material on Governance Decisions

JAMAICA

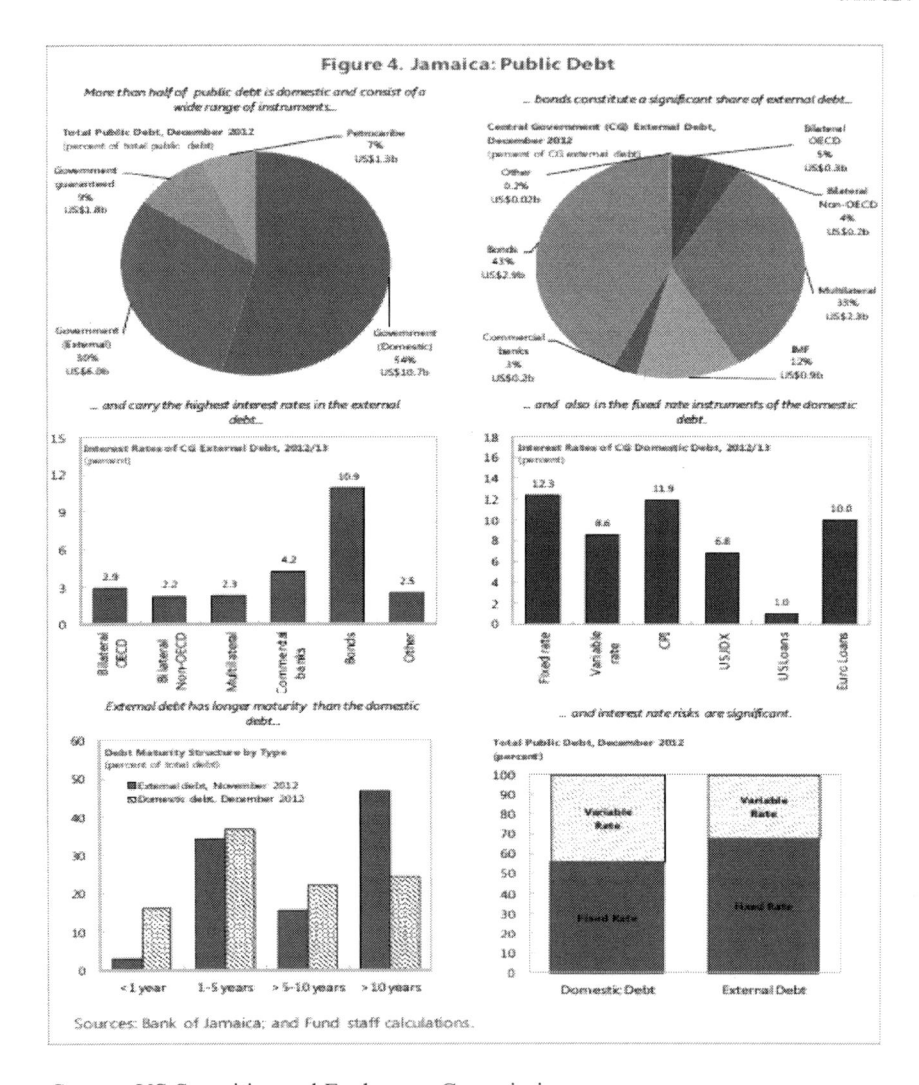

Figure 4. Jamaica: Public Debt

Source: US Securities and Exchanges Commission

Table 1 Government Guarantees of Interest to Study - 2000-2010

Ministry Paper No.	Title of Ministry Paper	Comments
29/2010 $150m	Loan from DBJ to JBDC	DBJ Pays own loan
56/2010 US$340m	China Exim Bank – JDIP	GOJ Pays interest
65/2010 Euro	Loan to DBJ from Venezuela to NROCC	Loan prepaid/
82/2010 US$20m	Loan to Students Loan Bureau	SLB Pays
009/2009 US4127.7	Loan for CAP to ALCOA	
14/2009 US$60m	Loan from EICB & CDB for NMIA	NMIA Pays Own
18/2009 US$2.75m	loan from CDB to UWI	UWI Pays Own
23/2009 J$425m	Loan from BNS to JUTC	
45/2009 Euro 204.4m	Loan from DBJ to NROCC (duplicate)	Loan prepaid/
51/2009 US$101.8m	Loan to AIR JA LTD - Assumed by GOJ,	Assumed by GOJ,
20/2009 US$10m	Loan from BNP Paribas to NWC - NW	NWC Pays
67/2009 US$37m	Loan from NCB to Central Water and	
68/2009 US$79m	Loan from DBJ to NROCC - ancillary to	NROCC Pays
99/2009	Loan from EKSPORT KREDIT HSBC -	PAJ Pays own
110/2009	Loan to NWC for water supply	NWC Pays own
117/2009	Loan to NWC for water supply	NWC Pays own
121/2009 US$1.8B	Loan from Private Placement via NCB for	GOJ Pays obo Air
39/2008 US$175m	Loan to Port Authority of Jamaica – PAJ	PAJ Pays
001/2007 $600m	Loan from BNS to DBJ	DBJ Pays
27/2007 Euro	Loan for NWC	NWC Pays
28/2007	Loan to Air Jamaica Ltd	GOJ Pays
61/2007 Euro 20m	Loan from European Union - A Grant of JAMPRO to implement the PSDP	
009/2006	Loan to Port Authority of Jamaica - PAJ to	PAJ Pays
012/2006	Amendment to Government Guarantee of plc. and PAJ	PAJ Pays
75/2006	Loan from members of the JBA to Students	SLB Pays own
87/2006 US$200m	Bond Issue - Clarendon Alumina	Assumed by GOJOJ
91/2006	Management of Loan Proceeds under Petro and Venezuela	
94/2006 US$70.34m	Reallocation of Loans and Government BNS Ja. Ltd - for Port Authority of Ja.	PAJ Pays own
003/2005	Loan from BNP Paribas to NWC - NW	NWC Pays
010/2005 US$20m	Loan from NCB to NWC - Martha Brae to	NWC Pays
51/2005	GOJ – IADB	
60/2005	Petro Caribe Energy Cooperation	
65/2005	Loan from IDB to NWC	NWC Pays
71/2005	Loan from RBTT JA Ltd to JUTC	JUTC Pays own
92/2005 US$44m	loan from BNS Ja Ltd to Port Authority for	PAJ Pays
002/2004 US$75m	Loan to NROOC for Phase 1 of HW2000	Repaid
005/2004 US$16m	Loan from NCB to Petroleum Corp. of Ja to	
42/2004	GOJ/IDB/ICT Project	
46/2004 US$28.7m	Amending Loan Agreement: GOJ/CDB	GOJ Pays loan
001/2003	Amendment of Loan Agreement Btwn Reflect increase from US$21,531,822 to	PAJ Pays own
003/2003 US$75m	Issuance of Infrastructure Bonds by	
24/2003 Euro 90m	Loan to Sugar Co. of Ja. Ltd - SCF to fund	GOJ repaid -

327

	to Sugar Industry	
50/2003	Loan from National Insurance Fund - NIS Health Fund	
53/2003 US$5m	Line of Credit between DBJ and OPEC On lending to Approved Financial	DBJ Pays own
75/2003 $41750m	Loan from BNS JA. Ltd to SCJ HW2000	GOJ Pays
008/2002	Payment Obligations of NROCC under	
18/2002	Commerzbank and PAJ	PAJ Pays
84/2002	5th Industrial Line of Credit to DBJ from Development	DBJ Pays own
75/2001	Loan - Credit Facility via BNS for SCJ	
44/2001	Improving the Quality of Governance	
002/2000	Loan to Support Sugar Industry	
68/2000	Loan from Conclear Ltd to Air Jamaica	GOJ Repaid
69/2000	Loan from European Investment Bank and	
73/2000	Loan to Bauxite and Alumina Trading	
84/2000	Loan Agreement Between GOJ & IBRD - Adjustment Programme	GOJ Pays

Source: Ministry of Finance (Jamaica) Debt Management Unit

Table 2 Some Costly (Mostly Infeasible) Projects and Programmes

PROJECT /PROGRAMME	Governance Decision	Touted Benefit /Objective/ Purpose	COST in US$	COST in J$	YR	SOURCE
JAMAICA WOOLENS	Loan left on books after 1962 elections	None stated	£700,000	1,400,000	1962	(Sangster 1962, 327)
LUANA	To develop Luana Oil Refinery between Jamaica & Mexico; presented in 1976; funds invested with JNIC lost	To increase production to meet national goals		16,000,000	1976	(Vaz 1981); also in Gleaner Archives Nov. 30, 1979
SPRING PLAINS 600 acre agricultural experiment	To diversify into winter vegetables - over 3 years (introduced by PM Seaga - May 10th 1983)	To replace sugarcane and banana with winter vegetables - Strawberries, Orchard Fruits		48,000,000	1983	(Ahmed 2001, 9)
Power Barge from Guam (Pearnel Charles)	Purportedly capable of producing only 10 of its 25 megawatts of power-generating capacity.	Reduction in energy cost in Jamaica	6,800,000	22,440,000	1983	Charles - March 1983
Reform of Secondary Education Project	World Bank Loan to increase students' performance at the secondary level	Improvement in quality, equity and access to education at the secondary level ...	8,800,000	287,760,000	1993	Patterson (1993);
HW2000/NROCC Phase 1 Melrose to Williamsfield leg	Design, build and transfer agreement signed with Tran-Jamaican Highway Limited, the concessionaire.	Substantial reduction in travel time & transportation costs; new development along the corridor; 2% increase in GDP growth; J$7 B in revenues; US$107 M in net FEX earning - medium term; & 54,000 jobs (Patterson 1999)	393,000,000	16,278,060,000	1999	Patterson (1999)
HW2000/NROCC Global Bonds due 2024	Global Bond issued with accumulated interest to maturity in	To complete Phase 2 of HW2000-Caymanas to Ocho Rios	652,712,000	56,133,232,000		(Oppenheimer 2014); FGFS; (US SEC 2012)

	2024	leg				
INTEC – NetServ	Government IT expansion programme, and; loans to set up Call Centers	Ministry Paulwell promised 40,000 jobs (< 800 jobs created)		3,900,000,000	2001	Paulwell 2001;
CLARENDON ALUM PROD. (CAPJAM)	Capital Expansion as part of Joint Venture with Alcoa	Proposal that Min. Davies said would have returned the company to profitability	115,000,000	7,722,250,000	2006	Golding (2009)
CAPJAM Global Bonds due in 2021	Global Bond issued with accumulated interest to maturity in 2021	Issued to restructure CAP's indebtedness	453,640,000	30,461,926,000		Oppenheimer (2014); FGFS; US SEC (2012)
HW2000 Phase 2	To complete the Kingston to Ocho Rios leg	Economic benefit from Kingston to Negril (Thame 2006)		13,200,000,000	2006	Thame (2012)
Trelawny Multi-Purpose Stadium	To build stadium for the Cricket World Cup	Development of Sports Tourism…	30,000,000	2,688,000,000	2006	Golding, Dec. 17, 2009
Sligoville Stadium	To build stadium for the Cricket World Cup	To enhance sports, heritage and eco-tourism in Sligoville		248,000,000	2006	Observer
CLARENDON ALUM PROD	As at December 2008 the total indebtedness of CAP was US$504 million (Golding 2009).	Accumulated debt to 2008	504,000,000	40,556,000,000	2008	Golding (2009)
HW2000 - NROCC – Interest (plus cost to issue and service NROCC debt)	$368 M in 2006/2007; $849 M in 2007/2008, and; projected to be $1.69 B in 2008/2009	See above		2,907,000,000	2008	(Shaw 2008)
Inner-City Housing Programme (ICHP) -	NHT funded development in PM Simpson-Miller's South West St. Andrew constituency	To provide housing for residents in PM's constituency		337,000,000	2008	Foster (2006) ; (Golding 2008,3)
Sugar Company of Jamaica (SCJ)	Debt Servicing plus costs absorbed by GOJ (Shaw 2007/2008)- $21 B reported by Shaw (2007) + $2 B	To support SCJ's operations…		27,000,000,000	2008	Shaw (2007)

		per yr to 2010/11 ($6 B)					
Jamaica Producers	To provide insurance support after Hurricane Dean	To coax banana farmers back into production (mainly JP Foods)		300,000,000		2008	Myers 2008
NHT ARREARS left by Simpson-Miller	Cost of Statutory Deduction withdrawn and unpaid	Unexplained		10,000,000,000		2008	Golding (2008)
Ian Flemming Airport	To provide easy access to the North Coast Tourist Resort (Ocho Rios etc); for private and small scale commercial aircraft	To increase tourism; ease of access and egress	300,000,000	2,688,000,000		2009	Thame 2011
Career Advancement Programme (CAP Edu)	To assist persons between 16 and 18 years to make them employable, by taking them through grades 12 and 13 in a senior school system.	Improvement in quality, equity and access to education at the secondary level ... **2 students certified competent**		390,800,000		2009	Holness (2009)
Falmouth Cruise Ship Pier - joint GOJ/PAJ and Royal Caribbean Cruise Lines (RCCL) project.	Government Guaranteed loan for HSBC Bank plc (US), for a loan of US$121.65 million for the Cruise Ship Terminal.	To host the new Genesis class mega vessels recently introduced into the cruise industry by RCCL Int. (WB 2011, 254); promised 800,000 disembarking passengers	122,000,000	10,474,920,000		2010	Shaw, Sep. 16, 2009
HW2000 - NROCC - Cost Overrun to Jan. 2011	Financial Support for HW2000	Cost Overrun plus interest charges from indexing bonds to inflation - 2.907 B + 10 B		10,000,000,000		2010	
Sandals Whitehouse	Sale of Hotel - GOJ sold the US$120M property for US$40M; then reportedly loaned hotelier	Divestment ...	80,000,000	6,880,000,000		2011	http://jamaica-gleaner.com/gleaner/20110116/business/business1.ht

	US$32M to make the purchase					ml
Air Jamaica	To divest Air Jamaica in 2011	Divestment - to remove Air Jamaica from GOJ's books		14,000,000,000	2011	Jackson (2011)
Air Jamaica Global Bonds due in 2015	Global Bond issued with accumulated interest to maturity in 2015	For financial restructuring - to revive the airline	629,850,000	40,675,713,000		Sources: Oppenheimer (2014); FGFS; US SEC (2012)
Air Jamaica Global Bonds due in 2027	Global Bond issued with accumulated interest to maturity in 2027	To meet Air Jamaica's obligations	328,130,000	23,172,540,600		Sources: Oppenheimer (2014); FGFS; US SEC (2012)
FINSAC	To restructure 'failed banks' and 'regulate' the Jamaican Financial sector	To save accounts, insurance policies and pension funds in insurance companies, valued at $19 billion (Davies 2001)		140,000,000,000	2002	World Bank (2011)
CLARENDON ALUM PROD. (CAP)	Formed in 1985 in response to the closure of the JAMALCO ... subsidized by GOJ up to 2013/14	Losses from operations- IMF (2011) estimated losses from CAP UP TO 2012	360,000,000,	39,600,000,000	2012	IMF (2011)
Liquified Natural Gas	To reduce the cost of energy in Jamaica	Lower energy cost	2,800,000	249,200,000	2012	Thompson 2012
Palisadoes Shoreline Project	To upgrade the corridor along the Norman Manley International Airport		65,400,000	6,473,946,000.00	2012	Observer
Montego Bay Conference Center (MBCC)	Construction cost - funded by the Government and the EXIM Bank of China in 2011	"[B]randed as a major outlet to garner foreign exchange from the lucrative meetings and conventions market"	51,700,000	4,808,100,000	2012	Mark Titus, Sunday Gleaner, Feb. 10, 2013
MBCC	Maintenance Cost	monthly maintenance cost of $30 M x 12 months	30,000,000	360,000,000	2012	(Titus, 2013)
MBCC	Contracted	Cost:	76,000	7,068,000	201	Gleaner (2013)

					2	
	company to market facility	US$80.000 per year **less** Revenue: US$4000 to 2013				
NHT	To support GOJ budget, and; close IMF deal	Budgetary support – 2013		11,000,000,000	2013	Decision by Simpson-Miller admin; $11B/yr to be taken over 4 yrs
HW2000	HW2000 - cost overrun	"$21.4 billion up to March 31, 2011 compared to the original target of $10.6 billion" (Thame 2012).		10,800,000,000	2012	Thame (2012)
TOTAL				**533,685,955,600**		

Source: Hansard (1960-2012); MOFP; Gleaner; Observer; Oppenheimer; US SEC; IMF; WB; Summarized from PhD Thesis – C. Smith

INDEX

INDEX

Accountability, 10, 11, 15, 19, 26, 28, 39, 41, 43, 75, 92, 109, 135, 152, 236, 237, 239, 241-2, 245-47, 253, 255, 275-78, 284-85, 287
Agriculture, 51, 77, 86, 110, 120, 122-3, 139, 144, 149, 200
Argentina, 57, 172-74, 228-29
Asia(n), 25, 44, 52, 54, 58, 11, 123, 125, 168, 170, 175, 220, 244, 287
Auditor General, 3, 196-98, 206, 208, 253, 257
Bank of Jamaica,/BOJ, 3, 5, 62, 131, 133, 143, 148, 151, 158, 161, 190, 206, 226-27, 234, 256-57
Barro, 66-70
Barrow, 110-11, 231
Bauxite, 77, 86, 98120, 139, 146, 199-200, 202-03, 145
Brain Drain, 97, 105, 126
Britain, xiv, 2, 7, 22, 35, 47, 60, 72, 77, 110-11, 125-26, 128, 140, 143, 170, 172, 289
Budget Deficit, 21, 31, 59, 60, 65, 67, 69, 72, 73, 119, 147, 149, 225
Capital Projects, 70, 185, 199-200, 208
Central Bank, xii, 13, 61-62, 77, 106, 110, 116-19, 131, 133, 156, 163, 174, 190, 217, 227, 233, 245-6
Channel, 13-15, 23, 66, 93, 128, 253, 259, 270,

Character, 6, 23, 26, 37, 105, 130, 178, 211, 245, 262, 284, 288,
Characteristics, 8, 11, 18, 19, 34, 76, 83, 128, 225, 244, 262-63, 277-78, 288
China, 13, 16, 21, 45, 56-57, 78, 165-7, 169, 197, 327,, 332-33
Comparator(s), xiv, 10, 75-76, 108-9, 113, 125-28, 178, 212-13, 230
Consensus Orientation, 11, 246, 251, 260, 272
Constitution(al), 9, 14-15, 19, 36, 43, 57, 82, 85-6, 91, 110, 125-6, 158, 162, 164-5, 194, 243, 261
Contractor General, 3, 208, 253-54, 258, 260
Corruption, ix, x, xiv,, 1, 3, 10, 14-15, 18, 20, 26, 28, 32, 75, 93, 98, 102, 107-9, 123, 212, 230, 236-8, 246-7, 251-58, 268, 277, 285
Cost Minimization, 70
COVID-19, 2, 46, 100, 107, 135, 161, 167
Crime, xii, 310, 102, 107, 185, 206, 212, 252, 267-9
Currency, 2, 11, 62, 72-3, 115, 117-18, 139, 144, 147, 160, 168, 177, 179, 181-3, 205, 20-11, 213, 221, 225-28, 230-1, 234
Current Account, 35, 61, 121, 168, 231-2
Cusan, 56
Debt Ceiling, 158

Debt-to-GDP, 1-2, 4, 12, 46, 54, 77, 93, 98, 100, 103, 106, 110, 131, 145, 149, 159, 166-7, 171-2, 174, 178, 181-2, 188, 190-1, 205, 213, 215-21, 233, 280, 286
Deficit Financing, 26, 41, 43, 65-6
Dependency, 15, 51, 53, 81-82, 237
Divestment, 38, 152, 154, 201, 204, 279, 327, 332
Director of Public Prosecution/DPP, 161, 253, 257, 259
Economic Development, 1, 20, 23, 58, 74, 112, 134, 140, 197-8, 208, 236, 286-7
Effectiveness and Efficiency, 11, 162, 245, 247-8, 261, 264-5, 270, 275, 277-8
Electoral, 3, 14-15, 36, 80, 97, 144, 178, 247, 258-9
Equity and Inclusiveness, 11, 40, 246, 251, 274-5, 277-8, 284-5, 329, 331
Ethics, 40, 126
Ethical, 14, 33, 36, 37, 284
European Union/EU, 13, 60, 130, 132, 170, 172, 175, 327
Exchange Rate, 2, 12, 20-21, 61, 71, 73, 98, 115, 118-19, 121, 135, 139-40, 159, 165, 173, 190-91, 213, 221, 225-29, 231, 235
Export(s), x, 35, 39, 50, 52, 86, 102, 121-25, 131, 144, 146, 149, 166, 168, 206, 211, 215, 231-3, 236
Federation, 86, 111, 125

Finance Minister/MOF, 1-2, 5, 22-23, 27, 87, 89, 97, 100, 102-3, 117, 133, 141, 148-9, 159-60, 163, 167, 179, 195-96, 220-21, 234, 245, 252, 255, 260
FINSAC, 74, 103, 117, 134, 149, 152-58, 163, 187, 193-94, 202, 205, 211, 217, 254, 279-82, 332
Fiscal Balance, 73, 144-45, 206, 225
Fiscal Policy, 12, 14, 26, 61, 66, 68, 70, 74,, 96, 115-16, 126, 139, 161, 165, 70, 172, 234, 286
Fitch, 2
Foreign Direct Investment/FDI, 23, 49, 86, 119, 122, 124, 144, 207
Foreign Exchange, 2, 71, 106, 115, 117-19, 121, 139-42, 146, 148-49, 151, 181, 197, 205, 226-28, 231, 332
Free Zone, 47, 99, 120-21, 207-8
Government Guarantee, 94, 168, 196-97, 202, 204, 327, 331
Governance Dividend, 107
Gross Domestic Product, 16, 24, 46, 74, 100, 120, 230
Government of Jamaica, 2, 5, 27, 62, 65, 117, 133-35, 149, 162, 184, 186, 188, 196, 200-1, 247, 254
Gross Fixed Capital, 136-7, 166, 184, 190-1, 206-9
Hansard, 3, 40, 65, 73, 86, 102, 105, 134, 194, 199, 206, 208, 245, 256, 333

Harrod-Domar, 48-49, 51, 62
Heterodox, 44-45, 287
Highway 2000/HW2000, 158, 273, 279, 282
Hobbes, 33-34, 56, 258
Human Capital, x, 1, 3, 15, 22, 31, 50, 63, 65, 79, 100, 107, 112, 122, 137, 169, 188, 190, 183, 206-7, 209, 212, 225, 284
Human Development, 9, 27, 40, 94, 126, 119, 189, 220-21
Import, 102, 119-22, 125, 141-42, 153, 155-56, 160, 163, 186, 189, 197, 247-48, 253, 279, 289, 327
International Monetary Fund/IMF3, 97, 99, 101, 104, 112, 117-18, 131, 135-75, 181-82, 185, 194, 203, 206, 216-18, 227-231, 244, 250, 279, 285
IMF Agreement, 60, 97, 141, 149, 159, 168, 175
Industrialization, 21, 48-9, 50, 52, 82, 86, 98, 119-20, 147, 169, 206, 213
Infrastructure, ix, xiv, 3, 4, 5, 18, 28, 30, 60, 92, 106, 130, 139, 166, 188, 197, 207-9, 328
Institutional Economics/Economists, 26, 32, 42, 44, 74, 127-8, 238
Investments, ix, xiv, 23, 31, 47-48, 50, 73, 79, 107, 112, 114, 119, 124, 133, 146, 157, 166, 196, 207, 216, 224, 238, 254
Jamaica Debt Exchange/JDX, 4, 69, 103, 131, 134, 159, 179, 279, 283

Japan, 21, 111, 124, 150, 165-67, 169, 183
Leadership, 1, 6, 57, 76, 81-83, 87, 89, 91-92, 113, 127, 159
Legislative, 15, 30, 32, 38, 40, 77, 85, 116, 162, 212, 252
Local Registered Stock/LRS, 131, 154-55, 162, 211
Lockean, 52
Manufacturing, 86, 110, 112, 120, 122-3, 166, 168, 236
Maturity Profile, 12, 20, 70, 179-81
Member of Parliament, 40, 93, 95, 120, 136, 138, 257, 261, 270
Mexico, 132, 173-74
Migration, 97, 105, 107
Mining, xiv, 200, 202-3
Ministry Paper, 134, 159, 194, 202, 204, 208
Mixed Method, xiii, 8, 288
Monetary Policy, 12, 14, 62, 72, 73, 115-19, 132-33, 234-35
Moral, 14, 29, 41, 56, 74, 118
National Housing Trust/NHT, 95-96, 197, 331-33
National Debt Exchange/NDX 4, 69, 70, 160, 180-83, 284
Net International Reserves/NIR 144, 149, 159, 226
Nurkse, 21, 26, 31, 50-51, 127, 165, 167, 170
Oil, 1, 3, 21-22, 110, 113, 139-41, 146, 197, 199, 222, 233, 258, 329
Orthodox, 42, 44-45, 60, 287
Parliamentarian, 82, 91, 95, 152, 202, 243, 247, 284, 287

Participation, 11, 26, 37, 39-41, 64, 124, 242-45, 248-51, 263-64, 273, 277, 284, 287
Pension, 103-5, 112-14, 154, 161, 170, 202, 332
Per Capita GDP/GDP per Capita, xiv, 1, 19, 77, 101-2, 107-8, 110, 113, 149, 168, 172, 190, 213, 221-3, 225, 235
Plantation, 26, 35, 51-52, 75, 82-83, 128
Population Ageing/Ageing, 104, 113-14, 170
Portfolio, 12, 69, 70-71, 114, 143, 152-3, 166, 179, 181-82, 225,
Premier, 83, 84-87, 98, 110, 119, 136
Primary Balance, 7, 73
Profligacy, xiv, 15, 22, 32, 96, 98, 152, 177, 196, 199-200, 221, 23, 237, 254-57, 285
Public Finance, 12, 59, 61, 74, 128, 171, 246
Public Policy, 10, 37-41, 74, 248
Regime, 17, 58, 61, 80, 97, 102, 148, 151052, 173, 225, 228
Remittance, 105-7, 158,
Republic, ix, 125-26, 243
Responsiveness, 11, 246, 261, 270-1, 284
Ricardo, 29, 31-32, 35, 51, 61, 66-67, 70, 145, 286
Rule of Law, x, 10-11, 19, 28, 57, 109, 135, 190-91, 206, 212, 237, 246, 251-53, 255, 266-68, 277-78, 285
Seignorage, 61-62, 143
Social Policy, 30, 58, 92-95, 104

Social Services, 22, 28-31, 90, 93, 184-91, 223, 252
South Korea, 16, 45, 54, 57, 124, 130, 165, 167-70, 175
Stabilization, 3-4, 21, 66, 117, 143, 172, 218,
Standard and Poor's, 230
State Capture10, 32, 37, 39, 108, 285
Structural Adjustment, 3, 21, 143, 149
Structural Transformation 28, 49
Sustainable Development, xii, 7, 26-28, 31, 37, 40, 65, 104-5, 161, 211, 260, 273, 284-85
Taxation, 43, 62-69, 74, 103
Tax-Smoothing, 67
Tobin, 69-70
Trade Balance, 121, 147-48, 150, 231
Transparency, 11, 15, 19, 20, 26, 28, 75, 126, 135, 152-3, 175, 193, 212, 236, 246, 258-60, 269-70, 277-79, 284-85
Transparency International, 28, 236, 238, 277, 279,
Treasury bill, 131-34, 148, 162, 164, 175, 219
Triangulation, 245, 277
Westminster, 34-36, 125
Whitehall, 34-35
World Governance Indicators/WGI, 8, 10, 20, 40, 108-9, 236-7, 239-41